PRIME TIME,
PRIME MOVERS

The Television Series
Robert J. Thompson, *Series Editor*

PRIME TIME, PRIME MOVERS

— — — — — — — —

From *I Love Lucy* to
L.A. Law — America's Greatest
TV Shows and the People
Who Created Them

— — —

David Marc and Robert J. Thompson

SYRACUSE UNIVERSITY PRESS

Our sincere thanks to the following people, who helped us make this book: Peggy Leith Anderson, Lucille and Ed Fulmer, Gary Fleder, Irv Goodman, Grant Graybeal, Nancy Izuno, Doris and Takumi Izuno, Melanie Jackson, Tom O'Dea, Gregg Oppenheimer, Christopher Pawelski, Roy Restivo, Kim Swindle, and Christopher Sturgeon.

Special thanks go to J. Fred MacDonald, an indispensable source of knowledge, advice, and assistance.

Material in this book concerning Aaron Spelling was originally written by the authors as a catalog essay for an exhibition of the Museum of Television and Radio. We thank Ron Simon and all our friends at the museum for permission to use that material here.

This book was originally published in 1992 by Little, Brown and Co.

The paper used in this publication meets the minimum requirements of American National Standard for Information Sciences—Permanence of Paper for Printed Library Materials, ANSI Z39.48-1984. ∞™

Library of Congress Cataloging-in-Publication Data
Marc, David.

    Prime time, prime movers : from I love Lucy to L.A. law —America's greatest TV shows and the people who created them / David Marc and Robert J. Thompson.

       p. cm. — (The television series)

    Originally published: Boston : Little, Brown, 1992.

    Includes bibliographical references and index.

    ISBN 0-8156-0311-8 (paper : acid-free paper)

    1. Television programs—United States—History.

2. Television broadcasting—United States—History.

3. Television broadcasting—United States—Biography.

I. Thompson, Robert J., 1959–   . II. Title. III. Series.

PN1992.3.U5M264   1995

791.45′75′0973—dc20   95-1812

Manufactured in the United States of America

To Tom O'Dea

and

to Nancy

Contents

PRIME TIME, PRIME MOVERS

Introduction

Who is the author of *Hamlet?* What a simple and silly question. People who have never even seen the play — people who don't even know what it's about — can tell you that William Shakespeare wrote it. But who is the author of *Miami Vice?* Millions of viewers, some of whom are capable of becoming more engrossed in the pastel adventures of Crockett and Tubbs than in the gray tones of their own lives, can only reply with blank stares.

Perhaps it was inevitable that drama, like so many of civilization's amenities, would find itself in danger of becoming a faceless assembly-line product in the twentieth century. If renowned chefs once cooked dinners for gourmets at restaurants, if reputable tailors once made suits of clothing for gentlefolk, if acclaimed architects once designed homes for important families, whom shall we credit with that Quarter-Pounder at McDonald's? or a three-piece pinstripe on the rack at Sears? or the third split-level on the right at Winding Lane Estates? Fast-food corporations, retailing chains, and real estate development companies are often given credit for these things. But the fact remains that abstract corporate entities cannot create things. That is still something only people can do.

Despite the rapid refinement of tools that we like to think of as the spiral of modern technology, the artistic act still thoroughly depends on the conscious effort of the individual creator. The human sensitivities that wrestle with the music of a line of dialogue or that sculpt the angle of a camera shot or that animate a performance with humor or pathos cannot yet be synthesized in computer programs. Even in production modes that employ dozens of specialists, individual people — for the lack of a better term in English, let us call them *auteurs* — must finally take responsibility for making the scores of decisions that determine the character of every moment of a televised drama. The elements of personal style that emerge from such choices remain beyond the purview of what can be accomplished by interoffice memos, programmable machines, or generic inertia.

Despite all odds, the necessity — as well as the mystique — of the individual artist has survived the late industrial age. By some measures, it is resurgent. The growing desire of marketers to slap "designer labels" on every kind of mass-produced product from evening gowns to ice cream cones provides evidence of an increasing public awareness that the mass-culture apparatus is not some kind of self-sustaining engine but, rather, a distribution system for the products of a new class of designers and artists. Though there can be no doubt that the relationship of artist to audience has been altered by the nature of mass-distributed culture, it has not been destroyed. Surely if we can attribute the cut of our blue jeans to authorial influences, we can do at least as much for the substance of our national drama — television. Familiarity with the identities and biographies of the people who have created the most popular body of story-telling in history will surely help us understand their handiwork. The need for such understanding is compelling. The work of TV producers has come to dominate the American imagination and, increasingly, the world's imagination of America.

During the 1950s, as television was finding its place in the American living room (and bedroom and dining room and kitchen and den and basement and hospital ward and bus station . . .), the culture seemed to be enjoying a kind of honeymoon with postindustrial anonymity. A new variation on the American dream crystallized out of the atomic mushroom at Hiroshima. One fine morning a man in a gray flannel suit awoke in a Levittown housing tract. He kissed a happy homemaker and 2.3 children good-bye, jumped in an enormous station wagon with power everything, and drove off to a downtown skyscraper to make enough money to pay off the mortgage and keep the refrigerator stocked with an endless supply of high-cholesterol, high-sugar, and high-sodium foods. Perhaps twenty years of economic depression, followed by global war, followed by the relentless threat of thermonuclear destruction had led many Americans to crave the simple pleasures of harmony, adaptation, and conformity that were implicit in such a life.

The fledgling television industry grew up hand in hand with this Cold War mentality. With the Hollywood Ten doing time in federal prison and everyone from stars to gaffers losing jobs over "political indiscretions," the logic of sheer survival may help to explain why the behind-the-scenes artists who were cutting and pasting and dreaming up the form of the new entertainment-industrial complex were not particularly keen on achieving public notoriety. Fame, among its many consequences, invites scrutiny; every celebrity in a mass culture is also a potential scapegoat for some public grievance. Born in the frenzy of the postwar Red scare, and prone by its very nature to charges of "invading" the American home, the TV industry found itself particularly vulnerable on this account.

A few exceptions dared show their faces. Jack Webb, whose law-and-order homilies put him on the right side of J. Edgar Hoover, did not hesitate to chisel his insignia into the end of each episode of *Dragnet*. Pioneer television slapstick clowns such as Red Skelton and Jackie Gleason gambled little by taking authorship credits for the shows on which they appeared as the star attractions. For "thriller" anthology producers, such as Alfred Hitchcock and Rod Serling, authorial identification was tantamount to good business sense; their very names were so closely identified with the generic properties of their productions as to become potent, perhaps indispensable, marketing tools. But most producers had to be more careful. Morbidly meticulous, the McCarthyite witch-hunters might somehow detect pinkish hues even in the starkest black-and-white tableaux of domestic situation comedy. In such an atmosphere, the behind-the-camera masterminds of the early television programs seemed only too happy to keep a low profile and cash the expanding checks of an expanding industry in an expanding economy.

The legacy of this birthright outlived the particular political circumstances that had spawned it. By the 1960s TV shows were just taken for granted as the products of three mythic bicoastal corporate oracles known as CBS, NBC, and ABC. It was as if no one knew that Ernest Hemingway had written *For Whom the Bell Tolls*, but knew instead that the publisher of the novel was Scribners. Even those patient viewers whose attention spans allowed them to sit through the closing credits crawl of a television program were apt to find the information offered on the screen to be indecipherable. Producer?

Director? Executive producer? Assistant director? Created by? Developed by? These terms were — and remain — virtually meaningless to most viewers.

Meanwhile, television continued to grow in influence. Old and honored newspapers and magazines collapsed as the medium displaced print as the primary source of public information. Downtown film palaces and neighborhood cinemas closed or went porno as TV established its preeminence over the movies as the technological stage upon which the national drama was enacted. Yet somehow, despite the democratic pretensions of American culture, no one seemed to think it strange that this new medium was creating a popular body of dramatic fiction that consisted largely of "unsigned" works. With little or no academic study of TV taking place, the basic bibliographic tasks essential to the health and growth of any art — and ultimately of any literate civilization — were being ignored.

It is worth noting that the movies had gone through a similar initiation into American culture. It was not until the end of the studio era that the problem of authorial anonymity in Hollywood was seriously addressed by an American critic. In 1968, more than forty years after pictures began talking, Andrew Sarris completed his landmark auteur study, *The American Cinema* (Dutton), a book that is still in print. Following a model of French criticism, Sarris complained about American indifference to the issue of film authorship. While the French spoke of a film such as *Stagecoach* as a "John Ford movie," Americans, including most reviewers and commentators, were more likely to call it a "John Wayne movie." "To put it bluntly," wrote Sarris, "many alleged authorities on film disguise their ignorance of American cinema as a form of intellectual superiority."

Sarris's point was well taken. What critic would dare review a book without mentioning the name of its author? The very heart and soul of the artistic act is the communication of a creator's emotion, perception, and thought to an audience. To deny the animating influence of the creator's personality in a film is to place it (and, by implication, the entire medium) outside the realm of art. The Sarris book, with its critical essays on dozens of American film directors and its valuable listings of their "complete works," did more than any other book during a decade of voracious film criticism to help to thoroughly accomplish the integration of the American cinema into the orbit of Western arts and letters.

Though movies and TV had made their industrial peace by the end of the 1950s, the two media remained alienated from each other in the world of cultural criticism. The film departments that grew up during the sixties at colleges and universities virtuously offered auteur courses on the Westerns of Sam Peckinpah or the populist comedies of Frank Capra, but just as judiciously these newly legitimated academic enterprises ignored and avoided the TV Westerns and situation comedies that had all but displaced those film genres from the popular cultural roles they had enjoyed less than a generation previously. The revolutionaries had taken the palace, but their first priority seemed to be the institutionalization of their own prejudices. There is perhaps no more efficient way of establishing one's own status in American culture than to reject the credentials of a more recent arrival to the neighborhood.

It was not until the 1970s that the study of television as culture began in earnest. In *TV: The Most Popular Art* (Anchor, 1974), Horace Newcomb offered a humanistic critique of popular commercial TV programs that was organized as a series of genre studies: the sitcom, the soap opera, the action/adventure show, and so on. A year later Newcomb, as editor, brought out *Television: The Critical View* (Oxford, 1975), an anthology of essays by humanities scholars, social scientists, and free-lance writers. That collection, now in a fourth edition, was a tremendous success in the academic market, filling a real need among a generation of students and teachers who were intimately familiar with television language, mythology, drama, and manners, but who, for lack of just such a book, could not "officially" study their own commonly shared visual culture in the print-oriented world of the classroom.

It was not until 1983, however, that Newcomb, now the de facto founder of an emerging school of American television criticism, directly addressed the issue of television authorship. Proclaiming television, in the title of the book, to be *The Producer's Medium* (Oxford), Newcomb and Robert S. Alley offered readers a series of revealing interviews with, and critical essays about, some of American television's most important and prolific video artists, including Quinn Martin, David Victor, John Mantley, Earl Hamner, Norman Lear, and Garry Marshall. Collaborative production teams such as Richard Levinson and William Link, and James L. Brooks, Allan Burns, and Grant Tinker, were covered as well.

The Producer's Medium had two particularly significant virtues. First, the interviews with the various producers firmly established the primacy of the producer as the auteur of the American commercial television series. As early as 1971, Muriel Cantor had demonstrated this point on a theoretical level in her book *The Hollywood TV Producer* (Basic). But the Newcomb and Alley study was replete with anecdotes and observations from specific working producers. These personal oral histories had the effect of translating a theory into an undeniable assumption about how television production functioned. Before publication of *The Producer's Medium,* for example, Christopher Wicking and Tise Vahimagi authored a reference text, *The American Vein: Directors and Directions in Television* (Dutton, 1979), that was entirely based on the erroneous assumption of the TV director as auteur. The writers, who were cinema critics off on a lark in TV-land, did not even think it necessary to argue their basic premise.

Second, and more important for most people interested in understanding television, the critical sketches offered by Newcomb and Alley constituted a potent statement on the application of auteur theory to American television. They demonstrated that despite the gigantic constituent corporate bureaucracies of this most massive of mass media — networks, advertising agencies, production companies, ratings organizations, federal regulatory authorities — the autobiographical visions of individuals did manage to break through onto the television screen, just as the personal visions of artists had managed to reach expression in the older, preelectronic arts. Were these visions mitigated or, in effect, edited by television's trilateral nature as industry, technology, and art? Certainly. But when and where had an art ever developed independently of other factors?

In this book we intend to offer readers a guide to the work of several of the most important creative personalities that have shaped American entertainment-television programming. It has been our aim to treat these TV-makers with the same measures of respect and critical scrutiny that are customarily accorded to artists working in almost any other medium. Inevitably, some emerge from the critical process looking better than others. We hope that these essays will be particularly meaningful to people who watch television with some regularity. After all, the majority of series that we discuss — or for that matter, many of the series that have been produced for the medium — continue to be available on a daily basis in reruns. The geometrical expansion of the channel spectrum made possible by cable has made potential video historians out of all viewers and accomplished amateur critics out of tens of thousands.

The serious couch potato will no doubt wonder why chapters on certain pet favorites are missing. Why is short shrift given to such prolific and popular sitcommakers as Harry Ackerman (e.g. *Bewitched*) and Don Fedderson (e.g. *My Three Sons*)? Why have we virtually ignored the dramatic and televisual breakthroughs of Bruce Paltrow in *The White Shadow* and *St. Elsewhere?* How could we even begin to discuss video creativity without devoting at least a chapter to the performance works of Ernie Kovacs? To all these charges we plead guilty — with an explanation. It was never our intention to write a "complete guide" to anything. We have chosen our subjects by a synthesis of two general criteria: the boldness of their brush-strokes, and the influence they have wielded in terms of affecting the development of the genres they have wrestled with. For reasons that are obvious to anyone who has put in a few hours in front of the set, some of the most creative personalities to work in the medium have remained among the least influential.

Academic thought-control freaks and others who have not been party to the insight that all in life is process will be particularly disappointed to learn that we are not offering a foolproof method for identifying and verifying television authorship. Instead, we have labored under the assumption that entire areas of human endeavor and consciousness — including this one — persist in which empirical scientific method need not apply. Instead, we have watched a lot of television, read on our subjects what we could find, and attempted to deduce and examine the threads of continuity that might lend some sensible framework to a particular producer's career and its role in the careers of other producers.

In his early-TV-era essay, "Notes Toward the Definition of Culture," T. S. Eliot makes the point that no culture can achieve coherence without the large-scale sharing of a common story concerning the origin and purpose of humanity. Without generally accepted beliefs about the nature of life on Earth, how can we judge, for example, if the actions of a character are heroic or cowardly? Surely Hamlet's soliloquy means something different to a Roman Catholic than it does to an atheist or a Japanese Shinto. The ratio of chaos to coherence in American television drama is very much tied up in this issue.

To the extent that TV offers an intelligible representation of reality to the viewer, the medium explains much about how one ought to act, think, and feel in the recognizable situations that occasionally crystallize from the fog of living. The valor of the relationship of parent to child, for example, in the Huxtable home on *Cosby* is made so obvious that it seems more like common sense than dramatic contrivance. No less can be said about the evil of any government that the *Mission: Impossible* team was ever sent to destroy. In this way, television has taken on a moral and therefore a religious function. Its sweetly didactic sermons are certainly among the most listened to in history.

Communion, another religious function, is casually performed by television as well. The image of an individual or even a family watching TV seems to imply physical atomization. But that only serves to make the communion of the sharing of the story by millions all the more phenomenal. The congregation cum audience achieves an electronic connection and then substantiates that miracle through discussion of the episode the next day at work, at school, or at the supermarket. Did you see *thirtysomething* last night? Yes . . . yes . . . yes. . . . Common witness to a story from a higher source is verified; exchange of interpretations follows.

One strategy for maintaining rational control while living in the thrall of such ritualistic behavior is to take an occasional stab at the demystification of the oracle. We offer this look at television producers in that spirit. If at times we seem to waffle between ironic detachment and the self-righteous espousal of true believers, then we can claim success in publicly expressing the ambiguities that haunt our own private relationships with our sets.

Norman Lear claims to have based the character of Archie Bunker on his own bigoted, cantankerous father. Aaron Spelling, the producer of such critically despised series as *The Love Boat* and *Fantasy Island,* won the prestigious Eugene O'Neill Award for his one-act productions as a student playwright at Southern Methodist University. Jackie Gleason claims to have modeled the set of *The Honeymooners* after the Brooklyn tenement apartment in which he grew up. Paul Henning, the creator/producer of *The Beverly Hillbillies* and *Green Acres,* grew up in modest circumstances in Missouri but went on to become a multimillionaire in Southern California. Can these things be dismissed as mere coincidences in deference to theories about the inherently collaborative nature of mass-culture products? Who are the authors of American television? How are their biographies manifest in their creations? Who influenced them? How did they influence each other? We hope to demonstrate to readers that whatever else TV programs may be, they are not images that simply materialize out of thin air. They may even be human expressions born of human experiences.

PART ONE

Comedy

1. FROM PERFORMER AUTHORSHIP TO PRODUCER'S GENRE

When a new communications invention is introduced to the public, it is usually greeted as an improvement of an older one. Radio, for example, was heralded as a "wireless" telegraph. Silent films, by advertising themselves as "photoplays," proclaimed an instant heritage in the traditional theater. Synchronous sound was originally presented to audiences as a system for automating the musical scores that had previously been played by live performers sitting at the edges of the silent screens. But in each case, the initial perception of the innovation as mere enhancement of an older communications system was forgotten in the face of the revolutionary aesthetic possibilities that began to materialize from the practice of the new technology. Radio, silent film, and sound film each achieved the status of a peculiar dramatic art in its own right. What had seemed like a refinement in transmission technique gradually revealed itself as a distinctively new medium of expression.

And so it was with television. Sold to the public as "radio with pictures" and proclaimed by optimists as an instrument that could bring theater, dance, opera, symphony, and cinema right into the living room of the common person, TV promptly demonstrated — to the irrevocable consternation of some — that its compelling contribution to culture would consist chiefly of itself. Today, with television out of the laboratory for barely a half century, we are already witness to a further recapitulation of this historical ritual. Cable television has been hailed as a culturally messianic technology capable of putting Ingmar Bergman, Tom Stoppard, and Martha Graham into Every-consumer's castle. In practice it has had far more success showering its subscribers with MTV, the Home Shopping Club, and pay-per-view wrestling events.

In the late 1940s the building of a national television system seemed to open up a bottomless pit of opportunities for the American entertainment industry. Among the first marvels of the new technology was its seemingly miraculous resuscitation of vaudeville. Vaudeville — which can loosely be defined as the live presentation of a sequence of variety acts on a proscenium stage — had flourished across America from approximately the 1880s to the 1920s. Rapid and dependable transcontinental railroad transportation had allowed for the industrialization of regional circus and carnival novelty acts into a salable urban entertainment commodity. Large companies (known as "circuits"), dominated by Keith-Albee of Boston, organized troupes of singers, dancers, comedians, acrobats, ventriloquists, trained animal acts, and so on, booking them on tours of strings of cities across the continent. Clearly a step above the carnival tent in terms of Victorian gentility — but clearly a step beneath the "legitimate theater" of the narrative stage play as well — vaudeville presented a first historical opportunity for large classes of immigrant peasants from around the world to try out American democracy by buying a ticket, entering a theater, and sitting down (like a mensch) to be entertained by professionals.

But vaudeville, like so many celebrated institutions of American popular entertainment, would die young at the hands of spiraling technology. The late-nineteenth-century transportation improvements that had allowed both performers and patrons to nonchalantly arrive at the vaudeville theaters for scheduled daily performances were soon eclipsed by twentieth-century communications inventions. The motion picture offered both producer and distributor unprecedented opportunities for cost cutting and quality control. Early films were themselves exhibited to audiences as vaudeville novelties, or as the cultural historian Robert C. Toll put it in *The Entertainment Machine*, "Movies [originally] became part of American show business as an 'act' on vaudeville bills."

By putting the same mechanically reproduced "act" in a can bound for Peoria as in a can bound for Chicago, the emerging corporate components of the entertainment-industrial complex found themselves in a position, for the first time, to market a truly national product. The great Al Jolson showed up for work each day in Omaha and Chattanooga as easily as in New York or Los Angeles. And to boot, he was as fresh and sassy at a Monday matinee as he was at the Saturday night late show. Nobody need settle for a "B" troupe or a "B" performance in a land where all members of the audience were created equal. A labor-intensive, transportation-based artform, vaudeville found itself at fatal disadvantage in the emerging age of capital-intensive communications. Perhaps as penance for the patricide, a whole genre of American movie musicals arose in the thirties that was dedicated to nothing less than a romantic celebration of the vaudeville period, which became for all intents and purposes the biblical era of modern mass culture.

Some twenty years after the talkies had sounded its death knell, vaudeville seemed to miraculously rematerialize on early television. Taking the form of what became known as the "comedy-variety show," it was ubiquitous during the formative years of the medium. In 1948, on the heels of the astounding success of Milton Berle, whose Tuesday-night show often pulled two-thirds of the existing TV audience, the William Morris Agency took out a two-page advertisement in *Variety* proclaiming "Vaudeville is Back . . . Wanted — Variety Artists from all corners of the globe." In 1951, following Berle's third straight season as the star of the highest-rated show on television, NBC signed the baggy-pants comedian to an unprecedented thirty-year contract. It seemed as if old vaudeville had returned from the dead to become a foundational genre of the newest and most technologically impressive of entertainment media.

But "vaudeo," as some critics called it, was a relatively short-lived phenomenon. By the late 1950s the comedy-variety show had already faded from dominance. During the sixties and seventies, only a few old favorites managed to hold on. The cancellation of *The Carol Burnett Show* in 1979 apparently marked the extinction of the classical comedy-variety hour from prime-time television. Even in the 1990s, with scores of cable outlets scrambling to fill their schedules with reruns of old forgotten sitcoms and moribund copshows, telecasts of comedy-variety shows — new or old — are very hard to find.

In retrospect, the experience of vaudeville comedians on early TV turned out to be something very much akin to that of the vaudeville stars that had come to the silent cinema at the turn of the century. Charlie Chaplin, Buster Keaton, Harold Lloyd, Fatty Arbuckle, and a handful of other performers had synthesized and developed a vibrant artform in the fertile chaos of an industry that had not yet defined its artistic limitations by the implementation of marketing formulas. At midcentury, Berle, Sid Caesar, Ernie Kovacs, Jackie Gleason, Red Skelton, and their cohorts did something similar on the black-and-white television screen. For approximately a decade they probed and tickled the new medium, searching for its character, practicing the clown's art, making new fun of the eternal vanities with their shiny new toy. But the networks, like the movie studios before them, eventually settled for profit-maximization formulas that, by their very nature, sought to minimize the serendipity of individual performance. In a time-tested spirit of American artistic enterprise, the networks proclaimed the pioneer comedians geniuses and proceeded to kick them out of the business. Vaudeville was, once again, dead (or, at the very least, it became a grant-funded refugee in the performance spaces of museums of postmodern art). The sitcom, a narrative genre in which individual performance was structurally subjugated to the editing control of the producer, instead became the dominant form of prime-time comedy.

An examination of the vaudeo period leaves the viewer with a clear impression that comedy-variety shows were so thoroughly invested with the personal styles of individual performers that the host/comedian was able to assert effective authorial control over his or her entire show. Berle, for example, not only starred in a live, hour-long weekly broadcast but collaborated with his writers, auditioned his guest acts, and arranged the sequence of presentation. He even wrote the Texaco commercials, which were part of the continuous flow of the hour rather than the breakaways that are used today. Known alternately as Mr. Television, Uncle Miltie, and the Thief of Badgags, Berle overpowered the production with a personality spawned in the proverbial steamer trunk.

Milton Berlinger was born in Harlem on July 12, 1908. His tenement neighbors on 118th Street and Lenox Avenue included Georgie Jessel. Raised as a child performer, Berle was a veteran of the vaudeville circuits by the time he was a teenager. During the thirties, as vaudeville shriveled in the dual shadows of talking pictures and the Great Depression, Berle took a shot at Hollywood, but with little success. By the forties he was working mostly as a nightclub emcee in the New York area. The sudden appearance of television after World War II came as salvation to his entire ilk of pie-in-the-face stage comics.

Berle was capable of whipping up a manic presence on live television. He particularly delighted in zigzagging across a kind of psychological neutral zone that he had created to divide his distensibly vulgar comic approaches from the oppressive, apologetic professions of sincerity required by a medium as mass as TV. Berle depended for humor on such basic vaudeville sources as transvestism, potty jokes, bad puns, and the gratuitous display of physically challenged people (dwarfs, giants, and the obese were prominent among his supporting troupe). But at the same time, he was forced to recognize that his "show" was no longer confined to the "house" in which it was performed. Whitebread perimeters had to be put around the giddy slapstick. After all, these images of cross-dressing and tushy-shaking were being piped directly to the American family hearth. After milking a transvestite gag for whatever it was worth, a repentant Berle would abruptly pull off his wig and assure the audience that he knew he had done wrong — but had only done so in the holy service of making them laugh. Propriety recovered, he would then proceed to introduce a child violin prodigy who would come out on stage and play two and a half minutes of Mozart in front of the curtain before the next commercial. The audience, which knew culture when it was presented to them, applauded wildly.

In 1949, the heyday of Berle's popularity, there were approximately one million television sets in the United States, and about 40 percent of these were located in the New York metropolitan area. But this was all about to change with the start of a new decade. Between 1952 and 1954 the number of TV stations more than tripled from 108 to 354. Berle's "shpritzing" style, replete with Yiddishisms, top-heavy with references to Broadway personalities, and generally designed to capture the attention of an already overstimulated megalopolitan population, would not survive the spread of television into the heartland. Stuck with a long-term contract, NBC tried everything to save its investment in Berle, tinkering with his format, scaling down his program to a half hour, even making him the host of a bowling show. Nothing worked. By the 1960s the network was often paying Mr. Television to stay at home in his own living room. Sid Caesar and Jack Carter, two other Jewish vaudeville "shpritzers" who had briefly flourished in the TV vaudeville revival, met up with much the same fate.

Richard "Red" Skelton, born in Vincennes, Indiana, in 1905, never quite got the press that Milton Berle or Sid Caesar did, but that may be for much the same reason that Hank Aaron, playing in Milwaukee and (pre–Ted Turner) Atlanta, never got the headlines accorded Mickey Mantle or Willie Mays in New York during the 1950s. Also born into a show-business family, Red was the son of Joseph Skelton, a clown for Hagenbeck and Wallace, a traveling circus that toured the tank towns of the Upper Mississippi Valley. The elder Skelton died of alcoholism some two months before Red's birth. Ida Mae Skelton found work in Vincennes as a charwoman at the Pantheon, a local vaudeville house, raising her four sons in a two-room shack along the banks of the Wabash River.

In *Red Skelton: An Unauthorized Biography,* Arthur Marx (son of Groucho) asserts that Skelton had a lifelong sense of comic vocation. The legacy of his father, as well as the time he spent hanging around backstage at the Pantheon, put him in contact with the world of show business, such as it was in small-town Indiana. As a child he met several touring stars, including Ed Wynn and Eddie Cantor. At the age of twelve, Skelton ran away from home to become best boy and apprentice to the title player of Doc Lewis's Patent Medicine Show. In the days before TV, credit cards, and 800 numbers, performers such as Lewis traversed the continent selling miracle potions — usually one half myth, the other half alcohol — in rural towns and villages. Paying as much for the entertainment as for the medicine, the locals would shell out up to a dollar a bottle for a good pitchman's rap. As Doc Lewis's novitiate, Red sang and danced in blackface to attract a crowd, bottled the magic elixir in the back of the wagon and, perhaps most important, kept the horses ready for a quick getaway after the show.

Skelton would make good use of this earthy, backroads show-biz education, playing either dopey good-hearts or slick-talking glad-handers throughout his career in vaudeville and in Hollywood feature films. Premiering on television in 1951, *The Red Skelton Show* would be a fixture in prime time for the next twenty years. In sharp contrast to Berle's sharp-tongued freneticism, Skelton offered cordial, deliberately paced monologues, which usually included pantomime bits, broadstroke mimicry, and especially parodies of inebriation. The body of the show each week consisted of a forty-minute, commercially interrupted mega-sketch in which Skelton would play one of his familiar signature characters: Freddie the Freeloader, a wiseguy hobo dressed in Chaplin clothing; Clem Kadiddlehopper, a backwoods rube who straddled the line between a portrayal of plausibly stupid innocence and a mockery of the mentally deficient; the Mean Widdle Kid, whose child's cruelty is made all the more grotesque wrapped in the package of an adult's body; or Sheriff Deadeye, a drunken and corrupt Western frontier lawman.

These narrative sketches were short on plot and long on slapstick. The custard pie, the exaggerated double take, and the banana peel were among the primary tools of Skelton's trade. He often cracked up his guest stars, midsketch, and just as often broke up in laughter himself as he delivered lines. This clownish lack of respect for the genteel pretension of the proscenium illusion was capped each week by the star's appearance at the end of the show. He would walk out in front of the closed stage curtain, half in costume, makeup dripping from his face, to deliver his sign-off line, "Good night and God bless. . . ."

Skelton managed to flourish throughout the sixties, but he ultimately could not survive the death of comedy-variety as a genre. In 1964 his hour-long show was reduced to thirty minutes. The star kept the loyalty of his aging audience but demonstrated little appeal for a new generation of television viewers who seemed to regard vaudeo as a corny remnant of the black-and-white era. In 1970, despite a Number Seven finish in the prime-time Nielsens, CBS dropped Red Skelton as part of a revamping of its prime-time schedule to capture a younger audience. NBC, the network that had originally carried Skelton in the early fifties, picked up the half-hour show, only to cancel it two seasons later.

If Milton Berle brought to television the "hellzapoppin' " vaudeville style associated with immigrant performers such as Ole Olsen and Chick Johnson, and Red Skelton practiced the more studied mimicry of a Buster Keaton, Jackie Gleason synthesized elements of both styles, making him perhaps the epitome of the vaudeo-age performers. As boisterous a stand-up *tummler* as Berle, he was more than willing to shake his ample fanny to get a laugh. Yet at the same time, in the style of Skelton, he developed a portfolio of familiar sketch characters, moving back and forth across the vaudeo proscenium between host and fictive personae.

John Herbert "Jackie" Gleason was born in Brooklyn in 1916. Like Red Skelton and so many other comedians, he did not enjoy an idyllic childhood. His alcoholic father abandoned the family when Jackie was eight. His older brother Clemence died of consumption soon after. Mae Gleason brought up Jackie in tenement poverty; she died when he was nineteen. Never finishing high school, Gleason plunged into the entertainment world during the 1930s. With vaudeville already on the ropes, he found most of his early opportunities emceeing the talent shows that were held at local movie theaters to help bring in customers for the main attraction: the films. He eventually graduated to nightclub work at small dives in the New York area, where he became known as "Jumpin' Jack Gleason."

Gleason got what seemed to be a big break in 1941 when Jack Warner, on a visit to New York, caught his act at a Manhattan nightspot called Club 18. Warner signed the young "fatman comic" to a studio contract and brought him out to Hollywood. But the studio was not kind to Gleason. Lost in a series of second-rate parts in third-rate pictures, he returned to New York in the late forties to resume his nightclub career just at the time when such entertainment was going into steep decline at the hands of the expanding television networks.

Television, however, would prove to be a godsend for Jackie Gleason. In the late forties, with Berle riding the crest of his popularity on NBC, the other three networks made their bids to cash in on the variety-hour craze. *Toast of the Town* premiered on CBS in 1948. Later known as *The Ed Sullivan Show*, it was perhaps the purest example of televised vaudeville. Sullivan, a longtime Broadway gossip columnist for the *New York Daily News*, presented a succession of widely diverse acts, ranging from pop singers and stand-up comedians to circus acts and the Bolshoi Ballet, all mixed together under the holy banner of entertainment.

In 1949 ABC found its way into variety programming with *Paul Whiteman's TV Teen Club*, a talent contest featuring amateur teenage acts and emceed by the big band leader. The Whiteman program, which played on Saturday nights for five seasons, was the jumping-off point for several stars, including pop singer Bobby Rydell. Dick Clark got his first show-business break with Whiteman; he delivered the Tootsie Roll commercials.

That same season the DuMont network premiered its entry in the variety sweepstakes, *Cavalcade of Stars* starring Jack Carter. Carter, a New York Jew with Catskills credentials, was as feverishly hyperactive as Berle. TV historians Tim Brooks and Earle Marsh note that "Carter . . . maintained a lightning pace throughout the 60 minutes, mugging, tossing off gags, and working with the guests in skits. Just as he began to build a following, NBC stole him away in February 1950, to front the first hour of its *Saturday Night Revue*, on the same night as *Cavalcade*." DuMont replaced Carter with another manic comic, Jerry Lester. But as soon as Lester demonstrated commercial promise, he too was stolen away. Lester departed *Cavalcade* to become the host of *Broadway Open House*, NBC's original late-night series, a direct ancestor of *The Tonight Show*. Again left in the lurch, DuMont turned to yet a third New York comic, Jackie Gleason.

The opportunity proved to be the turning point in Gleason's career. As the host and featured player of *Cavalcade of Stars*, he created the characters that would sustain him through twenty years of prime-time

television: The Poor Soul, his pantomime tramp; Reginald Van Gleason III, his slumkid's fantasy of exalted wealth; and of course, his
most memorable invention, Ralph Kramden, the blustering, egotistical Brooklyn bus driver. To the surprise of everyone, the relatively
unknown nightclub comic who had bombed in the movies was on his
way to becoming a national star. True to DuMont's hapless destiny,
CBS president William Paley stole Gleason away at the first hint of
success. DuMont left the air forever in 1955.

The Jackie Gleason Show premiered on CBS in the fall of 1952; it
would run on the network (with several interruptions and alterations)
until 1970. Gleason was perhaps the most bombastic of all vaudeo
presences. A shameless, even proud, nouveau, he wore flashy clothes,
surrounded himself with chorus girls (known as "Glea Girls"), sipped
booze from a coffee cup for inspiration, and danced across the stage
flaunting his expansive rolls of flesh. "He is a heavy man," observed
the critic Gilbert Seldes in The Public Arts, "with the traditional
belief of heavy men in their own lightness and grace."

After schmoozing a bit with the audience in front of the curtain,
Gleason would suddenly announce, "And away we go . . . ," introducing a commercial to be followed by a half dozen or more short
comedy sketches, peppered with guest singers and other variety acts.
By the midfifties Gleason had established himself as a prominent
figure in American popular culture. Of all his various continuing
sketches and routines, none was quite so popular as "The Honeymooners." Ralph Kramden's fist-thumping threats to send Alice to
the moon stood alone in a video world of domestic comedy otherwise
suffocating in the harmonious suburban sitcom banalities of Ozzie and
Harriet and Father Knows Best. The comedy of exasperation performed by Gleason and Art Carney made Ralph Kramden and Ed
Norton the TV equivalent of Laurel and Hardy.

In 1955–56, seeking to ease the workload of producing a live variety
show each week, Gleason split his Saturday-night hour on CBS into
two segments. The early half hour, from 8:00 to 8:30, would be called
Stage Show, a musical variety series starring bandleaders Tommy and
Jimmy Dorsey as alternating hosts, and featuring the June Taylor
Dancers and other Gleason-show familiars, though Gleason himself
did not appear. The second half hour would consist of The Honey-
mooners, a filmed sitcom version of the Ralph Kramden sketch that
Gleason had been developing since he first appeared live on Du-
Mont's Cavalcade.

The credits crawl at the end of each episode of The Honeymooners contains a clear and unambiguous message concerning authorship: "Entire Production Supervised by Jackie Gleason." Gleason had personally cast the show, hired the production personnel, and even designed the set. Employing several teams of writers, he collaborated on a particular script with one group or the other but remained the only writer who retained input on every script in the series.

Despite the fact that *The Honeymooners* (the sitcom, that is) lasted only one season, the show remains Gleason's most revered and popular work. More viewers have seen reruns of those thirty-nine half hours than have seen, or perhaps even heard of, the twenty-odd seasons of comedy-variety work done by the star. This demonstrates an important point about industry economics that would have a permanent effect on production genres. By the 1960s it had become clear that the real money in television, at least for producers, was to be made in rerun residuals.

The sitcom, with its "timeless" didactic narratives on the foibles and frailties of family life and social relations, turned out to be a gold mine in this regard, while comedy-variety, with its slant toward the style of the moment and topical content, proved a poor product for the syndication market. As a result, Berle, Skelton, Caesar, and other stars of the comedy-variety era who never made sitcoms are relatively unknown today among younger viewers. Their work appears occasionally on PBS tributes or in college broadcasting courses or in museum retrospectives. But Gleason, by virtue of that one season of situation comedy, is a universally recognized figure, still available on the homescreen — and still putting up ratings points for stations and sponsors.

There is also some reason to believe that comedy-variety, by its very nature, never had a real chance to survive as a television genre, even from the point of view of the performer. The unprecedented ubiquity of TV proved to be an unbearable burden for the comedian. A good vaudevillian at the turn of the century might take a routine on the road for two years or more before needing new material. This, of course, was not, nor could it be, the case with television. A joke told on TV becomes instantly obsolete. Twenty or thirty million people have heard it and are likely to tell it to so many millions more. The demand for new material, week after week, proved to be insurmountable even for the most hyperactive of the comedy-variety stars. In his autobiography, Milton Berle complained bitterly about the unrelenting pace of work in vaudeo: "I felt drained, finished, washed up, and terribly tired. . . . Seven solid years of live television when it was really live, seven years of going seven days a week trying to make each week's show better, bigger, and funnier than the week before — and for what? To end up axed. . . ."

Though Gleason lasted a decade longer than Berle, in some ways the gradual disintegration of his television career was more pathetic than Berle's rapid fall from grace. By the early sixties it had already become apparent that Gleason was creatively burned out. His Saturday-night show, now titled *Jackie Gleason's American Scene Magazine*, became a series of empty imitations of the vital work he had done in the fifties. Especially miserable were the hour-long revivals of "The Honeymooners" sketches that he initiated. The poignancy of Ralph's frustrated aspirations somehow got lost in the shuffle of the rewrites. Dreadful plotlines that undermined the basic tensions of the series were introduced. The Kramdens and the Nortons went vacationing in Europe. Atrocious Broadway-style musical numbers were added to the plots. The tight compact rhythms of the old sketches were lost in a stretched-out sixty-minute format. When the *Gleason Show* was finally canceled in 1970, it was a tired old shadow of the star's past glories.

Carol Burnett, the heartiest survivor of the vaudeo era, was born in 1933, too late to have ever traveled the vaudeville circuits. She was, however, among the greatest exponents of vaudeo, in terms of both artistic and commercial successes. She made her entrance into TV comedy-variety in the late fifties as a supporting regular in the cast of *The Garry Moore Show,* a classic New York comedy-variety hour. By the 1970s *The Carol Burnett Show* was often the only comedy-variety show to be found on the prime-time schedules of any of the networks. Burnett even managed to carry her own brand of sketch comedy into the 1990s with *Carol and Company,* an experimental anthology that gave her the chance to play a different character each week, in the old comedy-variety style.

A native Texan, the gangly yet graceful comedienne grew up in Los Angeles and studied theater at U.C.L.A. She broke into show business in New York, working nightclubs and the Broadway stage during the early fifties. When loud and loose, her style suggested the "big mouth" tones of a Martha Raye or a Rose Marie. But Carol Burnett could also be sedate, even regal, à la Ann Sothern or Eve Arden. She cut a prismatic figure of the American female clown: at once a slapstick mama and a refined lady of the stage. One moment she was wearing an evening gown and singing selections from *West Side Story* or *Carousel*. An instant later she was shouting, "Hey, watch it, Buster," while manhandling a masher. Her low/high range — hamburgers and caviar, soap opera and light operetta —

speaks of a peculiarly American synthesis of the genteel and the organic, of concomitant urges to be both extraordinarily excellent and democratically familiar.

Burnett debuted her own weekly series on CBS in the fall of 1967. It was in many respects the fifties comedy-variety hour reincarnate. Though industry wisdom was otherwise abandoning this format as an outmoded relic of TV's past, in the hands of Burnett and her producer/husband, Joe Hamilton, fresh new weekly comedy-variety sketch material would continue to be presented in prime time for a dozen more seasons. The premiere episode would not differ radically from the farewell show twelve years later. Carol came out at the top of the hour to take questions from the studio audience, as if to extend the warm-up right into air time. The segment became a Burnett trademark. The presentational bracketing it provided to the show served to remind the viewer that the laughs and even the occasional show-stopping applause that one heard were not sound effects but the reactions of people in a theater — a throwback to vaudeville.

The regulars on her first show would become familiar faces to Carol Burnett fans. They included announcer Lyle Waggoner, who would stay on until 1976, when he took an opportunity to become *Wonder Woman*'s sidekick; Harvey Korman, who would be Carol's principal sketch partner until he made the mistake of leaving to try his own variety hour on ABC; and Vicki Lawrence, who would not only remain with Carol for the entire production run but would, in a sense, help the show outlive its cancellation by spinning off a sitcom, *Mama's Family*, from one of its most popular sketches.

Years before late-night comedy shows such as *Saturday Night Live* and *SCTV* made spoofs of Hollywood movies and TV sitcoms popular among the upscale cognoscenti, Burnett was turning them out week after week for her prime-time audience. Andy Warhol, who particularly enjoyed the show's ability to caricature the styles of period movie genres and television commercials, was proud to call *The Carol Burnett Show* his favorite television program. But despite this extraordinary accolade, the series never cultivated the aura of "hipness" that would become the hallmark of the late-night satire shows. The *Burnett Show*'s sketch comedy was painted with brushstrokes a bit too broad for the Kultur crowd (and its music was tilted too heavily toward Tin Pan Alley for many younger viewers). When Carol played Joan Crawford, she wore the shoulder pads of a Chicago Bears lineman. When Carol played "Shirley Dimple," she slobbered over the lollipops, and her slip showed. Generally speaking, the sight gag took precedence over other forms of humor, and this will always make some people nervous.

Burnett built a stable of popular video sketch characters during the seventies, much as Gleason and Skelton had done some twenty years earlier. Of all her creations, her masterpiece — her Ralph Kramden — was Eunice Higgins. Indeed, as was the case with Gleason's Brooklyn bus driver, Eunice was a tormented working-class American, in her case a housewife, whose dreams of wealth and class are somehow thwarted by all the economic and cultural realities that she encounters. Married to a hardware salesman (Korman) whose ambition does not overleap a cold six-pack and reruns of *Gunsmoke*, living under the tyranny of a battle-ax mother (Lawrence) whose raison d'etre is to belittle her, Eunice is both citizen and spiritual prisoner of Raytown, U.S.A., a miserable little burg located somewhere in the heart of American mass-culture darkness.

Historically speaking, Carol Burnett was the last star of TV comedy-variety; from a critical point of view, she was probably the greatest. All efforts to revive the genre since Burnett — notably *The Dolly Parton Show* and *The Tracey Ullman Show* — have been measured against her standard.

In cataloging the demise of comedy-variety — and the decisive passing of TV comedy authorship from the hands of the performer to the producer — it is worth noting that the presentation of vaudeville on television also survived in a subgenre of situation comedy that concerns the personal lives of comedy-variety performers. This narrative technique is similar to that of the "backstage musicals" made in Hollywood during the thirties and forties that concerned the lives of vaudevillians (e.g. *Yankee Doodle Dandy, The Barkleys of Broadway, The Seven Little Foys*).

Backstage sitcoms appeared on television almost immediately, as vaudeville veterans, including Jack Benny and the team of George Burns and Gracie Allen, created television programs that attempted to synthesize elements of the vaudeville stage into sitcom structure. *The George Burns and Gracie Allen Show* (CBS, 1950–58) was, on its face, a typical domestic situation comedy set in a familiar-looking suburban-type home, complete with a son in college and a pair of wacky neighbors. But George and Gracie played themselves — a pair of vaudevillians who are the stars of a television show. George thought nothing of interrupting the sitcom dialogue to do several minutes of stand-up in direct address to the audience. After the climax of the hysterically flimsy sitcom plot, George and Gracie would come out on the lip of the theater stage to perform one of their old vaudeville routines.

The Jack Benny Program (CBS, 1950–65) played with the mixing of sitcom and comedy-variety formats in a somewhat different way. Jack started the show on a vaudeville stage, doing stand-up, playing the violin, or making jokes with his regulars or his guest stars. Then, using a commercial as a segue, he would suddenly reappear in a sitcom that observed the conventions of fourth-wall proscenium drama. Now, instead of being Jack Benny, the host of a vaudeo show, he was the fictional Jack Benny, a cheapskate bachelor attended to by a servant named Rochester (played by an actor, Eddie Anderson). After the climax of the sitcom plot, he would saunter out in front of the curtain again as the "real" Jack Benny to schmooze with the audience and say his good-byes.

Several attempts have been made over the years to imitate the half-vaudeo, half-sitcom model as practiced by Burns and Allen and Benny. In 1979, for example, only two seasons after the cancellation of her fantastically successful sitcom, Mary Tyler Moore tried something like this. In *The Mary Tyler Moore Hour*, she played the role of Mary McKinnon, the host of a TV comedy-variety hour. The program moved back and forth between the presentation of the variety "acts" on the show-within-a-show and the representation of Mary McKinnon's personal life. It failed miserably. A more recent and somewhat more successful example is *It's Garry Shandling's Show*, in which Garry Shandling was featured in the role of Garry Shandling, a comedian. Like George Burns playing George Burns in the *Burns and Allen Show*, Shandling readily violates fourth-wall illusion, doing stand-up bits in direct address to the audience, usually making fun of the banalities of the sitcom plot, and then stepping back into character.

A more common technique for integrating comedy-variety into narrative, serial television has been the straight "show-biz family" sitcom, which allows vaudeville shtick to be imbedded into dramatic structure. Examples include *Make Room for Daddy*, in which Danny Thomas plays Danny Williams, a nightclub singer and comedian; *The Dick Van Dyke Show*, in which Van Dyke plays the role of Rob Petrie, a writer for a TV comedy-variety show; and, of course, *I Love Lucy*, in which Desi Arnaz plays Ricky Ricardo, the emcee and bandleader at the Tropicana Club, a New York nightspot.

In 1952 *I Love Lucy* became the first sitcom to finish Number One in the Nielsen ratings: the most popular show on American TV. Among the programs it beat out for that honor were a slew of comedy-variety shows, including *The Texaco Star Theater with Milton Berle, Arthur Godfrey and Friends,* and *The Red Buttons Show.* Perhaps the best way to understand the collapse of the comedy-variety show — and the dominance of situation comedy in prime time — is to look at the career of Lucille Ball, the greatest comedy star ever produced by the medium. On paper, Ball was a prototypical comedy-variety star: a slapstick comedienne who could put over sight gags, double takes, and novelty song-and-dance with the best of them. The fact that she made her success in situation comedy sealed the contrasting fates of the two genres.

Over the years Lucille Ball performed a repertoire of vaudeville and silent-era cinema routines on television that rivals the work of any of the comedy-variety stars of the fifties. These "acts" are the centerpieces of hundreds of episodes of *I Love Lucy.* The famous speedup at the chocolate factory recalls Chaplin on the assemblyline in *Modern Times.* In another episode, Lucy thinks that everyone has forgotten her birthday and, despondent, wanders through Central Park doing tramp bits. Lucy goes for a glaucoma test on the same day that she is supposed to perform a dance number in a jitterbug revue down at the Club and ends up getting thrown all over the stage.

A closer look at the history of *I Love Lucy*'s genesis and production reveals that some authorship credit for the program also goes to Desi Arnaz, Lucy's real-life husband and onstage second banana. In his study "Desilu, *I Love Lucy,* and the Rise of Network TV," cultural historian Thomas Schatz documents the key role of Arnaz in setting up the vehicle for Ball. But while Lucy and Desi had produced their own vaudeville acts and had coordinated the writing of a TV series pilot, the real creative force behind *I Love Lucy* was its creator-writer-producer, Jess Oppenheimer, who helped to forge a model for television comedy authorship that remains intact to this day.

In 1950 CBS chairman William Paley asked Lucille Ball to move her successful Los Angeles-based radio program, *My Favorite Husband,* to the television network. At the time, the few dramatic comedies (i.e. sitcoms) that were on television were performed live in New York for Eastern and Central audiences, and then kinescopes (films of the live TV monitors) were shown to West Coast audiences three hours later. Ball, however, did not want to leave Los Angeles. For one thing, her husband was a successful bandleader in Southern California with a popular local radio program. Moreover, she was in her late thirties and hoping to become pregnant, and she and Desi wanted to raise their family in Los Angeles rather than in New York. Eventually CBS agreed to do a show from L.A., a decision that was just the beginning of an industry-wide migration of prime time program production to the West Coast.

The network was anxious to get Jess Oppenheimer to create the show because of the success he had had as head writer, producer, and director of Lucy's radio series. *My Favorite Husband* had debuted in July of 1948 but remained sponsorless as the fall approached. Oppenheimer wrote a single script for the series that changed its direction in subtle but important ways. He gave Lucy's character, Liz Cooper, a personality clearly foreshadowing that of Lucy Ricardo. Based on this script, Oppenheimer was given an exclusive seven-year contract with CBS and made the boss of *My Favorite Husband*, which two months later was being fully sponsored by General Foods.

Oppenheimer created *I Love Lucy* along with Madelyn Pugh and Bob Carroll, Jr., both of whom had also written for *My Favorite Husband*. A pilot was produced in March, 1951, and Philip Morris had signed up as sponsor within forty-eight hours. A few changes were made and the series began on October 15, 1951. While Oppenheimer had rehearsed a prototype of Lucy Ricardo's character in *My Favorite Husband*, *I Love Lucy* was an entirely new show. Desi Arnaz played Lucy's bandleader husband, Ricky, and Vivian Vance and William Frawley were cast as their neighbors, Ethel and Fred Mertz. With Ricky as a nightclub emcee, Lucy as an eternal show-business wannabe, and the Mertzes as a retired husband-and-wife vaudeville team, more than ample opportunities for vaudeo scenes were imbedded into the sitcom narrative.

The production of *I Love Lucy* utilized techniques that had only recently been developed but that would soon become standard operating procedure for the sitcom genre. Rather than broadcasting live, *I Love Lucy* was shot with multiple cameras in front of a live audience. This technique was invented by Al Simon in 1950 for use on CBS's *Truth or Consequences*. Simon was hired as *I Love Lucy*'s production manager, and he in turn hired Karl Freund, Fritz Lang's cameraman for *Metropolis*, who devised a lighting system appropriate to this new production technique.

I Love Lucy became a watershed in the history of television, and specifically in the development of television comedy. Its popularity, including its four Number One Nielsen seasons, helped establish the sitcom as the dominant genre for the presentation of comedy in the medium. A look at the ratings of almost any season since demonstrates that this principle still stands. Of equal importance, however, is the way in which the show represents the emerging importance of the producer. As co-creator, head writer, and producer of *I Love Lucy*, Jess Oppenheimer was a "hyphenate" of the kind that would come to dominate series television making in the years to come.

2. PAUL HENNING

Corn King

Though William Shakespeare's name is probably better known in America than Paul Henning's, it is doubtful that the same could be said of the two dramatists' work. Despite Henning's remarkable personal anonymity, the distinctive comic style that he developed during thirty-five years of writing, creating, and producing situation comedy for radio and television has become intimately familiar to scores of millions of listeners and viewers. In the mid-1960s several ordinary weekly episodes of his masterwork, _The Beverly Hillbillies_ (CBS, 1962–71), achieved Nielsen ratings comparable to those of Super Bowls. The show was arguably the most popular comedy produced in any medium in the history of American culture.

Paul Henning was born in 1911 in Independence, Missouri. Working as a soda jerk in a local drugstore, he served up phosphates to local customers, who included Harry Truman. During the shank of the Depression, he supported his studies at the Kansas City School of Law by working as a sound-effects man, disc jockey, singer, and scriptwriter for local radio station KMBC. Though Henning did receive a law degree in 1937, he would never actually get around to hanging out a shingle. Much to his amazement, an unsolicited manuscript, which he had written during his spare time, was accepted for production by *The Fibber McGee and Molly Show,* a popular prime-time network radio sitcom. An invitation to join the program's salaried writing staff followed. Thus finding the stagedoor ajar, Henning could not resist slipping into show business. He took the job and moved to Chicago, where *Fibber McGee* was based, effectively abandoning his aspirations for a career as an attorney.

In 1940 Henning left the Midwest for Los Angeles, finding work as a radio sketch writer with Rudy Vallee's weekly comedy-variety hour. Hollywood would remain his home — as well as the focus of much of his comedy — for the balance of his career. Henning returned to sitcom work after World War II, winning a prestigious staff position with *The George Burns and Gracie Allen Show,* a blue-chip radio program that had stood atop the ratings for almost two decades. When George and Gracie were persuaded by William Paley to jump from NBC Radio to CBS Television in 1948, the show's writers came along in the package deal. Like many radio workers, Henning would learn the ropes of TV production in whirling-dervishlike on-the-job training.

During his years with *Burns and Allen,* Henning came under the tutelage of Fred de Cordova, a veteran of film and radio, who would go on to become Johnny Carson's longtime director on *The Tonight Show.* De Cordova encouraged Henning to develop his own personal comic insistences and to write them into the show. In one cluster of episodes, for example, George and Gracie's son Ronnie strikes up a friendship with a naïve hillbilly schoolmate, who is suitably awed by the big-city charms of Los Angeles as well as by Ronnie's suave cosmopolitanism. When a beautiful hillbilly sister shows up from the backwoods, Ronnie promptly falls head over heels in love with her. In retrospect, these characters and their situational functions suggest prototypical sketches of the characters that would become Jethro and Elly May in *The Beverly Hillbillies.* It was also during the mid-1950s that Henning and his fellow *Burns and Allen* writer Stanley Shapiro created the crackerbarrel comic persona of "Charlie Weaver" for stand-up comedian Cliff Arquette. Arquette would appear in public only as "Charlie Weaver" for the rest of his career, which included a long stint in the lower-right corner box of the original *Hollywood Squares.*

In 1955 Henning concluded his long association with George Burns and Gracie Allen to create and produce a series of his own: *The Bob Cummings Show* (a retooling of an earlier series, *Love That Bob!*). The sitcom featured leading man Bob Cummings as Bob Collins, a Hollywood bachelor who shares a house with his widowed sister

Margaret (Rosemary DeCamp) and her teenage son Chuck (Dwayne Hickman).

A fashion photographer, Bob is a kind of edited-for-television incarnation of the 1950s playboy figure. He chases — and usually catches (though never on-screen) — the gorgeous models who pass through the doors of his Sunset Strip studio. Sister Margaret, however, is determined to raise her son in a style more closely akin to the traditional middle-American home life that she and Bob knew as children. Chuck, the Missouri boy transplanted to West Coast Gomorrah, embodies what was gradually crystallizing as Henning's chief paradigm. Though he idolizes his Uncle Bob's slick L.A. lifestyle, he is forced to toe the line by his old-fashioned mom.

Despite his reasonable IQ, Chuck's fascination with the Southern California dolce vita anticipates the similar reaction of *The Hillbillies'* Jethro, another young man stuck at this same cultural crossroads. Henning also gives us Grampa Collins (played in gray wig by Cummings), a minor character who occasionally flies out to California in his World War I biplane to visit the family. Grampa Collins is an augur of *The Hillbillies'* Granny. Beyond these particulars, the tenor and tone of lighthearted sarcasm that would characterize Henning's critique of contemporary life in *The Beverly Hillbillies* and in his other big hits were already manifest in *Love That Bob!*

One of Henning's most original and hilarious comic archetypes would also emerge as part of the Cummings show: the character of Pamela Livingston, played by Nancy Kulp. An ectomorphic intellectual, Pamela is a hopeless devotée of les beaux artes set adrift among the mesomorphic airheads of fast-lane L.A. Her quest for erotic satisfaction (i.e. a night on Mulholland Drive with Bob) is an exercise in painful frustration, a kind of sitcomic shadow mime of Thomas Mann's *Death in Venice*. Though thoroughly capable of quoting the collected wisdom of Western civilization at will, Pamela is simply no match in the eyes of Bob (or of any of his bachelor friends) for the zaftig nincompoops that crowd the waiting room of the photography studio. Kulp would remain a Henning stock player for most of her career, reprising the Pamela Livingston role as the dowdy Miss Jane Hathaway on Henning's next program — and his greatest hit — *The Beverly Hillbillies*.

After playing with contrasts between "rubes" and "city slickers" in one way or another for many years, Henning finally created a vehicle fully based on this contrast in *The Beverly Hillbillies*. "I've wanted to write something about these lovable people ever since [childhood]," he told the press in promotional material accompanying the show's debut in the fall of 1962. He constructed the series around Jed Clampett, whom he described as "the patriarch of the hillbilly clan." The show was an instant and unqualified commercial success for CBS, cracking into the Nielsen Top Ten after only a few weeks on the air. Its premise, summarized in the show's themesong, is a recognizable adaptation of a textbook American parable.

In the song's epic recapitulation of a generic American dream, Henning offers the story of a rugged individual dirt farmer who plows his way through the fertile fields of the New World to the Oz of millionairedom. The Puritan basis of the customary myth, however, has been remade for television — and the change has a distinctly TV feel: the rigors of hard work have been removed from the process. No Horatio Alger, Jed Clampett simply pulls the trigger of his shotgun and, as if spinning the Wheel of Fortune, his bullet lands on twenty-five million dollars in oil.

Henning further confounds mythic consistency by opening each episode of *The Beverly Hillbillies* with a visual image conjured from no less a tragic tale than John Steinbeck's *Grapes of Wrath* (via the John Ford film adaptation). As with the Joads, we see the Clampetts loading up their quaint belongings for the trek out West; like Steinbeck's Grampa Joad, Henning's Granny must be forcibly carried out of the house in her rocking chair and tied to the back of the flatbed truck. The image that follows, however, deviates sharply from the Steinbeck story. Omitting any hint of the dusty trials of the Joads' Depression-era transcontinental struggle, Henning presents us with the Clampetts as automatic boomtime sixties arrivistes, tooling down the palm-tree-lined streets of Beverly Hills, the breeze blowing in their faces.

"Jed Clampett was to be a tall man of simple, homespun honesty and dignity — the kind of Ozark mountaineer I knew as a boy," Henning told the press on the occasion of the series premiere. "I had Buddy Ebsen in mind from the beginning. I knew he'd been a dancer, with all kinds of grace and presence, who really knew how to carry himself."

A Jeffersonian yeoman imbued with a dose of instinctual moral wisdom, Jed is reluctant to leave Ozark arcadia for the concrete jungle of Los Angeles. Like Abe Lincoln, however, he is finally compelled to move to the city by a dedicated sense of obligation to others. Two factors sway him: 1) his daughter Elly May (Donna Douglas) has reached majority as a maiden, and her best hope for marriage as she advances into her twenties is to find a city boy; and 2) his nephew Jethro Bodine (Max Baer, Jr.) has reached adulthood without having settled on a career, and it is hoped that his grade-school education might serve him better in the postindustrial job market than in the subsistence agronomy of the hills.

Granny (Irene Ryan) is even more indisposed to be uprooted from the ancestral soil than Jed. Her apprehensions about dislocation will, in fact, prove to be perfectly justified over the span of the more than two hundred episodes that will follow. A spirited enemy of postindustrial culture, she is severely displaced in cosmopolitan California. Her considerable folk talents as a chef, domestic artisan, and health-care worker will go largely unappreciated in a society where the worthiness of the individual is measured by quantity of leisure time rather than quality of work. She refuses to have servants. She makes her own soap. She wears no makeup. For this, her neighbors regard her as a lunatic, especially Mrs. Drysdale (Harriet MacGibbon), who is forced to tolerate her in order to keep the Clampett millions deposited in her husband's bank. Raymond Bailey plays the urban banker Milburn Drysdale, whose personal greed is extravagantly contrapuntal to Jed's salt-of-the-earth selflessness.

The Beverly Hillbillies was the highest-rated program on television during its premiere season of 1962–63. This phenomenal success catapulted Henning to the top of the TV industry. He immediately capitalized on his new standing with a *Hillbillies* spin-off, which was ready for telecast by the start of the very next season. In *Petticoat Junction*, Henning shifts locale back to the hills. Bea Benadaret, who had worked with Henning for years as next-door neighbor Blanche Morton on *The George Burns and Gracie Allen Show*, was chosen for the role of Kate Bradley. The widowed mother of three postpubescent daughters, Kate is matriarch of a small family-run hotel located along a rural railroad spur on the line connecting Hooterville to Pixley.

The narrative focus of this series was once again a battle between the righteous world of country folk and the corrupt, money-driven modern world. The warm family way of life lived by the Bradleys at the Shady Rest Hotel is constantly threatened by railroad vice president Homer Bedloe (Charles Lane), who wants to close the "inefficient" branch line, without regard for the human damage it would do. Edgar Buchanan, a veteran Hollywood character actor, is exceptional as Kate's lazy and cantankerous Uncle Joe, a kind of geriatric vision of who Jethro might have become had he not been miraculously blessed with instant millions. By the end of the season, Paul Henning could claim creator-producer credits to two of the top four programs in the Nielsen ratings.

Henning was on a roll. His next project, *Green Acres,* which he produced in collaboration with Jay Sommers, was his most artistically aggressive. Though ostensibly the third installment of his Hillbilly trilogy, *Green Acres* abandoned the plodding sitcom conventions of *The Beverly Hillbillies* and *Petticoat Junction,* spilling over into a form of narrative discourse that has already become the subject of several doctoral dissertations. Or, as Nick at Nite (Nickelodeon cable network) put it in a series of 1990 promos for its reruns of *Green Acres,* "It's not stupid . . . it's surrealism!"

As utterly self-reflexive as any program ever aired on network TV, *Green Acres* was built upon reversals of the popular sitcom styles and trends of the twenty-five years of the genre's history that preceded it. On the most obvious level, the show is a plain and simple narrative mirror of *The Beverly Hillbillies:* in the *Hillbillies,* poor country folk miraculously become rich and move to a mansion in the city; in *Green Acres,* rich city folk purposefully give up a life of luxury and move to the country to live in rural squalor. But the series also contains within it a reversal of another major hit of the day, *Bewitched.* If Samantha Stevens is a paranormal female inserted into a "normal" suburban setting, Oliver Douglas (Eddie Albert) is a "normal" male inserted into a paranormal rural setting.

Douglas, a Wall Street attorney with a deep-seated penchant for the romance of Jeffersonian democracy, decides one day to give up his New York law practice and penthouse apartment for the ascetic satisfactions of forty acres and a mule. His aristocratic Hungarian émigré wife Lisa (Eva Gabor) protests, "Dahling, I love you, but give me Park Avenue!" Oliver's definition of democracy, however, does not extend to the marriage contract, and the Douglases ride off in their massive pre-energy-crisis Lincoln convertible to start anew in the fresh green breast of Hooterville, U.S.A.

Hoping to fill the frame of a Grant Wood painting, Oliver instead finds himself in the midst of something more in the style of Salvador Dali. Seeking a community of like-minded righteous yeomen, he encounters Mr. Haney (Pat Buttram), a ruthless rural conman who hornswoggles him into buying a ramshackle old farmhouse; Hank Kimball (Alvy Moore), a double-talking county agent whose discourses on plant and animal husbandry rival the lectures of a semiotics professor; and next-door neighbors Fred and Doris Ziffel (Hank Patterson and Barbara Pepper), a childless couple who are raising a young pig named Arnold as if it were their son.

The major problem plaguing the Harvard-educated Oliver in his attempt to drop out of the rat race is that he continues to maintain modern urban man's faith in cause-and-effect logic, a template of reality that does not apply in the fertile crescent that stretches from Hooterville to Pixley. Determined to spread the gospel of scientific positivism, Oliver reads books on modern American agriculture and spends his money on the items necessary to practice it. At harvest time, however, the lawyer finds he must continue to live off his New York bank account while his poor "backward" neighbors get on as they always have.

Lisa, though pining for Bloomingdale's, has a relatively easier time adjusting to life in the country. When not working on a batch of her famous hotcakes, she becomes involved in the cultural life of Hooterville: In one episode, she imports a symphony conductor to the tiny rural village; in another, she opens a state-of-the-art beauty salon in the back of Sam Drucker's General Store. Her lack of agricultural knowledge leaves her genuinely charmed when one of the chickens starts laying square eggs or when Arnold the Pig expresses romantic love for Mr. Haney's bassett hound Cynthia. Oliver, meanwhile, is driven mad by these violations of Cartesian reality.

The passage of time tended to push the lighthearted surrealism of the early episodes of *Green Acres* into the burlesque science fiction zone. Some stand-out episodes include "Double Drick," in which Oliver's faulty wiring job of the farmhouse causes a ripple in the national electric power grid that blacks out New York City; "The Reincarnation of Eb," in which Lisa believes that their hired hand (Tom Lester) has died and come back as a dog; and "Oliver and the Cornstalk," in which the Jolly Green Giant pays a visit to the Douglas farm. There is nothing intrinsically "magical" in the narrative structure of *Green Acres* — no alien, no witch, no genie, no monsters, as in other popular series of the period. Magic, however, seems to be doing good business on TV, and Henning gratuitously synthesizes it into the program.

As in *Bewitched*, *Green Acres* occasionally alludes — with a broad smile — to the cultural gut-wrenching that America is going through during the years of the program's production. In "The Liberation Movement," Lisa gets a sudden attack of political consciousness and takes over the farm, forcing Oliver to do the housework; this was a kind of updated postsixties retelling of the archetypal sitcom episode in which husbands and wives trade places (e.g. *I Love Lucy*, *The Honeymooners*, et al.). In "The Great Mayoralty Campaign," Lisa runs against Oliver when he attempts to become the mayor of Hooterville. Most notably, there is an implicit political subtext in the overall premise of the series, which is Oliver's "dropping out" of a privileged position in the Establishment to live off the land by the fruits of his own labor. This is brought full cycle in the prescient final episode of *Green Acres:* Hooterville secedes from the Union in a revolt following a tax increase — and crowns Oliver as its first *king.* So much for Jeffersonian democracy and/or sixties idealism.

After a decade of commercial success, all three of Henning's sitcoms were unceremoniously dumped by CBS in the early seventies, as part of the network's attempt to wipe its schedule clean of "rural-oriented" programming. Network President Jim Aubrey instituted the purge with the idea of going after younger and more affluent audiences. Relatively sophisticated sitcoms, aimed at these audiences, such as *The Mary Tyler Moore Show, All in the Family,* and *M*A*S*H* would dominate the CBS lineup — and the ratings — by 1972. Henning, arguably the most successful television producer of the 1960s, would not produce another series.

PAUL HENNING: SELECTED VIDEOGRAPHY

Early Writing Credits

The George Burns and Gracie Allen Show (CBS, 1950–58)
The Dennis Day Show (NBC, 1953–54)
The Ray Bolger Show (ABC, 1953–55)
The Real McCoys (ABC/CBS, 1957–63)

Series Creator-Producer

The Bob Cummings Show (syndicated title: *Love That Bob!*) (NBC/
    CBS, 1955–59)
The Beverly Hillbillies (CBS, 1962–71)
Petticoat Junction (CBS, 1963–70)
Green Acres (CBS, 1965–71)

Movie Made for Television

The Return of the Beverly Hillbillies (CBS, 1981)

3. SHERWOOD SCHWARTZ

— — — — — — — — —

An Empire of His Own

The nuances separating bona fide primitivism from embarrassing infantilism can be recognized, in most cases, without benefit of extraordinary analytic skills. On rare occasions, however, the boundaries prove elusive. In this regard, TV producer Sherwood Schwartz must be counted among such perplexing figures as painter Grandma Moses and *régie du cinema* Jerry Lewis. That a single sitcomic sensibility could conceive of and produce a work as indigenous to the American personality as *Gilligan's Island* is remarkable enough. That this same aesthetic vision might then manage to eclipse itself with no less a surgical strike into the national psyche than *The Brady Bunch* is a feat that frankly tests the plasticity of critical imagination in the waning years of the twentieth century.

Like so many of his producer/creator colleagues, Sherwood Schwartz launched a rewarding career in broadcasting as a scriptwriter. Raised in Passaic, New Jersey, he graduated with a premed degree from New York University and went on to take a master's in the biological sciences. But this early academic interest in the study of the physical realities gradually surrendered to more fanciful concerns. Spurred on by his older brother Al, who had established himself as a Hollywood writer, Schwartz supplied comic radio scripts to *The*

Bob Hope Show, where he worked as a staff writer for four years. With the Second World War in progress, he then joined the Armed Forces network. He soon got in on the ground floor of the TV bonanza, contributing multiple episodes to such salt-of-the-earth sitcoms as *I Married Joan* (NBC, 1952–55) and *My Favorite Martian* (CBS, 1963–66).

In these early days of television, with situation comedy still sharing the spotlight with comedy-variety, Schwartz also wrote material for several variety-show hosts. In 1961 he received his first Emmy (outstanding writing in a comedy series) in recognition of his work for *The Red Skelton Show.* As Skelton's head writer, Schwartz cranked out weekly slapstick routines for the comedian's repertoire of comic personae, including Freddie the Freeloader and Clem Kadiddle-hopper. But by the midsixties, comedy-variety had gone into its fatal tailspin. Following the example of Carl Reiner and other surviving c-v veterans, Schwartz committed himself fully to situation comedy.

In a cryptically instructive book titled *Inside Gilligan's Island,* Schwartz cites two formative experiences in the conceptualization of the series that would make him famous: 1) a boyhood obsession with Daniel Defoe's eighteenth-century shipwreck novel *Robinson Crusoe;* and 2) an oral report assignment he had been given by an NYU psychology professor on the subject of what tools might be most useful if stranded on a desert island. Already well known in Hollywood as a veteran prime-time gag writer — and armed with his Emmy — Schwartz was able to bring together a deal between CBS, United Artists, and Phil Silvers's Gladasya Productions for the making of the *Gilligan* pilot.

Describing *Gilligan's Island* as "comedy on top, allegory underneath," Schwartz recalls the project as an attempt to present broadly drawn stereotypes of diverse characters. The narrative focuses on two dramatic questions: how might modern individuals, nurtured in a high-tech environment, survive in primitive society? and how would members of radically different social groups manage to interact if forced to do so? Schwartz was not ashamed to discuss his sitcom in terms usually reserved for narrative genres of higher pedigree. In 1963, while pitching the show to network brass, he claims to have disarmed CBS Chairman William Paley by insisting that his dramatic aim in *Gilligan's Island* was to portray "a social microcosm."

The idea of a lighthearted social critique of modern affluence and technology was already doing quite well at the cash register for CBS, as evidenced by the success of Paul Henning's *The Beverly Hillbillies,* which had finished Number One in the prime-time Nielsens during each of its first two seasons. Of course CBS programming chief James Aubrey was aware of this and generally sympathetic to Schwartz's project, but he feared that the same seven castaways on the same island each week would limit plotline development too severely. Aubrey suggested that the series be retitled "Gilligan's Travels" and that the concept be revised to feature Gilligan and The Skipper taking out a new group of guest stars on a charter cruise in each episode: a kind of proto–*Love Boat* meets a *Lord Jim/Gulliver's Travels* knockoff.

When Schwartz balked at the changes, Aubrey agreed to allow him to continue with the *Gilligan* project as originally planned. But hedging his bets, the network honcho also decided to oversee the development of another sitcom, based on his own revision of Schwartz's concept. *The Baileys of Balboa* starred Paul Ford (who had played Colonel Hall on the old "Sergeant Bilko" show) in the role of the skipper, and the locale was moved from the South Pacific to a small Southern California fishing town. Aubrey's show premiered two days before *Gilligan's Island*; it did not last the season. *Gilligan's Island* immediately cracked the Top Twenty and would go on to a successful three-year production run and, more impressive, ubiquitous and perhaps eternal syndication.

The critics were not particularly amused. Throwing caution to the winds, Rick Dubrow of UPI was moved by the *Gilligan's Island* premiere to write, "It is impossible that a more inept, moronic or humorless show has ever appeared on the home tube." Jack Gould of the *New York Times* called it "the most preposterous situation comedy of the season." Schwartz was frankly angry about these disparaging reactions to his work. The tone of his resentment is well captured in this comment, which he made to *TV Guide* reporter Richard Warren Lewis at the end of the 1964–65 season: "Here are the same men who are forever saying, 'For Heaven's sake, won't somebody give us something other than the wife, the husband, and the two children?' So you bring something else to the tube and you read very good reviews about the husband, and the wife and the two kids with the same old story lines. They're yelling and crying for a fresh approach. You give them a fresh approach, they kill you and praise the guy who's doing the same old thing."

Though most contemporary critics still dismiss *Gilligan's Island* as a hopelessly derriere-garde sitcom produced during a hopelessly derriere-garde period of TV programming, there is evidence to support the view that the show had some significant effect on the overall development of televisual narrative technique. At a time when sitcoms were typically structured upon orthodox nuclear family or, in some fringe cases, "roommate" relationships, Schwartz was pioneering a dramatic matrix built upon the emerging cultural concept of the "support group": a collection of demographically diverse characters thrown together by circumstance and forced to become an ersatz "family" in order to survive. A decade later, sitcoms such as *The Mary Tyler Moore Show, Barney Miller,* and *Taxi* would win critical acclaim for their development of "ensemble" structures. But in terms of video framework, how different were the WJM Newsroom, the Twelfth Precinct Stationhouse, or the Sunshine Taxi Garage from "The Island"? The physical resemblance of *M*A*S*H's* 4077th hospital camp is more obvious. It might even be said that some of the highly respected hour-long dramas of the eighties, such as *Hill Street Blues, St. Elsewhere,* and *L.A. Law,* owe some kind of debt to Sherwood Schwartz in this regard.

Given this ensemble structure, the casting of *Gilligan's Island* was a crucial step in production. Bob Denver, who assumed the title role, was already familiar to the sitcom-viewing public. He had won distinction as the only "beatnik" character ever to appear as a regular on a TV comedy series: Maynard G. Krebs, the best friend of the title character in Rod Amateau's *The Many Loves of Dobie Gillis* (CBS, 1959–63), a sitcom based on the literary characters created by Max Shulman. An early proponent of sweatshirt chic, the goateed Maynard was a good-hearted, if simple-minded, sidekick to the preppie-but-schleppie Dobie. It might be said that Denver simply dropped the bongo drums, changed costumes, and reprised the Maynard role as Gilligan, sidekick to The Skipper.

The Skipper was a more hotly contested role. The short list for the helm of the ill-fated S.S. *Minnow* included actors who would benefit from flunking the audition and actors who would not; Carroll O'Connor and Jerry Van Dyke were among the failed candidates. Alan Hale, Jr., a veteran of dozens of Hollywood "B" comedies, was finally chosen for the part. As rotund and perennially exasperated as Gilligan was skinny and dim-witted, Hale offered a blustering, aggressive sitcom Oliver Hardy to Denver's passive and terminally confused Stan Laurel.

The other cast members were remarkably unidimensional, more like embodiments of particular character traits than whole characters. Ginger, played by Tina Louise, is identified in the series theme song as "The Movie Star." A kind of K-Mart Venus, the sultry Ginger speaks only the language of love (though, it should be noted, this is a somewhat monosyllabic dialect in early-sixties TV). Mary Ann (Dawn

Wells) is her foil. The personification of Innocence, she is a small-town American beauty in blue jeans, set in bas-relief against Ginger's Mae West-ish femme-fatality. The juxtaposition is a kind of female precursor to the Sam Malone–Woody Boyd pairing on *Cheers* some twenty years later. The Professor (Russell Johnson) is Scientia, the competent voice of empirical reason crying out among the otherwise foolish, inane, and inept.

The most famous of the cast members was Jim Backus, for whom Schwartz had expressly tailored the role of multimillionaire Thurston Howell III. The producer and the actor had worked together for over twenty years, tracing their collaborative efforts to radio. On *The Alan Young Show*, Backus had portrayed Hubert Updyke ("a man so rich he had one chauffeur for right turns, and one for left"). Moving to TV together, Schwartz wrote episode scripts for *I Married Joan*, on which Backus was featured as Judge Davis, the star's husband. Other well-to-do characters played by Backus include James Dean's negligent father in Nicholas Ray's *Rebel Without a Cause* and the cartoon voice of the nearsighted Mr. Magoo. Natalie Schafer, perennially typecast as a bubbleheaded moneybags, played Mrs. Lovey Howell.

If Thurston and Lovey Howell bore some resemblance to Milburn and Margaret Drysdale of *The Beverly Hillbillies*, this was only one of several such comparisons that can reasonably be made between the two CBS sitcoms. Mary Ann, who hailed from Homers Corners, Kansas, begs comparison with the beautiful, sweet, and virtuous Elly May Clampett, who grew up in Bug Tussle, somewhere outside of Hooterville. Each sitcom also sported a theme song, written by its producer, that carefully spelled the origins of the comic situation.

Gilligan's Island was an immediate hit. In spite of the fact that its scheduled slot was changed every season it was in production, it managed never once to lose its time period. So why then was the series canceled after only three years, while *The Beverly Hillbillies*, to name one apropos example, lasted for nine? In Schwartz's view, it was CBS Chairman William Paley's personal sense of embarrassment about *Gilligan's Island* that sank the *S.S. Minnow*. (Indeed, it is conjectured that the ship was named to conjure the specter of FCC Chairman Newton N. Minow, who had offered the famous characterization of American television as "a vast wasteland" in 1961.) While other top brass happily approved renewal for a fourth season based on black ink at the bottom line, Paley personally vetoed the critically disclaimed series in order to make way for the renewal of *Gunsmoke*, a prestigious "adult western" that had been airing since the radio era.

Remarkably, however, for such a relatively short-lived series, *Gilligan's Island* just would not go gently into that good night. Based on the consistent popularity of the syndicated reruns, which did especially well during the four o'clock weekday "children's hour," the dormant castaways found animation in two cartoon series. *The New Adventures of Gilligan* (ABC, 1974–77) simply continued the storylines of the original show in cartoon form. *Gilligan's Planet* (CBS, 1982–83) updated the now epic tale by trading in the uncharted island for an uncharted planet: The Professor builds a rocket from odds and ends around the island but gives it too much power, thus propelling the castaways past their planned destination of Hawaii into outer space.

As if all this were not enough, Schwartz personally produced and wrote three made-for-TV *Gilligan* sequels, all of which aired in prime time on NBC. Though the sitcom had been out of production for over a decade, six of the seven original actors returned for these reunion films. Only Tina Louise, who had also declined the voiceover role of Ginger in the cartoon programs, was unwilling to reprise her role; she was replaced by Judith Baldwin.

In *Rescue from Gilligan's Island* (1978), Schwartz mercifully returned the castaways to civilization, only to mercilessly strand them back on The Island again before the episode's end. Despite threatening skies, they just can't resist the chance to take a nostalgic cruise to the site of their thirteen years of captivity. Despite the title's promise of narrative climax, this development readily set up the next two-hour episode.

The Castaways on Gilligan's Island (1979) was on the air within a year. This time The Professor reconstructs the wreckage of a World War II bomber into an escape plane. But once again the myth of Sisyphus prevails. Aghast at the malaise-ridden society they discover in Jimmy Carter's stagflation-ridden America, they voluntarily return to the island and seek to become Reagan-era entrepreneurs. With easy access to Thurston Howell's now double-digit inflated millions, they turn The Island into a fabulous seaside resort, with the Castaways Hotel as its centerpiece. Programs such as *Fantasy Island* and *The Love Boat* (both by Aaron Spelling, see Chapter 15) were popular that season, and Schwartz was clearly bucking for a new series based on this format.

Both Schwartz and NBC, however, agreed to wait for the numbers on one more Gilligan movie-of-the-week before returning the saga to the regular weekly lineup. This final piece of Schwartz's late-Gilligan trilogy took a bizarre turn, possibly an indication that the aging concept was entering into some kind of inevitable baroque decay. In *The Harlem Globetrotters on Gilligan's Island* (1981), Schwartz brought the famous exhibition basketball team to The Island to appear at the Castaways Hotel. The Globetrotters, however, get mixed up with an evil mad genius scientist (Martin Landau), who is intent on taking over the world with a newly discovered element called Supremium, which can only be found (you guessed it) on The Island. Somehow, with programs such as *Cheers, Family Ties,* and *Hill Street Blues* looming larger in Grant Tinker's plans for the NBC of the eighties, there just didn't seem to be an amenable slot for Schwartz's impossibly downscale vision.

Though Sherwood Schwartz found himself again critically berated and commercially rejected as a purveyor of moronic content, the passage of time would reveal him once more as an influential innovator. All three Gilligan movies had done well in the ratings and, regardless of NBC's lack of interest in a new series, the sitcom "reunion movie," a phenomenon conceived and executed by Sherwood Schwartz, would soon establish itself as a familiar and lucrative programming genre. Within the next several years, similar projects were produced with the casts of such chestnuts as *The Andy Griffith Show, Father Knows Best, The Beverly Hillbillies,* and *Leave It to Beaver.* The form even expanded its base in the sitcom to include reunion films for such dramas as *Marcus Welby, M.D.* and *The Mod Squad.* Schwartz had made a salient point about the penetration of television series into the consciousness of the American viewing public.

The long and sometimes tortured history of *Gilligan's Island* is, by itself, not the story of Sherwood Schwartz's career. Even while *Gilligan* was still in production, Schwartz launched another series, *It's About Time* (CBS, 1966–67), a sitcom about two American astronauts (Frank Aletter and Jack Mullaney) who accidentally crash through the time barrier and become marooned in the past with a family of prehistoric cave-dwellers: Gronk (Joe E. Ross, late of Nat Hiken's *Car 54, Where Are You?*), Shad (Imogene Coca, once the partner of Sid Caesar), and their two children Mlor and Breer.

It's About Time seemed to have a winning recipe. Schwartz combined the basic stock of his own *Gilligan's Island* concept (castaways) with elements from other contemporary hits such as *The Flintstones* (prehistorical setting), *I Dream of Jeannie* (astronauts), and *The Beverly Hillbillies* (ancients versus moderns). However, the series seemed to bump into the very problems that James Aubrey had incorrectly predicted for *Gilligan*. The premise was just too narrow for the development of storylines. In an attempt to salvage the show, Schwartz tried a turnabout, à la Henning's *Beverly Hillbillies/Green Acres* reversal: the astronauts make it back to the twentieth century but accidentally bring the cave family along for the ride. Another of Schwartz's brothers, Elroy, who had written episodes of *Gilligan's Island*, was brought in for the rescue. But it was to no avail; CBS refused to renew *It's About Time*.

Schwartz's next — and by most standard measures greatest — hit was *The Brady Bunch* (ABC, 1969–74). If it was youth the networks wanted, Schwartz was determined to show he could deliver the market. He took an old, proven idea — a grafted family (*Make Room for Daddy*, *The Lucy Show*, *Family Affair*, et al.) — and demographically spruced it up for the seventies by providing three male/female pairs of kids at regular age intervals, plus a far-out, postsixties mom and dad, and a Hazel-like all-purpose servant and nanny.

The Brady kids filled a vacuum of national identification for America's youth as the Vietnam War wound down to its ignominious end. Greg (Barry Williams), the oldest boy, was at one point receiving as many as six thousand fan letters a week, while Marcia (Maureen McCormick), the oldest girl, could change the female grooming habits of entire junior high schools with a new hairdo. The middle kids, Jan (Eve Plumb) and Peter (Christopher Knight), achieved puberty along with their audience; while the "babies" of the family, the lisping Cindy (Susan Olsen) and the hyperactive Bobby (Mike Lookinland), could do naught but "play nice" even as American children were just saying "yes" to other activities at younger and younger ages.

The adults were no less demographically winsome. We are offered Mike, the father (Robert Reed), a white middle-class architect with a quasi-Afro hairdo and a post-Kennedy propensity for vigorously youthful activity; mother Carol (Florence Henderson), a pre–Mary Tyler Moore-ish perky wifette who had apparently cornered the market on bell-bottomed polyester pants suits; and maid Alice (Ann B. Davis), a welcomed proletarian visitor to this otherwise impenetrable bourgeois fortress. The Brady marriage was a positive omen of the coming age of corporate mergers.

As with *Gilligan's Island*, the cancellation of *The Brady Bunch* turned out to be more like a new beginning for the concept than an end. *The Brady Kids* was already a part of the ABC Saturday-morning cartoon schedule from 1972 to 1974. *The Brady Bunch Hour* (ABC, 1977) was a remarkable self-reflexive backstage musical in which Mike forsakes architecture to manage the family, which has by now moved to the beach and gotten its own network variety show. The original cast remained intact, except for Eve Plumb, who was replaced by Geri Reischl in the role of Jan.

Plumb returned, however, for *The Brady Brides* (NBC, 1981), which concerned the adult married lives of two of the girls: Marcia has gotten hitched to a mellow dude named Wally Logan, while Jan has nabbed Philip Covington III, an incorrigible anal retentive over-achiever. Unable to afford individual homes of their own, the two couples share a house, an arrangement that has been facilitated for them by the now post–Mary Tyler Moore-ish Mrs. Brady, who is pursuing a career as a real estate agent.

The quick death of *The Brady Brides* was merely a setback for the seemingly indefatigable concept. *A Very Brady Christmas* (CBS, 1988) achieved higher ratings than any individual episode of any of the Brady series had ever managed. In 1990 CBS and Schwartz got together on yet another mutation, perhaps the most remarkable of all: *The Bradys* was described in its developmental stages as aspiring to the form of ABC's *thirtysomething:* Jan suffering fertility problems; Bobby facing paralysis after an auto-racing accident. The possibilities seemed as bottomless as the depth of American neurosis: Greg taking Prozac for midlife crisis? Marcia wracked by Epstein-Barre? Like *Gilligan's Island, The Brady Bunch* even achieved category status on *Remote Control* (MTV, 1988–90). In 1991, a theatrical group in Chicago began performing actual Brady Bunch scripts on the legitimate stage.

Schwartz also had his share of prime-time failures. *Harper Valley P.T.A.* (NBC, 1981–82) is a classic example of TV derivation and recombinance. The sitcom was adapted from a 1978 movie starring Barbara Eden, which in turn had been adapted from the narrative of a 1968 hit song written by Tom T. Hall and recorded by Jeannie C. Riley. The story concerned Stella Johnson, an outspoken, free-thinking, free-loving woman in a small Ohio town who joins the PTA in an effort to expose the hypocrisies of its stuffy, hypocritical members. The series was reworked after the first year. Major changes included the title (to simply *Harper Valley*) and a new producer (Schwartz left); only four more episodes were ever made.

His other minor efforts are all tied to his two big hits in one way or another. In *Dusty's Trail* (syndicated, 1973–74) Schwartz brought back Bob Denver as Dusty, the lovable-but-incompetent scout for a nineteenth-century wagon train. Not surprisingly, the group of settlers becomes hopelessly lost on the Western frontier. The Skipper rematerialized as the Wagon Master (Forrest Tucker). The Millionaire and his Wife? Mr. and Mrs. Brookhaven, a couple of snooty Boston Brahmins. The Movie Star? Lulu, an aspiring showgirl. Mary Ann? Betsy, an idealistic young school teacher. In a stunning break with convention, the seventh passenger, Andy, is not a Professor.

Schwartz would eventually try Bob Denver in two more aborted projects: *The Invisible Woman,* in which Denver plays the biochemist who invents a secret elixir that can turn his niece invisible, and *Scamps,* which cast Denver as a starving writer who opens a day-care center in his home to generate some much-needed cash.

In *Kelly's Kids,* Schwartz attempted to bring a little belated relevance to *The Brady Bunch.* A childless couple (Ken Barry and Brooke Bundy) adopts three children: one white, one black, one Amerasian. The demographically eclectic family was introduced to the public on a 1974 *Brady Bunch* episode, but it never found a place on the network schedule. Schwartz would try this concept once more in *Together We Stand* (CBS, 1986–87), which starred Elliot Gould as the patriarch of another genetically unrelated family. Schwartz left after the pilot, at which time desperate writers killed off Gould's character and renamed the series *Nothing Is Easy,* transforming the show into a single-parent vehicle; but this was to no avail.

Big John, Little John (NBC, 1976–77) was a filmed sitcom expressly made by Schwartz for the network's Saturday-morning chldren's schedule, following his *Gilligan* cartoon spin-off successes. Herb Edelman plays a middle-aged science teacher who stumbles upon an elixir that causes him to temporarily turn into a twelve-year-old boy (Robbie Rist). Despite the failure of the project, Schwartz once again proved himself ahead of his time. His idea of doing a filmed, as opposed to animated, series for Saturday morning would become popular about ten years later; examples include *Pee-Wee's Playhouse* and *Saved by the Bell.* The very concept of *Big John, Little John* would be the foundation of an entire subgenre of age-reversal, kid-oriented movie comedies in the late eighties: *Big; Eighteen Again; Vice Versa; Like Father, Like Son.*

Schwartz published his book *Inside Gilligan's Island: From Creation to Syndication* in 1988, dedicating the book to his brother Al ("without whom I may never have become a writer"), his wife Mildred ("It was her constant help, encouragement and reassurance that enabled me to endure . . .") and, most notably, "to Bob Denver, Alan Hale, Jim Backus, Natalie Schafer, Tina Louise, Russell Johnson, and Dawn Wells who . . . have brought, and continue to bring, laughter and entertainment into the homes of millions of people all over the world."

SHERWOOD SCHWARTZ: SELECTED VIDEOGRAPHY

Early Writing Credits

The Red Skelton Show (NBC/CBS, 1951–71)
I Married Joan (NBC, 1952–55)
My Favorite Martian (CBS, 1963–66)

Series

Gilligan's Island (CBS, 1964–67)
It's About Time (CBS, 1966–67)
The Brady Bunch (ABC, 1969–74)
The Brady Kids (ABC, 1972–74)
Dusty's Trail (syndicated, 1973–74)
The New Adventures of Gilligan (ABC, 1974–77)
Big John, Little John (NBC, 1976–77)
Harper Valley P.T.A. (NBC, 1981–82)
The Brady Brides (ABC, 1981)
Gilligan's Planet (ABC, 1982–83)
Together We Stand/Nothing Is Easy (CBS, 1986–87)
The Bradys (CBS, 1990)

Movies Made for Television

Rescue from Gilligan's Island (NBC, 1978)
The Castaways on Gilligan's Island (NBC, 1979)
The Brady Girls Get Married (NBC, 1981)
The Harlem Globetrotters on Gilligan's Island (NBC, 1981)
The Invisible Woman (NBC, 1983)
A Very Brady Christmas (CBS, 1988)

4. NORMAN LEAR

——— —— —— —— —— —— —— —

A Post-McCarthy Sitcom

The first off-camera American television production personality to emerge as a widely known public figure, Norman Lear forever changed the tone and tenor of situation comedy, and perhaps all of prime time, with a series of critically acclaimed smash hits during the 1970s that included *All in the Family, Sanford and Son, Maude,* and *The Jeffersons.* While holding fast to the traditional structural features of American domestic comedy as it had developed on radio and television, Lear expanded the thematic concerns of the genre into previously unexplored realms. Forsaking standard content plotting axioms (the chastening of errant children, the consequences of forgotten wedding anniversaries, and so on), Lear tackled such highly charged issues as racism, sexism, sexual preferentialism, economic uncertainty, the generation gap, and a wide array of subjects that had previously seemed beyond the ken of situation comedy.

Not satisfied merely to break taboo for the purpose of displaying personal irreverence, Lear informed his comic dramas with a foursquare political liberalism — a didactic aesthetic that proved to be as controversial as his subject matter. By consistently embedding authorial advocacy into plot and characterization on issues ranging from abortion and homosexuality to foreign policy and Watergate,

Lear helped dispel the belief that situation comedy was an intrinsically superficial form that could only support its own status quo. Furthermore, through his ratings successes, the producer proved beyond doubt that a weekly commercial television series could in fact serve as a vehicle for personal expression.

Born in 1922 in New Haven, Connecticut, Lear studied communications at Emerson College in Boston and served in the Army Air Corps during World War II. Upon his return from the service, he found work in the infant television industry writing for comedy-variety shows. Lear's blackout sketches for NBC's *Ford Star Revue* in 1951 caught the attention of Jerry Lewis, who put the young writer on salary to supply material for the comedy team of Dean Martin and Jerry Lewis. This initial phase of Lear's career reached a peak in the late fifties, when he served as a director and as a principal writer for network comedy-variety stars including Martha Raye, George Gobel, Carol Channing, and Don Rickles.

By the end of the fifties, however, Norman Lear had left TV work in favor of theatrical film production. Like many other behind-the-scenes comic talents who had helped to pioneer the new medium (Neil Simon and Woody Allen head the list), Lear found the unremitting commercial and political pressures of weekly episodic television too stultifying an atmosphere for personal artistic development. Television had by now displaced the movies as the primary storytelling medium in American culture. As a consequence of TV's rise to dominance, the commercial stakes of program production had spiraled to the point where the playfulness and experimentation of first-generation comedy stars, such as Sid Caesar and Steve Allen, was being swept aside in favor of "safe" squeaky-clean family situation comedies, such as *Father Knows Best, The Donna Reed Show,* and *Leave It to Beaver.* In 1959 Lear produced a pilot for a sitcom titled *Band of Gold,* which starred James Franciscus and Suzanne Pleshette playing a different married or unmarried couple each week; the program was considered too "experimental" and was never broadcast. That was, for the moment, the last straw.

The movies, on the other hand, as a result of their diminished importance in the age of television, seemed to be loosening up as an artistic medium during the 1960s. The studio system, with its rigid control of stars, scripts, and every phase of creative activity, had in effect collapsed. The old "production code," which had functioned as a de facto censorship mechanism since the 1930s, was no longer enforced; film directors gained increasing license to do whatever they could to draw people out of their easy chairs and into theater seats.

Hoping to take advantage of this situation, Lear formed Tandem Productions, a partnership with Bud Yorkin. The two proceeded to write and produce Hollywood feature films for over a decade. The results, however, were less than distinguished, either critically or at the box office. Tandem films included such lightweight fare as *Come Blow Your Horn*, 1963; *It's Never Too Late*, 1965; *Divorce, American Style*, 1967; *The Night They Raided Minsky's*, 1968; and *Cold Turkey*, 1971. Somehow, Lear's heart — or perhaps his soul — remained in tube work.

Meanwhile the constrictions of prime-time television that had alienated him showed no signs of loosening up. Political assassinations, ghetto street riots, Vietnam combat footage, and antiwar demonstrations dominated the news in the sixties. But despite all this "material," satirical drama was nowhere to be found on the networks. Instead, sitcom viewers were fed a steady diet of shows such as *The Beverly Hillbillies, Here's Lucy,* and *Andy Griffith.* The yawning gap between the emerging realities of American family life and what was being represented on TV sitcoms was unattractive to some viewers — especially younger, more educated viewers, who were coming into their own as important consumers whom advertisers wanted to reach.

Lear contemplated a daring return to prime-time television that would ignore the conventional wisdom of providing audiences with what insiders called "least objectionable" programming. His idea was to do an American adaptation of a British sitcom, Johnny Speight's *Till Death Us Do Part,* which had been built around the generational conflicts between a bigoted middle-aged man and his live-in son-in-law. He tried to sell the innovative concept to ABC in 1968, but the network honchos were too timid to make a deal, despite the fact that ABC, as the last-place network, had relatively little to lose.

Paradoxically, it was CBS, the top-rated network, that was more receptive to Lear's proposal. With cable just on the horizon, CBS president Robert Wood seemed to grasp the growing importance of target demographics in TV economics, even if his colleagues at the other networks could not. Much to the amazement of many industry executives, Wood blithely canceled CBS ratings winners, including all three of Paul Henning's sitcoms (see Chapter 2), in favor of brash new material that might capture upscale viewers. *The Mary Tyler Moore Show* and *M*A*S*H* were among Wood's pet projects. Lear's *All in the Family* popped up as a midseason replacement in January of 1971.

Poor ratings during that initial winter seemed to back the predictions of the programming conservatives who believed that the

American TV audience would never go for such controversial fare. But throughout the spring and summer, the previously forbidden words and themes that were aired on *All in the Family* attracted free publicity in the form of dozens of newspaper and magazine articles. Wood prevailed and gave the Lear sitcom another shot the following fall. He wasn't sorry. *All in the Family* became the top-rated show on television for an unprecedented five seasons in a row.

Archie Bunker (Carroll O'Connor) was a sitcom character unlike any who had appeared before him. Liberally lacing his illiberal diatribes with complaints against "your coloreds, your Hebes, your gay homosexuals, and your broads who want to take over the world," Archie was clearly a foil to everything that Lear stood for. Yet public reaction provoked heated debate over the meaning of the text. While some saw *All in the Family* as a long-needed exposé of American boorishness, intolerance, and bigotry, others gleefully plastered their bumpers with Archie Bunker for President signs, finding a hero in the opinionated hardhat from Queens, New York. Was Lear providing the culture with therapy for its maladies, or was he, despite his intentions, lending a kind of legitimacy to the very things he most despised?

"Bigotry," Lear told a *Playboy* interviewer, "is most insidious — and common — when it occurs in otherwise lovable people. I abhor bigotry, but I think it's important to understand where it comes from, to realize there are more areas of agreement between people like Archie and people like me than there are areas of disagreement." He admitted that Archie, a loading-dock worker who occasionally worked nights driving a cab, was modeled more along the lines of his own father, an appliance salesman, than after the main character of *Till Death Us Do Part.*

The working-class setting of *All in the Family* was unusual in the 1970s; in fact, it was something of a throwback to the 1950s, when sitcoms such as *The Honeymooners* and *The Life of Riley* were still in production. Like his blue-collar predecessors, Archie Bunker was loud and prone to malapropisms. But, unlike a Ralph Kramden who pursued hare-brained, get-rich-quick schemes as he waited for his ship to come in, Archie suffered the real-life indignities of an erratic economy that led to layoffs, inflation, union give-backs, and a myriad of other distinctly non-sitcomic problems. In the face of it all, he seemed content to sit back in his easy chair with a beer in front of the TV set, a position from which he could practice his own special brand of freedom of speech.

Wife Edith (Jean Stapleton), though a bit acerbic in some of the early episodes, was mostly played as a simple-minded martyr. Not inclined to argue with her husband's pettinesses, she was too decent a soul to be supportive of his worst excesses. Archie was the bread-winner, and she fussed over him and catered to his every need, but she liked people too much to share his prejudices. Gloria (Sally Struthers), Archie's daughter, was more combative, refusing to let Archie's sexist or racist or otherwise politically incorrect remarks pass without challenge. But Archie's main antagonist was Gloria's husband, Mike Stivic (Rob Reiner), a doctoral student in the social sciences whom Archie preferred to call "Meathead" or, occasionally, "Polack."

Mike and Gloria, the young, politically liberal, baby-boomer couple, often seemed to be the mouthpieces for Lear's point of view. But at the same time, Lear made sure not to overidealize them. Mike, especially, was the target of authorial barbs. It was often while gorging himself at the Bunker dinner table with food paid for by Archie's hard work at the loading dock that he would enrage his father-in-law with his agnosticism, his antiwar sentiments, and his kind words for blacks, feminists, gays, and anyone else on Archie's hit list.

Lear had created a new sitcom style with the show. He had even shaken up conventional production wisdom by videotaping the episodes in front of live audiences at a time when most sitcoms were being filmed, with mechanical laughs added in the editing room. But it was surely the ratings rather than the fresh look or the crisp dialogue of *All in the Family* that had network executives screaming for more. Lear responded by going into production with a host of spin-offs that soon peppered the CBS schedule. *Maude* was the first of these, and it pushed the frontier of prime-time content beyond the limits of the program that spawned it. The title character was Edith Bunker's "ultraliberal" cousin Maude Findlay (Beatrice Arthur), a well-to-do matron from suburban Westchester who was working on her fourth marriage. (Only two years earlier CBS was refusing to allow divorced characters on its comedies; see Chapter 5.) Viewers of the series saw Maude get an abortion and go through menopause (hot flashes — right in the middle of a sitcom!), while her husband, Walter (Bill Macy), suffered from alcoholism and underwent a nervous break-down. If *All in the Family* had broken new ground by introducing dialogues on race, class, gender, and politics into a sitcom, *Maude* brought these same issues right into the heart of the same upscale suburban territory that had once been the province of shows such as *Hazel* and *Bewitched*.

In his next spin-off, *Good Times*, Lear returned to the inner city. The show follows Maude's maid Florida Evans (Esther Rolle) and her family to an apartment in a high-rise Chicago housing project. Though it was the first American television series ever to be set in such a locale, *Good Times* turned out to be one of the less pungent Lear sitcoms in terms of social criticism.

In the early seasons of the show, much attention had been given to good-parenting themes, with Florida and her husband James (John Amos) struggling to instill proper values in their three children despite the hardships of big-city ghetto life. In these episodes the Evanses seem more like a primitive version of the Huxtables than a family created by the producer who had given the world the Bunkers. But cast changes riddled the show. First John Amos left the series. While the absence of the father might have been pursued as a social issue in its own right, the series instead switched emphasis toward featuring a kind of shrieking "rank-out" humor, a comic strategy that was proving popular on another Lear sitcom about an Afro-American family, *Sanford and Son* (see below).

J.J. (Jimmie Walker), the Evanses' eldest son, became the focus of *Good Times*, and Walker emerged as the series' breakaway star. A jive-talking conniver, J.J. strutted before the camera, proclaiming his sexual prowess and periodically letting go his signature exclamation, "DY-NO-MITE!" To some critics, J.J. at times seemed like a character right out of *Amos 'n' Andy*. Stories centered on the other characters, such as younger brother Michael (Ralph Carter), a sensitive and serious "A" student played against ghetto stereotype, became increasingly rare. Esther Rolle, *Good Times'* original star, left the show, citing its new direction.

Whatever its shortcomings, *Good Times* was part of the return of black actors and characters to situation comedy in the 1970s, after a period of almost two decades during which the only blacks seen regularly in the genre had been in servant roles or in minor supporting parts. Norman Lear had, in fact, engineered the renaissance of black situation comedy almost singlehandedly. *The Jeffersons*, a third spin-off traceable to *All in the Family*, was also a predominantly black show. Starring Sherman Hemsley and Isabel Sanford in the title roles, the series concerned the Bunkers' upwardly mobile black neighbors who make it big in the dry-cleaning business and move to a luxury building on the posh Upper East Side of Manhattan.

George Jefferson was in many ways a black Archie Bunker, spouting his own catalog of prejudices with similar gusto. And he had much to shout about, as Lear continued to break new ground in sitcom content. Tom and Helen Willis, who lived upstairs, were the first interracial couple ever to appear as regular characters in a sitcom.

Moreover, their daughter Jennie begins dating Lionel Jefferson, and the young couple, much to George's chagrin, eventually marry. Simultaneously hungry for acceptance in the world he has entered and wary of its phoniness and pretenses, George embodies a sitcom crisis that shares structural similarities with the dilemma of Jed Clampett in *The Beverly Hillbillies*. As in *All in the Family*, the husband's excesses stand in contrast to the wife's moderation. Like Edith, Louise Jefferson is ruled by her nonideological decency and has a much easier time making friends.

Sanford and Son was another popular black sitcom produced by Norman Lear. Not a spin-off of *All in the Family*, the show was created by Lear and his Tandem Productions film partner Bud Yorkin as a vehicle for comedian Redd Foxx. Premiering on NBC as a midseason replacement only a year after *All in the Family* had hit the air, the show was also an adaptation of a British series. This time Lear transformed a Cockney junk dealer (from the British series *Steptoe and Son*) into Fred Sanford, a cantankerous aging black widower who lives with his son Lamont (Demond Wilson) in the Watts section of Los Angeles. Put-down humor was the linchpin of the show, as the sharp-tongued Foxx did his thing with a throng of regular characters — black, white, Hispanic, and Asian.

Sanford and Son was a Top Ten hit as long as it remained in production. But following the 1976–77 season, its fifth, Redd Foxx left the program to become host of his own comedy-variety series on ABC. This turned out to be a mistake for Foxx, as it has been for so many others who have attempted to revive that moribund genre. Costar Demond Wilson also departed when NBC refused to meet his salary demands. A new show, *Sanford Arms*, was spun off with the remaining regulars, but without Redd Foxx, the sitcom could not hold its audience.

Like *Sanford and Son*, *One Day at a Time* was a major Lear hit that was not narratively related to *All in the Family*. It was, however, more in line with the peculiar kind of sitcom social realism that Lear had developed in his three-way saga of the Bunkers, the Findlays, and the Jeffersons. Bonnie Franklin starred as Ann Romano, the first divorced single parent in the history of the American sitcom. A feisty, fortyish woman thrust back into the work force after the collapse of her marriage, Ann moves to a small apartment in Indianapolis with her two teenaged daughters. Her no-nonsense approaches to dealing with the problems that life has dealt her are aesthetically counterbalanced by the apartment building's bumbling janitor Schneider (Pat Harrington, Jr.), a middle-aged self-proclaimed macho man most often seen with a tool belt around his waist and a pack of Camels rolled up in the sleeve of his T-shirt.

Like Archie Bunker, Ann Romano is introduced to audiences as a working-class character suffering from a variety of economic inequities and societal ills. But in each case the character is "saved" by Lear before the series ends, in a very American Dream–like way. In the final seasons of *All in the Family*, following Edith's death, Archie buys the neighborhood bar, turning it — and the sitcom — into *Archie Bunker's Place*. Similarly, Ann Romano sees her fortunes improve as she moves up, over the course of the series, from the status of exploited office worker to an executive position with an advertising agency. Conservative critics of Norman Lear's "radical liberalism" might do well to consider the apple-pie endings provided by the producer for Archie Bunker and Ann Romano, not to mention the bootstrap entrepreneurial triumph of George Jefferson.

Amid all these smash hits, Lear also had his share of bombs: *Hot L Baltimore*, adapted from an off-Broadway play, was set in the lobby of a has-been grand hotel. Its regular characters included a Colombian prostitute and a gay couple. *The Dumplings*, based on a comic strip, was a lesson in tolerance toward the obese, focusing on an enormous couple, played by James Coco and Geraldine Brooks, who run a lunch counter in Manhattan. *All's Fair* starred Richard Crenna and Bernadette Peters as a conservative political columnist and liberal photographer involved in a stormy inner-Beltway romance. *A Year at the Top* featured Paul Shaffer and Greg Evigan as a pair of pop songwriters from Idaho who come to Hollywood, where they are repeatedly tempted by the son of the Devil — who also happens to be their agent — to sell their souls to reach the top of the charts. Lear even teamed up with Alex Haley to produce *Palmerstown, U.S.A.*, an hour-long dramatic series concerning the friendship of two nine-year-old boys, one black, one white, in small-town Tennessee during the Depression. None of these shows lasted a season.

Norman Lear sitcoms continued to dominate the prime-time ratings through the midseventies, but as the decade wore on, viewers — and consequently network executives — gradually lost interest. By the late seventies, the sentimental, politically toothless humor of Garry Marshall (see Chapter 6) was displacing Lear at the top of the heap. Initially undaunted, Lear's response was to attempt ever more innovative projects and to bypass the network bureaucrats if necessary.

Mary Hartman, Mary Hartman was the most famous of Lear's off-network projects. A five-nights-a-week send-up of soap operas, the series was set in the mythical town of Fernwood, Ohio. A look at *Mary Hartman* today reveals a program that looks more like David Lynch's *Twin Peaks* than anything ever produced by Irna Phillips or Agnes Nixon (see Chapters 26 and 27). Mary (Louise Lasser) was a character deeply influenced, to say the least, by a lifetime of television watching — a dreamy couch potato obsessed with the waxy buildup gathering on her kitchen linoleum. Her husband was impotent; her sister was a slut; her grandfather, complete with trenchcoat, was given to exposing himself in public.

As a commercial television property, *Mary Hartman* suffered from what turned out to be insurmountable obstacles. In markets where it was carried, the show was programmed late at night — sometimes in the wee hours — because of its "blue" material. Moreover, in many areas it wasn't carried by any local stations at all, and this was of crucial importance for national coverage in the primitive days before satellite cable. In less than a year, Louise Lasser departed and the series stumbled into free-fall. Spin-off surgery was attempted. *Fernwood Forever* pushed the same storylines forward without the Mary Hartman character. *Fernwood 2-Night* was a fictional talkshow, starring Martin Mull and Fred Willard, broadcast from the town's TV station. The talkshow was moved to California and became *America 2-Night*. The patient, however, could not be saved.

A less well remembered Lear project was *All That Glitters*, also developed for Monday-through-Friday first-run syndication. Defying most recognizable TV genres, this dimly lit drama was a kind of comic soap opera in which all traditional male/female gender roles have been reversed. It was gone in a matter of months.

Apparently Lear had run up against the limits of innovation that the traffic would allow in commercial television. He turned away from on-line production and instead moved toward front-office work. His studio, T.A.T. (an acronym culled from a Yiddish saying that literally means "to put your ass on the line"), had generated enormous profits from *All in the Family* and its spin-offs over the years, and he used this capital to buy a controlling interest in another production company, Avco-Embassy. This studio in turn generated several major hits of its own, including *Diff'rent Strokes* (NBC, 1978–86), about an Upper East Side Manhattan millionaire who adopts two black orphans, and *The Facts of Life* (NBC, 1979–87), set at a girls' boarding school in New York's Hudson River Valley. Both of these sitcoms lacked the sturm und drang of Lear's contentious style, but they were fully consistent with the kinds of social concerns he had shown in his own work. Episodes typically dealt with the evils of racism, sexual hypocrisy, and so on.

With the election of Ronald Reagan to the White House in 1980, Lear increasingly gave his personal energies to People for the American Way, an organization he had helped to create, which was dedicated to the public promotion of liberal political values. The producer's one attempt at reviving his vintage style during the eighties was a sitcom for ABC titled *A.K.A. Pablo*, which starred Paul Rodriguez as a young Chicano comedian, brimming over with ethnic jokes and wisecracks, who lives at home with his staid, traditionalist parents. Only five episodes were ever aired.

In 1991, much to the surprise of everyone, Norman Lear's name was suddenly heard again on prime-time television, as he attempted a comeback with a new program, *Sunday Dinner*. CBS, the network with whom he had built mutually advantageous successes during the seventies, aired the program on Sunday nights, in the time slot that *All in the Family* had briefly held. In fact, "best of" reruns of what was now the old Archie Bunker chestnut were hammocked in with *Sunday Dinner*, offering viewers, in effect, a "Norman Lear hour."

Sunday Dinner was clearly an attempt by Lear to revive his signature style of *All in the Family* and *Maude*, though concessions were made to contemporary cultural circumstances. Each week widower Ben Benedict (Robert Loggia) is reunited with his three adult children, his granddaughter, and his sister for a traditional family Sunday meal — presumably mirroring the activities of the audience. Ben, however, is approaching sixty and he is engaged to a woman named T.T. (Teri Hatcher), who happens to be twenty-six years his junior. In classic Lear fashion, the series unfolds in a succession of intergenerational squabbles about sex and politics, current events and religion, social mores and personal foibles. Interestingly, Lear himself is now married to a woman who is quite a bit younger than he is, and *Sunday Dinner* may well be his most autobiographical work of all.

Sunday Dinner also indicates a greater interest by Lear in spiritual matters since the days when Mike Stivic's agnostic pronouncements seemed to be his final say on the subject. T.T. regularly engages in out-loud prayer to God, whom she addresses as "Chief." Her New Agey theology falls somewhere between Ralph Waldo Emerson and the Naropa Institute, leading to conflicts with Ben's sister (Marion Mercer), a devout follower of the old-time religion, as well as with Ben's daughter (Martha Gehman), an indignantly enlightened research scientist given to atheistic thinking.

Despite intense publicity, *Sunday Dinner* failed to garner sufficient ratings and was canceled after a brief summer run. Yet whatever the fate of any new projects he may attempt, Norman Lear's place in American broadcast history has long been steadfastly secure. Many of the freedoms from censorship that the producers of situation comedies have taken for granted for decades now can be directly traced to Lear's extraordinary success in popularizing franker discussions of the social realities of American life. What sitcom today *doesn't* have a divorced character? or an ethnically diverse cast? or an outspoken bigot? or some vestige of a Lear innovation as part of its conventional structure? Indeed, it takes little more than a brief look at a rerun of just about any sitcom to ascertain whether, in historical terms, the series is a "pre–Norman Lear" or a "post–Norman Lear" show.

NORMAN LEAR: SELECTED VIDEOGRAPHY

Early Writing Credits

The Ford Star Revue (NBC, 1950–51)
Honestly Celeste! (CBS, 1954)
The Martha Raye Show (NBC, 1955–56)

Series

All in the Family (CBS, 1971–79)
Sanford and Son (NBC, 1972–77)
Maude (CBS, 1972–78)
Good Times (CBS, 1974–79)
The Jeffersons (CBS, 1975–85)
Hot L Baltimore (ABC, 1975)
One Day at a Time (CBS, 1975–84)
The Dumplings (NBC, 1976)
The Nancy Walker Show (ABC, 1976)
All's Fair (CBS, 1976–77)
Mary Hartman, Mary Hartman (syndicated, 1976–78)
Fernwood Forever (syndicated, 1977–78)
A Year at the Top (CBS, 1977)
The Keane Brothers (CBS, 1977)
All That Glitters (syndicated, 1977)
Fernwood 2-Night (syndicated, 1978)
America 2-Night (syndicated, 1978)
In the Beginning (CBS, 1978)
Apple Pie (ABC, 1978)
Hangin' In (CBS, 1979)

Archie Bunker's Place (CBS, 1979–83)
The Baxters (syndicated, 1979–81)
A.K.A. Pablo (ABC, 1985)
Sunday Dinner (CBS, 1991)

Movie Made for Television

Heartsounds (ABC, 1984)

5. JAMES L. BROOKS

_____

An American Comedy of Manners

Viewers were witness to sweeping changes in the aesthetics of television narrative during the 1970s. With the generation born during the television era emerging as the controlling force of the mass-consumer dollar, with cable beginning to thread its way through the national nervous system, and with the radio- and movie-based stars of TV's pioneer era gradually fading from view, the tone that television had established during its first quarter century seemed dated. The heritage of McCarthyism had made weekly episodic television seem Victorian to younger viewers who had grown up in a rock 'n' roll culture that had flattered their bohemian fantasies. Formidable changes would have to be made in the sitcom if the genre was going to capture the interest of viewers who associated *Leave It to Beaver* and *The Donna Reed Show* with their own prepubescence.

The provocative dialogue and deliberately innovative plot concerns of the Norman Lear shows (see Chapter 4) grabbed most of the media attention given to the overhaul of the TV sitcom that went on during the early seventies. But of no less importance in reshaping dramatic comedy on television was MTM Enterprises, the studio headed by Grant Tinker, which produced such seventies hits as *Mary Tyler Moore*, *Bob Newhart* (the Chicago show), and *Rhoda*. TV historian

Les Brown has referred to James L. Brooks and his MTM partner Allan Burns as the "resident geniuses" of that studio during the seventies. A close look at contemporary prime-time programming some two decades later provides evidence for the argument that Brooks's contributions to the TV sitcom renaissance of the seventies were perhaps the most influential and enduring innovations of all.

James L. Brooks was born in Brooklyn in 1940. He dropped out of New York University in the early sixties and found a job as a writer for CBS News. Like Norman Lear, Paul Henning, and several other producers, Brooks would find a way to make use of situation comedy as a means of autobiographical expression, in his case mythologizing his early work experiences at CBS into the newsroom of a local Minneapolis television station in *The Mary Tyler Moore Show*.

After a brief try at documentary work with David Wolper Productions (see Chapter 28), Brooks entered the world of prime-time fiction as the creator of *Room 222* (ABC, 1969–74). Part of a tidal wave of "relevant" dramas in the late sixties, the show was set in the classroom of Pete Dixon (Lloyd Hanes), a history teacher at Walt Whitman High in Los Angeles. The fact that Mr. Dixon was black was itself a salient indicator of "relevance," a term that referred as much to the breaking of TV's own set of self-imposed racial and sexual taboos as it did to the portrayal of any other particular aspect of society. The appropriately named Whitman High could also boast a Yiddish-spouting Jewish principal in Seymour Kaufman (Michael Constantine), a black guidance counselor in Liz McIntyre (Denise Nicholas), and a freshly graduated idealistic young WASP teacher in Alice Johnson (Karen Valentine). Sexual freedom, the generation gap, drug use, civil rights, and the war in Vietnam were all topics under discussion in *Room 222*. Brooks had collaborated on *Room 222* with producer Gene Reynolds, and each would move on to do influential sitcom work that would shape the future character of prime-time TV: Reynolds as the main creative force behind *M*A*S*H* following Larry Gelbart's departure from daily involvement with that series, and Brooks as a creator of *The Mary Tyler Moore Show*.

Brooks crafted the show as a vehicle for Mary Tyler Moore, who until this time had mainly been known for her role as second banana to the star of Carl Reiner's *The Dick Van Dyke Show* (CBS, 1961–66). The situation was originally conceived by Brooks as the story of a recently divorced small-town Midwestern woman setting out "to make it on her own" in the rough-and-tumble world of broadcast journalism. But the young producer ran into serious opposition to this concept from network management. Michael Dann, CBS's chief programmer during this period, argued that a divorcée was inherently too controversial a figure to be the heroine of a weekly comedy. Brooks and Burns were forced to rewrite Mary Richards into a woman who had broken a longtime engagement and decided to move to Minneapolis from her hometown.

Dann, who had piloted CBS at the top for years with such slapshtick sitcoms as *The Beverly Hillbillies* and *Here's Lucy,* was soon gone from Black Rock. But by the middle of the seventies divorced characters had become as familiar a sight in sitcoms as wacky neighbors. Not only would Norman Lear hit the Top Twelve in 1975 with his divorcée sitcom *One Day at a Time,* but Brooks would be able to divorce Lou Grant (Ed Asner) from his wife, midseries, in the third year of *The Mary Tyler Moore Show* as well. Brooks would also go on to create and produce *Rhoda,* which included in its storylines both the marriage and the divorce of the principal character.

The significance of the marketability of the Mary Richards character cannot be overestimated in terms of the development of target demographics in the mass market. Up until Mary, the primacy of nuclear-family lifestyle had been uncontested in sitcom narrative. The occasional single women who had dared show their faces in sitcoms — English teacher Connie Brooks (Eve Arden) in *Our Miss Brooks* or *Private Secretary* Susie McNamara (Ann Sothern) or comedy writer Sally Rogers (Rose Marie) in *The Dick Van Dyke Show* — were all self-consciously desperate to "snare" husbands. More recently Ann Marie (Marlo Thomas) of *That Girl* had carried around her fiancé Donald (Ted Bessell) like some kind of reassuring albatross. But Mary Richards was pretty and perky, and apparently willing to pursue a love life without sanctified legal commitment. She dated a man and then dropped him and then dated another. She seemed to be simultaneously on The Pill *and* getting coffee for her boss. She became the cover girl of the lonely crowd during the stagflation era.

The Mary Tyler Moore Show and its commercial success became the foundation of MTM Enterprises as a studio. Many of the show's characteristics — the emphases on single people and the workplace, the large ensemble cast, the self-conscious hipnesses of dialogue and plot-resolution styles — became studio trademarks, and indeed Brooks and Burns can be credited with much of the company's style. *Rhoda,* which follows Mary Richards's best friend and neighbor back in her native New York City, was spun off in 1974. Rhoda Morgenstern (Valerie Harper) had originally been introduced on *The MTM Show* as a wisecracking, overweight Jewish woman who has fled her overprotective Bronx mother to try to make it as a department store window dresser in downtown Minneapolis. She returns to New York, triumphant in both life and art, with her own sitcom, as a slimmed-down, self-confident wisecracking Jewish career woman who meets and marries a handsome building demolition expert named Joe (David Groh). Married life, however, soon proves boring for both Rhoda and her audience, and, as if the world of the sitcom had somehow adopted the legal code of the state of Nevada in the midseventies, the two are divorced. The supporting cast included Nancy Walker as the mother and Julie Kavner as sister Brenda.

Phyllis, a second *MTM* spin-off, starred Cloris Leachman as Mary's hopelessly hipoisie landlord, Phyllis Lindstrom. In her own series, Phyllis, who has enjoyed the material comforts of the wife of a professional, suddenly finds herself widowed in middle age with a teenage daughter. She moves to San Francisco to live with her late husband Lars's family, who frankly were never too crazy about her in the first place. The sarcasm and intercharacter hostilities make *Phyllis* in some ways the most interesting of the trilogy. For example, in *The Mary Tyler Moore Show* Brooks had been particularly innovative in the introduction of the patently annoying Ted Baxter character (Ted Knight). Ted's vanity and insensitivity, combined with his undeserved astronomical salary, created threads of resentment and hostility between him and the other regulars. In *Phyllis* we find this hostility taken a step further in Mother Dexter (Judith Lowry), Lars's white-haired, sharp-tongued grandmother, who frankly resents the intrusion of Phyllis into her home and makes no secret of it. By some measures, the pathetic Phyllis is the annoying character and the irascible Mother Dexter is the endearing one.

In addition to these three "career woman" sitcoms, Brooks and Burns created and produced *Paul Sand in Friends and Lovers* (CBS, 1974–75) at MTM. This short-lived series concerned Robert Dreyfuss (Sand), a young single man who is a bass violinist for the Boston Symphony Orchestra. A sensitive, shy, romantic, artistic bachelor, the character can be seen as a male complement to Mary Richards. His reluctances and passivities broke as many sitcom taboos concerning the behavior of single male sitcom heroes as Mary had concerning the behavior of single sitcom women. Perhaps because it lacked the energy supplied by the inferred feminist issues underpinning Mary, *Friends and Lovers* failed to gain an audience, even though it was slyly hammocked by CBS between *All in the Family* and *The Mary Tyler Moore Show* on the network's famous Saturday-night baby-boomer sitcom lineup of the midseventies.

If MTM Enterprises began its life as TV's high-quality sitcom factory during the seventies, by the eighties it had become better known for the production of high-quality hour-long dramatic series. Brooks took part in this transformation as the executive producer of *Lou Grant* (1977–82), a cusp program that was instrumental in the studio's migration across genre borders. *Lou Grant* was arguably the most unusual spin-off in the history of American broadcasting: a sitcom character was transferred virtually intact to the world of the prime-time dramatic series.

Lou Grant, the father figure of the workplace family of *The Mary Tyler Moore Show*, fired from his job as producer of the *Six O'Clock News* in the final episode of the show by WJM-TV's new owner (incompetent Ted was, of course, the only one who got to keep his job), confronts his midlife career crisis. He decides to return to print journalism and finds a job as city editor of the mythical *Los Angeles Tribune*. Focusing on contemporary issues of muckraking journalism (and the problems of successfully presenting it to a commercial audience), *Lou Grant* gave Brooks a chance to return to his insistent personal concern with the function of commercialized mass-media news operations in American culture. Brooks would make an even deeper thrust into the subject some ten years later as the director and writer of the movie *Broadcast News* (1987), a satiric exposé of the foibles of a network news operation that featured the triumph of an airhead pretty boy over a dedicated journalist.

Brooks's unprecedented adaptation of a sitcom character to TV's version of a serious drama was seamlessly smooth. As in sitcom Minneapolis, Lou Grant found himself in the center of a workplace family in dramatic Los Angeles. In this case the sitcomic Mary, Murray, Ted, and Sue Ann were replaced by a cast of post-Watergate characters whose ancestors can be traced to late-forties Hollywood newspaper films: Joe Rossi (Robert Walden) and Billie Newman (Linda Kelsey), a pair of idealistic pup reporters, each out to change the world with a typewriter and a dream; the uncompromising grande dame owner and publisher of the *Tribune*, Mrs. Pynchon (Nancy Marchand), a soft-hearted citizen and hard-headed businesswoman whose need to sell newspapers does not completely blind her to the responsibilities of the owner of a printing press in a democracy; Animal (Daryl Anderson), a sockless postsixties Weegee whose mind never seems close by but whose camera is never far away from trouble; and Charlie Hume (Mason Adams), the crusty editor-in-chief of the *Trib*, who must navigate the narrow channel between Lou's journalistic instincts and Mrs. Pynchon's determination to keep the venerable *Tribune* alive in the age of the television bite.

Lou Grant took on the vital issues of its day with as much fervor as any weekly commercial television series since Reginald Rose's *The Defenders* (CBS, 1961–65). Episodes typically dealt with such hot topics as the treatment of Vietnam veterans, nursing home care for the elderly, the careless disposal of toxic wastes, and the activities of neo-Nazi groups. In terms of the development of Brooks's career portfolio, *The Mary Tyler Moore Show* had met *Room 222*.

In 1977 Brooks left MTM and went to Paramount, where he would join such MTM sitcom alumni as James Burrows, David Lloyd, Ed. Weinberger, Stan Daniels, Davis Davis, and Glen and Les Charles. In their various capacities as series creators, writers, and producers, the team would collectively continue to develop the sitcom aesthetic they had begun at MTM, even as MTM itself was abandoning situation comedy to concentrate on hour-long continuing dramas such as *Lou Grant*, *The White Shadow*, *Hill Street Blues*, and *St. Elsewhere*. Paramount, meanwhile, would emerge from having little or no prime-time TV identity to become the honored home of such high-Q sitcoms as *Taxi*, *Cheers*, *The Associates*, and *Brothers*.

Taxi (ABC, 1978–81; NBC, 1981–83), which Brooks cocreated with Weinberger, Daniels, and Davis, was a "workplace family" sitcom about a New York City taxi garage. Despite its blue-collar setting, the show attracted the demographically upscale audience that had always been supportive of the MTM properties. Most of the characters of *Taxi* are, at least in their own minds, only driving cabs while waiting for breaks in other, more glamorous pursuits: a would-be actor (Jeff Conaway), a would-be prizefighter (Tony Danza), a would-be art gallery owner (Marilu Henner). The one full-time, dedicated cab driver, Alex Rieger (Judd Hirsch), is a kind of working-class philosophe, a blue-collar intellectual who is simply not interested in pursuing the material benefits of the "better" (i.e. white-collar) job that his obvious mental abilities might get him. Jim Ignatowski (Christopher Lloyd) is a different kind of refugee from the sixties, a burned-out acid freak who seems to have only enough brain cells left to drive a cab. All of these characters seemed to strike a nerve or two with *Taxi*'s audience, members of a generation that had graduated an unprecedented number of unemployable liberal arts majors from the nation's colleges. Louie DePalma (Danny DeVito), as grotesque and insensitive a boss as one was likely to work for in either art or life, presided over this abused collection of upright and sensitive victims. Louie, as a sitcom miscreant cast from the MTM mold, transcended the pretensions of Ted Baxter, happy homemaker Sue Ann Nivens, or even Mother Dexter in terms of pure sleaze factor.

The relative complexity of *Taxi*'s ironic plotlines, the allusive, plugged-in tone of its dialogue, and the not overly sweetened taste of its moral position are all definitive traits of Brooks's work. When ABC canceled the show in the spring of 1980, NBC picked it up as part of its attempt to create a "quality" image for the network, which had in recent years found itself floundering in third place. *Taxi* gained a slot on NBC's Thursday-night schedule ("The best night of television on television," as the network promo described it), along with such shows as *Fame, Hill Street Blues*, and *Cheers*.

The Associates (ABC, 1979–80), the story of three young law school graduates in their first year at a Wall Street firm, was a kind of yuppie-side-down version of *Taxi*. Though the series was a quick commercial failure (only nine episodes were even aired by ABC), it remains a prescient artifact that highlights Brooks's genius for understanding American cultural drift. With the coming of Reaganism, Wall Street chic would soon cast its three-piece pallor over American society. Films such as *Wall Street* and *Working Girl*, as well as TV series such as *L.A. Law* and *thirtysomething*, would all ride the crest of this new mythological trope to become mainstream pop cultural hits in the eighties. *The Associates* was perhaps half a dozen years ahead of its time; in fact, reruns of the thirteen episodes that were made tended to pop up on cable throughout the decade.

Like many of television's most creative minds, Brooks began to turn his attention to the movies at the height of his TV career. He had already done two films, both of which premiered on television. *Thursday's Game* (1974), which he wrote and produced while still at MTM, was a star-studded comedy about the personal and professional problems (the two never being very far apart in the Brooks world) of a group who played a regular Thursday-night poker game. The cast included such MTM familiars as Bob Newhart, Valerie Harper, Cloris Leachman, and Nancy Walker. Originally intended for theatrical release, the film was temporarily shelved and then released as an ABC movie-of-the-week. *Cindy* (1978), which Brooks cowrote and coproduced with a minyan of *MTM Show* and *Taxi* colleagues, was an adaptation of the Cinderella fairy tale — with an all-black cast, set in Harlem during the Second World War.

Brooks finally achieved theatrical release in 1979 with *Starting Over*, which he personally adapted from a Dan Wakefield novel. His film career went on to hit spectacular heights. In 1983 he won the Best Picture Oscar, as well as additional Oscars in writing and direction, for *Terms of Endearment*, which he adapted from the Larry McMurtry novel. With this kind of industry-wide recognition of his talents, Brooks gained the clout to produce a spate of theatrical films. One of them was *Just Between Friends,* which marked his return to MTM Enterprises as a producer. His old partner Allan Burns directed, and the film starred none other than Mary herself.

Brooks's most significant movie to date has been *Broadcast News* (1987), which he wrote, directed, and produced, and which brought him back to his oldest and apparently dearest theme: TV news production. Though the clash of responsible journalism and the bottom line in the crucible of the TV newsroom had been explored in the conflicts between the brainless, egotistical Ted and the Lou/Mary/Murray coalition of self-respecting professionals, in *Broadcast News* Brooks was able to get beyond the mere examination of personality clashes (though the film certainly contains its share of these) to some of the more perplexing social implications of the commodification of information.

Brooks returned to television production when his company, Gracie Films, developed *The Tracey Ullman Show* (Fox, 1987–90) for the new Fox network. Brooks served as executive producer, but much of the style of this performance-oriented variety vehicle was provided by its star. Ullman, along with an ensemble cast that included Julie Kavner (late of *Rhoda*), played an assortment of roles in a series of comedy skits set in a half-hour format. There had not been a successful comedy-variety show in production for American prime-time television since the old *Carol Burnett Show*, and *Tracey Ullman* was the most interesting and successful attempt that had yet been made to revive the form. Eschewing the traditional vaudeville-type stage that had been in use for c-v programs since the glory days of Milton Berle and Red Skelton, *The Tracey Ullman Show* was emphatically more cinematic than theatrical. It was as if the star were showing a collection of her short film works each week, rather than trooping out a stage show. The various skits were full of satiric thrusts on middle-class foibles of the type that a Brooks audience had come to expect. The show was produced by Heide Perlman, an extraordinary young talent who had written many of the best scripts for *Cheers*.

The Tracey Ullman Show used a series of very short cartoons by Matt Groening, an artist who at that point was better known for his newspaper comic strip "Life in Hell." Brooks, an admirer of Groening's work, had been responsible for selling Fox on this innovative animated segue structure for *Tracey Ullman*. In 1990 Brooks convinced Fox to spin off the Groening cartoon characters into their own half-hour series, *The Simpsons*, which immediately became the Fox network's biggest hit as well as a sudden national marketing bonanza.

Making powerful use of the convention of the animated cartoon as a "children's" form, *The Simpsons* has gone on to provide some of the most pungent social and political satire that has ever been seen on American television. Many of the best scripts for *The Simpsons* have been written by Brooks's coproducer, Sam Simon.

James L. Brooks has personally collected over the course of his career three Oscars, nine Emmys, a Humanitas Award, and a Writers Guild Award. His series have received multiple Golden Globes and Peabodys. But perhaps most remarkable in a business where Mammon and the Muse are usually engaged in abusive, bitter, and mutually damaging struggles, Brooks has established an indisputable reputation as the sensibility behind a funny, intelligent, incisive, and original comedy of American manners, while turning out a string of solid hits that would be the envy of any Hollywood cut-and-paste hack.

JAMES L. BROOKS: SELECTED VIDEOGRAPHY

Series

Room 222 (ABC, 1969–74)
The Mary Tyler Moore Show (CBS, 1970–77)
Paul Sand in Friends and Lovers (CBS, 1974–75)
Rhoda (CBS, 1974–78)
Lou Grant (CBS, 1977–82)
Taxi (various, 1978–83)
The Associates (ABC, 1979–80)
The Tracey Ullman Show (Fox, 1987–90)
The Simpsons (Fox, 1990–present)

Movies Made for Television

Thursday's Game (ABC, 1974)
Cindy (ABC, 1978)

6. GARRY MARSHALL

Back to the Future

There are three names commonly associated with ABC's rise to the top of the prime-time ratings during the mid-1970s after three uninterrupted decades as the "third network": Fred Silverman, the programming strategist who was raided from the management ranks of front-running CBS; Aaron Spelling (see Chapter 15), who supplied ABC with a string of racially and sexually integrated crime series that defined the tenor of action/adventure; and Garry Marshall, who retrieved situation comedy from its flirtation with social realities and brought it back to its white-picket-fence suburban home.

While sitcom producers such as Lear, Brooks, and Gelbart will be remembered for "reinventing" the oft-maligned genre during the 1970s, the numbers show that as the decade drew to a close it was Garry Marshall whose shows were commanding the highest ratings. During the 1978–79 season, for example, he accomplished the unprecedented feat of producing four out of the five top-rated programs in prime-time television, all of which were sitcoms for ABC: *Happy Days, Laverne and Shirley, Mork and Mindy,* and *Angie.*

Born in New York City in 1934 and raised in the Bronx, Garry Marshall grew up in a home on the margins of show business: his father was an industrial filmmaker and his mother was a dance instructor. Hoping for a career as a newspaper reporter, Marshall went off to Chicago to study at Northwestern University. During his student years, his affinity for print journalism expanded to include broadcast journalism as well. Receiving his bachelor's degree from Northwestern in 1956, he served in Korea as a producer for Armed Forces Radio.

Marshall returned to New York after his hitch in the army, where he found a job as a copy boy for the *New York Daily News*. But a growing proclivity for comedy writing soon eclipsed journalism in his career plans. While still working for the *News* he managed to establish a free-lance career as a joke writer. His clients during the late fifties came to include such notables as Jack Paar, then host of NBC's *Tonight Show*, and stand-up comedians Rip Taylor, Phil Foster, and Bill "Jose Jimenez" Dana. In the early sixties, he gave up newspaper work completely to take a job as a staff writer for *The Joey Bishop Show*, an easily forgettable turn-of-the-decade self-reflexive sitcom, which starred America's most deadly deadpan as the host of a fictional late-night TV talkshow. It was while working for Bishop that Marshall first teamed with cowriter Jerry Belson. The collaboration would prove a major turning point in Marshall's career.

Garry Marshall and Jerry Belson emerged as a bread-and-butter sitcom writing team during the early sixties, turning out scripts for such blue-chip CBS stars as Lucille Ball (by now in her post-Desi phase), Danny Thomas, and Dick Van Dyke. The pair occasionally even strayed from sitcom work to pen dramatic material for an assortment of prime-time network programs, including *Bob Hope's Chrysler Theatre* (a surviving dramatic anthology) and *I Spy* (an action/adventure hour starring Bill Cosby and Robert Culp). They even attempted to break the circumscribed borders of prime-time TV with a Broadway stage play, *The Roast* (1967), and two Hollywood films, *How Sweet It Is* (1968) and *The Grasshopper* (1970). In the seventies, however, Marshall would focus his undivided attention on sitcom production.

Garry Marshall's career as a producer took shape during his continuing writing partnership with Belson. Their first joint authorial project, however, was something of a flop. *Hey Landlord* (NBC, 1966–67) costarred Will Hutchins as Woody, a fair-haired boy from Ohio who inherits a brownstone in Manhattan and moves to the big city to become a writer, and Sandy Baron as Chuck, a fast-talking native New Yorker with aspirations to become a stand-up comic. The show barely lasted the season, but it managed to serve as a kind of dress rehearsal for Marshall's next effort, *The Odd Couple*, which would also be built around the concept of contrasting roommates sharing space in Manhattan.

The Odd Couple (ABC, 1970–75) was, of course, based on Neil Simon's hit Broadway play and Hollywood movie of the same name. Though Simon did not participate directly in the making of the TV series, he did implicitly offer his approval of Marshall's sitcom adaptation by making a cameo appearance on the show during its fourth season. The premise of the program was succinctly stated each week by a disembodied documentary narrator who asked viewers the question, "Can two divorced men share an apartment without driving each other crazy?"

Tony Randall played Felix Unger, the cultured, genteel, pathologically anal retentive professional photographer, while Jack Klugman was featured as Oscar Madison, the unrefined and unrepentantly anal expressive sports writer whom Felix moves in with after the collapse of his marriage. The concept, though adapted directly from the Simon play, was not in and of itself new to TV situation comedy. Felix and Oscar most readily resembled the twin teenage roommate/cousins played a decade earlier by Patty Duke on *The Patty Duke Show:* the mannered Cathy (who "adores the minuet, the Ballets Russes, and crepes suzette") and the impulsive Patty (who "loves to rock and roll/ a hot dog makes her lose control").

Both Randall and Klugman would win Emmys for their performances on *The Odd Couple.* But curiously, while it was both critically acclaimed and a survivor of five years on prime-time television, as well as being a successful property in syndication, the show did not exactly qualify as a full-fledged hit during its production run. It never, for example, managed to finish among the top twenty-five programs in the Nielsen ratings.

How did *The Odd Couple* manage to stay on the air so long with such mediocre ratings? Marshall offers this explanation for the show's seemingly anomalous track record. First of all, it aired during a period of television history when ABC was still routinely running a distant third place to its corporate competitors; the network's standards for success in those days were simply not quite as rigorous as those at CBS or NBC. Consequently, *The Odd Couple*'s second-place finishes in its time slot were actually palatable to the ABC programming department; they were used to finishing third. As for the reason that the program failed to capture a truly impressive mass audience — despite big stars and the familiarity bred by longevity — Marshall enumerates a more profound analysis that relates directly to his personal development as a *sitcomiste.* To the degree that *The Odd Couple* was a relatively sophisticated and complex series, it was distinctly lacking in what Marshall characterized as "kid appeal." *The Odd Couple* was not only devoid of child regulars but it also lacked the fashionable childish features of the day, such as witches, genies, and extraterrestrials.

Though other sitcoms throughout television history, including military sitcoms (e.g. *M*A*S*H*) and "career girl" sitcoms (e.g. *Rhoda*), had been successful without children in their casts, Marshall had come to agree with Fred Silverman that the "nag factor" of children was of critical importance in controlling family viewing choices. "I have three children," Marshall explained in a 1979 interview with critic Stuart Kaminsky, "and I had a lot of trouble finding something to watch with them. The best thing was to take them out to a Disney movie, but I was tired of watching a raccoon lick a duck for an hour and a half." A glance at Marshall's subsequent portfolio indicates that he resolved not to get caught short of "kid appeal" again.

Even if *The Odd Couple* could not be considered a bona fide "hit," the show had fostered Garry Marshall's emergence as a distinct authorial voice in prime time. "My organization mostly started with *The Odd Couple*," Marshall told Rip Stock, the author of *Odd Couple Mania*. The show "is my strongest memory, because then I worked every single day, every script, every word, I went over every edit. Every scene I was on top of, because I was literally producing that show. As the other shows came about, *Happy Days, Laverne and Shirley*, and *Mork and Mindy*, I became more of a supervising producer."

Marshall's next creation, *The Little People* (NBC, 1972–74), was clearly an attempt at refining *The Odd Couple*'s structure in a way that might attract younger viewers. The series concerned a father-and-daughter pediatrician team practicing medicine at a free clinic on the Hawaiian island of Oahu. Brian Keith starred as an informal, unceremonious Oscar-like dad, while Shelley Fabares played his straitlaced daughter, a stuffy young doctor who evinced the primness of a Felix. While this "odd" pair of unmarried roommates could argue with each other, have separate romantic attachments, and still be ready to reaffirm their mutual love and respect at the end of the half hour, they also had the advantage of sharing an office that was conveniently and regularly overrun with children of all descriptions.

The show met with poor Nielsen response, but ABC gave Marshall a shot at saving the property with midseason revisions. To this end, he changed the name of the program to *The Brian Keith Show* and introduced two new characters, both of whom were well-known Felix-like sitcom character actors: Roger Bowen, who had most recently played Hamilton Majors, Jr., the nerdy boss of the factory on the CBS sitcom *Arnie*, joined the cast as Dr. Austin Chaffee; and Nancy Kulp, fresh from her nine-year stint on *The Beverly Hillbillies* as that irrepressible partisan of culture, bank secretary, and bird-watcher extraordinaire Miss Jane Hathaway, came on board as the wealthy Mrs. Gruber, the widowed benefactor of the free clinic. But this strategy of Brian Keith as a kind of Oscar Madison on Valium, hounded by no less than three Felixes, failed to boost the ratings and the series was canceled.

Happy Days (ABC, 1974–85) was Marshall's next show; it would prove to be one of the greatest hits in TV history. The development of the project can be traced back to a 1971 Marshall concept, originally titled "New Family in Town." Set in a 1950s home on the day of the arrival of the family's first television set, the pilot featured Ron Howard and Marion Ross, both of whom would star in *Happy Days*, in the roles of a teenage son and his mother. The story was woven into the anthology comedy series *Love, American Style* under the title "Love and the Happy Day." ABC, however, failed to give the go-ahead for series production.

Hollywood legend has it that George Lucas, then a young film director fresh from the U.S.C. Cinema-TV School, just happened to catch Marshall's episode of *Love, American Style* and was so impressed by Ron Howard's performance as "the typical American teen-ager" that he cast Howard in the starring role of his hit film *American Graffiti* based on the TV appearance. Whether the details of the story are true or not, the box office success of the Lucas film revived ABC's interest in Ron Howard; a deal was struck with Marshall for the show that eventually would be known as *Happy Days*.

The premiere of *Happy Days* signaled the beginning of a new sitcom marketing strategy that would help lift ABC, at long last, out of the ratings cellar it had occupied for three decades. CBS had built its dominance in the early seventies by attracting younger viewers with shows such as *All in the Family, Mary Tyler Moore*, and *M*A*S*H*. ABC had at first attempted its usual strategy of copying the leader. Its "age of relevance" knockoffs, however, met with little success.

In the wake of the success of *All in the Family*, ABC had tried *The Corner Bar* (1972–73), produced by Alan King and Howard Morris. The show included such à la mode sitcom characters as blacks, Jews, hardhats, and even a homosexual. Though tried twice as a summer replacement, the show failed to make the fall schedule on both occasions. In another attempt at relevance, ABC made a deal directly with Norman Lear. But the show that resulted, *Hot L Baltimore* (1975), based on an off-Broadway play, was one of Lear's few failures during his unprecedented string of successes for CBS and NBC. Marshall offered the network an alternative from its unhappy struggle with relevance.

Like *M*A*S*H*, then in its third season, *Happy Days* was set in the 1950s. Its focus, however, was not upon the human trials and miseries of the Korean War but, rather, on the coming-of-age crises of teenagers along the booming homefront. Eschewing the stench of charred flesh in Asia in favor of the sizzle of hamburgers on the grill at a Milwaukee drive-in, *Happy Days* was an epic recounting of a mythic golden moment in American mass culture, just as that moment was defining itself as lost in post-Vietnam/post-Watergate malaise. If Norman Lear and Larry Gelbart had reimagined the situation comedy as an instrument to explore such hot topics as racism, abortion, and substance abuse, Marshall seemed more concerned with a nostalgic revisiting of malt shops, making out, first cars, and garage bands. Marshall had conjured a legendary America of innocent love among newly affordable washing machines.

Happy Days was ostensibly a sketch of the life of Richie Cunningham (Ron Howard) and his family, which consisted of Dad (Tom Bosley), a hardware store owner and the salt of the Midwestern earth; Mom (Marion Ross), a housewife and proud of it; and snotty little sister Joanie (Erin Moran). Early on there was also basketball-wielding, monosyllabic older brother Chuck, but he was erased from collective memory as part of cast changes made after the second season. Richie's social life was anchored at Arnold's Drive-In, where he hung out with his friends Potsie Weber (Anson Williams) and Ralph Malph (Donny Most) and consulted with his leather-jacketed mentor Fonzie (Henry Winkler).

Marshall demonstrated considerable savvy as a producer by continually planning and executing narrative strategies that made — and kept — the show a hit over the course of its eleven-year production run. The first and most important such move was the dropping of Chuck and the subsequent cultivation of Arthur Fonzarelli from a peripheral character whose name did not even appear in the opening credits to a major regular. The Fonz would not merely fill the void of a big-brother function for "typical male teenager" Richie; he would eventually become the dominant character of the entire *Happy Days* legend.

Fonzie had originally been envisioned by Marshall — and portrayed by Winkler — as a brooding, rebellious dropout. A kind of sitcomic James Dean, he was a 1950s American master of the masculine arts — a drop of Brando, a pinch of Elvis, a smudge of motorcycle grease — capable of making young girls swoon with a bored, if not very angry, stare. During story development, the character had been named "Marscharelli," which was Marshall's own pre-show-business Bronx family name.

The apparent disjunctions and the substantive continuities between the earnest, squeaky-clean Richie and the implicitly felonious Fonzarelli added up to an "odd couple" that became the matrix of much of the show's humor and narrative structure. Richie, who chased girls and "made out" with post–Norman Lear abandon, played Wally Cleaver to Fonzie's post–Norman Lear Eddie Haskell. Marshall once described Richie and The Fonz in terms of Tom Sawyer and Huckleberry Finn; further critical scrutiny might imagine the show as "*The Odd Couple* meets *Rebel Without a Cause*."

The sitcom by its very nature is an ameliorative dramatic genre. Diametrical paradigmatic structural conflicts — husband vs. wife, neighbor vs. neighbor, generation vs. generation, hip vs. square or whatever — are imbedded into the larger tale-telling framework of any given series. The trick of the week is to resolve the particular conflict of a sitcom episode without resolving the overall conflict, so that the recurrence of that overall conflict in the next episode remains credible. When a show is extremely successful — and therefore long-lived — this becomes particularly difficult. How many times can Richie learn that Fonzie's humane inner values far outweigh his déclassé exterior in importance? How many times can Fonzie learn that Richie's outward squareness is no indication of his inner state?

Marshall solved this basic dilemma in *Happy Days* by gradually rewarding The Fonz with entrée into the bourgeois world of the Cunninghams, while still allowing him the privilege of sexual potency, as symbolized by his omnipresent leather jacket and motorcycle. His first step away from alienation came when he moved into a room in the middle-class Cunningham home. Whereas in the early episodes he had disassembled and reassembled his motorcycle in ritual Zen practice, he eventually became a commercial garage mechanic. Whereas in the early episodes he would casually rip off Arnold's Drive-In by striking the jukebox with his fist to make it play, he later became a managing owner of the restaurant. Whereas once he was the indomitable scourge of all authority figures, he eventually went back to school, became a teacher, and in a bit of comic overkill, ended the series as the dean of boys at the local high school. Like Lear's

Archie Bunker, who miraculously recovered from an early diagnosis of terminal loading dock proletarianism to become the proprietor of his very own bar and grill, Marshall's Fonzie graduated from holding court in the men's room at Arnold's to become a model pillar of the community: a fine career marked by rapid advancement and personal growth. The Fonz's saving grace? He never took off his leather jacket, not even while serving as the dean of boys.

Were the lessons lived by The Fonz lost on his adoring public? Hardly. In a 1979 episode, Richie convinces Fonzie to get a library card. That week, according to the American Library Association, thousands of new library cards were applied for across the country. The ALA has used videotapes of that *Happy Days* episode as part of library-card recruitment drives.

Happy Days might have gone on forever, if not for the burgeoning career aspirations of Ron Howard. Howard, who had grown up in front of the nation as Andy Griffith's boy Opie in Mayberry during the sixties before reaching puberty in 1950s Milwaukee, left *Happy Days* in 1981 to pursue a career as a film director. His works would include such hits as *Splash* and *Cocoon*. The departure of Richie — he was graduated from college, drafted into the army, and shipped out to Greenland — effectively turned the series into "The Fonzie Show." A host of new characters was introduced. They included Mom's nephew Roger (Ted McGinley), a suave Yale preppie meant to be Fonzie's complement in a new "odd couple" configuration; Chachi, Fonzie's leather-jacketed nephew and protégé; and Lori Beth (Lynda Goodfriend), who married Richie, gave birth to a child, and knitted on the homefront while hubby was busy protecting the free world from Communism.

Happy Days became the most popular show on American television in the late seventies. It would spend eight of its eleven prime-time seasons in the Nielsen Top Twenty; rerun syndication should continue to be ubiquitous into the twenty-first century. As was the case with Sherwood Schwartz's *Gilligan's Island*, the sitcom's popularity with the eleven-to-seventeen-year-old crowd led to a Saturday morning cartoon series, *The Fonz and the Happy Days Gang* (ABC, 1980–82), which had the animated characters traveling via a time machine in a desperate search for 1957 Milwaukee. Moreover, *Happy Days* became the germinating center of an expanding Marshall cosmology, from which three other prime-time series were spun off; two of them became major hits.

The first of these was *Laverne and Shirley*. Laverne De Fazio was played by Penny Marshall, Garry's sister, who had also worked in the family sitcom business as Myrna Turner, Oscar Madison's secretary on *The Odd Couple.* Cindy Williams, who had costarred with Ron Howard in *American Graffiti,* played her roommate, Shirley Feeney. Laverne and Shirley originally had been introduced to the public on several *Happy Days* episodes in 1975 as friends of The Fonz. The following season they premiered in their own show. Once again the setting was Milwaukee during the Eisenhower era. The focus, however, shifted from the tree-lined expanses of the Cunninghams' suburban neighborhood to a basement apartment in a working-class precinct of the city, adjacent to the Shotz Brewery, where Laverne and Shirley — two single working girls — toiled for hourly wages as bottle cappers.

Laverne and Shirley was in some ways a reworking of the 1950s white working-class sitcom that had informed such chestnuts as *The Life of Riley* and *The Honeymooners.* The fact that *Laverne and Shirley* was set during the same period as these shows only added to that impression. It was as if America had once been home to a blue-collar class that was now part of some nostalgic past to be remembered from the middle-class present. Working-class life for *Laverne and Shirley* is portrayed as comically drab, wholesomely gray, and utterly satisfying to the degree that it allows those who live it to exercise their incorrigibly American capacity to dream of a better day. As was the case with Ralph Kramden and Norton or with Chester Riley and Gillis, Laverne and Shirley — this time women — plot their escape from working-class misery only to learn that the greatest joy in life is in the plotting.

Once again Marshall had resurrected an *Odd Couple* structure, this time lacing it with "zany female" slapstick elements, of the kind he had written for *The Lucy Show* during the previous decade. Goofy Laverne and less goofy Shirley, downscale versions of Lucy Carmichael and Viv, schemed to get respectable dates and to find new jobs that might positively impact their fragile senses of dignity and self-esteem. The amorous advances of their "loser" neighbors, Lenny and Squiggy (Michael McKean and David L. Lander), were of no help in this regard. Marshall also reached back into his pre–*Happy Days* bag of tricks to cast comedian Phil Foster as Laverne's father.

Set on the ABC Tuesday-night schedule following Number One *Happy Days,* and further boosted by occasional cross-series visits from The Fonz, *Laverne and Shirley* became an instant hit and even surpassed *Happy Days* at the top of the ratings by the end of the 1977–78 season. If the public was amused, the critics were not. Having been encouraged by the popularity of the innovative sitcoms of the early seventies, TV commentators lambasted Marshall for what was viewed as a return to sitcom neanderthalism. Fred Silverman, the ABC programming chief who had been instrumental in backing the Marshall shows, at one point responded by alluding to the critique of class manners implicit in *Laverne and Shirley* as comparable to the eighteenth-century French dramas of Molière.

After a decline in the show's ratings during the 1979–80 season, Marshall came up with a characteristic plan to reinvigorate the concept. He moved the "girls" from Milwaukee to Burbank, where, in what perhaps can be seen as another Lucyesque stroke, they would try to break into show business. The change was made with righteous sitcom alacrity. In the tradition of Fred and Ethel following the Ricardos from Manhattan to Connecticut, Lenny and Squiggy dutifully relocated from Milwaukee to Southern California.

Like *Happy Days*, *Laverne and Shirley* outlived its concept and survived to crumble through a period of baroque decay. A Saturday-morning cartoon series, which featured the girls in the army under the command of a talking-pig drill sergeant named Squeally, came and went. By the final season, Cindy Williams had left the series (just as Ron Howard had left *Happy Days*), and the Shirley-less Laverne was knocked out of the top twenty-five by the feisty Mr. T, who had materialized as her ratings opposition on NBC's *The A-Team*.

The other notable *Happy Days* spin-off was inaugurated in an episode titled "My Favorite Orkan," a self-reflexive tip of the Marshall camera to *My Favorite Martian*, an early sixties sitcom of similar narrative design. In this dreamlike 1978 segment, Richie is chosen by aliens to be the subject of interterrestrial anthropology experiments on the planet Ork. More significant, Marshall offered the national audience its first good look at a bright young comedian named Robin Williams who had been cast in the role of the alien. The episode tested so well that ABC gave the go-ahead for a new series to begin the following fall. By the end of its first season, *Mork and Mindy* was the third-highest-rated show on TV, trailing just behind two other ABC sitcoms, *Laverne and Shirley* and *Three's Company*.

In the series, Mork is exiled from his emotionless, laughterless planet because he displays a mutant sense of humor. He is sent as a passenger in a giant egg to Boulder, Colorado, where his assignment is to observe and report on the local customs of the natives. Upon arrival he befriends Earthwoman Mindy McConnell (Pam Dawber), a cute-as-a-button, straight-as-an-arrow sales clerk in her dad's downtown record store. Mork sat on chairs upside down, drank beverages through his finger, made strange noises, and effected a persona that lay somewhere between a San Francisco street entertainer and a borscht-belt *tummler*. *Mork and Mindy? The Odd Couple* goes intergalactic.

The kids, as they say, loved it. Before long schoolyards across America resounded with such Orkan sayings as "Nanu, nanu" (Goodbye) and "Shazbat!" (Oh, shit!). Each episode was packaged like a child's fable, complete with a moral, which Mork would deliver in his weekly reports to his superior, Orson. Traditional sitcomic lessons on jealousy, honesty, charity, and, of course, the primacy of love abounded, all neatly reviewed in a way that would have impressed Aesop.

If Marshall had seen *The Odd Couple* live beyond the means of its relatively meager ratings to a prosperous five-year production run, he would have just the opposite experience with *Mork and Mindy*. Even as the show was scoring spectacular ratings during the 1978–79 season — and even as Robin Williams was distinguishing himself as a major bankable star — ABC executives were concocting ideas to further capitalize on the property that would eventually contribute to the show's astonishingly rapid demise. First of all, despite *Mork's* demonstrated popularity, major cast changes were made for the 1979–80 season. Dad and the record store disappeared, along with a bunch of minor characters; Mork and Mindy threw caution to the wind and moved in together in a small Mary Tyler Moore-ish apartment. Second, in an effort to bolster ABC's traditionally weak Sunday lineup, the show was removed from its dominant Thursday slot.

As a result the sitcom went into spectacular commercial free-fall, losing almost half its audience over the course of a single season. *Mork and Mindy* plunged from third in the national Nielsens to twenty-sixth. A mad scramble was made to return it to its original time slot and to undo some of the changes: forty-ninth place for 1981–82. During the final season, in a typical sitcom last-gasp ploy, the pair were married. They take a surrealistic honeymoon on Ork. Mork gets pregnant and gives birth to Mearth (Jonathan Winters), who springs full grown from an egg that emerges from Mork's belly button. The result? Sixtieth place and cancellation at the end of the 1983–84 season.

Though *Mork and Mindy* had originally been introduced in a *Happy Days* episode, the series was only nominally a spin-off; there were no crossover characters or episodes, as there had been with *Laverne and Shirley*. There was, however, to be one more *Happy Days* spin-off that would be adapted directly from the show's plot. *Joanie Loves*

Chachi (ABC, 1982–83) followed the relationship of Richie's sister (Erin Moran) and Fonzie's protégé (Scott Baio). With the sixties finally dawning on Milwaukee, the young couple decide to move to Chicago and get their own pad so they can seek their fortune as pop singers. Musical numbers were introduced into the sitcom, à la the scenes down at the Tropicana in *I Love Lucy*. A kind of nonoedipal *Partridge Family*, the show scored great ratings during its premiere season before mysteriously plummeting into the Nielsen netherworld the following fall. Marshall cut his losses by reintegrating the Joanie and Chachi characters into *Happy Days;* the parent sitcom had outlived all three of its progeny.

Mork and Mindy and *Joanie Loves Chachi* were not the only quick fizzles that were tarnishing the producer's reputation. In 1979 Marshall had tried a non-*Happy Days*-related sitcom, *Angie*, a remarkably short-lived rocket whose payload proved to be made of wax. In yet another variation of the *Odd Couple* theme, the title character, Angie Falco (Donna Pescow), is a blue-collar waitress at a Philadelphia coffee shop who marries a customer, Brad Benson (Robert Hays), a Main Line millionaire who occupies his idle time as a pediatrician. The in-laws have trouble getting along; in one episode they even face off on *Family Feud*, complete with guest star Richard Dawson. In the spring of 1979, Marshall reached the apex of his commercial TV career: *Laverne and Shirley* finished Number One; *Happy Days* and *Mork and Mindy* tied for Number Three; and *Angie* was Number Five.

Two Marshall failures are perhaps worth mentioning, one early in his TV career, the other a kind of fitting farewell. *Me and the Chimp* (CBS, 1972) concerned a typical American family who adopt an orphaned chimpanzee, which they are bringing up in their typical suburban home. *Me and the Chimp* starred Ted Bessell and Buttons in the respective title roles. Critics Harry Castleman and Walter Podrazik went so far as to characterize the show as "a low-water mark in western civilization." This may or may not be a fair statement, but suffice it to say that *Me and the Chimp* was a clear step backward from *The Hathaways* (ABC, 1961–62), which had featured Jack Weston and Peggy Cass as a childless couple who are bringing up an entire family of chimpanzees.

The other dud was perhaps Marshall's final — and most up-front — remake of *The Odd Couple*. Coming full cycle from his half dozen odd-couple variations on a theme, in 1982 Marshall produced *The New Odd Couple*, an all-black remake starring Ron Glass and Demond Wilson as Felix and Oscar. The show did not fare better than the last all-black sitcom adaptation of a Neil Simon play, *Barefoot in the Park* (ABC, 1970–71), which Marshall also produced, and was canceled before the end of the season.

In the 1980s Marshall, like so many others before him who struck it rich in video, turned his focus away from television toward the movies. He has directed, produced and, in some instances, written such theatrical film releases as *Young Doctors in Love* (1982), *The Flamingo Kid* (1984), *Nothing in Common* (1986), *Overboard* (1987), *Beaches* (1989), and *Pretty Woman* (1990), many of which play variations on the odd-couple theme. He even appeared as an actor in Albert Brooks's *Lost in America* (1985). What little television work Marshall has done since the transition has come in the form of attempts to adapt his own film projects into TV sitcoms.

It is perhaps a testament to Garry Marshall's leadership and competence that so many of the people who have worked with him have gone on to successful careers as TV producers and film directors. Bob Boyett and Tom Miller, for example, went on to form their own company and to produce *Perfect Strangers*, yet another odd-couple knockoff. Many of Marshall's stars and protégés, including Ron Howard, Penny Marshall, Henry Winkler, and Anson Williams, have gone on to distinguished directing careers in Hollywood movies and television.

In looking back at his work in television, Marshall is more forthcoming about his philosophy than most televisionmakers have cared to be. In accepting the Lifetime Achievement Prize from the American Comedy Awards in 1990, he commented, "A lot of times they put down television saying, 'It's the lowest common denominator.' It's the only medium that can reach the lowest common denominator. To get up in the morning and say, 'I'm gonna make some rich, smart, successful people laugh,' — that's not what I do. I think, let them get their own laughs. I like to make people laugh who come off a hard job, they had a long day, they want to sit down and have a good time. . . . If television is the education of the American public, then I am recess."

GARRY MARSHALL: SELECTED VIDEOGRAPHY

Early Writing Credits

The Danny Thomas Show (ABC/CBS, 1953–64)
The Tonight Show starring Jack Paar (NBC, 1957–62)
The Dick Van Dyke Show (CBS, 1961–66)
The Joey Bishop Show (NBC/CBS, 1961–65)

The Bill Dana Show (NBC, 1963–65)
Bob Hope Presents the Chrysler Theatre (NBC, 1963–67)
Gomer Pyle, U.S.M.C. (CBS, 1964–70)

Series

Hey Landlord (NBC, 1966–67)
Barefoot in the Park (ABC, 1970–71)
The Odd Couple (ABC, 1970–75)
Me and the Chimp (CBS, 1972)
The Little People (NBC, 1972–74)
Happy Days (ABC, 1974–84)
Laverne and Shirley (ABC, 1976–83)
Blansky's Beauties (ABC, 1977)
Mork and Mindy (ABC, 1978–82)
Who's Watching the Kids? (NBC, 1978)
Angie (ABC, 1979–80)
Joanie Loves Chachi (ABC, 1982–83)
The New Odd Couple (ABC, 1982–83)

Movie Made for Television

Evil Roy Slade (NBC, 1972)

Ad Campaign

Classic Coke (1988)

7. SUSAN HARRIS

Seriously Funny

While women have been ubiquitous on the homescreen from Lucy and the June Taylor Dancers to Roseanne and *Designing Women*, the overwhelming majority of the characters they have played, lines they have spoken, and stories they have enacted have been conceived behind the scenes by men. There have been several noteworthy exceptions. During the infancy of the medium, Gertrude Berg, who came to American broadcasting from the Yiddish-language stage, created, starred in, and maintained considerable authorial control over her long-running sitcom, *The Goldbergs*. Writer-producers such as Irna Phillips and Agnes Nixon (see Chapters 26 and 27) pioneered an entire genre by shaping the character of the daytime soap opera with such programs as *As the World Turns, The Guiding Light,* and *One Life to Live*. For the most part, however, the script of any given American television show was — and is — more likely to have been typed by a woman than composed by her.

It was only during the 1980s that the names of women began to appear with any frequency in the prime-time network credits crawl. *Cagney and Lacey* (CBS, 1982–88), the first police show in TV history to gather a predominantly female audience, was created by Barbara Corday, who was consequently rewarded with a vice presidency at

CBS. Other women who have realized work in prime time include Diane English (see next chapter), creator and executive producer of the smash sitcom *Murphy Brown*, and Terry Louise Fisher, who collaborated with Steven Bochco in the conceptualization of such shows as *L.A. Law* and *Hooperman*.

Among the originators of shows by and about women, however, no single personality has been more prolific or exerted more influence on the art and the industry of television than Susan Harris. Harris grew up in New York's suburban Westchester County, the daughter of an accountant and a homemaker. An "A" student and cheerleader in high school, she went on to study English literature at Cornell and then later at New York University. But she never received a degree.

In 1969 Harris broke into the business by writing an episode script for *Then Came Bronson*. This short-lived NBC series concerned a newspaper reporter (Michael Parks) who is compelled to reconsider the meaning of life after the suicide of his best friend. A quintessential pre–Michael J. Fox period piece, the program follows Bronson as he quits his job, gives away all of his bourgeois possessions, and rides his dead friend's motorcycle around the country helping people: a kind of two-wheeled reprise of *Route 66*. A friend with connections on the *Bronson* set shepherded the script to the producer and Harris had launched her career as a television writer with a forty-five-hundred-dollar sale.

Perhaps her most formative experience as a writer was gained at Norman Lear's Tandem Productions during the halcyon days of the "relevant" sitcom in the mid-1970s. When *Maude* was spun off from *All in the Family*, Harris became a powerful force in shaping the new hit, which at times eclipsed even the saga of Archie Bunker in terms of public controversy. Maude Findlay (Beatrice Arthur) was Edith Bunker's cousin from the haute suburban reaches of Harris's native Westchester County. Alternately enjoying and enduring her fourth marriage, Maude was committed rhetorically to any and all causes on the left side of Hubert Humphrey, making her a kind of political mirror image of the reactionary Archie Bunker. To Maude, as we learn in the series themesong, "Lady Godiva was a freedom rider."

The show went further than any of the Lear sitcoms in its presentation of previously verboten material. A woman in her late forties, Maude spent her six years in prime time living on the edge of sitcom taboo: she tried to talk her husband into getting a vasectomy; she became pregnant and had an abortion; she went through on-camera menopause, complete with hot flashes in living color. No bodily fluid or bodily function seemed too base a subject for a *Maude* episode.

The abortion story, written by Harris as a two-parter, caused a particular sensation, and the public ruckus turned the otherwise obscure writer into a minor celebrity. In part one, the aging Maude kills the rabbit and must come to grips with the problem. The following week, after much agonizing (including a bevy of concessions to the soundness of the antiabortion point of view), Maude chooses to end the pregnancy, a decision that she emphatically acknowledges "may not be the right one for everyone."

Though as executive producer of *Maude* Norman Lear retained ultimate authorial power, Susan Harris became identified with the show as the writer of its two most controversial episodes. To the degree that *Maude* was a hit — it finished in the Nielsen Top Ten during its first four seasons — she became perceived as a hot creative property. Wooed by then struggling NBC, Harris was given the opportunity to present her first full-fledged work with the premiere of *Fay,* a sitcom focused on a woman in her fifties who divorces her husband of twenty-four years when she catches him in the arms of a young manicurist named Cookie.

Though *Fay* was probably the most critically acclaimed series of the 1975–76 season, it was canceled by the network after only three episodes. The program, which debuted during the midst of the "family viewing" battle of the midseventies, was an unfortunate victim of the political moment. At the 1975 convention of the National Association of Broadcasters, member stations adopted a proposal by CBS President Arthur Taylor agreeing to designate the first hour of prime time each evening to programs "appropriate for a family audience." This self-censorship by the networks was designed to stem complaints about growing bawdiness and violence in prime-time programming. If the 8:00–9:00 P.M. (Eastern) hour were kept "clean," so the reasoning went, the networks might find themselves under less scrutiny during the later hours of the evening. Though the policy was eventually scrapped (in no small part due to a lawsuit brought by Norman Lear and the Writers Guild), *Fay* was one of the casualties of the brief experiment. Awkwardly shoved into an 8:30 slot, the show was trapped between its emphatically adult themes and a sudden and unwanted obligation to adhere to the newly instituted family-viewing principles. NBC stubbornly — and inexplicably — refused to consider a time change. Paul Klein, the network's chief programmer, was well known for his advocacy of "least objectionable" programming, a marketing theory that makes avoidance of controversy a top priority. It is not unreasonable to speculate that the early time slot was Klein's way of sabotaging *Fay.*

Harris and her partner/husband, Paul Junger Witt, found themselves between a political rock and an aesthetic hard place. The changes that were being forced upon the series were simply incompatible with the authorial concept. When Harris first began to develop the show, she wanted to present a story about the fears and vulnerabilities of a late-middle-aged woman who suddenly finds herself without a husband. NBC executives had expressed sympathy for the idea but were full of "suggestions" for insuring the show's popularity: they insisted on shaving ten years off Fay's age and making her more glamorous and physically appealing than Harris had intended. Key storylines were nixed by the network: Fay was not allowed a scene in bed with her ex-husband; Fay was refused permission to fall in love with an impotent man. Lines were cut from — and new lines were awkwardly dubbed into — the finished pilot episode to change an affair Fay was having to a "serious relationship."

Series star Lee Grant was herself no stranger to censorship controversies; she had been among the victims of the McCarthy-era blacklists some two decades earlier. Learning of *Fay*'s cancellation only minutes before an appearance with Johnny Carson, she used *The Tonight Show* as a forum to rail against the NBC executives who had sabotaged the project. Susan Harris made public her own response to the situation on a PBS documentary that aired several months later: "After that experience, I would really like to be writing something else. I find it very frustrating. I don't like having to write *down*, which is what I have to do now. I'm working on a play and I hope to write my way out of television." This was not, however, to be. The "Family Hour" soon became a footnote in broadcasting textbooks, and an ascendant ABC came forward to make Susan Harris an offer she could not refuse.

During the stagflation year of 1977 the nation's supermarkets were witness to a craze for austerely labeled "generic" products, and the title of Harris's new sitcom, *Soap*, was very much in the spirit of that moment. (*Family*, also an ABC show, had been the smash of the previous season.) *Soap* indeed resembled a daytime soap opera, but it was, beneath the plain white packaging, a raunchy satirical synthesis of two genres — the sitcom and the soap opera — after the fashion of Norman Lear's *Mary Hartman, Mary Hartman* (syndicated, 1976–78), a show that never achieved network distribution during its production run.

On the face of it, *Soap* was the ongoing saga of two Connecticut families — the upper-crust Tates and the blue-collar Campbells — who were uneasily joined together by marriage. But the series soon established multiple soap-operatic narrative lines that branched out in a hundred directions. Some of the themes that Harris managed to cram into its half-hour episodes included homosexuality, impotence, incest, premarital sex, adultery, racial stereotyping, satanism, transsexualism, and transvestism. Based solely on preseason publicity, ABC received over thirty thousand letters protesting *Soap* before it even aired. Following the series' actual debut, organizations including the U.S. Catholic Conference, the Southern Baptist Convention, the Catholic League for Civil Rights, and the usually tolerant National Council of Churches joined in with vehement attacks. When the Gay Task Force joined the fray to criticize the show's portrayal of the homosexual character Jodie Dallas (Billy Crystal), it became evident that Harris had managed to alienate viewers across a broad range of the political spectrum, to say the very least.

When the dust settled, seven major advertisers had dropped out of sponsorship, fifteen ABC affiliates were refusing to air the series during prime time (and instead bumped it into less lucrative late-night slots), and twenty other stations were refusing to carry *Soap* at all. The network attempted concessions. ABC programming chief Fred Silverman, borrowing a philosophical thought from the Hays Commission, publicly announced that no character in the series would ever be rewarded for "tawdry or immoral" acts. A viewer warning was added at the beginning of each episode, advising "parental discretion." Silverman even went so far as to characterize the program as "socially redeeming."

As has so often been the case in American popular culture, calls for censorship from the political margins only served to create a mainstream appetite to find out what all the fuss was about. Despite — or perhaps because of — the furor it raised, *Soap* was the highest-rated new show of the 1977–78 season, finishing Number Thirteen in the Nielsens. It would rank among the top twenty during three of its four years in production. Harris had established her reputation as a television auteur. She had created *Soap*, supervised its production, written many of its scripts, and even appeared on-screen in the role of the prostitute Babette in several episodes.

Following the example of her mentor Norman Lear, Harris was quick to follow her first authorial success with a spin-off that focused on a black character. Just as *The Jeffersons* had outlived *All in the Family*, *Benson* (ABC, 1979–86), would enjoy a longer, if somewhat quieter, production run than *Soap*. Robert Guillaume starred in the title role of the erstwhile cool and rational servant whose duties as chief cook and bottle washer for a well-to-do family of white neurotics must often transcend the confines of the pantry into the realm of the spiritual. In the new show Benson left the service of the Tates to run the household of the governor of the state; he quickly established himself as a kind of power behind the throne.

Following the success of *Benson*, Harris and her partners, Paul Witt and Tony Thomas, met with several disappointments. *I'm a Big Girl Now* (ABC, 1980–81) starred Diane Canova (who had played Corinne Tate on *Soap*) as a divorced mother of a young daughter who moves in with her divorced father to form a nontraditional household: a kind of intergenerational *Odd Couple*. In 1982 the production trio tried again with *It Takes Two*, starring Patty Duke and Richard Crenna as a pre-*Cosby*, pre-*thirtysomething* lawyer/doctor married couple surviving the slings and arrows of outrageous yuppie angst. Neither series won renewal.

In *Hail to the Chief* (ABC, 1985), Harris attempted to recapture some of the controversial flavor of *Soap*. The sitcom starred Patty Duke as Julia Mansfield, the first female president of the United States. Finding a new context for one of her favorite dramatic metaphors, Harris chose to afflict Julia's "first gentleman" Oliver Mansfield (Ted Bessel) with impotence. The ensemble cast was pure *Soap:* a sexy tennis pro, an omniscient butler, a flamboyant homosexual, a raving minister, a sensible black man, an unrepentant Satanist. But American television had changed radically since the premiere of *Soap* some seven years earlier. The growth of cable TV had established far more shocking phenomena as commonplace on the American homescreen. *Hail to the Chief* did not stimulate anything like the public outcry that greeted *Soap*, but neither did it manage any of the publicity that surrounds such controversy. It was canceled after only seven episodes.

Only weeks after the final airing of *Hail to the Chief*, NBC debuted Harris's next effort, *The Golden Girls*, a series about four older women seeking both financial and emotional social security by throwing their lot together as roommates in the retirement mecca of Miami, Florida. This sitcom would win Harris her greatest critical accolades and prove to be her greatest commercial success as well.

Focusing on four single older women, *The Golden Girls* was an ideal vehicle to carry many of Harris's career-long concerns into the 1990s. In Dorothy Zbornak (Beatrice Arthur) Harris achieved much of what she had originally intended for the ill-fated *Fay*. As was the case with Fay, Dorothy's long marriage had culminated in divorce when her husband betrayed her for a younger woman. But Dorothy was older and less glamorous than the Lee Grant of 1975, making her situation more urgent and potentially more tragic. Her ability to survive — and to flourish occasionally — is challenged by some very unsitcomlike bouts with anxiety, including a two-parter during which she undergoes clinical depression.

Dorothy's roommates are two other veterans from the golden age of the "relevant" sitcom. Rue McClanahan, who played Bea Arthur's next-door neighbor on *Maude*, resurfaces as Blanche Devereaux, a well-preserved Southern belle whose sexual exploits, both past and present, provide an image of the older woman that fights against stereotype. Offering a kind of comical takeoff on Tennessee Williams's Blanche Dubois, with a bit of Maggie the Cat thrown in for good measure, McClanahan often steals the show with her unabashed bawdiness. Rose (Betty White), by contrast, is an innocent widow from St. Olaf, Minnesota, a character conjured from the heart of Garrison Keillor's Lake Wobegon. Driving her roommates to distraction with incomprehensible didactic allegories of small-town Scandinavian life in the northern Midwest, Rose not only provides a stark contrast to the ribald Blanche but also stands as a self-reflexive allusion to that other sitcomic Minnesotan played by Betty White during the seventies: Sue Ann Nivens, the lascivious and conniving Happy Homemaker of *The Mary Tyler Moore Show*.

A fourth member of the household is Dorothy's mother Sophia (Estelle Getty), a Sicilian-born octogenarian who moves into the house after a nursing-home fire. Because of a stroke, we are told, Sophia has been robbed of the ability to be diplomatic with people (in other words, she cannot help but speak the truth), thus giving her dispensation to issue one-liners that no other character would dare utter. Though Sophia is often celebrated by critics as a radically innovative character, she is in some ways merely a fuller, more satisfying realization of an earlier Harris character, The Major, a shell-shocked veteran of World War I who was part of the Tate household on *Soap*.

In a demographics-conscious decade that seemed intent on pandering to the tastes of upscale thirty-five-to-forty-nine-year-old babyboomers, with shows such as *Hill Street Blues* and *thirtysomething,* the odds seemed to be stacked against the success of a show like *The Golden Girls*. A sitcom featuring widows and stroke victims on primetime TV? Nevertheless, the series achieved Top Ten status in its premiere season and proceeded to climb from seventh to fifth to fourth during its first three years. Not only did the show win a faithful following among viewers over fifty-five, as might be expected, but it did astonishingly well among younger adults as well. Demographically, in fact, *The Golden Girls* may be a prescient sign of things to come. If contemporary yuppies enjoy the show now because it demonstrates that their parents can get along quite well on their own (that is, without moving in or taking up residence in an expensive and depressing nursing home), *The Golden Girls* also begins to explore a somewhat happier ending for the boomers themselves. Is it possible that getting old will mean moving in with roommates and going out on dates? Is it possible that old age could be, well, just like going back to college?

Showing little interest in the neo-whitebread chic occasioned by the successes of sitcoms such as *Cosby* and *Growing Pains*, Harris has continued in *The Golden Girls* to explore the socially conscious and often controversial themes that she has insisted upon since her days as a writer for the Lear group: Rose befriends a lesbian; Blanche misses her period and thinks she is pregnant but is only experiencing menopause; Dorothy's son is engaged to marry a black woman. The result has been a showering of Emmys for Susan Harris.

In 1988 Harris further broadened her cosmology of senior-citizen life in Miami by spinning off *Empty Nest*, a kind of male version of *The Golden Girls*, with roots in the original *Fay* concept. To play the aging spouseless protagonist, Dr. Harry Weston, Harris cast *Soap* alumnus Richard Mulligan. Having enjoyed the security of a long and successful marriage, Dr. Weston attempts to pick up the pieces following the death of his wife. Though clearly a component of the Harris portfolio, *Empty Nest* is in some ways a kinder, gentler sitcom than viewers have come to expect from the often rambunctious Harris. Though Mulligan's Harry Weston can wisecrack with the best of them, his sarcasm never reaches the extremes of a Maude or a Dorothy but is, rather, tempered by the gentle, loving memory he cherishes of his late wife. There is, perhaps, an implied role reversal between the aggressive cynical women of *Golden Girls* — Dorothy, Blanche, and Sophia — and the accepting passivity of the male physician.

While Blanche is chasing men and Dorothy is wishing that she could, we find Harry rejecting the advances of a beautiful and eager woman when he realizes that he is simply unprepared to begin a new sexual relationship. While *The Golden Girls* typically bicker and argue with their children, Harry is much more affectionate with his daughters Barbara (Kristy McNichol) and Carol (Dinah Manoff). Harry's antagonist on *Empty Nest* is his next-door neighbor Charlie, played by David Leisure, who first gained public attention as the shamelessly deceitful pitchman Joe Isuzu. His vanity license plate reads SEXGUY. Having set *Empty Nest* in the same Miami neighborhood that is home to *The Golden Girls*, Harris has provided herself with the opportunity to develop complex intertextual themes across the Saturday-evening hour that the two sitcoms share.

Susan Harris's legacy to the sitcom far outstrips the remarkable breakthroughs she accomplished as a female auteur and entrepreneur in an utterly male-dominated art and industry. Almost singlehandedly she kept alive the spirit of social consciousness and conscience that had briefly infused the genre during the seventies but had subsequently fallen out of favor during the Reagan era.

SUSAN HARRIS: SELECTED VIDEOGRAPHY

Early Writing Credits

All in the Family (CBS, 1971–79)
Maude (CBS, 1972–78)

Series

Fay (NBC, 1975–76)
Soap (ABC, 1977–81)
Benson (ABC, 1979–86)
I'm a Big Girl Now (ABC, 1980–81)
It Takes Two (ABC, 1982–83)
Hail to the Chief (ABC, 1985)
The Golden Girls (NBC, 1985–present)
Empty Nest (NBC, 1988–present)
Nurses (NBC, 1991–present)
Good and Evil (ABC, 1991–present)

8. DIANE ENGLISH

_____ _____ _____ _____ _____ _____ _____ _____

The Superwoman as Comic Hero

It is generally acknowledged that James L. Brooks (see Chapter 5) and Allan Burns, the creator-producers of *The Mary Tyler Moore Show*, reinvented the sitcom persona of the single, upscale working woman during the 1970s. The model of the pitiable spinster was put to rest in favor of a positive and independent image that more accurately took into account the lives and aspirations of post–World War II American women. But if Brooks and Burns cut the wood, no one has sculpted the mythic figure of the post–Mary Richards sitcom woman in greater detail than Diane English.

A native of Buffalo, New York, Diane English attended Buffalo State College, where she majored in education and minored in theater arts. She taught high school for a year, in 1970, then moved to New York City. There she first met with public attention as a TV critic for *Vogue* magazine, where she wrote a TV column for over three years. In a career move more readily associated with French cinema than American television, however, English gave up her role as a critic to try her hand at production. In 1980 she adapted *The Lathe of Heaven*, a science-fiction novel by Ursula K. LeGuin, into PBS's first feature-length made-for-TV movie. The script won her a Writers Guild Award nomination. Moving over to commercial production, she wrote scripts for several network TV movies and weekly series before achieving authorial status as creator, producer, and writer of *Foley Square* (CBS, 1985–86). It would be the first of a trilogy of career-woman sitcoms that English would produce for CBS over the next decade.

Foley Square established the signature of the producer's sitcom vision. Alex Harrigan (Margaret Colin) is a woman working in a profession that had once been considered a male domain; like all of English's sitcom heroines, she carries a sexually ambiguous first name as if to reiterate the point metaphorically. An assistant district attorney in New York City, Alex wears Reebok sneakers along with her conservative suit as she journeys each morning by subway from her tasteful Upper West Side brownstone to the Criminal Court Building in Lower Manhattan's Foley Square. Barely thirty years old (her thirtieth birthday is actually the subject of an early episode), Alex cannot help but compulsively glance at her ticking bio-clock even as she prosecutes an endless procession of thieves, murderers, and rapists. Unmarried, and entertaining no immediate prospects, Alex's love life is the soft underbelly of her otherwise stalwart yuppie existence. How many times can she be called away from a date — or even from bed in flagrante — to take a confession or attend an autopsy before her entire social life disintegrates completely?

At home Alex was supplied with a requisite sitcomic neighbor/confidant, but in a reversal of sexual role conformity her pal turns out to be a man, Peter Newman (Michael Lembeck). At the office Alex worked under the no-nonsense Lou Grant-ish D.A. Jesse Steinberg (Hector Elizondo), along with two other Assistant D.A.s: Carter DeVries (Sanford Jensen), an unctuous careerist sporting a power tie; and Molly Dobbs (Cathy Silvers), a starry-eyed Yalie from rural New Hampshire. "Mole," a free-lance video artist who squeezed in tapings of confessions and crime scenes between bar mitzvahs and sweet sixteens, was played by John Lovitz; had *Foley Square* been renewed, he might never have gone on to *Saturday Night Live* fame the following season.

English's next project was *My Sister Sam* (CBS, 1986–88). Once again the story focuses on a twenty-nine-year-old single woman, with a sexually ambiguous first name, living in an apartment in a large cosmopolitan city, who is trying to make it in "a man's world" (in this case, as a photographer). Pam Dawber, who had played second banana to Robin Williams for four years on *Mork and Mindy,* was cast in the title role of Samantha Russell. English even went so far as to supply her with a male next-door neighbor/confidant; the part went to David

Naughton, who was better known as the "I'm a Pepper; you're a Pepper" guy from the soft-drink commercials.

The storylines of *My Sister Sam* germinated from Sam's relationship with her sixteen-year-old sister Patti (the late Rebecca Schaeffer), who moves in following the death of their parents. This new addition to the otherwise footloose-and-fancy-free bachelorette's San Francisco loft/photography studio causes Sam's identity to oscillate between poles of young urban professional self-absorption and selfless parental responsibility. If the plot sounds a bit like a feminist remake of *Bachelor Father, Love That Bob!,* or *Family Affair,* there is also ample evidence in the form of census data that allows *My Sister Sam* to be seen, even in reruns, as a hyperbolic allegory of a crisis that many "Me Generation" women were going through during the 1980s with their actual bio-kids.

In one episode Patti begs Sam to let her invite her new-wave boyfriend to a genteel yuppie party that Sam is about to throw. But clients will be there, for heaven's sake. The boyfriend shows up anyway. Sam's anger turns to instant if somewhat guilty self-gratification as the boyfriend — wild young guy that he is — makes a pass at her. Not only does her ego get stroked but there's also proof that her parental instinct about the boyfriend being dangerous was correct all along! Now *there's* a happy ending for a Perrier drinker.

Foley Square lasted for only fourteen episodes, and *My Sister Sam* was gone after two seasons. But English's third series, *Murphy Brown* (CBS, 1988–present), became a bona fide hit. Entering into professional partnership with her husband, Joel Shukovsky, English created and frequently writes for the series. As always, her work was critically acclaimed for its sophisticated, ironic, and even self-reflexive wit. But this time she had also triumphed at the cash register. Network research revealed that *Murphy Brown* was not only scoring well but was also drawing viewer loyalty from that legendary target market of "shop-till-you-drop" eighteen-to-forty-nine-year-old upscale viewers.

The mold that English had cast during her previous two series remains intact in *Murphy Brown.* Murphy (Candice Bergen) is, of course, single and attractive. Outdoing both Alex and Sam in terms of professional glamor, she is the coanchor of a weekly network newsmagazine called *FYI.* Her home? A tasteful rowhouse in the Georgetown section of Washington, D.C. A recovering alcoholic à la Frank Furillo and a graduate of the Betty Ford Clinic who used to chain smoke in the manner of her idol Edward R. Murrow, Murphy has crossed the generational divide beyond the thirtysomethings of Alex and Sam. More accomplished than her predecessors, Murphy decorates her office with magazine covers that feature her, including an issue of *People* magazine bearing the headline story, "Murphy Brown: Fabulous at Forty."

The supporting cast is populated with familiar denizens of the post–Mary Richards sitcommunity. Jim Dial (Charles Kimbrough), the senior anchor of *FYI*, puffs up and blusters a bit in the style of Ted Baxter, but, unlike Ted, he proves to be a competent newsman. Coanchor Corky Sherwood (Faith Ford) is a female riff on the narcissistic Ted; a former Miss America competitor, she coordinated a closet onstage at Atlantic City for the talent competition. Reporter Frank Fontana (Joe Regalbuto), like Murray Slaughter, serves as the star's balding surrogate brother. A Lou Grant figure, however, is conspicuous by its absence. Instead, *FYI*'s boss is executive producer Miles Silverberg (Grant Shaud). A young make-a-million-bucks-before-you're-thirty go-getter, the Miles character owes more to Michael J. Fox than Ed Asner.

Murphy Brown has succeeded in life far beyond the modest dreams of Mary Richards. In fact, she probably would have given much to have Mary as her secretary. One of the running jokes of the show is her inability to find a steady assistant. The revolving door of secretaries has included an Elvis impersonator and the proprietor of a phone sex service who coolly conducted business on Murphy's private line. At home, like Alex and Sam, Murphy has a male confidant. Eldin (Robert Pastorelli) is a housepainter who has been working on Murphy's place since the series began. He began by painting a mural on her kitchen ceiling titled, "Scenes from the Industrial Revolution," and year after year he continues to spread dropcloths with no end in sight. As an available shoulder to cry on, he is a best-friend fantasy from beyond the valley of such dolls as Rhoda and Phyllis.

English has placed a bar in *Murphy Brown*, providing the series with a third regular location between the poles of workplace and home. At Phil's the well-paid communications workers that are responsible for *FYI* — journalists, executives, and blue-collar technicians — relax in extended-workplace-family bliss. The proprietor of Phil's is a salt-of-the-earth ironist (Pat Corley) who seems to know everything from impending changes in network personnel to who's *shtupping* whom this week in the Audience Research Department. If the *FYI* studio resembles *MTM*'s Channel 12 Newsroom, and Murphy's haute bourgeois urban nest recalls Alex's apartment on *Foley Square*, the scenes at Phil's closely resemble the ties-loosened camaraderie to be found in *Cheers*.

English's style in *Murphy Brown* proudly exhibits the same video self-consciousness that has characterized such well-written shows as *St. Elsewhere* and *Moonlighting*. *Murphy Brown* (again like *The MTM Show*) is after all a TV show about a TV show. Self-reflexive flourishes at medium (TV) and genre (sitcom) mark the narrative events that divide the commercials. For example, in a "sweeps" month episode the gang plans a sensationalistic show featuring Murphy interviewing a group of prostitutes; the strategy works for both *FYI* and *Murphy Brown* as Nielsens rise in both art and life.

The stage world–real world confusions are carried to an extreme in an episode in which *FYI*'s network develops a sitcom based on Murphy Brown's "real" life. Morgan Fairchild guest-stars as Julia St. Martin, who spends time on the *FYI* set to do method-acting research on Murphy for her title role in a new sitcom titled *Kelly Green*. The line between reality and fiction reaches vanishing point. A hackneyed sitcom opening credits, developed especially for this episode, replaces *Murphy Brown*'s normally austere cold start. Murphy then makes a cameo appearance in the pilot episode of *Kelly Green*. Murphy does poorly as an actress, and in one scene she caresses the Emmy she has won for TV journalism as solace. (Shortly after this episode was filmed Candice Bergen would, in so-called real life, win an Emmy for best actress in a comedy for her portrayal of Murphy Brown.) As if all this were not enough, Connie Chung shows up at the end of the episode to chastise Murphy for appearing on a sitcom. "Once you cross the line," says Connie, who in fact is crossing that very line as she speaks, "you undermine your credibility."

Diane English has won tremendous critical praise for her biggest commercial success. In its first season, *Murphy Brown* was nominated for no fewer than eleven Emmys, winning four. English personally took home an Emmy for writing the pilot episode. The series has also won a Golden Globe Award for best comedy series. In some ways, Diane English's sitcoms approach stories about women in much the same way that *The Cosby Show* approaches stories about blacks. What would have once been the subject of the drama has now become its setting. While all of English's main characters break with traditional stereotypes, that breakage is itself never the subject of a given episode. In earlier sitcoms that addressed issues of gender this was not the case. Shows such as *One Day at a Time* and *Alice*, to name two prominent examples, were often vigorously didactic in this regard, making direct attacks on sexism and sexist institutions. But the lives of Alex, Sam, and Murphy seem to take place in the aftermath, as opposed to the trenches, of a revolution.

DIANE ENGLISH: SELECTED VIDEOGRAPHY

Series

Call to Glory (CBS, 1984–85)
Foley Square (CBS, 1985–86)
My Sister Sam (CBS, 1986–88)
Murphy Brown (CBS, 1988–present)

Movies Made for Television

The Lathe of Heaven (PBS, 1980)
My Life As a Man (NBC, 1984)
Classified Love (CBS, 1986)

9. MARCY CARSEY AND TOM WERNER

The Family Moderne

At the end of the 1989–90 season, three of the top five shows in the Nielsen ratings belonged to the production team of Marcy Carsey and Tom Werner. It had been more than a decade since a studio had pulled off this kind of coup (see Chapter 6, on Garry Marshall). According to ratings projections, over 120 million Americans — almost half the country — tuned in each week to Carsey-Werner situation comedies: *The Cosby Show, A Different World,* and *Roseanne.*

The Carsey-Werner style is in some ways a throwback to an older sitcom technique pioneered in the fifties with such programs as *I Love Lucy, I Married Joan,* and *The Burns and Allen Show.* A well-known star, with an established comic persona, is the featured player and the basic building block of the series. This focal character is placed in a familiar, even emphatically banal sitcom setting. Most of the program's storylines and humor derive from the unconventionally conventional persona's peculiar reactions to an endless series of confrontations with recognizable life situations: Cliff Huxtable (Bill Cosby) discovers a gray hair. Roseanne (Roseanne Barr) must punish her daughter for staying out late. Jackie (Jackie Mason) goes out with a shiksa, much to the dismay of his mother.

Carsey and Werner are not hands-on "hyphenate" producers but, rather, are more aptly described as impresario auteurs, after the fashion of a Lee Rich (see Chapter 18). As executive producers, they select a star and a broad premise, hire the off-camera and on-camera personnel to realize the concept, and maintain a kind of quality control over the series by reviewing episode scripts on a week-to-week basis. They have cast five sitcoms from this mold to date: *Oh, Madeline* (ABC, 1983–84), starring Madeline Kahn; *The Cosby Show* (NBC, 1984–present); *Roseanne* (ABC, 1988–present), starring Roseanne Barr; *Chicken Soup* (ABC, 1989), starring Jackie Mason; and *Davis Rules* (ABC, 1991), starring Jonathan Winters. With the prime-time comedy-variety show for all intents and purposes a dead genre, the creation of a sitcom for a comedian is absolutely essential for any stand-up who wishes to reach a national audience on a regular basis. In each of the sitcoms mentioned above, Carsey and Werner collaborated directly with the star comic in constructing a customized performance-oriented proscenium showcase for weekly television.

Marcia Carsey was born in South Weymouth, Massachusetts, on November 21, 1944. After graduating from the University of New Hampshire, she moved to New York City and pursued a well-worn if somewhat meandering path up the mountain of the TV industry. Starting out as an NBC tour guide in the Rockefeller Center complex, she went on to do a stint as a "gopher" on the set of the *Tonight Show* before Johnny Carson moved the program to the West Coast. She left NBC to work for an advertising agency and also did freelance work reading scripts for studios and acting in commercials. In 1974 Michael Eisner hired her as a program executive in the comedy department at ABC in Los Angeles, and this proved to be a significant career breakaway. Within two years she was promoted to vice president of Prime Time Comedy Development and then vice president of Prime Time Comedy and Variety Programs. By the age of thirty-five she was the ABC senior vice president in charge of all prime-time series.

Though half a dozen years younger than his partner, Tom Werner arrived at ABC a year earlier than Carsey. A native New Yorker, Werner attended Harvard, where he majored in government and tried his hand at documentary filmmaking before taking a job at ABC as a junior researcher. By 1979 he, too, had risen in the executive ranks and found himself working directly under Carsey.

Carsey and Werner enjoyed the pleasures of the executive suites at ABC during the network's halcyon days of the late seventies. Comedy had played a particularly important role in ABC's rise from the bottom of the ratings to the top, and the two young programmers were prime strategists in this successful campaign. As so often happens in these types of management situations in the mass-culture industries, the young superexecs became intent on leaving the bureaucratic network rat race to produce their own programs. For most, independent production seems like a more gratifying profession, but it only turns out to be more lucrative for some. Carsey departed first, in December 1980, to create the Carsey Company. Less than a year later, Werner followed and Carsey–Werner Productions was in business.

Respectful of the ratings as well as the critical successes achieved by Norman Lear during the 1970s with adaptations of British sitcoms, their first series, *Oh, Madeline,* was an adaptation of a British show titled *Pig in the Middle.* Madeline Kahn stars as a bored suburban housewife who systematically dives headfirst into every trendy fad she can find: Maude Findlay meets Lucy Ricardo. Madeline's husband of ten years is Charlie (James Sloyan), a writer of trashy romance novels who works under the nom de plume of "Crystal Love." Simultaneously jealous and contemptuous of Charlie's career, Madeline immerses herself in fashionable causes and more-fashionable diets. Doris (Jesse Welles) is the Ethel-like wacky neighbor. Despite the lively slapstick of its proven star, *Oh, Madeline* couldn't handle the competition of the *CBS Tuesday Night Movie,* and it lasted for only eighteen episodes. The wunderkinds' new independent production company seemed off to a slow start.

All of that changed, however, with the premiere of *The Cosby Show* the following September. One of a handful of TV's all-time greatest hits, *Cosby* would dominate the balance of the eighties and continue into the nineties as the most-watched half hour in all of prime time. Carsey and Werner had fancied finding a vehicle for Bill Cosby since their days in the brass at ABC. Lifelong fans of Cosby's record-album stand-up routines, which mined rich veins of American family humor, the producers saw in Cosby's eye for domestic detail a natural sensibility for the nuclear-family sitcom. But Cosby had been involved in his share of prime-time series before. These included a costarring role in a popular action-adventure show in the sixties (*I Spy*), a failed comedy-variety hour in the seventies (*Cos*), and even a previous sitcom, *The Bill Cosby Show* (NBC, 1969–71), in which the comedian played Chet Kincaid, a gym teacher in a lower-middle-class Los Angeles high school. Cosby, who holds a doctorate in education from the University of Massachusetts, had also worked in children's programming, including both commercial cartoons (*Fat Albert and the Cosby Kids*) and noncommercial educational TV (*The Electric Company*).

With Cosby's commercial viability for prime time somewhat in question, Carsey and Werner's *Cosby Show* was turned down flat by both ABC and CBS before Brandon Tartikoff, head of NBC Entertainment, finally bit on the concept. Tartikoff would himself play a major role in the early development of the show, as would Cosby, who retained a variety of authorial contract concessions. The first season's writing team included Ed. Weinberger and Michael Leeson, both of whom shared creator credits with Bill Cosby. It is clear that Carsey and Werner were not so much the hands-on sitcommakers of *The Cosby Show* as the dealmakers who had engineered Bill Cosby's triumphant return to prime-time television. *The Cosby Show* marked the first triumph of this specific production style for Carsey and Werner. They would carry it into their subsequent projects.

Plain old commercial success is usually enough to make any TV show a darling of the industry. But *The Cosby Show*'s success provided its producers, its stars, its network and, some would say, American culture as a whole, with something extra in the self-congratulations department. Here was a popular show with a black cast that avoided the three traditional dead ends of network attempts at black prime-time programming: Uncle Tom-ish shuffling (e.g. *Amos 'n' Andy*, *Beulah*), machinegun put-down humor (e.g. *Sanford and Son*, *What's Happening?*), and inner-city criminality (e.g. almost all copshows since the late sixties). Instead there were the Huxtables, a post-Watergate *Father Knows Best* family, awash in family love, nose deep in traditional values. Here was a doctor dad, a lawyer mom (Phylicia Rashad), and five children sent by God from heaven. As if all this were not enough, dress the kids up in designer fashions and inspire them with hipper-than-thou attitudes to remind viewers of just how far we have all come since the ancient days of Wally and the Beaver.

Like *The Jeffersons* (CBS, 1975–85), the Huxtables are indeed a black family that has made it. But they are no vulgar nouveaux. Instead of moving into an Upper East Side high rise, they choose a spacious, well-appointed townhouse in that least pretentious of places on the map of American urban mythology, Brooklyn. From Cliff's technicolor sweaters to Denise's Third World chic, the Huxtable life is a page torn from a glossy magazine. Despite their duties as doctor and lawyer, Dad and Mom have a bottomless pit of quality time for Denise, Theo, Vanessa, Rudy, and even married daughter Sandra and her husband, Elvin.

It is perhaps easy to forget that *The Cosby Show* not only broke ground in the portrayal of the African-American family in situation comedy, but it also played an instrumental role in resuscitating the sitcom, which very much seemed like a genre on the ropes in the early eighties. Since *I Love Lucy* had finished Number One in 1951, sitcoms had consistently constituted a hefty share of the Nielsen Top Ten. However, in the early eighties, sitcoms began to disappear from the charmed circle of ratings winners. By 1983–84, the season before *Cosby*'s premiere, only one sitcom, *Kate & Allie* (at Number Eight), could be found in the Top Ten. *Cosby* reversed that trend, not only with its own popularity but also with its spin-off (*A Different World*) and its successful imitators. *Growing Pains* (ABC, 1985–present), for example, with its M.D. father, anchorwoman mother, and neo-squeaky siblings, is probably best understood as a "white" knockoff of *Cosby*.

A *Different World* debuted in 1987. This series followed Denise Huxtable off to Hillman College, the predominantly black school from which both her father and grandfather had graduated, and which she had chosen over several Ivy League options. In some ways the spin-off simply expanded the time slot into a "Cosby Hour." The lack of a nuclear family setting for A *Different World* was compensated for with a network of dormitory supervisors, teachers, and coaches serving *in Cosby parentis* with the same set of values and lighthearted humor that dominated the Huxtable household. Its time slot — immediately following the Number One–rated parent show — and frequent crossover characters appearing from the original virtually guaranteed A *Different World*'s success, despite some early creative problems.

Several personal and professional circumstances resulted in Lisa Bonet's departure from A *Different World* during the show's first season, not the least of which was Bonet's pregnancy, which promised to present a very un-Cosby-like dilemma for the show, Dr. Huxtable's credentials as an obstetrician notwithstanding. Debbie Allen, the real-life sister of Phylicia Rashad, was brought in by Carsey and Werner as the new producer. Allen was well known to TV viewers as the on-camera dancing teacher on *Fame* (NBC/syndicated, 1982–87). But she had also been an important creative force behind the scenes of that show. Allen managed to develop A *Different World* away from its earlier structure as a vehicle for Bonet toward a *Fame*-like repertory style, which made full use of what were originally supposed to have been "supporting" characters.

Thus an entire troupe of previously unknown young actors would emerge as stars: Jasmine Guy as Whitley Gilbert, a black Southern belle whose feminine affectations rivaled those of *The Golden Girls*' Blanche Devereaux (Rue McClanahan); Kadeem Hardison as the self-anointed Mr. Cool, Dwayne Wayne; and Dawnn Lewis as Jaleesa Vinson, a twenty-six-year-old freshman divorcée who has little patience for the adolescent high jinks of her roommates.

Carsey and Werner struck with a third major hit in 1988. This time they worked with a younger and not quite so well known comic, Roseanne Barr, to produce *Roseanne* for ABC. Barr, the self-described "domestic goddess," had created a kind of "housewife from hell" persona that had been packing them in on the comedy club circuit for several years. NBC was offered the sitcom first, but in this case Brandon Tartikoff decided to pass. ABC took the show and suddenly *Cosby* had a rival at the top of the ratings, and *Married . . . With Children* (Fox, 1987–present) had a rival for denunciations from the fundamentalist pulpit.

Like *Oh, Madeline*, *Roseanne* follows the life of a housewife. If *Cosby*'s "hook" was that it focused on a black middle-class rather than a white middle-class family, *Roseanne*'s "hook" was that it focused on a white working-class rather than a white middle-class family. Roseanne and Dan Connor are, of course, not the first proletarians to come lumbering across the homescreen. They are the heirs to a long and honored tradition that goes back to Ralph and Alice Kramden, Chester and Peg Riley, and Fred and Wilma Flintstone. Whereas in these earlier programs only the husband was overweight, that distinction is now shared in an age conscious of sexual equality. Like their more recent ancestors, Archie and Edith Bunker, Roseanne and Dan (John Goodman) are shown to live lives more at the mercy of the economic system than these earlier blue-collar sitcomites. Dan gets irregular construction work when it's available; Roseanne is the more consistent breadwinner for the family of five. Her jobs have taken her to an assemblyline at a plastics factory, a fast-food counter, and a state-of-the-art tacky beauty salon. Through all this, however, she must always be ready for a second shift, in her capacity as "domestic goddess."

Instead of the tasteful original paintings by contemporary black artists that hang on the wall of the Huxtable home, the art-of-choice at chez Roseanne includes a mass-produced print of a group of dogs dressed as humans playing poker. But despite the cosmetic differences between *Cosby* and *Roseanne*, similarities may be more substantial. Under all the crude redneck posturing and shrieking, the members of the Connor family retain the same capacities for love and family bonding that hold the Huxtables together. Roseanne and Dan tease each other mercilessly with a vulgarity that would shock Cliff and Clair Huxtable (and probably send Ward and June Cleaver off into his-and-her swoons). But underneath all their psychological squalor and physiological cellulite, they are just as dedicated to each other and to their children as any sitcom couple that ever hit the air.

A story in the *New York Times Magazine* as well as most supermarket tabloids have reported that Roseanne Barr exercises a kind of despotic control over the tone and content of the show, "with virtually no intercession by Carsey or Werner." Matt Williams, *Roseanne*'s creator, and Jeff Harris each quit the job of executive producer, in turn, over disputes with the star. Jay Daniel, the show's third executive producer, contritely admitted to the *Times* that Barr "knows the character better than anyone on the show." Bill Cosby may have been the darling of the industry during the eighties, and Roseanne Barr its enfant terrible, but ultimately the style and content of both of their programs are similarly structured by the dominant persona of the star.

After one show featuring an upper-middle-class family of black professionals, and then another built around a domineering overweight white woman in a working-class setting, Carsey and Werner continued to develop their portfolio of nontraditional sitcoms with *Chicken Soup* (ABC, 1990). This project starred Jackie Mason as a middle-aged Jewish man living with his mother, pursuing a romantic relationship with an Irish Catholic woman (Lynn Redgrave). Mason had recently won a Tony for his one-man show on Broadway, and all the signs seemed propitious. ABC placed *Chicken Soup* in the time slot right after *Roseanne* on its Tuesday-night schedule, hoping it could engineer the same kind of Carsey-Werner coup that NBC had pulled off on its Thursday-night lineup with *Cosby* and *A Different World*.

Strangely, the strategy both succeeded and failed. With *Roseanne* as its lead-in, *Chicken Soup* did well enough to finish in the Nielsen Top Ten for the season. But ABC canceled the show, nevertheless, after only eight episodes, explaining that the borscht-and-blarney humor of the sitcom just wasn't going anywhere. A closer look at the numbers, however, tells a somewhat less fuzzy and more quantitative story. Even with its powerhouse lead-in, *Chicken Soup* managed to lose a significant percentage of *Roseanne*'s audience. ABC was determined to find a property that could hold the audience with the same consistency that *A Different World* held *Cosby*. It is arguable some twenty years after *All in the Family* and its spin-offs whether a Jewish-Catholic romance remains a controversial topic for a sitcom, but Jackie Mason made several comments on the New York City mayoral election that were widely interpreted as racist, and that development certainly didn't help any. The cancellation of *Chicken Soup* recalls the cancellation of another sitcom about a Jewish–Irish Catholic love relationship, *Bridget Loves Bernie* (CBS, 1972–73), which finished fifth in the Nielsens but was also canceled in a haze of controversy. Jewish groups had protested the show for showing intermarriage in too benevolent a light. In this area, tolerance seems to have regressed since *Abie's Irish Rose*, the popular radio sitcom of the 1940s on this same subject.

Carsey and Werner's next outing was a show called *Grand*, which premiered on NBC in January 1990. Set in a Pennsylvania town where the major industry is a piano factory, *Grand* synthesizes the social-class focuses of *Cosby* and *Roseanne*. The show has even been compared with the BBC's *Upstairs, Downstairs*, in that it follows the upper and lower crusts of the factory town as they act among themselves and interact with each other. In its first half season, *Grand* was structured as a nighttime soap opera in the manner of *Dallas*, with several ongoing stories crossing episodic lines. There was talk of cancellation, but Carsey and Werner used the clout of *The Cosby Show*'s seventh-season renewal contract to insure a second chance for *Grand*. In turn, the network asked Carsey and Werner for more self-contained episodes, and the partners agreed. *Grand*, however, was axed in the middle of its second season.

As part of their original *Roseanne* deal with ABC, Carsey and Werner got the network's commitment for at least one new series. ABC was looking for an early prime-time property for family viewing. The partners' response was *Davis Rules*, a sitcom about a grade-school principal. Once again, the show was a vehicle for a veteran stand-up comedian, this time Jonathan Winters. Randy Quaid, whom Carsey and Werner had unsuccessfully tried to add to the cast of *Grand*, was given a costarring role.

Having paid their dues in network management, Carsey and Werner have exhibited great savvy in navigating the complex packaging and bargaining strategies that it takes to get a show off the drawing board and onto national air. In 1989, when ailing CBS was searching for a new president of its entertainment division, Carsey and Werner were seriously considered — as a team — for the job. The network was obviously hoping that a Carsey-Werner regime might have the same effect on it that NBC had gotten when it plucked Grant Tinker from MTM Enterprises during that production company's heyday. The idea had to be dropped, however, when it became evident that Carsey and Werner's contractual commitments to ABC and NBC in their capacities as producers presented insurmountable legal problems. But this little episode in corporate head-hunting strategy demonstrates the tremendous respect that has developed in the industry for the two hitmakers.

MARCY CARSEY AND TOM WERNER: SELECTED VIDEOGRAPHY

Series

Oh, Madeline (ABC, 1983–84)
The Cosby Show (NBC, 1984–present)
A Different World (NBC, 1987–present)
Roseanne (ABC, 1988–present)
Chicken Soup (ABC, 1989)
Grand (NBC, 1990–91)
Davis Rules (ABC, 1991)

Movie Made for Television

Single Bars, Single Women (ABC, 1984)

10. COMEDY

Honorable Mention

Danny Arnold

Originally a performer, Arnold worked as an actor and comedian in vaudeville, summer stock, and nightclubs. In the mid-1940s he gave up the spotlight for behind-the-scenes work as a sound effects editor in the movies. A decade later he was writing sketches for TV comedy-variety hosts such as Tennessee Ernie Ford and Rosemary Clooney, and episode scripts for sitcoms such as *The Real McCoys* and *Bewitched*. His first "creator/producer" credit was *My World and Welcome to It*, a collaboration with Sheldon Leonard that starred William Windom in an adaptation of a James Thurber piece about a daydreaming cartoonist. Arnold's biggest hit — and most widely respected work — was *Barney Miller*, a literate and humane comedy of manners set in the squadroom of a New York City police station.

William Asher

Asher made his reputation in Hollywood as the director of the half dozen or so Frankie Avalon/Annette Funicello beach movies. He simultaneously took various directing jobs in television, including many episodes of *I Love Lucy*. His biggest TV success came as the producer of the major TV hit *Bewitched* (ABC, 1964–72), which starred his wife Elizabeth Montgomery as a beautiful witch who trades in her broomstick for a suburban advertising executive and a quarter acre of crabgrass. Other Asher sitcoms include the TV adaptation of *Fibber McGee and Molly*, *The Paul Lynde Show*, and *Temperature's Rising*.

Linda Bloodworth-Thomason

Part of the generation of producers born during the TV era, Linda Bloodworth grew up among a family of lawyers in Poplar Bluff, Missouri. Deciding against law school, she headed West in the early seventies to seek her fortune in Hollywood. As a free-lance writer, she sold episode scripts to various running sitcoms, including *M*A*S*H* and *Rhoda*. Toward the end of the seventies, Bloodworth married a fellow Ozark native, Harry Thomason, and the two formed their own studio, Mozark Productions, staking out a speciality in creating sitcoms set in the contemporary South. Their first, *Filthy Rich* (CBS, 1982–83), was about a wealthy Memphis family. This tongue-in-cheek parody of *Dallas* only lasted a season, but its two stars, Delta Burke and Dixie Carter, were brought back by Bloodworth-Thomason in *Designing Women* (1986–present), a character-oriented sitcom set at a small interior-design company in Atlanta. This time she had a winner. Her formula? "Get four women together and listen to them talk," she told the *New York Times*. Moreover, the "talk" she refers to runs directly against genre stereotypes about the South and Southerners. The sharp-tongued dialogue heard at the Sugarbaker design firm goes far beyond the ken of anything ever heard at Floyd's Barber Shop in Mayberry or Sam Drucker's General Store in Hooterville. Bloodworth-Thomason followed with *Evening Shade* (CBS, 1991–present), starring Burt Reynolds and Marilu Henner as a small-town Arkansas couple. In 1990 CBS signed an agreement with Mozark for five new series over a period of eight years at a reported cost of approximately $45 million. It was the network's biggest deal ever with an independent studio.

Glen Charles, James Burrows, Les Charles

These partners have been the most artistically and commercially successful of the "graduates" of the school of *sitcomistes* that emerged from MTM Enterprises during the seventies. The Charles brothers are from Henderson, Nevada, and both took B.A.s in English from the University of the Redlands, while Burrows is a native Angelino who was educated at Oberlin and at Yale, where he took an M.F.A. from the School of Drama. Working in various capacities as writers and directors for James L. Brooks during the seventies on such hit shows as *Mary Tyler Moore*, *Bob Newhart*, and *Phyllis*, the three went on to form their own production company, which has turned out such literate, sophisticated hits as *Taxi* (various, 1978–83) and *Cheers* (NBC, 1982–present).

Don Fedderson

This native South Dakotan is one of American TV's unsung yeoman-producers. He has worked throughout the history of the medium as a producer of musical programs (e.g. *The Liberace Show*), dramas (e.g. *The Millionaire*), gameshows (e.g. *Do You Trust Your Wife?*, starring Johnny Carson), and sitcoms (e.g. three different shows starring Betty White in the 1950s). He is best known for *My Three Sons* (various, 1960–72), a sitcom featuring Fred MacMurray as the widowed father of three incorrigible boys. The male single parent became a Fedderson specialty. *Family Affair* (CBS, 1966–71) starred Brian Keith as a New York millionaire architect who inherits three orphaned kids from Indiana. In *To Rome with Love* (CBS, 1969–71), John Forsythe plays the bachelor father, a widower bringing up three daughters while teaching at an American university in Rome.

Larry Gelbart

Born in 1928, Gelbart grew up in Chicago and broke into radio during the 1940s. His early television career was devoted to writing jokes for comedians and talkshow hosts such as Bob Hope, Red Buttons, and Jack Paar. He was also a member of the famous writing staff assembled for Sid Caesar by producer Max Liebman (see below). Disgusted by the McCarthy-era witch-hunts and the stifling atmosphere they created in the American TV industry during the fifties, he fled to Britain, where he worked on a number of television projects. He was enticed to return to Hollywood by CBS to produce *M*A*S*H* (CBS, 1972–83), a sitcom whose irreverence for generic taboos was as startling as the profound love that an audience numbering in the tens of millions developed for it. Gelbart left day-to-day involvement with *M*A*S*H* in the midseventies to try other TV projects. But subsequent sitcom attempts, such as *United States*, *Roll Out!* and *Karen* were commercial failures. He turned his talents toward theatrically released feature films and did better with hits such as *Oh, God!* (1977) and *Tootsie* (1982).

Nat Hiken

A sketch writer for Milton Berle's *Texaco Star Theater* in the late 1940s, Hiken left comedy-variety work to produce two extraordinary sitcoms: *You'll Never Get Rich* (aka "Sergeant Bilko," CBS, 1955–59) and *Car 54, Where Are You?* (NBC, 1961–63). Both made during the sitcom's whitebread period, when suburban family comedies concerning the moral educations of unbearably cute children dominated the genre, the Hiken sitcoms were emphatically urban, ethnic, and sassy. Moreover, in an era when laughtracks were doing most of the laughing, Hiken's shows, one about a conman army sergeant, the other about a precinct full of inept Bronx cops, could be uproariously funny. Hiken also rowed against prevailing currents by his insistence on using black actors in nonservant roles. Nipsey Russell, for example, got his start in television as Officer Anderson in *Car 54*. Hiken died in 1968.

Sheldon Leonard

Born in New York City in 1907 and educated at Syracuse University, Sheldon Leonard became familiar to moviegoers in the 1930s as an archetypal underworld "heavy" in gangster films. By the start of the television era, however, he had largely given up acting for production work. In 1953 he formed a company in partnership with Danny Thomas to produce *Make Room for Daddy*, a sitcom starring Thomas as a nightclub entertainer and family man. The show ran for twelve years, winning several Emmys for Leonard. Other Leonard hits growing out of the Thomas partnership included a trio of rural sitcoms: *The Real McCoys, The Andy Griffith Show*, and *Gomer Pyle, U.S.M.C.* In the action/adventure category, Leonard produced *I Spy* (NBC, 1965–68), which was the first hour-long drama series to feature a black actor, Bill Cosby, in a starring role. Most critics consider *The Dick Van Dyke Show* to be Leonard's finest work. The sitcom was originally created by Carl Reiner and starred Reiner in the lead role of a comedy writer commuting between suburban family life and the midtown Manhattan show-business world. Then titled *Head of the Family*, the pilot was aired, but it was considered "too Jewish" by CBS brass. Leonard was brought in to "doctor" the property; his first move was to recast the lead role, taking it away from Reiner and awarding it to Dick Van Dyke. Leonard, Reiner, and Van Dyke then formed a partnership to coproduce the series.

Max Liebman

"The Ziegfeld of TV" was a well-known Broadway-show producer before moving over to television in the late forties. A dominant force in the comedy-variety vogue of early TV, he is often credited as being a behind-the-scenes inventor of the genre. Liebman produced dozens of musical comedy specials (or "spectaculars" as they were called), many of them under the banner of his own showcasing imprimatur, *Max Liebman Presents* (NBC, 1954–56). His masterpiece, however, was *Your Show of Shows* (NBC, 1950–54), which starred Sid Caesar and a troupe of regulars that included Imogene Coca, Carl Reiner, and Howard Morris. Liebman's genius for presenting talent on-screen was only outstripped by his ability to gather it off-screen. The remarkable writing staff of *Your Show of Shows* included such notables as Woody Allen, Selma Diamond, Neil Simon, Mel Brooks, and Larry Gelbart. Liebman, however, was unable to survive the decline of the comedy-variety format that he had helped to create. By the sixties there was little work left for him in prime-time television. He died in 1981 at the age of seventy-eight.

Lorne Michaels

Born and raised in Toronto, Michaels was writing and producing amateur comedy-variety stage shows before his graduation from the University of Toronto. He began his professional career writing radio and television comedy for Canadian Broadcasting Company shows, moving to the United States in the midsixties. In Hollywood he found work writing and producing variety specials for comics such as Phyllis Diller, Lily Tomlin, and Flip Wilson, and eventually won a staff job with the top-rated *Rowan and Martin's Laugh-In* (NBC, 1968–73). Michaels's big break came in 1975 when NBC tapped him to produce a new late-night weekly comedy revue designed to capture young upscale audiences. The result was *Saturday Night Live*. Mixing star guest hosts with musical acts and the sketch comedy of a troupe of comedians, many of them recruited from the Second City nightclubs in Chicago and Toronto, the show got off to a slow start. But gradually the "Not Ready for Prime Time Players" — Dan Aykroyd, Gilda Radner, John Belushi, Chevy Chase, Jane Curtin, Garrett Morris, and Bill Murray — developed into a first-class comedy repertory company, offering some of the freshest, most intelligent material ever produced for commercial television. Spoofs of commercials, game-shows, sitcoms, and other "normal" TV fare were among the show's greatest strengths. Michaels left *SNL* in the early eighties to attempt other projects but came back in 1987 to save the show from the doldrums it had entered during his absence.

Bob Mosher and Joe Connelly

This sitcom team broke into TV in the early days writing scripts for *Amos 'n' Andy,* a show created and produced by another team: Freeman Gosden and Charles Correll. Mosher and Connelly had two hit sitcoms of their own: *Leave It to Beaver* (various, 1957–63) and *The Munsters* (CBS, 1964–66), a pair of shows that have been ubiquitous, to say the least, in rerun syndication. Their most bizarre effort was certainly *Calvin and the Colonel* (ABC, 1961–62), a prime-time cartoon series about a couple of animals from the Deep South living in a Northern city. This show found Mosher and Connelly employing their old bosses Gosden and Correll as the voices of Calvin, a stupid bear, and The Colonel, a wily fox. Though the race of these cartoon characters was never mentioned, they seemed an awful lot like the stupid Andy and the wily Kingfish of *Amos 'n' Andy.*

PART TWO

Drama

11. THE GOLDEN AGE OF TELEVISION DRAMA

The Writer as Auteur

In The Age of Television, the drama critic Martin Esslin writes, "The time devoted by the average American adult male to watching dramatic materials on television amounts to over 12 hours per week, while the average American woman sees almost 16 hours of drama on television each week. That means that the average American adult sees the equivalent of *five to six full-length stage plays a week!*" Indeed, by such measure a typical American child is likely to have seen more drama before reaching puberty than the most avid theatergoer in Elizabethan London could have possibly witnessed in a lifetime.

But Esslin, like most critics, is anything but happy about what he calls "the drama explosion." Quantity has been achieved at the expense of quality. The culture factories of the entertainment-industrial complex have drawn the mythic wellspring dry and destroyed the aesthetic ecos. With no tale left untold, no message left unpreached, and no narrative structure left uncloned, sensation takes precedence over moral wisdom and relaxation displaces catharsis as the objective of dramatic art. "Nobody," he writes, "should be compelled to like the greatest art, the highest flights of the intellect, but everyone should at least have an opportunity to encounter them. Denial of access to these areas of human achievement on the most generally accessible medium of communication amounts to the denial of a basic human right. An extension of television to encompass the whole range of cultural activity must thus be regarded as, above all, the reestablishment of one of the greatest and most vital of human liberties."

*Re*establishment? Where and when was access to drama — or any form of culture — ever considered "a basic human right"? In the slave-holding societies of ancient Greece? In feudal Europe? In Victorian Britain? On planet Earth? The series of technological innovations that has given rise to cinema, radio, and television over the last hundred years has created the first opportunity in the history of civilization to establish anything like democratic accessibility to drama and other forms of culture. To challenge the quality of a drama created for a heterogeneous audience of tens of millions of people by the standards created to judge works performed in Peloponnesian amphitheaters for a few thousand members of the same social class is a perfunctory academic exercise. It is far from clear whether an episode of *Dallas* or *L.A. Law* even manages to meet Aristotle's minimal demand that a drama have "a beginning, a middle, and an end."

Perhaps a more fruitful way of understanding television drama lies in a consideration of how the function of drama has changed since it became the product of a household appliance. For one thing, formal drama had typically been a sacred or religious activity in most cultures throughout recorded history. The Greek plays were performed at harvest festivals as celebratory offerings to the gods; in the European Middle Ages, the passion plays at Easter constituted one of the few church-sanctioned occasions for drama. If culture was to become, as Matthew Arnold predicted, a fortress against the chaos of the post-Darwin universe, the republican theater that emerged in the late nineteenth century was a keystone of that newly consecrated structure; the secular-humanist faithful gave reverence, and even dressed appropriately to attend mass at the temple of the Muse.

Perhaps it was this very metaphorization of the religious function of theater that paved the way for drama to migrate down the primrose path from the sacred to the profane. The advent of the cinema was a significant transitional step in this regard. Here was an activity that took place in a theater. Yet any person might enter in the darkness at any time during the performance, dressed in rags or designer jogging clothes, and talk, munch on junk food, sleep, or perform even more radical bodily functions during the show. It is no wonder the movies were looked down upon as vulgar amusement by the exclusive theatergoing classes.

And yet, during the age of cinema, drama at least remained a public occasion. In front of the TV set this last bit of civic communion disintegrates. Having just completed an eight-hour shift in front of a video display terminal, bracketed by several more hours of fuming through the choke of traffic, swilling down bad coffee, and dealing with an office full of people doing likewise, the members of the television audience come home to the drama; they do not go out to it. Whether sprawled upon a Naugahyde couch in dirty underwear or pumping away on a stationary bicycle or even casually seated upon the domestic throne, the contemporary patrons of the drama might be prone to experience the fourth-wall illusion in ways that cannot be accounted for by criteria that were developed before the play became such a convenient thing.

Even the classical distinctions between tragedy and comedy that are the very foundation of Western drama criticism are difficult to apply to TV. In the weekly TV series, the hero is structurally protected from death. This may make perfect sense as a convention of situation comedy, but what about the copshow? A typical episode of a program such as *Miami Vice, Starsky and Hutch,* or *Police Woman* may contain murder, rape, child abuse, and/or multiple fatal car crashes. Yet at the end of the episode the viewer finds the series hero alive and well — with harmony restored to society to boot. This type of ending was once a defining feature of comedy. The only major prime-time genre structurally capable of presenting tragic drama is the made-for-TV movie, which is nonserial, allowing for the death of the hero. But even here tragedy is rare because many made-for-television movies are conceived of as pilots for series.

The continuing series has been the rule in television drama for decades now, but this was not always the case. During the first fifteen years or so of network telecast (a period ending at about 1960), the optimal commercial formats had not yet been clearly defined. Anthology showcases — programs that presented original, nonserial plays each week — were once as common as copshows or sitcoms. This period is often referred to as "the golden age of television drama." Not yet seen as an art itself, television was widely thought of as a transmission system for the presentation of bona fide arts — especially drama. In this "theater of the air" way of thinking, the writer, rather than the producer or director, was regarded as the primary creator of televised drama.

As a result, more than at any other time in the history of the medium, it was possible during the "golden age" for a TV writer to become a recognized artist or even a major celebrity. Authors such as Paddy Chayefsky, Reginald Rose, Rod Serling, Robert Alan Aurthur, and Gore Vidal were better known than any other behind-the-scenes TV personnel, in some cases sharing the public limelight with the actors and actresses who performed their work. Despite the general antagonism of the movie industry toward TV during this period, it was not unusual for the works of these television playwrights to be adapted into Hollywood feature films. Examples include several Oscar winners, such as *Marty* by Paddy Chayefsky, originally a 1953 episode of *Goodyear TV Playhouse* (NBC, 1951–60), and *Requiem for a Heavyweight* by Rod Serling, a 1956 episode of *Playhouse 90* (CBS, 1956–61).

The dominance of dialogue in early teletheater was one factor that helped to focus attention on the virtuosity of the writer. In these cheaply made productions, which were telecast live (often from hastily converted radio studios), there was little room for the visual sensations of car chases, shoot-outs, or even outdoor scenery. The typical mise-en-scène consisted of a few talking heads in a crowded little room. The logistics of directing live TV were too demanding to allow for much in the way of fancy directorial footwork. Production schedules for a given teleplay were typically less than a week long. Moreover, the commercial constraints of the medium often defined the look of a play to a greater degree than any particular director's camera style. Marketing wisdom demanded that viewers not be "distracted" from the stars they had tuned in to see — and usually that translated into close-ups, close-ups, and more close-ups. Talented novices such as George Roy Hill, Franklin Shaffner, John Frankenheimer, Sidney Lumet, and Daniel Petrie began their careers directing TV drama. But none of them achieved personal fame until making it in the movies. The attention instead went to Chayefsky, Rose, Serling, and the other writers.

According to broadcast historian Erik Barnouw, author of *Tube of Plenty*, the creative process of anthology drama went something like this: "The play was the thing. Actors were chosen to fit the play, not vice-versa. The anthology series said to the writer: 'Write us a play.' There were no specifications as to mood, characters, plot, style, or locale — at least not at first. . . . Except for such technical requirements [as studio size and length of program], *Philco Television Playhouse, Kraft Television Theatre*, and other anthology series began as carte-blanche invitations to writers — and writers responded."

Of course some golden-age writers were more "golden" than others. There is no point in overstating collective virtuosity. As has usually been the case with any artistic genre in any medium throughout recorded history, much of 1950s television drama was mediocre and most of it is forgotten. But given the general problems of working in this most commercial of all media, the fact that a handful of dramatists did create a handful of notable works is itself remarkable.

No writer personified the golden-age dramatists more than Paddy Chayefsky. Born Sidney Chayefsky in New York City to Jewish immigrant parents in 1923, he attended DeWitt Clinton High School in the Bronx and the City College of New York. He worked at various times as a semiprofessional football player for the Knightsbridge Trojans and as an apprentice in his uncle's print shop. After graduating from CCNY in 1943, he joined the army and was shipped out to Europe. As a member of the 104th Infantry Division, Chayefsky was wounded by a land mine in Germany and received the Purple Heart. While recuperating in a hospital bed in England, he wrote a musical comedy titled *No T.O. [time out] for Love* and played the lead role in a U.S.O. production of it. In 1945 he got his first screenwriting job, working on a script for a U.S. government-produced propaganda film titled *The True Glory*. After the war he went on to study at the Actor's Lab of Hollywood and eventually signed on as a script doctor for Universal-International, where he specialized in rewrites and added dialogue for the studio's endless stream of "B" pictures.

Not satisfied to merely turn screws on an assemblyline in a Hollywood factory, Chayefsky returned to New York to try his hand at radio drama. He authored scripts in the early fifties for *The Theatre Guild of the Air*, a long-running showcase for radio adaptations of Broadway plays, and for *The Cavalcade of America*, an anthology that specialized in dramatizing events from American history and literature. It was only an elevator trip from the network radio studios to their new TV production facilities, and Chayefsky spent several years working in both broadcast media.

His earliest TV credits were scripts for two live anthology programs: *Manhunt*, an NBC showcase built around adaptations of adventure short stories from books and magazines; and *Danger* (CBS, 1950–55), whose thematic focus was psychological drama, usually tied to murder mystery. *Danger* was reasonably high-toned as TV series went during the period. Its production staff included future stand-out film directors Sidney Lumet and John Frankenheimer, and its casts boasted the likes of such promising young performers as Jack Lemmon, Grace Kelly, Anthony Quinn, Carroll Baker, James Dean, and Paul Newman. Chayefsky's career-long inclination to set his work in the proletarian depths of New York City was already evident; his half-hour playlets for *Danger* included an episode titled *Murder Takes the "A" Train.*

Early in 1952 Chayefsky signed on as a staff writer for *The Goodyear–Philco Television Playhouse*, and it was here that he wrote some of his best scripts and made his breakthrough into public recognition. *Goodyear–Philco* was a typical network dramatic anthology. The program was sponsored on alternating weeks by the giant tiremaker and the home electronics company, both of whom were represented by the same ad agency, which technically "owned" the show's Sunday night ten-to-eleven o'clock NBC time period. This kind of arrangement was a key feature of golden-age drama production. At a time when such phrases as "boob tube" and "idiot box" were first entering the American vocabulary, the live TV play was considered a prestigious high-profile corporate investment; PBS, of course, did not even exist yet. The names of the industrial giants were splashed all over such projects: *General Electric Theater* (hosted by Ronald Reagan), *The U.S. Steel Hour, Ford Theatre, Plymouth Playhouse,* etc.

The advantage of full sponsorship was that a program did not necessarily have to get high ratings to stay on the air. The pleasure of a board of directors — or in some cases just a single executive — could keep it in production. In the early fifties, television had not yet penetrated half the households in the nation, and advertising rates were still quite affordable to these large companies. Thus the dramatist might theoretically be freed from Nielsen tyranny by a sympathetic corporate patron. But the disadvantage of full sponsorship was that the advertiser (and its advertising agency) retained extraordinary editorial say over the content of the writer's work. Paddy Chayefsky, for better or worse, was very much a creature of this Janus-faced system. During the 1952–53 season, Chayefsky saw the production of four of his plays on *Goodyear–Philco: Holiday Song, The Reluctant Citizen, Printer's Measure,* and, the most important of the quartet, *Marty.*

Chayefsky's protagonists were usually lower-middle-class men working in skilled manual professions (butchers and printers, to name two prominent examples). The dialogue spoken by these characters — and the problems they faced — were emphatically common and personal: loneliness, alienation, social pressure to conform. The technical requirements of live broadcast were a good fit with Chayefsky's dramatic gestalt: cramped urban living rooms, small working-class bars, neighborhood mom-and-pop stores. Car chases, big crowds, and location shots were strictly out of the question.

In this and many other ways *Marty* epitomizes its genre and remains a germinating artifact of its moment in television — and American — history. Like most golden-age teleplays, *Marty* strives to be emphatically realistic. Cigarette butts fill the ashtrays; people gratuitously bump into each other. The plot strives just as emphatically for psychological naturalism, though the thickly layered allusions to oedipal revelations and identity crises often fall off the edge of credibility into trickle-down psycho-babble. Despite its physical resemblance to 1930s social realism, the fifties teleplay consistently falls short of the ideological goals of that model. The golden age of television drama, it should be remembered, coincided with the golden age of Senator Joseph McCarthy.

Chayefsky unambiguously toes the political line in *Marty*. The play, for example, was set — as well as telecast — in 1953. Though a story about single working men during a period of universal male conscription, the Korean War is never mentioned. Though set in a working-class section of the Bronx during a time when tens of thousands of Southern blacks and Puerto Rican emigrants were arriving there, no minority characters appear, even in scenes set in public places.

The civil rights movement was kicking into high gear during the fifties, and the psychological effects of race prejudice were filling the literature of authors such as Richard Wright, James Baldwin, and Ralph Ellison. The subject was even penetrating the nation's movie theaters with such pictures as Elia Kazan's *Pinky* and Douglas Sirk's *Imitation of Life*. But neither the works of minority playwrights nor plays about minority problems, nor even references to the struggle against Jim Crow in the South, appeared in the self-proclaimed "serious" drama of 1950s American television.

In his study " 'Marty': Aesthetics vs. Medium," Kenneth Hey writes in great detail about the whys and wherefores of TV drama during the McCarthy era. Perhaps the most restricting dictum facing TV playwrights was the necessity to be "upbeat," to always leave their audiences with at least some semblance of a happy ending, no matter how the inner coherence of plot indicated otherwise. Effectively forced to steer clear of social issues, Chayefsky and his colleagues had to derive all the tensions in their plays from purely personal problems, as if such problems could ever be seriously considered outside their social contexts.

Marty concerns an Italian-American Bronx butcher (Rod Steiger) approaching middle age as a bachelor. Everyone around him asks why he's not married — his customers, his friends, and his mother (with whom he lives). In the opening scenes, the viewer immediately develops a sense of empathy for the homely, kindhearted title character. At one point Marty poignantly describes himself as "an ugly little man." "Whatever it is that women like," he tells his mother, "I just ain't got it."

Why are all these people badgering him? He is a kind and decent fellow, apparently not capable of harming a fly. Why won't everybody just leave him alone, a viewer might wonder. But over the course of the hour we learn that these are the wrong questions to ask. "Everybody," as the play turns out, is right. Marty *should*, in fact, get married, and his realization of this is the "moral" of the story. In the final scene of the play, he is about to call up Clara (Nancy Marchand), a woman whom he hopes will one day accept his proposal of marriage. The other bachelors tease him, calling her a "dog." His best buddy Angie, who is afraid of losing Marty's misery-loves-company companionship, tries to stop him. "When are *you* gonna get married?" Marty angrily shouts at Angie as he shuts the door to the telephone booth. Marty has finally adopted the point of view of his tormentors — and thus he finally becomes a man.

Conformity then is a happy ending. Things weren't as bad as Marty (and we) might have thought at the beginning of the play. Neither society nor any of its hallowed institutions is to be blamed for personal unhappiness. Several subplots reaffirm this. For example, Marty's Aunt Katerina, who lives with her son and daughter-in-law, is facing difficulties. The young couple have a small apartment and Katerina keeps "interfering" with their marriage. But the family, as an institution, is shown to be capable of solving this problem; Marty and his mother happily take Katerina in and provide her with a home. Even though they're far from rich, they make no mention of money. No nursing home horrors here.

Marty's mother wants him to get married, but when she sees the problems that Katerina is having with her daughter-in-law, she develops second thoughts based on a fear of being "cast out of her own home." She treats Clara rudely when they meet. But after going to Mass the next Sunday, she miraculously exits the church door and admits that she has been acting like "an old goat," encouraging Marty to go ahead and pursue Clara's hand. We don't know what the sermon might have been; all we need to know is that there's nothing like a visit to church to put the errant back on the righteous path.

The bottom line seems to be that Marty's humiliation over his bachelorhood is itself part of a just and natural mechanism to get him to do the "right" thing. The idea that it is his duty to society to get married is not questioned by the play. Marty's willingness to blame his depression on personal inadequacy turns out not to be neurotic but, rather, quite correct. No matter how much pain it causes him ("heartache" is the word he repeatedly uses), he must attempt to conform.

Marty contains at least one example of "full sponsorship" content control which is astounding in its pettiness. On the night that Marty meets Clara at a local dance hall, he offers to take her home, though he has no car. According to Chayefsky, in his original script Marty says that they better get going because "the subway trains run one every hour." At first Goodyear demanded that Marty have a car, because cars use tires. Chayefsky protested that it would be unrealistic for someone of Marty's social class in New York City during this period to own a car. So they compromised by changing the line so that Marty takes Clara home by bus, a vehicle that at least uses rubber tires.

Other examples of sponsor interference during the golden age were far more ludicrous. *Judgement at Nuremberg,* by Reginald Rose, a play about the Nazi war crimes trials, which was later adapted into a feature film starring Spencer Tracy, was first presented as a 1959 episode of *Playhouse 90.* The show was sponsored by the American Gas Association, and all references to lethal gas used in the concentration camps had to be deleted from the script! A less spectacular, but more typical, intrusion of this type was the policy of *The Lucky Strike Hour* that demanded that heroic characters including "attractive males and females" be shown smoking cigarettes in the course of normal activity. Criminals, on the other hand, were not to be shown smoking cigarettes.

By the early 1960s, network television had reached virtual saturation in the United States, and the three-network system was reaching new heights of money and power. Live drama had virtually disappeared, as expensive filmed series with recurring characters replaced the canceled anthology showcases. Prime-time advertising rates skyrocketed, and as a result full sponsorship became increasingly rare. Instead, the networks programmed as they pleased and sold "spot" or "cluster" commercials to advertisers who now had no say in production matters. Chayefsky became angered and embittered as the networks abandoned the genre to which he had devoted his career. He damned the industry that had made him famous and went on to become a Hollywood screenwriter. His most celebrated movie script would be *Network,* a 1976 film directed by his old TV collaborator Sidney Lumet, which is an impassioned satire directed against the entire American television industry.

*   *   *

Reginald Rose got less public attention than Chayefsky, but he was no less a significant creative force in early TV drama. Like Chayefsky, Rose was born in New York City during the twenties, the son of immigrant Jewish parents, and he attended the (then) tuition-free City College of New York. His most famous work was probably *Twelve Angry Men* (*Studio One*, 1954), a claustrophobic little teleplay concerning the deliberations of a jury in a homicide case. Bob Cummings and Norman Fell starred in the hour-long original, which was adapted by Sidney Lumet into a feature film some three years later, starring Lee J. Cobb and Henry Fonda. The script is a classic of American liberalism, circa the era of Adlai Stevenson. The jury is ready to convict a ghetto kid for the murder of his father. His crime is "obvious" to all the jury members — but one. The deliberations reveal that the rush to judgment of most of the jury members is born not out of the facts but out of personal prejudices. In the end, the persistence of the lone right-minded liberal prevails: not guilty.

A more revealing example from Rose's portfolio, at least in terms of the problems facing television playwrights, was *Thunder on Sycamore Street*, also presented in 1954 as an episode of *Studio One*. Rose's original script, written for presentation at a crucial point in the civil rights desegregation struggle, concerned the violent antagonism faced by a black family that moves into an all-white neighborhood. It was considered too hot a topic for television. In a comment accompanying the publication of the play, Rose writes, "One interesting point to note is this: Originally, *Thunder on Sycamore Street* was conceived as the story of a Negro who moves into a white community. This was unpalatable to the network since many of their stations are situated in Southern states, and it was felt that viewers might be appalled at the sight of a Negro as the beleaguered hero of a television drama. I felt that a compromise would weaken the play but I decided to make one anyway, hoping that the principle under observation was strong enough to arouse an audience, no matter what strata of society the mob's intended victim represented."

The casual tone of Rose's explanation is itself remarkable. In terms of the most cherished traditions of Western artists, he had sold out, pure and simple. Yet he argues, nonetheless, that, faced with the choice of ameliorating the story or not telling it at all, a revamped version at least brought up the "principle" of the right of Americans to live in the neighborhood of their choice. In any case, Rose's black family reached the TV cameras as a white man persecuted by his neighbors because he is an ex-convict.

Another Rose teleplay, *Tragedy in a Temporary Town* (1956), concerned a lynching in a trailer camp. Alcoa Aluminum Company, the show's sponsor, was upset because mobile homes are typically constructed out of aluminum and the company did not want to have its product associated with such a "controversial" topic. Rose again obliged and reset the story in rural wooden shacks, thus sacrificing the contemporary associations that he had purposely intended for this story on race relations.

Despite the travesties committed against his work, Rose persisted in pressing forward with his socially conscious television projects. Unlike Chayefsky, Rose chose to stay in television even after the anthology format began to die. In the early sixties he spun off one of his old *Studio One* scripts into a telefilm series: *The Defenders* (CBS, 1961–65). This courtroom drama starred E. G. Marshall and Robert Reed as affluent father-and-son law partners with a penchant for sticky *pro bono* work. The show was a landmark series and a prototype for the "relevance" movement in series teledrama, which was still the better part of a decade away. TV historians Tim Brooks and Earle Marsh wrote of *The Defenders:* "At a time when most TV entertainment series avoided any hint of controversy or topicality, [*The Defenders*] . . . addressed such real-life issues as abortion, mercy killing, and the U.S. government's restriction of a citizen's right to travel to unfriendly foreign countries. A January 1964 episode titled 'Blacklist' was TV's first hard look at its own practice of political blacklisting. . . ."

Of all the golden-age writers, none received anything approaching the public acclaim and affection that went to Rod Serling. Like Chayefsky and Rose, Serling was a New Yorker, but he was an Upstate product, born on Christmas Day 1924 in Syracuse and raised in nearby Binghamton, the eerie little Susquehanna River city in which many of his most bone-chilling playlets would be set. While earning a B.A. in English at Antioch College, he worked at several local radio stations in nearby Marion, Ohio, and after graduation set his sights on a career as a radio writer. In 1949 he made his own big break by entering a script in a national contest sponsored by a medical drama called *Dr. Christian* (CBS Radio, 1937–53); it was selected from hundreds of entries for production on the show.

In the early fifties he contributed scripts to some of television's most prestigious anthology series: *The U.S. Steel Hour, Studio One, Fireside Theatre, Lux Video Theatre,* and *Desilu Playhouse.* He won Emmys in 1955 for *Patterns (Kraft Theatre)*; in 1956 for *Requiem for a Heavyweight (Playhouse 90)*; in 1957 for *The Comedian (Playhouse*

90), and in 1963 for *It's Mental Work* (*Chrysler Theatre*). *Requiem for a Heavyweight* was adapted for the movies in 1962. The film version starred Anthony Quinn as a punch-drunk prizefighter on his way to Palookaville and Jackie Gleason as his manager.

Serling, of course, is best known — both in front of and behind the camera — for *The Twilight Zone*, which originally ran on CBS from 1959 to 1965. The weekly series outlasted virtually all of the golden-age drama showcases, and to this day *The Twilight Zone* remains the only anthology show in commercial rerun syndication. By focusing the program on the related themes of the occult and science fiction, and by moving over to filmed rather than live production, Serling found a way to continue to develop his personal dramatic aesthetic in prime time years after most of the other golden-age writers had been squeezed out of the medium (e.g. Chayefsky) or gone over to writing for regular series (e.g. Rose).

Each episode of *The Twilight Zone* opens with a view of the night sky serving as backdrop for Serling's staccato narration: "You're traveling through another dimension . . . a dimension not only of sight and sound, but of mind. . . ." Ticking clocks and ominous equations start flying around the screen as if this were the opening sequence of *The René Magritte Show* or *The Salvador Dali Theatre*. Silence. The camera descends on some poor schnook who is about to enter *the twilight zone*. Serling's on-screen appearance as narrator at the end of the establishing scene became his trademark.

The leitmotifs that dominate *The Twilight Zone* are the same ones that Serling had always been associated with: the thin line between ambition and hubris; the price of success (which often included a tête-à-tête with none other than Beelzebub himself); and the fading lives of fading celebrities, sports heroes, and movie stars. Politically liberal, emotionally romantic, and philosophically quasi-existential at times, *The Twilight Zone* was an ideal prime-time vehicle, attracting children with an overflow of macabre glitz and their parents with a surfeit of "heavy" message.

A typical *Twilight Zone* episode was "The Trade-Ins," which aired in 1962. The story takes place, as Serling's so often do, "sometime in the future." An elderly couple is being taken through a showroom by a salesman. What is he offering them? Furniture? Cars? Nothing quite so banal. He has new bodies for sale. Technology, it seems, now allows people to trade in wrinkled old bodies for shiny new ones. Here's something nice in an athlete for the gentleman . . . in a dancer for the lady. . . . Unfortunately, the couple in question is of modest means. They can only afford one body. What to do? The old man has the operation and, with his new body, he will get a job and make enough money to have his wife "done." Suddenly finding himself in his sleek new bod, however. . . . In any case, this one's a comedy of education, and the man gives up his new body so that he and his lifelong mate can follow the natural cycle of things. If Serling had a literary idol, it was probably O. Henry.

The Twilight Zone, more than any other remnant of golden-age TV drama, became a living part of American mythology. A Rod Serling imitation is de rigueur for stand-up mimics. The show's opening musical theme remains a signifier for the odd, the weird, and/or the crazy; it is casually invoked for this purpose in contemporary films, TV shows, and even rap songs.

In 1970 Serling returned to prime time with *Night Gallery,* a series that anthologized three narratively unrelated playlets into each hour-long episode. Serling once again appeared to introduce the stories, this time in an art gallery filled with televisual renderings of surrealistic paintings. But with its stories limited to about fifteen minutes in length, *Night Gallery* seemed a poor shadow of *The Twilight Zone* — and in some ways a pathetically abridged relic of the once mighty anthology genre.

Rod Serling died in 1975, but *The Twilight Zone* lives on. In 1983 directors John Landis, Joe Dante, Steven Spielberg, and George Miller each contributed a story to *Twilight Zone — The Movie.* The film was in part adapted from the old teleplays, recalling the golden-age practice that had resulted in such TV dramas as *Marty* and *Requiem for a Heavyweight* becoming Hollywood pictures. In 1985 CBS, floundering in last place, revived *The Twilight Zone* TV show, ending its twenty-year production hiatus; it ran on the network for two seasons. The several attempts that have been made at reviving anthology drama on television over the last few decades have mostly been attempts to copy the Serling formula. Examples include not only a new (third) syndicated version of *The Twilight Zone* but also such shows as Steven Spielberg's *Amazing Stories, Tales from the Crypt, Monsters,* and *Friday the 13th.*

In retrospect, the triumph of the episodic series over anthology drama seems logical. As marketing analysts and social psychologists achieved greater power in the industry, goals such as "viewer loyalty" and "habit formation pattern" revealed such notions as "a national theater" and "quality popular drama" as dreamy idealism from an era of innocence. Audience size and audience character are easier to predict when people know they can return week after week to the same characters and meet them with the same expectations. Series, which tend to reuse the same sets, stars, and production schedules, invite the economies of industrial production.

The role of the dramatic writer, however, became very different in the recurring series than it had been in the anthologies. The anthology writer in effect created his or her own little universe for an hour. Each play was an independent entity with its own characters, rules, and ambience. In contrast, series writers tend to be hired hands, itinerants fleshing out stories for someone else's creation according to someone else's established formula. That "someone else" is, of course, the producer. Parameters of character development, setting, attitude, and style are set by the producer before an episode of a continuing series is ever written or in many cases before the writer is even hired. A writer for *The Incredible Hulk*, for example, would have a great deal of trouble with a personal vision of an episode in which Dr. David Banner didn't manage to change into the Hulk — twice, once during the first half hour of the show, once during the second.

The made-for-TV movie, it can be argued, is the television dramatist's last possible authorial domain. But even here, so many of these two-hour films are conceived of by production companies as pilots for possible series that a writer is forced to take careful notice of which way the pen is pointing. Killing off a possible Top Ten show's star could give real meaning to the phrase "television tragedy." The only way a writer can hope to truly dominate a production in the system that has developed is by becoming a "hypenate." This industry term usually means a "creator-producer" who writes at least some episodes and retains editorial control over episodes written by the hired help.

Hyphenates are collectively the creative power élite of American video drama. Some TV writers have consolidated enormous power through the assumption of multiple production roles. Stephen J. Cannell, for example, is so hyphenated at this point that he is in a position to personally conceive of a program idea, personally finance and produce a pilot episode based on that concept, and personally maintain direct control of week-to-week production on the soundstage of his own studio. As if all this were not enough, he has recently begun the process of purchasing his own television stations. One day soon his only problem in getting a show on the air might be getting the left side of his brain to buy the concept from the right side of his brain.

Most of the television auteurs discussed in the following chapters, though not all, are writers who have expanded their control by becoming hyphenates. (Notable exceptions are Lee Rich, a consummate front-office man, and Jack Webb, whose roots are in acting.) The majority of television producers today are people who began their careers writing piecemeal for others and then "graduated" to creating and producing series of their own. One theory about why most critics hold such special animus for television shows is based on the idea that critics, who are after all writers, cannot forgive television for demystifying their own craft as the dominant creative influence in contemporary drama.

12. JACK WEBB

The Struggle Against Evil

During the 1950s, while virtually all other producers of episodic television remained anonymous to the public, Jack Webb stood alone as a widely recognized crimeshow auteur. This was certainly due in large part to the fact that he was also the star of his own hit show, *Dragnet,* as well as its behind-the-scenes mastermind. But there is also no disputing the distinctive style that Jack Webb developed in the public mind as a storyteller. As a series creator; as a producer, director, and writer; and as the chief executive of his own studio, Mark VII Productions, Webb was a crucial player in the adaptation of the cops-and-robbers legend for television. Sergeant Joe Friday, the staccato-voiced law-and-order missionary whom Webb created and portrayed, first for radio in the 1940s, then for TV in the fifties and sixties, remains a vital character in the myth of the American urban policeman.

Born April 2, 1920, in Santa Monica, California, Webb began his broadcasting career in the late thirties working in West Coast radio production. After serving as a bomber pilot in the Pacific during World War II, he returned stateside to become part of the lively commercial radio scene that was developing in San Francisco, producing a weekly show for the ABC network titled *One out of Seven* (1946). Initiating a format he would become known for throughout his career, Webb presented dramatizations of "true" stories freshly torn from the national newswire services. Each week *one* story from the previous *seven* days (hence the show's title) would be selected for instant adaptation. Webb was all over the production process from the beginning. He not only wrote scripts and served as the series' narrator, but he played one or even several of the characters on each episode as well.

One out of Seven provides an interesting illustration of the complex relationship of style and content in the work of a developing production personality in commercial broadcasting. The show was very much Webb's in the sense that it was insistently docudramatic and, in the context of the American airwaves, extremely outspoken in its politics. But while viewers of *Dragnet* (or other Webb productions such as *Adam 12* or *Emergency!*) might easily recognize the form and style of *One out of Seven*, they might be hard put to identify the radio program's political insistences. The principal focus of *One out of Seven* was racial injustice in American society. Webb himself played the roles, in dialect voices, of black, Jewish, and other ethnic characters who had been victimized by prejudice. Still grooving on the New Dealist, popular frontist elation that followed the defeat of the Axis, Webb, like many Americans, had not yet surrendered his soul to the Cold War McCarthyism that lay just around the historical corner.

Webb made his reputation in radio during the late forties primarily as a creator and portrayer of hardboiled detectives. His title characters included *Pat Novak, For Hire* (ABC, 1946, 1949); *Johnny Madero, Pier 23* (Mutual, 1947); and *Jeff Regan, Investigator* (CBS, 1948–50). Webb's peculiar style — the clipped speech, the impatience with personal idiosyncrasy, the command for "just the facts" — became an instant model for imitation. In 1949, for example, *Richard Diamond, Private Detective* premiered on NBC radio with a supporting character, "Pat Cosak," who was an obvious knockoff of Webb's Pat Novak. Over the years stand-up comedians began to imitate Webb, especially the Joe Friday character, precisely because he was so distinctive in a genre otherwise crowded with interchangeable clones. Other crimeshow producers, such as Roy Huggins (see Chapter 13), would even parody Webb scripts in their prime-time TV programs.

In 1947 Webb moved back to Los Angeles, the city that would remain his real-life as well as fictional headquarters for the rest of his career. He continued to work as an actor, taking roles in such films as *He Walks By Night* (1948), in which he plays a street cop, and *Sunset Boulevard* (1950), in which he plays the earnest young Hollywood assistant producer who almost loses his fiancée to William

Holden. But Webb increasingly gave priority to his career behind the camera. Forming his own company, Mark VII Productions, he sold a radio show to NBC in 1949 that would change the future of American broadcasting. Basing each script on an incident lifted directly from the daily precinct logbooks of the LAPD, *Dragnet* would become a radio hit, a TV hit, and a kind of permanent cosmological feature of American culture whose recognizability would allow it to be resurrected at will as a TV series and a feature-film subject decades after the end of its original production run.

By the time *Dragnet* expanded from radio to television in 1952, its format had already been firmly established with the public. The entire vehicle was clearly Webb's, as evidenced by the fact that three different actors would come and go as his partner between 1952 and 1959. In a schedule loaded with vaudeville stage variety shows and proscenium sitcoms, *Dragnet* proved that the filmed cop series could be a viable genre for prime-time television, despite the added expenses of action sequences. The show placed among the Top Ten during its first four seasons, finishing as high as second (to *I Love Lucy*) for 1953–54. The *Dragnet* musical theme ("Danger Ahead" by Walter Schuman) was recorded by the Ray Anthony Orchestra and released as a single in 1953. The show won its share of Emmys, including several "bests" in the Awards' ever-changing array of programming categories.

Dragnet follows the daily activities of Sgt. Joe Friday, the quintessential police operatchik. The program's status as "docudrama" (though this term had not yet entered the American language) is repeatedly and shamelessly emphasized. As if a radical rewriting of "Once upon a time," each episode begins with the voiceover announcement that "the story you are about to see is true. . . ." Webb, acting as narrator, punctuates the scenes with announcements of exact times and locations ("11:18 P.M.: we were working a stakeout at the corner of Pico and Union in Central Los Angeles . . ."). At the end of the half hour, the viewer is once again reminded of the story's indisputable verity as a disembodied voice announces the details of the outcome of the criminal's trial; without exception, all were guilty as charged. The credits boasted the support of the Los Angeles Police Department, whose seal was shown, full screen, and whose Chief William Parker gave Webb access to departmental files.

Friday and his partner spend a good portion of each episode doing routine police business: questioning suspects and witnesses, following leads, disposing of paperwork, walking into cul-de-sacs, and turning up red herrings. Most of the labor is tedious and unrewarding, sometimes it is downright degrading. But Friday is mercilessly loyal to the job. Even his humorless monotone ("That's where I come in; I carry a badge") is a kind of pledge by the harried policeman not to waste the taxpayers' time or money in his relentless prosecution of a Manichaean struggle against the unspeakable scum whose disregard for the law threatens the well-being of the City of Los Angeles and the United States of America.

Solving the video authorship puzzle is not a difficult task when it comes to *Dragnet*. Jack Webb created, produced, directed, wrote for, narrated, and starred in the program. He was even the CEO of the company that made the series. Webb also produced a few less-successful series during *Dragnet's* network production run. *Noah's Ark*, an early color series for NBC (which, as an RCA subsidiary, was committed to promoting the innovation), featured the exploits of two messianic veterinarians. Pushing his *Dragnet* formula to what seems like surrealist hyperbole, Webb culled the episode plots of *Noah's Ark* from actual files of the Southern California Veterinary Medical Association and the American Humane Society. He, of course, displayed the official seals of both organizations in the credits. Perhaps the struggle for justice for abused cats and mistreated boa constrictors lacked the tensions inherent in *Dragnet's* struggle against the evils perpetrated by criminals upon humans. In any case, the series folded after a single season in the spring of 1957.

Organized crime was the target of *The D.A.'s Man*, which followed the exploits of an ex–private eye working undercover for the New York district attorney's office to infiltrate the mob. It too bombed. A bit more memorable, but no more successful, was *Pete Kelly's Blues*. Webb had created and starred in the *Pete Kelly's Blues* radio series (NBC, 1951), and he had directed and starred in the *Pete Kelly's Blues* feature film (1955). The story was a period piece set during the Roaring Twenties, focusing on a jazz musician who worked at a Kansas City speakeasy. Pete Kelly was a hipster who wanted nothing more than to play his cornet. But like Webb himself, he learned that the artist could not afford to ignore evil. In the nightclub, Pete often found himself caught in the tentacles of unsavory underworld characters. Busy with *Dragnet*, Webb produced *Pete Kelly's Blues* but declined to play the title role as he had in the film.

In the early 1960s, with prime-time anthology drama in its death throes, General Electric decided to revamp its longtime anthology showcase, *General Electric Theater* (CBS, 1953–62). The new angle for the series would be that each story would be a "real life" adventure culled from the pages of *True* magazine. The company transferred

GE Theater's host, Ronald Reagan, to its political division and replaced him with Jack Webb — Mr. Docudrama himself — as the host of *General Electric True* (CBS, 1962–63).

But Webb would not have another true hit until he resurrected *Dragnet* in the late sixties. Having saturated American consciousness for close to twenty years with *Dragnet* the radio series, *Dragnet* the TV series, and *Dragnet* the feature film, Webb hit the streets of Los Angeles again with *Dragnet '67*. From a cultural historical perspective, the timing couldn't have been better. With sixties polarization bringing American society to the political cracking point, the old McCarthy-era extremism of *Dragnet* was given fresh life. The counterculture spawned by the Vietnam War provided Webb with a whole new range of pinko stereotypes to animate what had become the stilted tones of his fifties-style paranoia. Protesters, marijuana smokers, LSD-users, and even the occasional feminist or eco-nut showed up as obstacles to Friday's pledge "to protect . . . and to serve." Law-and-order fans cheered; hippies laughed out loud.

A few changes were in order for the revival. The episodes for the new *Dragnet* were shot in color, according to what had recently become network policy for all prime-time programming. Given the show's immutable black-and-white moral code, the color episodes tend to sacrifice a measure of the starkness that contributed so much punch to the original. Also in *Dragnet '67*, Friday was permanently teamed with Officer Bill Gannon (Harry Morgan), rather than the succession of partners he had worked with in the fifties. Morgan's grandfatherly mellowness complemented Webb's bulletheadedness. After his stint on *Dragnet*, Morgan would go on to play Colonel Potter on *M*A*S*H*, giving him the distinction of having costarred in what were arguably the most politically conservative and politically liberal half-hour series in the history of American television.

But the enduring message of the original *Dragnet* remained intact. Once again Webb, his company now working in partnership with Universal Television, took complete and comprehensive artistic control: creator, director, star. The LAPD Chief of Police's seal of approval was slapped on the end of each episode, as if it were Webb's own. The revived *Dragnet* was not quite as popular as the original, but it did place among the Top Twenty in the second of its three-season production run. The show also served as a pilot showcase for Webb's next generation of programming. Officer Jim Reed (Kent McCord) began appearing as a minor character in *Dragnet*; a year later he would be the costar of his own series.

Adam 12 (NBC, 1968–75) starred McCord and Martin Milner as

Reed and Malloy, two young uniformed Los Angeles police officers. The chief of police once again opened his files to Webb, and even served as technical advisor to the program. The series title, a bit of police jargon used as an official dispatch code for black-and-white unit "A-12," was ecto-Webb. While most copshows by the late sixties had gone over to the full-hour format, Webb continued to cultivate the half-hour structure for both *Dragnet* and *Adam 12*, perhaps as further emphasis of the laconic, action-oriented personalities of his policemen.

More significant, *Adam 12* remained a bastion of the poker-faced, white male studcop into the seventies, even as the video police force was becoming racially and sexually integrated in such programs as Aaron Spelling's *The Mod Squad* (see Chapter 15) and Cy Chermak's *Ironside*. It seemed as if the socially conscious liberal who had produced exposés of racial injustice for radio on *One out of Seven* had come full circle, as the last hold-out against black officers in his fictional police department. Webb's one concession to changing times and changing demographics in *Adam 12* was the relative youth of the featured cops. Considering the context that Webb had created for his work in *Dragnet*, this compromise did have the effect of lightening up the pressure in *Adam 12*. But there were still no black policemen; that would have to wait for *The New Adam 12* (syndicated, 1989–present), which was made after Webb's death. And there were still no women; that never happened.

Webb had cocreated *Adam 12* with R. A. Cinader. He took executive producer credit for the show, frequently writing and directing the episodes. Stephen J. Cannell (see Chapter 19) got his first big break when Webb hired him as story editor of *Adam 12*. Commenting on his old boss, Cannell told critic Gary Deeb, "The Jack Webb style of dialogue used to be . . . you'd write a line [on *Dragnet*] for Joe Friday to say to Gannon, 'I'll tell you one thing, she's never gonna do that again.' Jack would [then] break that up. He'd ask you to write it so Friday says, 'One thing's for sure.' And Gannon would say, 'How's that?' And Friday would say, 'That girl?' Gannon, 'Yeah?' Friday, 'She'll never do that again.' He'd make six lines out of one."

Adam 12 was a bona fide hit, playing for seven seasons in production. Hoping to do another character spin-off, Webb used Reed and Malloy as crossover guests to introduce his next show, *The D.A.*, a half-hour crimeshow that featured Robert Conrad in the title role. Harry Morgan, coming off the canceled *Dragnet* revival, was once again recruited by Webb as the sidekick figure. The courtroom scenes provided a new mise-en-scène for Webb's double-boiled docudramatic technique. Conrad, who had collaborated with Webb as a minor actor in *Red Nightmare,* a short McCarthyite cult classic film of the fifties, provided a Joe Friday–like voiceover narration. Unfortunately these gems of pre-neoconservative dialogue are likely to remain buried museum pieces; *The D.A.* was canceled after only several episodes.

O'Hara, U.S. Treasury starred David Janssen as Webb's first federal officer. In signature style, the producer secured the official cooperation and blessings of the Customs Service, the Secret Service, and the Division of Alcohol, Tobacco, and Firearms — and all other branches of the Department of the Treasury — in order to "authenticate" the series. Webb's first one-hour show, it was another ratings failure, the only one of Janssen's many career efforts (*Richard Diamond, The Fugitive, Harry O* among them) to be canceled in its first season. The following season Webb tried a Western setting. *Hec Ramsey* brought Richard Boone, who had starred in *Have Gun, Will Travel* (CBS, 1957–63), back to weekly television after a decade's absence. Dressed in chaps rather than a dull gray suit, Hec is a turn-of-the-century Joe Friday, solving crimes by the book in New Prospect, Oklahoma. Webb's resident sidekick, Harry Morgan, played Doc Coogan, a kind of tumbleweed Quincy who supplied the law officer with avant-garde medical clues. It was Mark VII's third bomb in a row.

Webb came up with a much-needed winner when he returned to the streets of Los Angeles with *Emergency!* in 1972. The series, cocreated with R. A. Cinader, was aired in hour-long episodes, but it is nevertheless very much a trilogy with *Dragnet* and *Adam 12.* Another tale of the L.A. civil service (told, of course, with the official authorization of the Departments of Fire and Hospitals), *Emergency!* followed the "day-in-the-life" shiftwork of two county paramedics: Roy DeSoto (Kevin Tighe) and John Gage (Randolph Mantooth). At the leisurely pace afforded by a fifty-two-minute episode, the more-than-just-two ambulance drivers ran into a variety of problems during any given episode that took the show from vexing social realism (fires, earthquakes, damaged power lines) to goofy video mayhem (a three-hundred-pound woman stuck in her girdle, a child stuck in a sewer drain, a magician stuck in a straitjacket). But as Webb had always assured *Dragnet* viewers, "This is the city: Los Angeles, California. . . ."

Emergency!, premiering on NBC in 1972, ran in production for five years as a weekly show and for two more seasons as a recurring made-for-television movie series (eight of these were made). Surprisingly, it never managed to reach Nielsen's Top Twenty-five over the course of those seven seasons. Its longevity can be at least partly explained by the fact that these were the extremely lean years at NBC, and the show's demonstrated popularity with young children was apparently enough to keep it running in prime time for the faltering network. Mark VII even produced a Saturday-morning cartoon version, *Emergency +4*, the studio's only animated series.

In 1975 ABC bought an *Emergency!* knockoff from Webb titled *Mobile One*. Here again we saw a roving crew of professionals speeding through the streets from disaster to disaster, but this time it was a local TV news crew. Jackie Cooper starred as Peter Campbell, ace reporter for station KONE. Though the show was clearly set in Webb's Los Angeles, no name was ever given to the setting, perhaps because the show could boast no official authorization from any government institution. Only a few episodes were ever made.

Of all the variations on the *Dragnet* theme, *Sierra* (1974) was probably the most interesting, at least from a political perspective. This time Webb brought the *Dragnet* format to the great outdoors, setting the series in mythical "Sierra National Park." Filmed on location at Yosemite, the series featured five rangers as they went about their daily business of rescuing tourists from bears, rockslides, and their own urban ignorance. Each episode ended, of course, with Webb's display of the seal of the U.S. National Park Service. Too late to cash in on the first Earth Day (1970) and too early for the environmental crises of the eighties, *Sierra* only lasted three months on the air.

There was a bit of poetic justice in Webb's last effort, *Project U.F.O.* (NBC, 1978–79). Having applied his peculiar form of docudrama everywhere from the streets of contemporary Los Angeles to the trails of the Old West, from the police department to the fire department, from a district attorney's office to a veterinarian's office, Webb made one final transformation on the model, sending it into outer space. The show was a series of dramatizations of cases from Project Blue Book, the U.S. Air Force's official file of unidentified flying object sightings. Webb was back as both executive producer and narrator. In his customary attempt to lend historical credibility to his work, he included among his production consultants the retired Air Force colonel who had been the officer in charge of the actual Project Blue Book for the Pentagon.

Jack Webb died on December 23, 1982, at the age of sixty-two.

JACK WEBB: SELECTED VIDEOGRAPHY

Series

Dragnet (NBC, 1952–59; 1967–70)
Noah's Ark (NBC, 1956–57)
The D.A.'s Man (NBC, 1959)
Pete Kelly's Blues (NBC, 1959)
General Electric True (CBS, 1962–63)
Adam 12 (NBC, 1968–75)
The D.A. (NBC, 1971–72)
O'Hara, U.S. Treasury (CBS, 1971–72)
Hec Ramsey (NBC, 1972–74)
Emergency! (NBC, 1972–77 as series; 1977–79, eight specials)
Chase (NBC, 1973–74)
Sierra (NBC, 1974)
Mobile One (ABC, 1975)
Sam (CBS, 1978)
Project U.F.O. (NBC, 1978–79)

Movies Made for Television

Red Nightmare (NBC, 1953)
The Log of the Black Pearl (NBC, 1975)
Little Mo (NBC, 1978)

13. ROY HUGGINS

Let Cooler Heads Prevail

Roy Huggins is a fundamental shaper of the image of the private eye that has developed in episodic television. The free-lance shamus, of course, had been on the case in the United States for most of the twentieth century. Baptized in the hardboiled fiction of Dashiell Hammett and Raymond Chandler, and canonized on the silver screen by actors such as Humphrey Bogart and Robert Mitchum, the streetwise small-time entrepreneurial gumshoe-for-hire is a uniquely American character. In contrast to his British cousin (epitomized by Conan Doyle's Sherlock Holmes), the classic American private investigator is no civic-minded gentleman of leisure but, rather, a working stiff who is in the business strictly for the money. Unlike his often hostile counterparts in local big-city police departments, he shies away from the self-righteous role of defender of the state and its social order; he is instead a rough-hewn individual, a loner whose laconic judgments concerning right and wrong are delivered as ironic digressions into personal viewpoint.

The networks were not quick to assimilate this particular mass-culture hero into weekly TV as they began their stewardship of the primary story-telling function in the years following the Second World War. Early TV crime was mostly the beat of bulletheaded crusader-cops such as *Dragnet*'s Joe Friday (Jack Webb), *M Squad*'s Frank Ballinger (Lee Marvin), and *Highway Patrol*'s Chief Dan Matthews (Broderick Crawford). The rare free-lancer who could be found on TV in the early days — *Martin Kane, Private Eye*, for example — tended to think and to act much like a police officer who just didn't happen to carry a badge.

Roy Huggins challenged the hegemony of these law-and-order martinets by inventing ways to adapt the more existential attitudes of the pulp fiction/movie private eye to the peculiar requirements of weekly television. The detectives he created, from Stu Bailey of *77 Sunset Strip* (ABC, 1958–64) to Jim Rockford of *The Rockford Files* (NBC, 1974–80), were kinder, gentler dudes than the messianic crime-fighters who typically packed heat for the network police forces. Relaxed and at home in Los Angeles, Miami, New Orleans, Honolulu, and other Sunbelt locales, Huggins's private eyes seemed to actually have personal lives outside their vocational callings. They frequented bars and nightclubs. They even went out with women instead of demanding "just the facts" from them.

Roy Huggins was born in Litelle, Washington, in 1914, the son of an Oregon lumberman. As a teenager he dropped out of the University of Oregon to move to Los Angeles in hopes of becoming a writer. He returned to school at U.C.L.A., where he earned a degree in political science, graduating summa cum laude and Phi Beta Kappa. Before finding his way into the visual media, Huggins achieved some success as a mystery writer, placing short stories in such magazines as *Esquire* and the *Saturday Evening Post* during the forties. He went on to publish three mystery novels: *The Double Take, Too Late for Tears*, and *Lovely Lady Pity Me*. Elements from these prose efforts would recombine and reappear in his movie and television work for decades. Huggins made the shift to screenwriting in 1949, when he signed a studio contract with Columbia Pictures. By 1952 he had written and directed a feature Western, *Hangman's Knot*, starring Randolph Scott.

A one-time member of the Communist Party (he resigned after the 1939 signing of the Nazi-Soviet pact), Huggins was called before the House Un-American Activities Committee in September of 1952. A "friendly witness," he confirmed the names of nineteen of his former party comrades under oath. Later he would renounce his cooperation with HUAC; for the rest of his career he would make frequent efforts to hire blacklisted writers, actors, and technicians for his productions.

By the late fifties the face of prime-time television was experiencing radical plastic surgery. The live New York studio productions that had been the mainstay of peak-hour programming during the pioneer years were quickly yielding to filmed series. Telefilms, as they were called, were more easily produced on the soundstages and in the streets of Los Angeles. The major motion picture studios, which had at first fought television with everything from contracts that forbade their stars from appearing on TV shows to the installation of air conditioning in theaters, began seeking mutual accommodations with the new medium as the outcome of the struggle between the two media was becoming increasingly evident. Warner Brothers and Disney, for example, both signed advantageous contracts with ABC, which up to this time had been the sick sister of the Big Three nets. ABC, in turn, began to come up with its first winners after a decade of woeful ratings performances.

Roy Huggins was a key creative personality in effecting this change-over in the look and feel of network television. One of the original producer/writers for Warner Brothers's newly formed television unit, he directly participated in the creation of several of the major hits that were fruits of the Warner-ABC deal. They included Westerns, such as *Cheyenne* (1955–63) and *Maverick* (1957–62), as well as private detective series, such as *77 Sunset Strip* (1958–64) and *Hawaiian Eye* (1959–63). Many industry historians agree that without these much-needed commercial successes ABC might well have succumbed to the fate of the DuMont network, which had gone bust only several years earlier.

Cheyenne had originally been part of an early rotating "umbrella" series (see Levinson and Link) titled *Warner Brothers Presents*, which also included two other titles: *Casablanca* and *King's Row*. All three were series adaptations of Warner Brothers feature films from the forties. Charles MacGraw had the unenviable task of substituting for Humphrey Bogart as Rick, the owner of *Casablanca*'s Club Americain. In *King's Row* (also a Huggins production), Jack Kelly played the part of a turn-of-the-century shrink, Dr. Parris Mitchell, whose small-town Midwestern constituency is mostly unconvinced of the efficacy of modern psychiatry. *Cheyenne* was the only one of the three to survive the first season of *Warner Brothers Presents*. But it was, indeed, an unqualified success: only the fourth ABC series ever to finish in the Nielsen Top Twenty.

Premiering during the same season as *Gunsmoke*, *Cheyenne* was part of the wave of "adult" Westerns that would achieve ratings dominance during the late fifties and early sixties. The show's hero was Cheyenne Bodie (Clint Walker), an Indian/Anglo half-breed.

Cheyenne had once been a frontier scout, but after the Civil War he had taken to wandering the West as a kind of alienated soldier of fortune. He roamed from town to town, from job to job, from woman to woman, and from gunfight to gunfight, a rootless displaced person in the emerging society of the half-conquered West. Bodie's "drop-outism" connected him to a strain of fifties culture that pointed more in the direction of James Dean, Marlon Brando, and Jack Kerouac than Jack Webb, J. Edgar Hoover, and John Foster Dulles.

In *Maverick* the full flower of Huggins's style would bloom. James Garner starred as Bret Maverick, a gambler, a rascal, and an unabashed advocate of his own personal safety and interests. Maverick was fond of quoting his "old Pappy" on this latter subject: "He who fights and runs away, lives to fight another day." Well aware that this philosophy was hardly typical of the Western hero, Huggins had quite purposely set out to "see how many rules we could break" in the show. *Maverick* was particularly instrumental in bringing an element of comedy to the TV Western; the genre had previously been stone-faced, to say the least.

By its second season, *Maverick* had sufficiently established itself with the public as to begin to take conscious potshots at the heart of sacred Western legends. In an episode titled "Gunshy," for example, Huggins offered a self-reflexive parody of *Gunsmoke*, the most popular — and most unrepentantly serious — Western on the air. It featured a comically poker-faced Mort Dooley (in place of *Gunsmoke*'s Matt Dillon) trying to run poor Bret Maverick out of Elwood (instead of Dodge City), Kansas. In a parody of *Bonanza* during *Maverick*'s fourth season, we see Joe Wheelwright's three sons, Moose, Henry, and Small Paul (i.e. Ben Cartwright's sons, Hoss, Adam, and Little Joe) at long last brought to the altar in a triple marriage ceremony.

Maverick cracked the Top Ten, finishing Number Six for 1958–59. The show also won an Emmy that year for best Western series. Perhaps the fact that a Western capable of parodying its own generic conventions won the Emmy that year was an omen of the impending decline of the genre. The human, rather than the ideal, dimensions of Huggins's Western hero was by no means an unintended happenstance. Having joined the Communist Party during the thirties because he saw it as the only force actively fighting fascism, Huggins quit the Party because of its authoritarian loyalty to the Soviet government. Having testified for HUAC in the early fifties, he regretted his cooperation with the government because of the Committee's authoritarian excesses. In his own experience, extremism in defense of movements or institutions had proved to be a vice. It was therefore no surprise that the Huggins hero was neither a marshal nor a sheriff, nor even an ideological rebel. Maverick watched out for Number One. If at times this attitude made him seem a bit like a hero, at other times it made him seem something closer to an outlaw. So be it.

Years later Huggins offered these observations, concerning the subject of heroism, to Victor Navasky in *Naming Names:* "I considered the possibility of being a hero and I couldn't quite make it. I said to myself, You know, I'd love to be a hero, I'd love to go to jail, except for one thing: Who the hell is going to take care of two small children, a mother, and a wife, all of whom are totally dependent on me? . . . The naming of names was probably the most unspeakable and heinous aspect of the Un-American Activities Committee. To cooperate with it in that aspect, even though the names had already been mentioned, was, I believe, the wrong thing to do. And that's the only part of my part in this thing that I really regret. I got caught off guard and I had a failure of nerve."

More adept at drawing a card from the deck than a gun from his holster, Bret Maverick, like his creator, was anything but the self-sacrificing superhuman "violent redeemer" of the mythological West. The series made a star of James Garner, who would continue to bring elements of Bret Maverick's antiheroic persona into many of the characters he would play throughout his career, including Jim Rockford, the contemporary Los Angeles private eye created for him by Huggins some twenty years later.

Huggins was extremely protective of the special qualities he had invested in Bret Maverick. He wrote "A Ten-Point Guide to Happiness When Writing or Directing a *Maverick*," a list of rules to remember that was distributed to all contributors involved in the show's writing and production. In it he delineated his vision of the series and its principal character, insisting among other things that Bret's principal motivation was to make "easy money" — rather than to necessarily do the right thing. Huggins characterized Bret as a "disorganization man" (referring to William Whyte's 1956 sociological study of middle-class conformity, *The Organization Man*). "Heavies" in the show were to be treated with some sympathy rather than the pure contempt they received in most contemporary TV shows.

During the first season of *Maverick*, with production running seriously behind schedule, the character of Bret's brother Bart Maverick (Jack Kelly) was introduced, giving the show a kind of internal umbrella format. One week the episode might concern Bret, with Bart not even appearing, and the next week vice-versa. On certain weeks both brothers would be involved together. When Garner chose to leave the show after its third season, he was replaced by cousin Beau (Roger Moore), who had come West from England. Moore quit in 1961 and another relative, Brent (Robert Colbert), joined the cast. By making the series a larger phenomenon than any of its stars, Huggins was able to avoid the tyranny that series stars often hold over producers.

If the moral ambiguity of *Maverick* was a self-conscious effort at personal self-expression in network television, Huggins's studio contract with Warners kept him busy cranking out stories for other types of heroes as well during this period, including several who were lacking in Maverick's existential outlook. For example, he was producing *Colt .45* (ABC, 1957–60) simultaneously with *Maverick*. Ironically, this series focused on a serious and dedicated undercover agent spying for the U.S. government in the Old West. The hero, Christopher Colt (Wayde Preston), was the son of the inventor of the famous revolver; he roamed the countryside posing as a gun salesman while tracking down the enemies of the moral order.

Huggins's next major hit, however, was very much in the quirky spirit of *Maverick*. *77 Sunset Strip* offered a decidedly mellower take on urban America's law-and-order problems than a viewer was likely to find elsewhere in prime time. The foreboding "dum-dee-dum-dum" of *Dragnet*, which had set the rhythm of TV crime since the early fifties, was conspicuously absent from the series. Instead a finger-snapping, beatniklike theme signified the show. The setting was a Hollywood detective agency on Sunset Boulevard that shared a driveway — and a lifestyle — with a swinging (circa 1958) bar-and-hangout named Dino's: Philip Marlowe meets the Rat Pack.

Stu Bailey (Efrem Zimbalist, Jr.) and Jeff Spencer (Roger Smith) were the debonair, martini-sipping shamuses. The supporting players consisted of their va-va-va-voom French switchboard operator Suzanne (Jacqueline Beer), a streetwise horseplayer named Roscoe (Louis Quinn) who had recently arrived from New York, and, most important, Kookie (Edd Byrnes), the hipster parking lot attendant at Dino's who became the show's teencult star.

A character midway in myth's journey from James Dean to The Fonz, Kookie spoke in a made-for-television dialect of hip. His most characteristic pose for the camera found him thrusting his hips forward while he combed his hair with one hand and checked the shape of his pompadour with the other. Byrnes's picture soon adorned the covers of teenybopper and mainstream magazines. At the height of his popularity Kookie was receiving as many as ten thousand fan letters a month. His recording of "Kookie, Kookie, Lend Me Your Comb" became a radio hit, reaching fourth position in the Billboard Top Forty in 1959–60. *77 Sunset Strip* finished Number Six in the Nielsen ratings that season. Success led to immediate and prolific cloning by the Warner/ABC partnership. The Huggins formula: a couple of "cool" private eyes, a "kookie" sidekick, a sexy secretary, and a Sunbelt location. The results over the next few seasons: *Bourbon Street Beat* (New Orleans), *Hawaiian Eye* (Honolulu), and *Surfside Six* (Miami).

The pilot for *77 Sunset Strip*, written by Huggins, was first presented to the public as an episode of *Conflict,* a Warners/ABC anthology series. The story of the "cool" West Coast detectives employed elements that Huggins had originally developed in his fiction writing. Later on Huggins would rewrite *Maverick* episodes into *77 Sunset Strip* plots and vice-versa. Bits and pieces of both programs would in turn show up in *The Rockford Files* fifteen years later. Huggins's ability to adapt and synthesize ideas across medium, genre, and time, and yet somehow invest these recombinations with a fresh inventiveness, proved to be the key to his success as a television producer.

Early Warner/ABC action-adventure shows, all done on short budgets, were notorious for major cast changes during their production runs. Clint Walker left *Cheyenne* over contract disputes and was replaced by Ty Hardin for a season, only to return to the series after a settlement. Donald May stepped in to replace Wayde Preston, midseries, on *Colt .45* under similar circumstances. The Maverick family gene pool seemed to generate a bottomless supply of suave young conmen whose first names began with the letter *B*, as actors moved through the cast's revolving door.

After its fifth season, *77 Sunset Strip* experienced the most radical of all these shake-ups. Jack Webb, the godfather of no-nonsense law-and-orderism, was assigned by Warner Brothers to replace Huggins as the executive producer of the series. Webb, as usual, meant business: Kookie, Roscoe, Suzanne, and Jeff Spencer were all unceremoniously fired. Even the theme music was changed; all traces of jazz were summarily snuffed out in favor of a Webbian dirge. Despite the title, which remained tagged onto the show, the Sunset Strip and Dino's both disappeared from the setting. In their stead, Webb offered his usual establishing shot of downtown "this is the city" Los Angeles. The sole remaining character from the Huggins years, Stu

Bailey, made a midlife career switch, giving up chasing bad guys on the streets of L.A. for the international espionage game. Webb launched the revamped show in September of 1963 with a five-part episode that took Stu around the world fighting Communist enemy agents. Viewers, especially the fourteen-year-old girls who tuned in to dig Kookie, must have been dumbfounded; the series went into ratings free-fall and it was canceled before the year was up.

Huggins's direct association with *77 Sunset Strip* had actually ended before Webb took control. But up to that time, the Huggins formula had been followed by the operatives who had replaced him. This highlights an important point about television authorship. More so than any other art, series television presents a producer with the opportunity to use drama as a medium of self-expression or to decline to do so, as he or she wishes. While many producers are, practically speaking, incapable of creating their own imprimaturs, others — such as Huggins and Webb — cannot seem to help but leave their personal signatures.

A similar conclusion can be drawn from another of Huggins's series concepts, *The Fugitive* (ABC, 1963–67). Huggins created and sold the idea for this series to ABC while still working for Warners. He left the studio, however, before *The Fugitive* went into production. The job of actually making the program fell to Quinn Martin. As with *77 Sunset Strip,* the switch from one strong authorial personality to another completely changed the politics of the drama. The mistreated, misunderstood, wandering-outlaw aspect of *The Fugitive* was right at the heart of Huggins's work. In the hands of Martin, however, the series switched emphasis to become a triumph of American justice (see next chapter).

Huggins left Warners to join Twentieth Century–Fox as a vice president in charge of production. After a very short stay, however, he moved into the second major phase in his career as a writer, producer, and executive at Universal Television. His first project as a producer at Universal brought him back to the Western. Huggins's *The Virginian* (NBC, 1962–71) was among the last horse operas to become a major hit in prime-time television. Very loosely based on Owen Wister's turn-of-the-century novel (and Victor Fleming's 1929 film starring Gary Cooper) about a young Southerner's rise to fortune in frontier Wyoming, the program starred James Drury in the title role and included in its changing cast of regulars such actors as Lee J. Cobb, Tim Matheson, Lee Majors, and Stewart Granger. It was one of television's first ninety-minute-long, weekly prime-time series, paving the way for other Universal/NBC projects such as *The Name of the Game* (1968–71) and *The NBC Mystery Movie* (1971–77).

As the executive in charge of production of the anthology series *Kraft Suspense Theater* (NBC, 1963–65), Huggins employed Robert Altman as an occasional writer, producer, and director. He also used *Kraft* to introduce the pilot for *Run for Your Life* (NBC, 1965–68), which was his attempt to remake *The Fugitive*. *Run for Your Life* starred Ben Gazzara as Paul Bryan, a successful, popular, good-looking lawyer who is suddenly diagnosed with a mysterious incurable disease, leaving him with only "several years" to live. He responds by abandoning his middle-class existence and taking to the road to live life to its fullest for the rest of his numbered days. In a sense, *The Fugitive*'s Lt. Philip Gerard (Barry Morse) is replaced by the specter of Death itself, as Bryan wanders the highways and byways in a desperate attempt to discover the meaning of his own essence on the American road. Not satisfied to merely administer production for Universal, Huggins often wrote many episodes of *Run for Your Life* under the pseudonym John Thomas James (the first names of his three sons).

The signature of John Thomas James would also appear in the writing credits of *The Lawyers* (NBC, 1969–72), a segment of a Universal umbrella series known as *The Bold Ones*. *The Bold Ones* was among the first wave of "relevance" programs during the late sixties that attempted to incorporate hot social issues from the news into prime-time series drama. The other segments of the trilogy were *The New Doctors* (medicine) and *The Senator* (politics). *The Lawyers* starred Burl Ives as Walter Nichols, a crusty veteran mouthpiece who goes into partnership with the young Darrell brothers, Brian (James Farentino) and Neil (Joseph Campanella). *The Lawyers* was also the first show of Public Arts Productions (PAP!), a new company founded by and headed by Huggins to coproduce series with Universal. The company name echoed the title of a book by Gilbert Seldes (*Public Arts*), the only major critic who had focused his life's work on the American broadcasting industry during the formative years of the radio and television industries.

Huggins returned to the Western for the last time in *Alias Smith and Jones*. Glen Larson (see Chapter 16) appeared in the credits as creator and producer, but the touch of Huggins, who was executive producer as well as the supplier of many of the storylines and an occasional writer (again as John Thomas James), is evident. Hannibal Heyes (Peter Deuel) and Kid Curry (Ben Murphy) are Western outlaws who are promised a pardon by the governor of the Wyoming territory if they can stay out of trouble for one year. (It is, of course, important to note that, like the Maverick brothers, they have never killed anybody except in self-defense.) The two adopt aliases — Smith and Jones — and roam the territory in anticipation of their pardons. Trouble, however, somehow manages to find them. As with Maverick, the emphasis is on comic irony rather than heroic bravado. *Alias Smith and Jones* is often read as a TV adaptation of George Roy Hill's *Butch Cassidy and the Sundance Kid* (1968). Perhaps *Butch Cassidy* is more correctly read as a cinema adaptation of Roy Huggins's *Maverick* (1957).

If Glen Larson learned the *Maverick* style from Huggins on *Alias Smith and Jones*, Stephen J. Cannell would come under Huggins's tutelage in *The Rockford Files* (NBC, 1974–80). Cannell (see Chapter 19) had previously worked under Huggins's executive leadership on urban crime series such as *Toma* and *Baretta*. Most of the credit for *The Rockford Files* usually goes to Cannell and, in terms of day-to-day involvement, rightfully so. But the ancestry of Jim Rockford in Huggins's oeuvre is undeniable. The contemporary Los Angeles detective was indeed a latter-day Bret Maverick. The fact that James Garner played both roles with similar tones of ironic aspersion only brought home the point. In Raymond Strait's biography of James Garner, Huggins told Strait: "Actually, *The Rockford Files* was simply *Maverick* as a modern-day private eye. That's all. Played by the same character. He was a guy who didn't like to put himself in danger. Didn't like to work too hard. Had a wry sense of humor. Somewhat cowardly. Was not a superman or superhero. . . . That's the way I came up with the character. Doing *Maverick* in modern-day circumstances meant that I had to have a guy who is kind of an outsider, which is why I made him a former convict."

The Outsider (NBC, 1968–69), a commercially unsuccessful series created midway between *Maverick* and *Rockford,* provides a glimpse at the evolving creative process that led from Bret to Jim. David Ross (Darren McGavin) has essentially the same biographical profile as Jim Rockford. An L.A. ex-con, he lives in a shabby apartment that is a kind of downtown version of Rockford's woeful trailer on the beach. Ross avoids fights when he can and most often takes one on the chin when he can't. Collecting fees from his clients is often as difficult as capturing wrongdoers. Though a ratings failure, *The Outsider* did manage to impress at least one viewer. Stephen J. Cannell claimed the show was a personal inspiration to him during the period of his trials as a struggling TV writer. He even wrote an unsolicited episode script for the show, though he was not able to break through the bureaucracy to get it read by Huggins. Several years later he dusted off that same manuscript and, now working in direct collaboration with Huggins, incorporated elements of it into the pilot episode of *The Rockford Files.*

During his years at Universal, Huggins mainly stuck to his specialties — the Western and the private detective series — but he did branch out into other types of projects as well. American car culture had always been a Huggins leitmotif, from the glitzy sports convertibles that would pull up in the driveway of Dino's in *77 Sunset Strip* to the trusty battle-worn Camaro in which Jim Rockford cruised the freeways of Southern California. This interest became the central focus of a trio of Huggins made-for-TV movies during the seventies: *The Challengers* (CBS, 1970) was an action film concerning race-car drivers competing on the Grand Prix circuit; *Drive Hard, Drive Fast* (NBC, 1973) was a murder mystery set in the auto-racing world; and *The Three Thousand Mile Chase* (NBC, 1977) was a transcontinental car chase across the United States featuring good guys outrunning bad guys to deliver a key prosecution witness to the authorities. *Wheels* (NBC, 1978), adapted by Huggins from the Arthur Hailey novel, was a ten-hour, soap-operatic miniseries set in the bedrooms and boardrooms of Detroit amid the inner workings of the American automobile industry.

Roy Huggins's career provides a distinct model of the hyphenate operative in commercial television production. Huggins wrote, created, directed, produced, executive produced, and even served as a studio administrator. No matter where he appeared in the chain of command, however, he managed to emerge as a coherent, identifiable creative force in the projects he was associated with. Over the years he not only moved vertically through the chain of command but laterally as well, doing stints at the television production divisions of such major suppliers as Warners, Fox, Universal, and Columbia. In 1984, at age seventy, he was hired by his former protégé Stephen J. Cannell to serve as executive producer of *Hunter,* yet another successful private-eye series that carries the imprimatur of the "Huggins touch."

ROY HUGGINS: SELECTED VIDEOGRAPHY

Series

King's Row (ABC, 1955–56)
Cheyenne (ABC, 1955–63)

Conflict (ABC, 1956–57)
Colt .45 (ABC, 1957–60)
Maverick (ABC, 1957–62)
77 Sunset Strip (ABC, 1958–64)
The Virginian (NBC, 1962–71)
The Fugitive (ABC, 1963–67)
Kraft Suspense Theater (NBC, 1963–65)
Run for Your Life (NBC, 1965–68)
The Outsider (NBC, 1968–69)
The Lawyers (NBC, 1969–72) (as part of *The Bold Ones*)
Alias Smith and Jones (ABC, 1971–73)
Cool Million (NBC, 1972–73)
Toma (ABC, 1973–74)
The Rockford Files (NBC, 1974–80)
Baretta (ABC, 1975–78)
City of Angels (NBC, 1976)
Blue Thunder (ABC, 1984)
Hunter (NBC, 1984–present)

Movies Made for Television and Miniseries

Any Second Now (NBC, 1969)
The Lonely Profession (NBC, 1969)
The Challengers (CBS, 1970)
The Young Country (ABC, 1970)
Sam Hill: Who Killed the Mysterious Mr. Foster? (NBC, 1971)
Do You Take This Stranger? (NBC, 1971)
How to Steal an Airplane (NBC, 1972)
Drive Hard, Drive Fast (NBC, 1973)
Set This Town on Fire, aka *Profane Comedy* (NBC, 1973)
The Story of Pretty Boy Floyd (ABC, 1974)
This Is the West That Was (NBC, 1974)
Captains and the King (NBC, 1976)
The Invasion of Johnson County (NBC, 1976)
The Courier: The Three Thousand Mile Chase (NBC, 1977)
Best Sellers: Arthur Hailey's "Wheels" (NBC, 1978)
The Jordan Chance (CBS, 1978)
The Last Convertible (NBC, 1979)

Sherwood Schwartz, producer/creator of *Gilligan's Island,* with his famous cast of castaways. Left to right: Russell Johnson, Alan Hale, Jr., Dawn Wells, Natalie Schafer, Jim Backus, Schwartz, director Jack Arnold, Tina Louise, and Bob Denver.

© Wayne Williams

Susan Harris, writer and producer of *Soap, Benson, The Golden Girls,* and *Empty Nest.*

James L. Brooks, writer and producer of *Room 222, The Mary Tyler Moore Show, Rhoda, The Tracey Ullman Show,* and *The Simpsons.*

© Kerry Hayes

Norman Lear, producer of *All in the Family, Sanford and Son, Maude,* and *The Jeffersons,* forever changed situation comedy by introducing social and political issues into the standard format.

Lear joins the cast of *The Jeffersons* to celebrate the taping of the 200th episode. Left to right: Marla Gibbs, Sherman Hemsley, Isabel Sanford, Lear, Ned Wertimer, Belinda Tolbert, Roxie Roker, and Franklin Cover.

Richard Levinson (left) and William Link created *Mannix, Columbo,* and *Murder, She Wrote.*

Stephen J. Cannell, creator, writer, and producer of *The A-Team, Riptide, Hunter,* and *Wiseguy.*

Jack Webb (above) worked in radio, often playing a hardboiled detective, before adapting the formula to television in the fifties as series creator, producer-director, and writer of *Dragnet.*

Right: Webb as *Dragnet's* Joe Friday.

© Ron Batsdorf

Lee Rich, dealmaker and packager supreme, has been executive producer of such hits as *The Waltons, Eight Is Enough, Dallas,* and *Falcon Crest.*

Aaron Spelling, with Linda Evans, at a 1986 party for cast and crew of *Dynasty.* Spelling also created *The Mod Squad, Starsky and Hutch, Charlie's Angels, The Love Boat,* and *Fantasy Island.*

Bettmann Photo Archives

David L. Wolper launched his TV career with *The Race for Space*. Later, he established the television miniseries with *Roots*, *Roots: The Next Generations*, and *The Thorn Birds*.

Steven Bochco, Emmy-winning creator of *Hill Street Blues* and cocreator of *L.A. Law*.

Mark Goodson, the king of gameshows; his creations include *What's My Line?*, *The Price Is Right*, *To Tell the Truth*, *Match Game*, and *Family Feud*.

Ken Burns stunned critics and audiences when thirty-nine million Americans tuned in his eleven-part miniseries, *The Civil War*, on PBS.

14. QUINN MARTIN

— — — — — — — — —

Republican Supersleuths

If widespread public awareness of television producers is a relatively recent phenomenon, the self-consciousness of the producers themselves has a somewhat longer history. Decades before Stephen J. Cannell slapped his picture onto the end of every episode of *Wiseguy*, or David Lynch made the rounds of talkshows to publicly ruminate on the aesthetic drift of *Twin Peaks*, there was at least one TV producer who was making calculated efforts to establish himself as a distinctive artist in the eyes of the viewing audience. Fans of such sixties hits as *The Fugitive* and *The F.B.I.* had not yet gotten through the opening credits of an episode before a booming voice informed them each week that what they were about to see was "a Quinn Martin Production." Over the course of the next hour they would be presented with introductory supers announcing the segments between the commercials as Act I, Act II, Act III, Act IV, and, of course, Epilogue.

Born in Los Angeles on May 22, 1927, and educated as an English major at Berkeley, Martin began his TV career writing teleplays for several of the golden-age anthology series, including *Four Star Playhouse* (CBS, 1952–56), *Fireside Theatre* (NBC, 1955–58), and *Desilu Playhouse* (CBS, 1958–60). A major break came when he was asked to write and produce a 1959 *Desilu* installment titled "The Untouchables," a violent tale of the 1930s Chicago underworld, which was adapted from Oscar Fraley's biography of a retired U.S. Treasury Department agent named Eliot Ness. When Desilu decided to develop *The Untouchables* into a series, Martin was asked to stay with the project as the show's line producer.

Framing the narrative progress of each episode with the "historically authoritative" interjections of Walter Winchell, the New York tabloid gossip columnist, Martin pioneered the docudramatic deus ex machina that future generations of television producers would typically use to invoke naturalistic legitimacy on scores of semiridiculous made-for-TV movies and action-adventure series episodes. Another innovation imbedded in this otherwise primitive-looking, Prohibition-era period piece was Martin's willingness to keep his villains alive so as to allow for long-term tensions to build up between cop and criminal. A personalized macroconflict between the ascetic, plainly dressed, laconic Eliot Ness (Robert Stack) and the loud-mouthed, gaudy, sneering Frank Nitti (Bruce Gordon) dwarfs the particulars of any single *Untouchables* episode. This technique would be resurrected to spectacular effect a quarter of a century later by producer Michael Mann (see Chapter 21) in his series *Crime Story* (NBC, 1987–89).

The Untouchables was at first a ratings bright spot for the eternally struggling third-place ABC, cracking Nielsen's Top Ten as the Number Eight show in prime time during the 1960–61 season. Despite commercial success, however, *The Untouchables* was controversial, to say the least, causing several problems for network management. For one thing, each episode was so thoroughly saturated with beatings, killings, maulings, and disfigurements that the show became the centerpiece of a congressional investigation into television violence, not to mention a favorite topic of sociology graduate students in search of thesis material; for another, Martin's willingness to tag his Chicago gangsters with Italian surnames provoked outrage and protest from the Italian-American community. These hot issues cooled, however, when NBC counterprogrammed *Sing Along with Mitch* against *The Untouchables*, humbling Ness, Nitti, and Martin to a dismal forty-first place on the charts during the 1962–63 season.

Just a week after the final episode of *The Untouchables* had aired, Martin brought out the first series made by his newly formed independent production company, QM Productions. *The Fugitive*, like *The Untouchables*, cultivated a soap-operatic long-term relationship between cop and criminal. In this case, however, the criminal turned out to be no criminal at all. *The Fugitive* followed the story of Dr. Richard Kimball (David Janssen), a man tried and convicted for the murder of his wife. While being transported to a death-row cell at the state penitentiary in the custody of Indiana State Police Lt. Philip Gerard (Barry Morse), Kimball manages to escape in the chaos of a train wreck. Gerard makes the recapture of Kimball his singleminded goal, much as Eliot Ness had focused his life on the capture of Frank Nitti. Again, Martin employed a disembodied narrator to goose along the often slow-paced progress of episodes. This time it was William Conrad, who had played Superman on the radio during the 1940s and who would work for Martin again in the title role of *Cannon* during the 1970s.

More interesting than Gerard's search for Kimball or than Kimball's search for "the one-armed man" whom he had seen fleeing the scene of his wife's murder is the picture of American social-class relations presented in the program. Kimball is in effect banished from his haute bourgeois life as a physician and forced to travel the highways and byways of what Jack Kerouac had recently called "the great American night." Kimball becomes a kind of shadowy lumpenproletarian, hitch-hiking from one town to the next, dressed in a blue-collar work shirt, taking odd jobs, and ultimately depending upon the kindnesses of strangers. Martin is sentimental, even romantic, about the values of the American working class. Waitresses and construction workers are glad to help out the incognito Kimball, who seems to be a quiet and decent loner, merely down on his luck. But there is also an element of patronization in this portrayal. Despite the genuine warmth and nurture that Kimball receives in the lower precincts of society, he cannot help but view his working-class protectors as anything more than simple hearts; he is determined to find a way to return to his proper place in the world of middle-class status. Ironically, it is Gerard, his nemesis and his middle-class equal, to whom he must prove himself.

Like *The Untouchables*, *The Fugitive* spent only one of its four seasons among the top-rated programs in prime time. Martin, how-ever, came up with a novel idea for ending the series that would prove to be a milestone in television history. Instead of letting the show die the usual unheralded death of a series pulled from produc-tion, he created a spectacular series climax. This dramatic grand finale aired in the summer of 1967; it was the single most-watched program in TV-series history, a record that would stand until the "Who Shot J.R.?" episode of *Dallas* topped it in 1980. Nearly 46 percent of American households tuned in to witness Dr. Richard Kimball cleared of all charges: Gerard shoots the one-armed man; the one-armed man confesses the murder of Mrs. Kimball to Gerard; the one-armed man leaps to his death from a water tower. The good doctor trades in his work shirt for a three-piece suit, dusts off his shingle, and all's right with the world. Martin's innovation, the bestowing of narrative closure on a long-running series by means of a climactic final episode, gradually became conventional. Future programs, including *The Mary Tyler Moore Show*, *M*A*S*H*, and *Newhart*, all went out of production in similar fashion.

The basic themes of *The Fugitive* were repeated by Martin and copied by others for years to come. In Kenneth Johnson's *The Incredible Hulk* (CBS, 1978–82), for example, Dr. David Banner is another physician who is banished from professional life to become a fugitive on the run in blue-collar America. This time, however, the fugitive is charged with his own murder and is pursued not by a cop but by a reporter for a sensationalistic tabloid. In terms of Quinn Martin's own work, an analogous storyline can be found in *The Immortal* (ABC, 1970–71). Here, a racing car driver (Christopher George) discovers he has special antibodies in his blood that make him immune to disease and decay, giving him the gift (which, of course, also turns out to be the curse) of immortality. He is pursued across America by a megalomaniacal aging billionaire who wants to steal his blood. (In *Hot Pursuit* [NBC, 1984], Kenneth Johnson virtually remakes *The Fugitive*, complete with the train-wreck escape of the wrongly accused. This time a husband-and-wife team of fugitives is chased across the country by police while trying to locate the wife's evil twin double who has framed her for murder. The series even manages to work a "one-eyed man" into the story!)

Twelve O'Clock High (ABC, 1964–67), Martin's next series, was one of a string of World War II series that aired on ABC during the midsixties (others included *Combat* and *Rat Patrol*). Adapted from a 1940s novel and movie of the same name, *Twelve O'Clock High* concerned the activities of an Army Air Corps bombardment group based near London. The original star of the series was Robert Lansing, who played the role of Brig. Gen. Frank Savage. Lansing, however, had his own ideas about the artistic directions that the series ought to take, and he proved incompatible with the strong authorial style of the producer. As a consequence, Martin had him shot down and killed at the end of the first season. This killing off of a principal character, midseries, not only further established Martin as a producer from whom viewers might expect the unexpected but also set a precedent for the bumping off of future uppity stars by producers.

The biggest hit of Quinn Martin's career was *The F.B.I.*, which played on ABC for nine seasons. This crime series celebrated authoritarian, jingoistic, cold-warrior values even as relatively anti-establishment comedy shows, such as *Rowan and Martin's Laugh-In* and *All in the Family*, were claiming huge followings in other prime-time slots. Martin's featured lawman, Inspector Lewis Erskine (Efrem Zimbalist, Jr.), like Federal Agent Eliot Ness before him, was stone-faced, efficient, and effective. In this sense both were perhaps spiritual descendants of Jack Webb's Los Angeles street cop, Sgt. Joe Friday.

As with all dramatic portrayals of the Bureau (including, for example, the 1959 feature film, *The F.B.I. Story*, starring Jimmy Stewart), the TV series was subject to the personal approval of J. Edgar Hoover, who reserved the right to approve each episode. The show's close ties to the Bureau were demonstrated in other ways as well. Some two decades before *America's Most Wanted* (Fox, 1988–present), Martin was adding a segment to the end of some *F.B.I.* episodes that would show "most wanted" posters on-screen and request information from the public, complete with telephone number. Among those featured in these appeals to the citizenry was James Earl Ray, the assassin of Dr. Martin Luther King, Jr. *The F.B.I.* became so imbedded in popular consciousness that even after the series was canceled, Martin was able to produce a pair of successful prime-time made-for-TV revival movies based on the series: *The FBI Versus Alvin Karpis, Public Enemy Number One* (1974), and *The FBI Versus the Ku Klux Klan* (1975).

Though Quinn Martin always insisted on defining himself as a "former ultraliberal" who had retreated to a position "a little left of center," the sense and substance of his television shows clearly put him on the right side of the aisle during the politically polarized sixties. His valorization of the Prohibition-era proto-narcs of *The Untouchables* and his worshipful portrait of the government's domestic intelligence community in *The F.B.I.* argued for the legitimacy of the very institutions that were being questioned most sharply during the sixties. Martin's FBI chased and captured Communist spies, kidnappers, counterfeiters, and other bona fide criminals; the Bureau was never shown harassing civil rights or peace groups, or gathering files on the personal lives of public figures.

Even *The Fugitive*, which after all was the story of a wrongly accused man, might have been open to more leftish implications, in the tradition of, say, Mervyn LeRoy's 1931 Warner Brothers film, *I Am a Fugitive from a Chain Gang*. However, it is the policeman,

Lieutenant Gerard, who captures the one-armed man and elicits his confession, thus freeing Kimball and redeeming the system from a potentially tragic mistake. *Twelve O'Clock High,* though fictionally set in the consensus polity of World War II, also held metaphoric implications for the times, as it came to the homescreen each week during the massive troop escalations of the Vietnam War.

If Quinn Martin's vision of the law-and-order struggle never quite reached the hysterical peaks scaled by Jack Webb in *Dragnet,* it came close in his next series, *The Invaders* (ABC, 1967–68). Architect David Vincent (Roy Thinnes) is minding his own business on an otherwise deserted country road one day when he bears witness to the arrival on Earth of a flying-saucer load of advance-guard alien colonists, all cleverly decked out in humanoid form. He, of course, must spend the rest of his life traveling from one town to the next in a frustrating attempt to convince an apathetic population of satisfied consumers that the aliens are indeed among us, infiltrating our most sacred and strategic institutions as they prepare their insidious take-over: a paranoid remake of *My Favorite Martian?* Dr. Richard Kimball meets Senator Joe McCarthy? *The Fugitive*–like feel of the show was augmented by Martin's use, once again, of the distinctively autocratic voice of William Conrad as the disembodied narrator.

The Invaders was a commercial failure, however, as was Martin's next program, *Dan August* (ABC, 1970–71), which starred Burt Reynolds as a police detective working in the small California town where he had grown up. The hook of Dan August was the special agony of a policeman forced to investigate, bust, and put away his lifelong friends and neighbors. The show was gone after a season, freeing Reynolds to take a stab at the movies, where he became an instant overnight box office sensation. Ironically, *Dan August* would do better in reruns than it had during its original production run. In 1973, and again during 1975, CBS aired network reruns of the series, which now could be promoted as featuring "Hollywood superstar" Burt Reynolds.

After stumbling a bit with these false starts, Martin rushed head-long into the seventies with a string of private-eye and copshow hits that would secure his place among the most successful producers in television history. The first of these was *Cannon.* By putting William Conrad in front of the camera, Martin both literally and figuratively broke the mold from which TV crimefighters had been cast. Terminally overweight, unrepentantly balding and, to put it kindly, intensely middle-aged, Frank Cannon was anything but the matinee-idol gumshoe of American dreams. Beyond that, he was the only regular character on the series: no young attractive sidekick, no young attractive secretary, no young attractive girlfriend, no young attractive contact and/or nemesis in the police department. He just drove around the episode in an enormous Lincoln Continental, grimly chasing after mesomorphic young criminals, collecting fees from satisfied customers, and ending each hour by stuffing his face with some Julia Child–like butter-and-mushrooms delicacy that, anywhere outside the realm of fiction, would have hardened his arteries and killed him long ago. Yet somehow Conrad survived to play (guess which) one of the title roles in *Jake and the Fatman* during the 1980s.

It was on an episode of *Cannon* that Martin spun off another of his mammoth hits, *Barnaby Jones* (CBS, 1973–80). Recalling a geriatric Buddy Ebsen from post–*Beverly Hillbillies* retirement to play the title role, Martin offered the public yet another prime-time private eye whose demographic profile strayed from the commercial wisdom of the day. Barnaby (like Ebsen himself) had been a happily retired Los Angeles senior citizen before the premiere of the series. The aging sleuth goes back into business, however, to avenge the death of his son. Realizing that he can still do the job with the best of them, he reopens shop as a private eye. Martin made use of Barnaby's age in much the same way that he had worked with Cannon's girth. The tough young criminals never fail to underestimate the wily, if frail-looking, old-timer. But Martin did retreat from the radical minimalism of the *Cannon* cast, affording Barnaby the regular assistance of former Miss America Lee Meriwether as his daughter-in-law Betty Jones, and Mark Shera as his young apprentice sidekick (and cousin) J. R. Jones.

Another Hollywood retiree rearmed and brought back to the TV screen during the seventies by QM Productions was Karl Malden, who played Detective Lt. Mike Stone in *The Streets of San Francisco* (ABC, 1972–77). But in this series Martin matched a reborn veteran star with an up-and-coming leading man, Michael Douglas, who played Stone's protégé, Inspector Steve Keller. The pair played out the high generation-gap dialogues of the early seventies, much as their contemporaries, Archie Bunker and Meathead, did in the sitcom *All in the Family*. Stone, as the name implied, was a grizzled no-nonsense veteran of twenty-three years on the force; Keller, by contrast, was a college-educated greenhorn, still wet behind the ears. While Stone saw policework as the Manichaean struggle of good versus evil, Keller was wont to spout an idealistic sociological analysis or two. During the final season of the show, Douglas decided to quit in order to pursue a career in the movies. Martin wrote him out of the series as resigning from the force to become a teacher, thus leaving the crime-ridden streets of San Francisco to be patrolled alone by his partner. This climax of the Stone-Keller debates left no doubt about where Martin stood on the issue of where the true interests of America's future security might lie.

Both costars would go on to even greater fame: the putty-nosed Malden profited from his renewed public visibility to become principal spokesperson for the American Express credit card. Douglas used the public familiarity he had gained on *Streets* as a jumping-off point for a movie career that would include such smash hit films during the eighties as *Fatal Attraction* and *Wall Street*.

Though Martin had tried to conjure American urban mythology dating back to the gangland-Chicago feel of *The Untouchables*, he made this an increasingly important feature of his work during the seventies, as budgets for episodic television expanded to allow for extensive outdoor shooting. *The Streets of San Francisco* were indeed the title players in that series, which featured spectacular car chases that scaled the concrete hills and valleys of the city by the bay. In *Banyon*, QM tried another period piece, going after the Spanish bungalow–palm tree ambience of 1930s Raymond Chandler Los Angeles. In *Caribe*, Martin presented two hip cops, one Afro, the other Anglo, who work the dangerous causeways and canals of Dade County, Florida — this some ten years before the premiere of Michael Mann's *Miami Vice*.

Martin also continued to cultivate the quasi-vigilantism he had propagated in *The F.B.I. Most Wanted*, set in contemporary Los Angeles, marked the reuniting of the producer with Robert Stack. This time Stack played Capt. Linc Evers, the head of an elite police unit charged with tracking down criminals on the mayor's secret "most wanted" hit list. *The Manhunter* featured Ken Howard as a Depression-era Idaho farmer who makes up the shortfall of plummeting potato prices by picking up some extra cash as a moonlighting bounty hunter.

By the late seventies the solid-citizen, no-nonsense, law-and-order heroes that had made QM Productions such an important supplier of programming to the networks for twenty years were finally wearing thin commercially. The glitzier, sexier, more lifestyle-contempo detectives, such as the ones found in Aaron Spelling's shows (e.g. *Starsky and Hutch, Charlie's Angels*) had grabbed center stage in prime time. Martin's audience was aging and shrinking. He attempted to respond by adding women and younger men and even socially conscious subtexts to his later efforts, but neither *Most Wanted* nor *The Manhunter* could manage the ratings to make it through a season. He produced a profusion of made-for-television detective movies during this period, hoping to spin off a successful new series — but the networks were no longer buying.

In 1977 Martin deviated, for the first time in decades, from his crime series area of expertise to try a *Twilight Zone*-like anthology series titled *Tales of the Unexpected*; it was canceled in a matter of weeks. When *Barnaby Jones* left the air after seven seasons in 1980, it marked the first time since the premiere of *The Untouchables* in 1959 that not a single Quinn Martin show was being aired over the networks in prime time.

Quinn Martin left the television business, selling QM Productions to Taft Broadcasting in 1978. As part of the sales agreement, he was forced to personally forswear TV production work for at least five years. Like his fictional character, Inspector Steve Keller of *The Streets of San Francisco*, he quit the daily wars "to enter teaching" at the University of San Diego at La Jolla. He died in 1989.

QUINN MARTIN: SELECTED VIDEOGRAPHY

Anthology Series

Four Star Playhouse (CBS, 1952–56) — writer
Fireside Theatre, aka *The Jane Wyman Show* (NBC, 1955–58) — writer
Westinghouse Desilu Playhouse (CBS, 1958–60) — writer, producer
Tales of the Unexpected (NBC, 1977) — executive producer

Series

The Untouchables (ABC, 1959–63)
The Fugitive (ABC, 1963–67)
Twelve O'Clock High (ABC, 1964–67)
The F.B.I. (ABC, 1965–74)
The Invaders (ABC, 1967–68)
Dan August (ABC, 1970–71)
Cannon (CBS, 1971–76)
The Streets of San Francisco (ABC, 1972–77)
Banyon (NBC, 1972–73)
Barnaby Jones (CBS, 1973–80)
The Manhunter (CBS, 1974–75)
Caribe (ABC, 1975)

Bert D'Angelo/Superstar (ABC, 1976)
Most Wanted (ABC, 1976–77)

Movies Made for Television

House on Greenapple Road (ABC, 1970)
The Face of Fear (CBS, 1971)
Travis Logan, D.A. (CBS, 1971)
Incident in San Francisco (ABC, 1971)
The FBI Story: The FBI Versus Alvin Karpis, Public Enemy Number One (CBS, 1974)
Murder or Mercy (ABC, 1974)
Panic on the 5:22 (ABC, 1974)
A Home of Our Own (CBS, 1975)
The Abduction of Saint Anne (ABC, 1975)
Crossfire (NBC, 1975)
Attack on Terror: The FBI Versus the Ku Klux Klan (CBS, 1975)
Brink's: The Great Robbery (CBS, 1976)
Law on the Land (NBC, 1976)
The City (NBC, 1977)
Code Name: Diamond Head (NBC, 1977) ·
The Hunted Lady (NBC, 1977)
Standing Tall (NBC, 1978)

15. AARON SPELLING

_____

Crime, Punishment, and Affirmative Action

Arguably the most prolific television auteur in the history of the medium, Aaron Spelling remains little more than a vaguely familiar name to most of his audience. Admirers of *Charlie's Angels* and *Dynasty* would probably be just as surprised as the sternest critics of those shows to learn that during the late forties, as a student playwright at Southern Methodist University, Spelling had won the prestigious Eugene O'Neill Award for his one-act productions. Degree in hand, the young native Texan left Dallas to seek his fortune on the Broadway stage. But his sojourn in New York proved only brief. He found a more congenial home in Hollywood, where he has been making his extraordinary devotions to the muse of mass culture ever since.

Like many popular American storytellers — George M. Cohan, D. W. Griffith, and Jack Webb, to name a few — the aspiring dramatist first found work in the entertainment industry as an actor, landing bit parts in several pioneer prime-time series, including Webb's original *Dragnet*. By the middle of the fifties, however, he had come down off the boards to take up his true vocation behind the scenes, writing scripts for such golden-age drama anthologies as *Four Star*

Playhouse, Dick Powell's Zane Grey Theater, Playhouse 90, and *The DuPont Show with June Allyson.*

Within a few years anthology drama was dying its much mourned death as a popular commercial genre, but Spelling was already showing a survivor's quick reflexes in a medium notorious for leaving the lethargic behind. Now a producer at Four Star Studio, he retooled for what had become the favored form of prime-time production: the continuing weekly series. *Johnny Ringo* (CBS, 1959–60) is notable among Spelling's early series failures. The Western starred Don Durant as a former gunslinger who had gone straight and become the sheriff of an Arizona town. Though *Johnny Ringo* was canceled during its first season, a decade later Spelling would repackage the show's concept of "the rehabilitated criminal as lawman" into a modern urban setting as *The Mod Squad.*

Spelling successfully completed his transition to weekly series production at Four Star with the first of his many copshows, *Burke's Law* (ABC, 1963–66). Starring Gene Barry as a millionaire Beverly Hills police detective who pursues criminals down the wide boulevards of Southern California in a chauffeured Rolls-Royce, *Burke's Law* foreshadows several future Spelling series. Amos Burke, the crimefighting blue-chip connoisseur of all things fine and expensive, is a video ancestor of Jonathan and Jennifer Hart (Robert Wagner and Stefanie Powers), the aristocratic sleuths of *Hart to Hart* (ABC, 1979–84). *Matt Houston* (ABC, 1982–85) suggests the Burke character as well, this time in the form of a bon vivant oil baron (Lee Horsley) who fights evil for fun between gushers.

Spelling used a *Burke's Law* episode to spin off a second crime series for Four Star, *Honey West* (ABC, 1965–66). Honey (Anne Francis) was an unlikely detective in a genre still modeled on the macho image of Joe Friday. She had been thrust by fate into the then exclusively male domain of crimefighting as a result of the sudden death of her father, whose private investigations agency she inherited. Though the show was renewed for only one more season, its premise points the way to the transformation of the network cops-and-robbers show that Spelling accomplished almost singlehandedly during the next decade in a string of hits he would deliver to ABC.

The Mod Squad (ABC, 1968–73), produced in partnership with Danny Thomas, was Spelling's first true ratings victory, finishing as high as Number Eleven in the Nielsens for 1970–71. The series proved to be a watershed for both its genre and its network, as well as for Aaron Spelling. During the late sixties, advertisers were anxious to court the emerging population bulge of eighteen-to-thirty-four-year-old boom babies. But this seemingly straightforward marketing problem had been complicated by the political and cultural turbulence of the late sixties. How could a mass story-telling medium such as television appeal to both the young and to their parents, when the two generations seemed locked into an endless cycle of confrontations over questions of war and peace, responsibility and freedom, and conformity and personal expression? The phrase "law and order" had, itself, become a buzzword for a political agenda.

Spelling addressed this crisis in crimeshow aesthetics by reconfiguring the lone, white, middle-aged Webbian police figure into a kind of popular-front youth troika composed of a middle-class white man (Pete), an independent white woman (Julie), and a young black man recently risen from the ghetto (Linc). This grand crimefighting alliance was headed by a desk-bound father figure (Captain Greer), a kind of aging Joe Friday now kicked upstairs to an advisory role, out of the path of screeching cars and flying bullets.

The Mod Squad bears some resemblance to Cy Chermak's *Ironside*, which had premiered on NBC a season earlier. But the differences between the two shows help define the Spelling touch. On *Ironside*, Chermak presents us with a demographically similar triumvirate of young new police heroes. But the members of Chermak's Class of '67 were painfully straight arrows: Ed (Don Galloway), a kindergarten *Dragnet* G-man; Eve (Barbara Anderson), a kind of iron police maiden; and Mark (Don Mitchell), a smiling youngster from the ghetto who joins the group as manservant to the wheelchair-bound "police genius," Chief of Detectives Robert T. Ironside (Raymond Burr). As the title of the show indicates, all the young cops were assistants to the traditional middle-aged white male star.

Spelling, on the other hand, gave youth its day. The members of his Squad had all joined the police force following juvenile run-ins with the law: Pete (Michael Cole), a rebellious son of well-to-do parents, had been arrested for stealing a car; Julie (Peggy Lipton), had been picked up for vagrancy; and Linc (Clarence Williams III), a poor kid from Watts, had been carried off in handcuffs during a race riot. All three were recruited into the force by Captain Greer (Tige Andrews) while being held in police custody.

A look at the promotional material surrounding the premiere of *The Mod Squad* in 1968 offers a compelling view of the level of confusion at the networks concerning the portrayal of the sixties "youth rebellion" in prime-time programming. "The police don't understand the now generation and the now generation doesn't dig the fuzz," proclaimed an ABC press release that fall. The solution? "Find some swinging young people who live the beat scene and get them to work for the cops." The beat scene? In 1968? The age of the ABC public relations department was showing.

The Mod Squad indeed strived mightily for the look and feel of sixties "relevance" as it plumbed the depths of the "generation gap." Spelling introduced the ambience of the evening news into the crimeshow, much as Norman Lear would do for the sitcom several years later with *All in the Family* and its spin-offs. Moreover, despite the seedy street world of drugs, prostitution, and worse that *The Mod Squad* presented, Spelling left viewers with two extremely optimistic messages: the young were assured that their idealism would be redeemed not by revolt but by integration into the system; the old were reassured that the center would hold against the implied threat of youthful anarchy.

Unlike most of Spelling's later shows, *The Mod Squad* was critically acclaimed, winning six Emmy Award nominations in its first season, barely losing out to *Marcus Welby, M.D.* for best dramatic series. The program also gained Spelling an exclusive contract with ABC, guaranteeing him and his new partner, former ABC executive Leonard Goldberg, at least one new series on the network schedule for each of the next three years (eventually this agreement was extended). This compact was put to quick and profitable use. The fresh themes introduced in *The Mod Squad* — the rehabilitation of errant youth, the assimilation of rebellious energies into the system, and the strengthening of the establishment through benevolent flexibility — revitalized the crimeshow genre and constituted the framework for a bevy of Spelling-Goldberg hits.

The first of these was *The Rookies* (ABC, 1972–76). In this series Pete, Julie, and Linc become Mike Danko (Sam Melville), Nurse Jill Danko (Kate Jackson), and Terry Webster (Georg Stanford Brown), all under the direction of a Captain Greer–like father figure, Lieutenant Ryker (Gerald S. O'Loughlin). A fourth (single) white male officer, Willie Gillis (Michael Ontkean), was added during the second season for romantic purposes. A bit more conservative than their progenitors, the young idealistic *Rookies* trade in *The Mod Squad*'s tie-dyed shirts and bell-bottoms for a set of shiny new uniforms. The next chapter in the Spelling-Goldberg police saga, *S.W.A.T.*, pushes even further in this direction. In this show, youth has been thoroughly disciplined and whipped into a paramilitary police strike force, complete with automatic rifles and tear-gas canisters. The final of the four cop operas to be set at Spelling's fictitious "S.C.P.D." stationhouse was *Starsky and Hutch* (ABC, 1975–79). Drawing back a bit from the excesses of *S.W.A.T.*, it cast David Soul and Paul Michael Glaser as a pair of fast-lane cops cruising the Strip in a Dodge muscle-car during the energy-crisis years.

If *The Mod Squad* and its clones had retold the story of the sixties youth rebellion as an epic of American political co-option, Spelling turned his attention toward a new, though related, set of concerns as the Reagan era approached. *Charlie's Angels* (ABC, 1976–81) is the story of three highly capable female crimefighters who had suffered as members of the police force, where institutional discrimination against women had saddled them with desk jobs. Much as Captain Greer had recruited alienated youth into satisfying public service during the sixties, Charlie, a millionaire entrepreneur, had plucked the Angels from public service into the newly revalorized private sector. Gloating over the government bureaucracy's inept misuse of the Angels during the show's opening sequence each week, the disembodied voice of Charlie (John Forsythe) tells us, "But I changed all that!" The rich entrepreneur had regained hero status in American culture.

In the process, Spelling had turned an implicitly feminist story into an explicit vehicle for the gratuitous display of the bodies of three women, played in the initial seasons by Kate Jackson, Jaclyn Smith, and Farrah Fawcett-Majors, who were gradually replaced by various models and starlets. Spelling followed suit with more wealthy crimefighters in *Hart to Hart* and *Matt Houston*.

Amid all the shootings and car chases of these cop and private-eye crimeshows, one series stands out as a distinct departure from the Spelling style: *Family* (ABC, 1976–80). This weekly hour-long drama, coproduced with Mike Nichols, began as a six-part miniseries. Its popularity, however, soon gained it a spot on the regular ABC lineup. As the program's self-consciously generic title indicates, the story focuses on the daily lives of an upper-middle-class suburban family. Lacking the violence and twisted metal that had characterized Spelling's familiar hits, *Family* charmed the critics, many of whom found it hard to believe that this effort at domestic social realism had come from the producer who had given prime-time television the *S.W.A.T.* team and Farrah Fawcett-Majors.

More surprises followed. In 1977 Spelling dissolved his partnership with Leonard Goldberg and ventured even further afield from crime drama. *The Love Boat*, his first comedy, was a smash hit that would change the face of prime time. Set in tropical climates and complete with an on-board swimming pool, the show could "jiggle" with the best of them, much to the theoretical delight of then ABC programming chief Fred Silverman. Moreover, *The Love Boat*'s revolutionary narrative structure would help prepare network television for the "target marketing" requirements of the cable era.

In *The Love Boat*, Spelling revised the traditional thirty-minute form of the TV situation comedy into an hour-long presentation of three segmented yet interwoven pieces, with different writers actually taking credits for each "sitcom-within-a-sitcom." One narrative line in a *Love Boat* episode might concern a marital spat targeted at older viewers; another might concern a young romance; a third could feature a child's problem. By presenting three coequal plots aimed at different points of viewer identification, Spelling could hope to appeal to disparate demographic groups; by actively intercutting between these plots over the course of a single episode, he could hope to keep all groups watching for the entire hour.

The boarding scene, which opened each episode, used the program's familiar recurring characters (Captain Stubing, Julie, Dr. Bricker, Gopher, and Isaac) to introduce the week's guest characters and the anthological plots. Though *The Love Boat* is rarely credited for its ingenuity, this ritual introductory sequence that Spelling developed for the show can be seen as a formal source for organizational conventions employed by some of the finest multiplot dramatic series of the eighties. Examples include the squadroom roll call that opens each *Hill Street Blues* episode and the partners' meeting similarly placed in *L.A. Law*.

Spelling capitalized further on this new formula with his next hit, *Fantasy Island* (ABC, 1978–84). Like Captain Stubing (Gavin MacLeod) and Julie (Lauren Tewes) of *The Love Boat*, Mr. Roarke (Ricardo Montalban) and Tattoo (Herve Villechaize) ritually greet the guest stars and introduce their problems to the audience as "dee plane" lands on the island at the top of the hour. Though it might be said that anthology drama had come to *Gilligan's Island*, Spelling preferred another analogy: "*Love Boat* and *Fantasy Island*," he told *TV Guide*, "they are all O. Henry short stories."

During the eighties Spelling continued to successfully dabble in several prime-time genres. With *T. J. Hooker* (ABC, 1982–87), he returned to the cops-and-robbers genre in which he had made his reputation some fifteen years earlier. *Hotel* (ABC, 1985–88) was described by critics as "a landlocked *Love Boat*" and "an indoors *Fantasy Island*." But the greatest of Aaron Spelling's eighties hits — perhaps the most popular work of his career — was *Dynasty* (ABC, 1981–89). Lee Rich's *Dallas* had premiered in 1978 and, once again, Spelling had read the Nielsen tea leaves correctly. He chose to conjure his blue-chip oil company and its viciously feuding family owners a time zone away across the West in the Rocky Mountain city of Denver. If sixties viewers had enjoyed watching *The Mod Squad* duke it out with a bunch of heroin dealers for the soul of the community, eighties viewers were treated to the spectacle of Alexis (Joan Collins) and Krystle (Linda Evans) wrestling in the mud for the amorous attentions and fiscal codicils of multibillionaire Blake Carrington (John Forsythe).

A leading member of the inner circle of big-time network television suppliers, Aaron Spelling has been both innovator and imitator, a ratings engineer whose success is as much derived from his ability to go with the flow as to change the course of the river. His twenty-year association with ABC must be counted as a primary factor in that company's rise from its once seemingly immutable position as the "third network" to a coequal competitor with NBC and CBS. Every time Spelling's limits seemed clear, he redefined them by taking on the challenges of another genre or style. If *The Colbys* (ABC, 1985–87) seemed like a safe extension of the proven formula of *Dynasty*, the same cannot be said of Aaron Spelling's 1988 series, *Heartbeat,* which concerned a women's health clinic and featured a lesbian doctor among its principal characters.

AARON SPELLING: SELECTED VIDEOGRAPHY

Series

Johnny Ringo (CBS, 1959–60)
The Dick Powell Show (NBC, 1961–63)
The Lloyd Bridges Show (CBS, 1962–63)
Burke's Law (ABC, 1963–66)
The Smothers Brothers Show (CBS, 1965–66)
Honey West (ABC, 1965–66)
The Danny Thomas Hour (NBC, 1967–68)
The Guns of Will Sonnet (ABC, 1967–69)
The Mod Squad (ABC, 1968–73)
The New People (ABC, 1969–70)
The Rookies (ABC, 1972–76)
Starsky and Hutch (ABC, 1975–79)
S.W.A.T. (ABC, 1975–76)
Charlie's Angels (ABC, 1976–81)
Family (ABC, 1976–80)
The Love Boat (ABC, 1977–87)
The San Pedro Beach Bums (ABC, 1977)

Fantasy Island (ABC, 1978–84)
Vega$ (ABC, 1978–81)
Friends (ABC, 1979)
Hart to Hart (ABC, 1979–84)
Strike Force (ABC, 1981–82)
Dynasty (ABC, 1981–89)
Matt Houston (ABC, 1982–85)
T. J. Hooker (ABC, 1982–87)
Hotel (ABC, 1983–88)
Glitter (ABC, 1984–85)
Finder of Lost Loves (ABC, 1984–85)
MacGruder and Loud (ABC, 1985)
Heartbeat (ABC, 1988)
Nightingales (NBC, 1989)

16. GLEN LARSON

Hacking Away

In the world of series television, the threshold separating extraordinary achievement from unceremonious yeomanship is often illusive. The familiar distinctions between genius and hack become buried in the sheer quantity of work required by the enterprise. Who but a maestro could have possibly produced such an impressive portfolio? Who but a dullard could have possibly cranked out all that product? These kinds of critical questions, originally asked to satisfy the curiosity of a preindustrial aesthetic, become not so much groundless as weightless in the context of the mass-distributed commercial arts.

A look at the work of Glen Larson offers an excellent case in point. A show-business original, Larson began his career as a teenage pop singer in the 1950s, earning three gold records as a member of The Four Preps, an AM Top Forty group much favored by the Pat Boone set. In the early 1960s, however, as adolescent androgeny suffered the inevitable outcome of its struggle with five o'clock shadow, Larson retreated behind the scenes to try his hand at television production. As a producer of action/adventure hours, he would eventually reach the charmed group of video auteurs who could claim multiple prime-time sales to all three networks.

Like so many of his most successful contemporaries, including Steve Bochco and Stephen J. Cannell (see Chapters 19 and 20), Larson learned the nuts and bolts of series production in the factorylike surroundings of Universal Television during the sixties. His early credits include a stint as a staff writer for Roy Huggins's *The Virginian* (NBC, 1962–71). A major break for Larson came in 1969 when he was given the chance by Universal to become the producer of an already running series, *It Takes a Thief* (ABC, 1968–70). The show was a spy vehicle starring Robert Wagner and Fred Astaire as former master criminals who had been recruited by the "SIA" to help fight fire with fire. From there, Larson was reassigned as the producer of *McCloud* (1970–77), one of the rotating components of *The NBC Mystery Movie* umbrella. This series starred Dennis Weaver as a New Mexico lawman on loan to the NYPD and was loosely based on *Coogan's Bluff*, a 1968 film starring Clint Eastwood as an Arizona cop chasing a bad guy through the ersatz grand canyons of Manhattan.

Having thus paid company dues for a decade, Larson's next project was his own. *Alias Smith and Jones* (ABC, 1971–73), created and produced by Glen Larson, was, until very recently, among the last TV Westerns to survive for more than a single season in prime time. In terms of form, the series can be seen in retrospect as a prototype of the cut-and-paste authorial style that would mark Larson's career, as well as a sounding board for many of his continuing thematic concerns and motifs. Borrowing the criminals-become-lawmen parable of *It Takes a Thief* and resetting it in the Western milieu of *The Virginian*, Larson fashioned a kind of television adaptation of one of the block-buster box-office films of the period: *Butch Cassidy and the Sundance Kid* (1969). Roy Huggins (see Chapter 13) was Larson's boss at Universal, and his influence can be felt in the series as well.

The action of *Alias Smith and Jones* takes place somewhere in the Aristotelian middle of the *Butch Cassidy* story. Hannibal Heyes (Peter Deuel) and Kid Curry (Ben Murphy) materialize in prime time as the video counterparts of Paul Newman and Robert Redford, two lovable, attractive rascals roaming the wide-open plains of frontier America. Sometimes the West is a garden and sometimes the West is a jungle, leaving suitably jagged boundaries between rugged individualism and reckless lawlessness for the episodes to explore.

The concept was, however, severely edited for television. Whereas Butch and Sundance attempt to simply walk away from their life of crime, Hannibal and The Kid receive more formal, state-sanctioned rehabilitation. At the beginning of each episode, we learn that the governor of the territory has *secretly* promised the boys a pardon for their many past crimes (no capital offenses involved, of course) if they can just keep out of mischief for a suitable period of time. Heyes and The Kid agree to these conditions, assuming new identities: Joshua Smith and Thaddeus Jones. Unfortunately, their past keeps catching up with them in the form of trigger-happy bounty hunters, bullet-headed lawmen, and former associates-in-crime who have not quite seen the light.

Though *Alias Smith and Jones* was unable to achieve Top Twenty-five ratings in its Thursday-night time slot, the series did make a respectable showing opposite NBC's *The Flip Wilson Show,* a rare hit comedy-variety hour that was the Number Two–rated program of the 1971–72 season. Though Westerns were generally fading from popularity during this period, last-place ABC decided to renew the series, hoping to boost ratings by adding Sally Field, fresh from her triumph as *The Flying Nun,* in the role of Clementine Hale, another rogue-turned-samaritan and the show's first female regular.

However, the most consequential change to occur during the show's second season was anything but planned by Larson. Peter Deuel was found dead of a self-inflicted gunshot wound to the head, apparently having committed suicide while watching an episode of *Alias Smith and Jones* on New Year's Eve. Larson scrambled to replace him, giving the role to Roger Davis, who had been serving as the show's disembodied narrator. But the series never quite recovered from this sudden shock and was canceled in January of its second season. (In an interesting, if somewhat macabre, footnote to the incident, another of Larson's stars would kill himself, midseries, when Jon-Erik Hexum accidentally shot himself in the head on the set of *Cover-Up* [CBS, 1984–85]; Hexum, too, was replaced, but once again the series could not survive the death of its star.)

Larson would not achieve his first bona fide commercial success until the midseventies, when he hit the bionic jackpot with *The Six Million Dollar Man* (ABC, 1974–78). Loosely based on *Cyborg,* a novel by Martin Caidin, the series followed the adventures of Col. Steve Austin (Lee Majors), an astronaut who is pulled from the wreckage of a missile crash and rebuilt with nonorganic parts. His career as an astronaut over, Austin dons an avocado leisure suit to become a robo-spy for the U.S. government.

Here, once again, Larson can be observed massaging his own concepts. *It Takes a Thief* had been structured around the relationship between a government bureaucrat and a roguish man of action. The clash of styles between nerdy Wallie Powers of the "SIA" and the suave Robert Wagner character recurred in the relationship between straitlaced Oscar Goldman of the "OSI" and the cowboyish Lee Majors. The show was a runaway hit, allowing ABC to spin off *The Bionic Woman* (1976–78).

This self-derivative formula became even more apparent in Larson's next series, *Switch* (CBS, 1975–78). Robert Wagner returned to work for the producer, this time playing Pete Ryan, a reformed conman who has become a good-guy private eye. Replacing Fred Astaire as Wagner's mentor was Eddie Albert, who played ex-bunco-squad cop Frank McBride. Just as *Alias Smith and Jones* had capitalized on the popularity of *Butch Cassidy and the Sundance Kid*, episodes of *Switch* were designed as miniversions of another movie blockbuster, *The Sting* (1973).

In 1976 Larson was asked by Universal to create a new element for its *NBC Mystery Movie* umbrella, which already included three rotating components: *Columbo, McMillan and Wife,* and *McCloud.* The result was *Quincy, M.E.,* one of the most remarkably banal series ever to appear in prime time. Starring Jack Klugman as a crimefighting L.A. County coroner, the series epitomizes the painful doldrums that beset the crimeshow genre between the burst of "relevance" in the late 1960s (*Mod Squad, Dragnet*) and the formal rehabilitation of the genre during the early 1980s (*Hill Street Blues, Miami Vice*). If *Marcus Welby, M.D.* had never lost a patient, *Quincy, M.E.* had never saved one. By the time Quincy arrived, the victim was already dead. In each episode, however, a crucial clue lay hidden in the decaying flesh of the deceased — a fruitful urine sample, a datable contusion, a singed follicle — allowing the whining, whimpering Klugman to nail the murderer with an empirical revelation. As if such forensic genius were not enough, Quincy insisted upon leaving his viewers with excruciatingly socially conscious tirades on such controversial subjects as steroid use among athletes or the dangers of slam dancing.

Larson's productivity accelerated in the wake of *Quincy's* success: *The Hardy Boys/Nancy Drew Mysteries* (ABC, 1977–79) was drawn from the pages of teenage literature; *Battlestar Gallactica* (ABC, 1978–79) looked a lot like George Lucas's *Star Wars; Buck Rogers in the 25th Century* (NBC, 1979–81) could trace its lineage to a comic strip, a movie serial, a radio show, and even a previous TV series of the same name; *B.J. and the Bear* (NBC, 1979–81) trod the path of Clint Eastwood's *Every Which Way But Loose; The Fall Guy* (ABC, 1981–86), starring Lee Majors, followed Burt Reynolds's *Hooper.* Adaptations or knockoffs? Blank-label copies or postmodern reiterations? Homages or plagiarisms? George Lucas apparently thought the latter; he sued Larson over *Battlestar Gallactica.*

Larson produced two series set in the rural South even as he was exploring the outer reaches of the universe. During the 1960s, rural series had reached a peak of popularity (see Chapter 2, Paul Henning). The election of President Jimmy Carter in 1976 signaled a minirevival of this subgenre that included *Carter Country* and *The Dukes of Hazzard*. Larson moved right in with *B.J. and the Bear*. The idea of pairing a good-old-boy truck driver with his pet ape in the cab of an eighteen-wheeler was freshly plucked from a recent Clint Eastwood flick, *Every Which Way But Loose*. Set in a town that might as well have been Plains, Georgia, the narrative was hung on the honest, independent driver's run-ins with the corrupt local police, à la *The Dukes of Hazzard*. The fate of *B.J. and the Bear* was not unlike that of *Alias Smith and Jones*. Ratings were poor, but NBC, now the new last-place network, added a female component to try to boost interest: seven jiggling pinup lady truckers. Displaying his ability as either a narrative ecologist or a cosmic junkman, Larson even managed a spin-off out of the ill-fated project, *The Misadventures of Sheriff Lobo* (NBC, 1979–81).

Larson began to hit stride again when he collaborated with Donald Bellisario to create the phenomenally successful *Magnum, P.I.* (CBS, 1980–88). In addition to being a ratings hit, *Magnum* was so finely crafted and allusion-laden that it became an all-time favorite of the critics. Such was the enthusiasm for the show that Professor Christopher Anderson of Indiana University characterized it as "one of the great achievements of twentieth-century culture." Had Larson finally transcended his reputation as a schlockmeister with this "trouble in paradise" tale of a Vietnam vet private eye whose existential anxiety dogs him through his professional investigations?

Not hardly. After helping work out and sell the *Magnum* concept to CBS, Larson left the series in the hands of Bellisario, rushing off to a more characteristic low-rent ratings jackpot: *The Fall Guy* (ABC, 1981–86). Three years after the cancellation of *The Six Million Dollar Man*, Larson called on Lee Majors once again to star in an action/adventure series. In this TV adaptation of the Burt Reynolds film *Hooper*, Majors plays the role of Colt Seavers, a Hollywood stuntman who moonlights between car crashes by chasing bail jumpers for a local collection agency headed by "T&A"-era specialist Heather Thomas. Larson's twenty-year association with Twentieth Century–Fox ended with *The Fall Guy*, marking his arrival as an independent supplier.

Larson attempted a trilogy of sci-fi concepts during the early eighties, only one of which was even moderately successful. In *Knight*

Rider (NBC, 1982–86), Michael Young, a police officer, is killed in the opening minutes of the pilot but is reconstructed by scientific geniuses. Though this may sound a lot like *The Six Million Dollar Man*, it does contain a Reagan-era departure: the givers of artificial life are not "big government" technocrats but, rather, the private sector research and development folks at Knight Industries.

Dying billionaire/industrialist/philanthropist/high-tech genius Wilton Knight has the badly mangled Michael fixed up and brought back to life. In a touch of apparently unselfconscious hubris, Wilton has the plastic surgeons model the rehauled cop after his own image as a young man. (Not surprisingly, he looked very much like a daytime soap-opera star.) Just before dying he rechristens the Frankenstein "Michael Knight" and charges the creature with the duty of carrying on his personal lifelong crusade for truth, justice, etc. under the guidance of his majordomo Devon Miles (Edward Mulhare). All of this is familiar Larson stuff: the reconstructed hero snatched from the jaws of death (*The Six Million Dollar Man*); a new identity for the rehabilitated crimefighting hero (*Alias Smith and Jones*); a genteel supervisor to direct the sometimes impulsive hero's actions (*It Takes a Thief*); and, of course, car chases galore (*The Fall Guy*).

Though not particularly bionic himself, Michael (David Hasselhoff) is given the technological advantage of a special edition Pontiac Trans Am (William Daniels) that includes such options as a bulletproof paint job, X-ray vision, autopilot, and an ironic, sarcastic personality. Daniels, as the disembodied voice of the Pontiac, talks about a lot more than just fastening seat belts and locking doors. The ability to plot shortcuts, access FBI files, counsel the driver in matters of romance, and speculate about the criminal mind are all included among his standard features.

Larson's next two sci-fi adventures, *Manimal* (NBC, 1983) and *Automan* (ABC, 1983–84), were quick and unmitigated failures. *Manimal* starred Simon MacCorkindale as an erudite professor of animal behavior at New York University who liked to solve crimes and right wrongs between classes. His advantage at this hobby lay in his ability to turn himself, at will, into a panther, a snake, or a hawk as the situation required. His dad had learned this technique from some unexplained New Age experience in the Central American jungle and passed it on to Simon before dying. Like *The Incredible Hulk* (CBS, 1978–82), the show offered at least two spectacular metamorphosis scenes per episode. The special effects used in the man-to-beast transformations were right out of recent movies such as *Cat People* (1981) and *An American Werewolf in London* (1982). NBC boasted in promotional announcements that *Manimal* would knock *Dallas* off the air in its Friday-night time slot; the opposite quickly proved true.

Similarly, bad ratings befell *Automan*. Desi Arnaz, Jr., whose own miraculous appearance had put him on the cover of the first issue of *TV Guide*, starred in the series as the nebbishy Walter Nebicher, a nerdy desk cop who specializes in computers. One day while pounding the keys in front of his VDT, Nebicher creates a near-letter-quality superhero in the form of Automan (Chuck Wagner), who materializes from a cathode ray tube assisted by state-of-the-art TV animation techniques. The brainy Walter and the handsome, athletic Automan combine to become a crimefighting team, aided in their work by Cursor, a computer-generated dot who follows them around like Jiminy Cricket.

Larson seemed to be getting nowhere in the 1980s. *Masquerade* (ABC, 1983–84) starred Rod Taylor as an operative of the "National Intelligence Agency" who recruits American tourists to perform spy missions while they are taking vacations abroad. *Cover-Up* (CBS, 1984–85) was not unrelated; it featured Jennifer O'Neill and Jon-Erik Hexum as U.S. government agents posing undercover as a photographer and her favorite high-fashion male model. The series' chances were mostly hung on Hexum's rising pinup-boy stardom. After his bizarre accidental death on the set, Larson attempted to save the program by casting Australian Tony Hamilton in the role of the pretty-boy model cum two-fisted agent, but Hexum proved too tough an act to follow. *Half Nelson* (NBC, 1985) was yet another Larson role-switching vehicle, with Joe Pesci as an aspiring actor who is forced to work as a security guard (and to therefore solve crimes) for Beverly Hills celebrities while waiting to be discovered. Pesci himself finally was discovered and won an Oscar for his performance in *Goodfellas* (1990). Larson, however, has not done nearly as well.

Desperately in need of a hit in the late eighties, Larson characteristically massaged one of his old concepts; in this case it was *Knight Rider*, which had been his last successful venture some three years earlier. NBC even went so far as to program *The Highwayman* (1988) in *Knight Rider*'s old time slot. In this go-around, the futuristic sports car is traded up (or perhaps down) to an even more preposterously spectacular truck. Not only was this vehicle bulletproof and computerized but it could also become a helicopter or turn invisible upon demand. To make the formula complete, Larson gave the series' mise-en-scène a popular-film look, which in this case he took from the *Mad Max* movies. Sam Jones played the title role of the TV series, with the Australian "personality" Jacko in the role of his sidekick, Jetto.

The two were apparently post–World War III-ish federal marshals patrolling the otherwise ungovernable American outback after the fashion of the Mel Gibson character in the *Mad Max* trilogy. As in *Knight Rider*, the cast was rounded out by a young black male technician who serviced the road needs of the supervehicle, a young white female scientist who serviced the more high-tech needs of the supervehicle, and an older white male administrator who ran the show from headquarters. Unlike *Knight Rider*, however, the series lasted only three months.

By the end of the eighties, Larson's style and substance seemed increasingly dated — even downright silly. The hour-long form seemed to be migrating toward upscale, educated viewers with self-consciously sophisticated dramas such as *St. Elsewhere*, *L.A. Law*, and *thirtysomething*. Larson, with his downscale comic-bookish action/adventure concepts, was in disarray.

GLEN LARSON: SELECTED VIDEOGRAPHY

Series

It Takes a Thief (ABC, 1968–70)
McCloud (NBC, 1970–77)
Alias Smith and Jones (ABC, 1971–73)
Get Christie Love! (ABC, 1974–75)
The Six Million Dollar Man (ABC, 1974–78)
Switch (CBS, 1975–78)
Quincy, M.E. (NBC, 1976–83)
The Hardy Boys/Nancy Drew Mysteries (ABC, 1977–79)
Battlestar Gallactica (ABC, 1978–80)
Sword of Justice (NBC, 1978–79)
B.J. and the Bear (NBC, 1979–81)
The Misadventures of Sheriff Lobo (NBC, 1979–81)
Buck Rogers in the 25th Century (NBC, 1979–81)
Magnum, P.I. (CBS, 1980–88) (coproduction with Donald Bellisario)
Fitz and Bones (NBC, 1981)
The Fall Guy (ABC, 1981–86)
Knight Rider (NBC, 1982–86)
Manimal (NBC, 1983)
Trauma Center (ABC, 1983)
Automan (ABC, 1983–84)
Masquerade (ABC, 1983–84)
Cover-Up (CBS, 1984–85)

Half Nelson (NBC, 1985)
The Highwayman (NBC, 1988)
P.S.I. Luv U (CBS, 1991–present)

Movies Made for Television

Benny and Barney: Las Vegas Undercover (NBC, 1977)
The Islander (CBS, 1978)
Evening in Byzantium (syndicated in two parts, 1978)
Battles — The Murder That Wouldn't Die (NBC, 1980)
Nightside (ABC, 1980)
Rooster (ABC, 1982)
Terror at Alcatraz (NBC, 1982)
In Like Flynn (ABC, 1985)

17. RICHARD LEVINSON AND WILLIAM LINK

The Rotating Umbrella

The word *literate* is not often used to describe American prime-time television, but it appears over and over again in reviews of the work of the TV production team of Richard Levinson and William Link. Both born in the Philadelphia area within eight months of each other, the partners began their long association as classmates in junior high school. In their jointly authored autobiographical memoir, *Stay Tuned: An Inside Look at the Making of Prime Time Television* (1981), they describe the strong bonds that were forged between them in the adolescent heat of American popular culture: "We grew up, middle-class children of radio and comic books, in the suburbs of Philadelphia during the forties and early fifties. Our tastes were formed well before the advent of television, and what we ingested by way of out-of-school influences was an eclectic mix of wonderful trash and high art, swallowed whole. Long before we met, each of us had frequented countless Saturday afternoon serials; we laughed at Abbott and Costello, worshipped Disney (happily unaware that he was out of vogue with the intellectuals); collected Superman and Captain Marvel comics — turning out our own hand-drawn versions on the side — and listened to everything from

Let's Pretend and *Jack Armstrong* to *Suspense, Escape,* and *Inner Sanctum."*

Despite (or perhaps because of; the debate rages on) their voracious appetites for pop, the boys were also excellent students on their way to Ivy League educations. Hemingway, Faulkner, Fitzgerald, Sartre, Camus, Shakespeare, Kafka, and Orwell were among the writers who shared shelf space on their walls with Dashiell Hammett, Raymond Chandler, L. Frank Baum, Ellery Queen, Erle Stanley Gardner, and Jules Verne. The two frequented the Philadelphia theaters, which often featured Broadway-bound tryouts, and they haunted the city's movie houses. Above all, they were avid devotees of prime-time radio drama. Their collaborative efforts as teenagers included their own homemade radio productions as well as short stories submitted (unsuccessfully) to such magazines as the *New Yorker* and the *Saturday Evening Post.* In their own words, "If there was a common thread to this experience, it was the love of popular culture in its many forms. As our tastes became more sophisticated we broadened and deepened the range of our reading, but even the major novelists and playwrights didn't have the same visceral appeal as the movies, the radio, and the popular songs. When television arrived on the scene it was not with the force of revelation; rather it was an easily integrated part of our everyday lives — it seemed an amalgam of everything we had been doing."

As students at the University of Pennsylvania, Levinson and Link wrote for various campus literary and humor magazines, worked as film critics for the *Daily Pennsylvanian,* founded their own mimeographed magazines, and wrote words and lyrics for several campus musicals. The pair even managed to obtain senior honors thesis credits for coauthoring a television script, which was quite an accomplishment at an Ivy League college during the fifties. Their first free-lance sale came while they were still at Penn, when an unsolicited short story was accepted for publication by *Ellery Queen's Mystery Magazine.* After graduation they moved to New York and continued to collaborate, producing two novels, an assortment of short stories, two professionally produced stage plays, two nonfiction books, and, eventually, five motion picture scripts.

But all through these early efforts in the more traditional — and more prestigious — venues of culture, the goal of their partnership remained the production of network television programs. Even after achieving some reputation as fiction writers by selling short stories to nationally distributed high-circulation magazines, including *Playboy* and *Alfred Hitchcock's Mystery Magazine,* they continued to humbly mail out their unsolicited teleplays to TV production companies. The golden age of television drama was in full swing, and the two desperately wanted to become part of that scene.

They finally managed a foot in the industry door in 1957 by selling a pair of scripts to *General Motors Presents,* a Canadian dramatic anthology series produced in Toronto. In 1959 *Westinghouse Desilu Playhouse* (CBS, 1958–60) bought another of their scripts, a development that inspired the partners to pull up stakes and make their move to the West Coast. Unfortunately, Levinson and Link had arrived in Hollywood just as the golden age of anthological TV drama was sputtering into historical disintegration. The young writers were forced, instead, to pay their video dues by cranking out episode scripts for weekly Westerns, including *Sugarfoot* (ABC, 1957–61) and *Wanted: Dead or Alive* (CBS, 1958–61), and for Roy Huggins's private-eye series (see Chapter 13), including *77 Sunset Strip* and *Hawaiian Eye.*

By late 1959 Levinson and Link had graduated to staff positions with Four Star Studio, a company founded by four aging Hollywood movie stars (Dick Powell, June Allyson, David Niven, and Charles Boyer), who were trying to find a way to cash in their film chips on the burgeoning television bonanza. At Four Star the two continued to work as a writing team and as script doctors for such shows as *Richard Diamond, Private Detective* and *Johnny Ringo* (which, incidentally, was Aaron Spelling's first producer credit). Four Star even gave them a shot at resuscitating anthology drama by letting them do scripts for *The DuPont Show with June Allyson* (CBS, 1959–61). But despite the appearances on the program of such major stars as Bette Davis, Ginger Rogers, and Harpo Marx — as well as occasional on-screen guest shots by each one of the Four Star partners — the show barely made it through a second season, a sure sign that live television theater had indeed become moribund.

Disappointed by the quality of the shoot-'em-up series, both urban and Western, that were knocking anthology dramas off network schedules, Levinson and Link became convinced that if they wished to do what they considered " 'good work' [it] could be done between the covers of a book or on the stage." So in the early sixties they took up a bicoastal existence, writing TV scripts in L.A. during the summers for such shows as *Dr. Kildare, Burke's Law, The Fugitive,* and *The Man from U.N.C.L.E.,* and using the profits from these ventures to support the stage plays and books they were writing in New York during the remainder of the year. The money kept rolling in from television, while the rejection letters from theater producers and publishers kept piling up on their desks. By the midsixties they came to terms with their talents and made a commitment to television, returning to year-round work in Hollywood, where they would flourish for the rest of their careers.

Having written episode scripts for other producers' series for over five years, Levinson and Link took their first "Created By" credits for *Jericho* (CBS, 1966–67), a project done with a third partner, Merwin A. Bloch. During the early and middle sixties ABC had achieved some success with World War II action series, including such shows as *Combat, Twelve O'Clock High,* and *Rat Patrol. Jericho* was to be CBS's attempt to break that monopoly. The series followed the exploits of three Allied agents working clandestinely behind Nazi lines: American psychological warfare authority Franklin Sheppard (Don Francks), British demolition specialist Nicholas Gage (John Leyton), and French munitions expert Jean-Gaston André (Marino Mase). Once again, however, Levinson and Link had missed the boat on a genre of prime-time television. The World War II action craze was fading just as they were delivering their entry into the sweepstakes. CBS was disappointed by the poor ratings and canceled the show in its first season.

In 1967 Levinson and Link ended their partnership with Bloch. Their first thoroughly independent effort would be an incontrovertible smash hit: *Mannix* (CBS, 1967–75). The original premise of the series concerned Joe Mannix (Mike Connors), a loner private eye who worked as an operative for Intertect, a large Los Angeles detective firm. Intertect boss Lou Wickersham (Joseph Campanella) continually insisted that Mannix use the firm's state-of-the-art technology (including computers) to solve cases, but Mannix preferred his own gritty hardboiled techniques to the company's high-tech solutions. Not surprising for American television, the old-fashioned instincts of the rugged individual consistently proved superior to newfangled collective strategies, even those of major corporations.

In the second season, Mannix left Intertect and opened his own detective agency in the mixed-usage building where he lived. Peggy Fair (Gail Fisher), the widow of Mannix's best friend, a policeman killed in the line of duty, joined the cast as the star's secretary and confidant. Ms. Fisher was among the first wave of black performers to win regular roles in prime-time network television during what amounted to the racial thaw of the 1968–69 season. (Others included Clarence Williams III as Linc in the police series *The Mod Squad* and Diahann Carroll in the title role of the sitcom *Julia.*) The changes improved the show's ratings. *Mannix* cracked the Top Twenty in its fourth season and then moved on to the Top Ten in 1972–73.

Mannix is perhaps best remembered for its excessive violence, during a period of excessive television violence. Car crashes, street shootings, and, especially, fistfights peppered each episode. The series managed to garner more than its share of criticism from academic researchers and citizen watchdog groups. Like most TV producers, Levinson and Link publicly claimed to be skeptical of the idea that violence on television motivated viewers toward violence. But unlike most of their colleagues, they took the criticisms to heart. They decided that in the future they would indeed strive to keep screen violence to a minimum in all their properties. Though it is debatable whether any acts of violence were ever averted in the so-called real world by this decision, it is clear that this strategy — murder mysteries without visible brutality — became an aesthetic linchpin of the Levinson and Link crimeshow. Their biggest hit, *Columbo* (NBC, 1971–77), is the sterling case in point.

Columbo, a series that film maestro Federico Fellini is reported to have walked out on dinner parties in order to watch, came to television through a circuitous route of adaptations. Partially inspired by G. K. Chesterton's Father Brown and by Dostoyevsky's Petrovich (from *Crime and Punishment*), Lieutenant Columbo's incubation began early in Levinson and Link's career. In 1960 the partners were hired to adapt one of the stories they had published in *Alfred Hitchcock's Mystery Magazine* for a short-lived anthology titled *The Chevy Mystery Show*. Thus Lieutenant Columbo, played by Bert Freed, made his first appearance on NBC more than a decade before the series that would bear his name.

Columbo's next incarnation came in the Levinson and Link stage play *Prescription: Murder*, which toured the United States and Canada during the early sixties. The show opened in San Francisco to mixed reviews but did good business at the box office across the continent. This time around Thomas Mitchell played Columbo, managing to steal the show on a daily basis from its star, Joseph Cotten, who played the murderer. This led the writers to midtour revisions that made the Columbo character more prominent in the script. The next step was an adaptation for television. Levinson and Link produced *Prescription: Murder* as a made-for-TV movie at Universal in 1967. The original shortlist for the role of the blue-collar police detective included Lee J. Cobb and Bing Crosby, but Peter Falk, the producers' third choice, finally won the role, a decision largely based on salary differentials. The first two-hour NBC *Columbo* telefilm registered numbers that put it among the ten highest-rated made-for-TV movies to date. Universal was all set to give Levinson and Link a series contract, but the idea was scrapped when Peter Falk declined the title role, expressing a desire to avoid the grind of weekly series production and instead continue his career in theater and cinema.

In the late sixties, however, Universal was experimenting with its new "umbrella" format, a showcasing idea that rotated any number of freestanding but thematically linked series in a regular weekly slot. Universal proposed *Columbo* as a constituent of its *NBC Sunday Mystery Movie* umbrella, offering Falk the chance to make six ninety-minute *Columbo* episodes rather than the usual twenty-four sixty-minute episodes. This time Falk went for the idea. A second two-hour pilot, *Ransom for a Dead Man,* with story by Levinson and Link, aired in March of 1971. Once again the ratings were good, and *Columbo* was inserted into the *Mystery Movie* rotation, along with *McMillan and Wife,* starring Rock Hudson and Susan St. James, and *McCloud,* starring Dennis Weaver.

Levinson and Link relished the umbrella format as a workable compromise between the anthological drama they had dreamed of doing and the quality-controlled genre programming that had become the reality of network television by the 1970s. The umbrella (or "wheel") series became their specialty, and there was plenty of such work to be done at Universal Television during this period. They wrote the pilot episode (along with Stuart Whitmore) for *McCloud;* they produced and wrote episodes for the various constituent series of *The Name of the Game;* they created *The Psychiatrist* segment for *Four in One;* and they wrote episodes of *The Lawyers* segment for *The Bold Ones.*

The success of *Columbo* was especially important in establishing a bankable reputation for Levinson and Link. The absence of violence from the popular series was pleasing to the networks, who were under continual criticism on this account. Furthermore, violence wasn't the only "action" that *Columbo* was free of. The erstwhile workaholic police lieutenant's life was devoid of on-screen sexual or even romantic entanglements. A crusty, middle-aged, working-class cop, Columbo never sheds his crumpled trenchcoat. All we know about his off-duty hours is that he is married to an unseen woman whom he only refers to as "the missus," or "my wife."

As if the absence of violence and sex were not a pleasing-enough deviation from postsixties copshow convention, this rotating component of *The NBC Mystery Movie* wasn't even a mystery. The killer was revealed in the opening moments of each episode, and the body of the program consisted of Columbo driving around in his dilapidated Peugeot 403 convertible interviewing witnesses while closing in on the too-smart-for-his-or-her-own-good killer: ninety minutes of highly rated network prime-time "action/adventure" dominated by talking heads! The money saved on car crashes alone was staggering.

Columbo's attractions were indeed its quirky defiances of copshow convention. Though set in Southern California, the show made little use of the sun-and-fun motifs that dominated Aaron Spelling shows such as *Starsky and Hutch* or *Charlie's Angels*. Though, of course, it never rained in Southern California, the lieutenant was never seen without his London Fog raincoat. Was he more conscious of the cultural myth of being a detective than he was of the natural world he lived in? He didn't even have a sidekick. But above all, Columbo was a working-class hero, an Italian-American with more than a hint of Brooklynese in his accent, who took particular delight in outfoxing the country club murderers who simply assumed their own intellectual superiority to the gritty proletarian.

After seven seasons, ratings had flattened and overhead costs were rising on the tail of Falk's incremental salary increases. The show was reluctantly canceled at the end of the 1978–79 season by NBC, which had finished third in the Nielsens that season and was more than nervous about giving up its proven entities. Fred Silverman, the network's new programming chief, contrived a plan to cash in on the public's familiarity with the Columbo name. He proposed *Mrs. Columbo*, starring Kate Mulgrew in the title role. Not wanting to ever reveal the identity of Columbo's disembodied missus, Levinson and Link refused to work on the project. But Universal owned the rights to the Columbo name and character, and the partners could do nothing but stand idly by as their carefully crafted dramatic cosmos was tinkered with.

The Mrs. Columbo who appeared on NBC in February of 1979 was glamorous and beautiful, played by an actress twenty-eight years younger than Peter Falk. Levinson and Link claimed they had always imagined "the missus" as "looking something like Maureen Stapleton." But during the late seventies, the period known in TV history as the "jiggle era," it was no surprise that Silverman and Universal had pursued a different look. Kate Columbo, it turned out, was a journalist for a newspaper in the San Fernando Valley suburbs of Los Angeles who somehow managed to find herself in the middle of a murder mystery each week.

According to the ratings, however, the public rejected these revisionist permutations of the Columbo myth. An unusually intense effort was made to fix the series, while Levinson and Link remained adamant about refusing to participate. First, Kate was divorced from Columbo, turning the show into *Kate Columbo*. Then it was decided that all association with Columbo would be dropped, turning Kate into Kate Callahan (her maiden name) and the show into *Kate the Detective* (its third title). Following one more title change (the desperately pitched *Kate Loves a Mystery*), the show died after only ten months of production. In 1988, when William Link brought *Columbo* back to life as part of a new rotating series for ABC, all references to Kate, the divorce, or any other detail from the fiasco were completely ignored, as Columbo (again played by Peter Falk) reverted to his customary allusions to the otherwise unseen missus.

The NBC Mystery Movie, which included *Columbo* among its components, did good business for the network, consistently finishing among the top-rated shows in prime time, including a high of Number Six in 1972–73. Levinson and Link were given the chance to put a second detective drama on NBC, and they used their newly won commercial capital to produce *The Adventures of Ellery Queen* (NBC, 1975–76). For the partners, who had been boyhood fans of the old Ellery Queen novels written by Frederick Dannay and Manfred Lee, and who had sold some of their early short stories to *Ellery Queen's Mystery Magazine*, the project was a labor of love. If Ellery was a hero that Levinson and Link could easily relate to, this is perhaps understandable. A writer of murder mysteries, the brilliant young scribbler uses his uncanny understanding of the "fictional" criminal mind to help his father, a police detective, solve "real-life" cases.

Actually, Ellery Queen was no stranger to the airwaves. Broadcast series bearing the name dated back to CBS radio in the 1930s. In 1950 the old DuMont network introduced *Ellery Queen* to TV. ABC purchased the property in 1951, changed the cast, and ran the show for another year. In 1958 NBC resuscitated it again, with George Nader in the title role. Some sixteen years after it had last been seen on network television, Levinson and Link resurrected Ellery once more, with Jim Hutton in the title role and David Wayne as his dad, Inspector Richard Queen. All the effort went for naught, however, as the complex, Sherlock Holmesian style of the show was swamped by its familiar, formulaic chase-and-shoot opposition, Quinn Martin's *The Streets of San Francisco*.

Another series created by Levinson and Link, *Stone* (ABC, 1980), starred Dennis Weaver as a Joseph Wambaugh–like cop who continues working on the force while writing best-selling detective novels. *Ellery Queen* had at least managed to last an entire season; *Stone* was gone in eight weeks. Failed series for all three networks followed: *Blacke's Magic* (NBC, 1986), starring Hal Linden as a retired magician-turned-detective and Harry Morgan as his helpful (see Richard Queen) father; *Hard Copy* (CBS, 1987), a series about a group of crime reporters at an L.A. newspaper; *Probe* (ABC, 1988), cocreated by Link and Isaac Asimov, concerning a young science genius (Parker Stevenson) who dedicates his high IQ toward the catching of crooks.

While Levinson and Link continued to create these weekly series in the 1980s, it was clear that their real interests lay elsewhere. Even the phenomenal ratings success of *Murder, She Wrote*, starring Angela Lansbury, which they had created for Universal Television in 1982, could not tempt them back into weekly series script work. The two well-read Ivy Leaguers fancied themselves as television playwrights, not cut-and-paste hacks. They continued to aspire to anthological as opposed to formulaic work. Though the old live anthology drama of the golden age was by now a closed chapter in television history, a new species of freestanding prime-time drama was rising that might redeem some of its promise: the made-for-TV movie. Though the *Columbo* series will surely stand as Levinson and Link's most popular and visible work, the two made their greatest contribution to the development of American TV aesthetics in their cultivation and refinement of the two-hour nonserial telefilm.

Mystery films, such as *Rehearsal for Murder* (CBS, 1982) and *Guilty Conscience* (CBS, 1985), capture Levinson and Link in their characteristic stride. Using surrogate "writer/detectives" as personae, playing games with the viewer's knowledge of generic convention, shocking the audience with reversals and counterreversals in the manner of Hitchcock, Levinson and Link created what was perhaps the only readily identifiable style in the made-for-television movie of the 1980s.

Rehearsal for Murder, for example, took place in large part on a theater stage. It included the multiple mirrors of a play within a play within a play within a play. At the end we learn that the entire film we have watched is itself a fiction staged by one of the characters to trap the murderer in the show's final scene. *Guilty Conscience* achieves similar narrative ambiguities by use of dream sequences and the depictions of various characters' inner fantasies. By the end of the telefilm, the line between the "fantasy" sequences and the "reality" sequences has become so blurred that an intelligent viewer must give up suspension of disbelief and revert to better judgment in order to remember that the whole film itself is a fiction.

Another movie-of-the-week, *My Sweet Charlie* (NBC, 1970), was among the first attempts in prime time at a serious drama on American race relations. Adapted from David Westheimer's novel and Broadway play of the same name, *My Sweet Charlie* featured Patty Duke as a pregnant, unmarried white Southerner on the run from her father. She meets up with a black lawyer (Al Freeman, Jr.) who is running from the law after killing a white man in self-defense at a civil rights demonstration. The uneducated white woman and the articulate black man are both full of racial animosities, but they become de facto allies while hiding out in an abandoned house in Texas. The film presented all kinds of problems for Universal management before it could be sold: controversial language (including use of the word *nigger*), and the fact that a white woman and a black man were living together in the same house, were both unprecedented prime-time phenomena. Moreover, the film featured long, turgid dialogues between the principals and was therefore considered "soft on action." NBC finally agreed to air the third cut of the film.

Levinson and Link received an Emmy for their script, and Patty Duke won the first Emmy ever given for a performance in a made-for-television movie. In terms of the bottom line, the ratings were high, causing the networks to take notice that TV movies might be something more than just two-hour pilots for potential series. The good numbers scored by *My Sweet Charlie* were arguably instrumental in opening up the two-hour "movie-of-the-week" blocks of prime time to the many issue-oriented films that have since become so thoroughly identified with the format.

Black-white relations continued to be a thematic insistence for Levinson and Link throughout their career. In 1973 they had created and produced a short-lived series for NBC titled *Tenafly*, which was the first — and remains one of only a very few — noncomedy television series to feature a black star without benefit of a white partner or sidekick. Harry Tenafly (James McEachin) was a private detective who was upwardly mobile, suburban, and middle class; little emphasis of any kind was placed on race. In 1981 Levinson and Link wrote and served as executive producers of *Crisis at Central High*, a two-hour docudrama based on the 1957 Supreme Court–ordered integration of the Little Rock, Arkansas, school system. Lamont Johnson, who had directed *My Sweet Charlie*, directed once again.

Credit for two of the most controversial telefilms ever aired on American television must also go to Levinson and Link. *That Certain Summer* (ABC, 1972) concerned the relationship between a divorced homosexual and his son. The gay father (Hal Holbrook) and his lover (Martin Sheen) were carefully portrayed as unexotic, "masculine," upper-middle-class adults. However, in the context of television history, it should be noted that the film was made at a time when the subject of divorce had only recently been introduced as a "hot" topic, and when the very mention of homosexuality in prime time was considered strictly taboo. NBC waffled on the project and finally opted to reject the film for telecast.

ABC, however, was still smarting from its recent decision to pass on Norman Lear's sitcom *All in the Family*. The network had rejected the show as too controversial in 1969, only to see it become the top-rated show on all of television for CBS two years later. ABC's chief telefilm executive, Barry Diller, expressed interest in *That Certain Summer,* and the project was revived. Changes, however, were demanded by Diller. The young son's age was changed from thirteen to twelve in an attempt to make the child a "safer" (i.e. less sexual) character. The following piece of dialogue had to be added to the final scene, in which the father sums up his experience to his young son: "A lot of people — most people I guess — think it's wrong . . . they say it's a sickness . . . they say it's something that has to be cured. Maybe they're right, I don't know. . . . I do know that it isn't easy. If I had a choice, it's not something I'd pick for myself." When the movie finally aired on ABC in November of 1972, it did not win high ratings, but neither did it cause much public outcry. Levinson and Link won the Best Television Script award from the Writers Guild, and Lamont Johnson won a Directors Guild of America Award.

Taking on yet another controversial issue, Levinson and Link wrote and produced *The Gun* (ABC, 1974), a telefilm that follows a single handgun as it is passed from owner to owner until it is eventually found by a young child who shoots himself (off-screen) in the final scene. *The Gun* contained an element of sardonic satire in that it aped the form of *The Yellow Rolls-Royce,* a lighthearted 1965 comedy starring Rex Harrison that similarly followed the social history of a luxury car. The partners had in fact expressed their views on gun control as early as 1959 in a script they did for *The Rebel,* a weekly Western. Johnny Yuma (Nick Adams) rides into a town in which all citizens have voluntarily surrendered their guns to the local clergyman. The disappearance of just one of the confiscated guns, however, causes all the citizens to reclaim their weapons, and eventually a child is (accidentally) shot.

Once again it was Barry Diller at ABC who supported Levinson and Link in the midst of controversy. The National Rifle Association found out about the film before it was aired and made some fuss, but ABC simply maintained a low profile and aired the film without fanfare. Whether it was due to the lack of promotion or because of public hostility or public indifference to the issue, or a combination of all three, *The Gun* scored low in the ratings. Curiously, in recent years it has found some following as a videostore rental.

By contrast, Levinson and Link's *The Execution of Private Slovik* (NBC, 1974) was a spectacularly promoted docudrama that won a huge audience and received a Peabody Award as well as nine Emmy nominations. Based on the book by William Bradford Huie and directed by Lamont Johnson, the telefilm explored the 1945 case of Eddie Slovik (Martin Sheen), the only American soldier to be executed for desertion since the Civil War. The story was told in generally sympathetic (or, it might be said, politically liberal) terms. Sheen portrayed Slovik as a likable if somewhat eccentric character whose death was a senseless tragedy caused by the inability of the bureaucracy to handle a nonconformist individual. Promoted by NBC with full-page newspaper ads featuring Sheen tied up, blindfolded, and ready to be shot, the show's ratings actually climbed throughout the two-and-a-half-hour broadcast, reaching a peak during the final fifteen minutes for the firing-squad scene.

The Storyteller (NBC, 1977) was an introspective dramatic essay on the issue of TV violence, which had been a concern for Levinson and Link since their own experience with *Mannix*. They wrote and produced this film in the self-conscious fashion that has become the outstanding identifiable characteristic of their work. The plot was inspired by several recent courtroom trials that had been prominent in the news. In one such case, a mother charged that the rape of her daughter was caused by the attackers' viewing of the TV movie *Born Innocent* (NBC, 1974). In another case, a murderer had used the psychological defense that he was motivated to kill by continual viewing of *Kojak* (CBS, 1973–78).

Levinson and Link's tale concerned a TV writer who accuses himself of responsibility for the death of a young boy. The writer has recently scripted a highly successful telefilm about arson, and there is evidence that the boy had been attempting a "copycat" crime at his school when he was consumed by the fire. *The Storyteller* provided an

articulate dramatic debate about the effects of television and about
the accountability of its creators while at the same time begging its
own question: among the millions of viewers watching the film, might
not an aberrant child out there somewhere be taking it as a cue to
copy the crime?

The Arab-Israeli conflict did not escape examination by Levinson
and Link. In *Terrorist on Trial: The United States of America v. Salim
Ajami* (CBS, 1988), they give us the story of an Arab (Robert Davi)
who kills five Americans, is captured in Europe, and then extradited
to the United States to stand trial. Basically a courtroom drama, the
film featured Sam Waterston as the prosecutor and Ron Leibman as
the defense attorney. Taking great pains to present two sides to the
story, Levinson and Link predictably managed to offend both Arab-
American and Jewish-American viewers. Much of the film's emotional
focus concerned the agony of the Jewish defense attorney, torn between his personal feelings and professional ethics. Levinson and Link
even employed, as special consultant to the project, Harvard Law
School professor Alan Dershowitz, an avowed Zionist who has repeatedly stated that he would defend a terrorist of any stripe if called
upon.

On March 12, 1987, during the filming of *Terrorist on Trial*, Richard Levinson died of a heart attack. William Link had lost his lifelong
friend and collaborator. Link has since remained involved in a variety
of projects, but the most successful of these has been the revival of
Columbo (ABC, 1988–present), for which he allows the credit of
"supervising producer." In the spring of 1991, Link's semiautobio-
graphical made-for-TV movie about a writer and the death of his
partner, *The Boys,* aired on ABC.

RICHARD LEVINSON AND WILLIAM LINK: SELECTED VIDEOGRAPHY

Series

ITINERANT WRITING

Alfred Hitchcock Presents (CBS/NBC, 1955–65)
Richard Diamond, Private Detective (CBS/NBC, 1957–60)
Sugarfoot (ABC, 1957–61)
Westinghouse Desilu Playhouse (CBS, 1958–60)
Wanted: Dead or Alive (CBS, 1958–61)
77 Sunset Strip (ABC, 1958–64)
The Rebel (ABC, 1959–61)

Bourbon Street Beat (ABC, 1959–60)
Johnny Ringo (CBS, 1959–60)
Black Saddle (various, 1959–60)
The DuPont Show with June Allyson (CBS, 1959–61)
Hawaiian Eye (ABC, 1959–63)
The Third Man (syndicated, 1959–60)
The Westerner (NBC, 1960)
Michael Shayne (NBC, 1960–61)
Chevy Mystery Show (NBC, 1960–61)
Dr. Kildare (NBC, 1961–66)
Stoney Burke (ABC, 1962–63)
Burke's Law (ABC, 1963–65)
The Fugitive (ABC, 1963–67)
Slattery's People (CBS, 1964–65)
The Rogues (NBC, 1964–65)
The Man from U.N.C.L.E. (NBC, 1964–68)

CREATING, WRITING, AND/OR PRODUCING,
EXECUTIVE PRODUCING

Jericho (CBS, 1966–67)
Mannix (CBS, 1967–75)
The Name of the Game (NBC, 1968–71)
McCloud (NBC, 1970–77)
Columbo (NBC, 1971–77)
The Psychiatrist (NBC, 1971)
Tenafly (NBC, 1973–74)
The Adventures of Ellery Queen (NBC, 1975–76)
Stone (ABC, 1980)
Murder, She Wrote (CBS, 1984–present)
Blacke's Magic (NBC, 1986)
Hard Copy (CBS, 1987)

Movies Made for Television

Istanbul Express (NBC, 1968)
Prescription: Murder (NBC, 1968)
The Whole World Is Watching (NBC, 1969)
Run a Crooked Mile (NBC, 1969)
Trial Run (NBC, 1969)
My Sweet Charlie (NBC, 1970)
Sam Hill: Who Killed the Mysterious Mr. Foster? (NBC, 1971)
Two on a Bench (ABC, 1971)

That Certain Summer (ABC, 1972)
Partners in Crime (NBC, 1973)
Tenafly (NBC, 1973)
Savage (NBC, 1973)
The Gun (ABC, 1974)
The Execution of Private Slovik (NBC, 1974)
Ellery Queen: Too Many Suspects (NBC, 1975)
A Cry for Help (ABC, 1975)
The Storyteller (NBC, 1977)
Charlie Cobb: Nice Night for a Hanging (NBC, 1977)
Murder by Natural Causes (CBS, 1979)
Crisis at Central High (CBS, 1981)
Take Your Best Shot (CBS, 1982)
Rehearsal for Murder (CBS, 1982)
Prototype (CBS, 1983)
The Guardian (HBO, 1984)
Guilty Conscience (CBS, 1985)
Vanishing Act (CBS, 1986)
Terrorist on Trial (CBS, 1988)

18. LEE RICH

Blood, Soap, and Dirty Laundry

Lee Rich differs from most of the producers discussed in this book in that he does not fit the usual mold of the "hyphenate" television-maker. Though he has served as executive producer — in effect, the boss — on scores of weekly series and made-for-television movie projects, he has never taken additional credits as creator, director, or writer for any of these. He is, rather, a supreme packager, a deal-maker, a bringer together of creative teams. Given the enormous complications of making TV deals, this is no small achievement. While certain thematic motifs do emerge from Rich's massive portfolio — the crucial role of the family in American life is chief among them — his work is probably more recognizable for the consistency of its production quality than anything else.

Born in Cleveland and educated at Ohio University in Athens, Rich moved to New York in the 1950s to begin a career in advertising. While still in his twenties he would attain a vice presidency in the TV department at Benton and Bowles, a Madison Avenue agency that was rapidly proving itself a spawning ground for many of the young executives who would come to dominate all aspects of the burgeoning television industry. In 1965, after a decade with the firm, he left Benton and Bowles to form his own production partnership, Mirisch-Rich

Television. The company made several sales to the networks in the mid-to-late sixties, including prime-time series such as *Rat Patrol* and *Hey Landlord,* and Saturday-morning cartoon shows such as *Super Six* and *Super President and Spy Shadow.* Not particularly happy with these results, he returned briefly to the advertising industry. But in 1969 Rich hooked up with another partner, Merv Adelson, to form a new company, Lorimar Productions. It would become one of the most successful production units in broadcasting history, placing at least one program among the top eleven ratings finishers every year for fifteen seasons in a row.

The Waltons (CBS, 1972–81) was the rocket that got Lorimar off the ground. Lee Rich's role in the making of *The Waltons* provided a model for his career as an executive producer. His function was more akin to that of an impresario than a hands-on auteur. Earl Hamner, Jr., created the series, which he had based on his autobiographical novel about an Appalachian upbringing in a large family in Schuyler, Virginia. Rich was high on the idea and he gave Hamner the creative space to work on it. Hamner wrote the pilot, which was a 1971 two-hour made-for-TV movie titled *The Homecoming: A Christmas Story.* Hamner even served as the unseen narrator in the film, the "inner voice" of the story's persona, John-Boy Walton (Richard Thomas).

During the early seventies, prime-time TV programming was experiencing the full force of the "relevance" wave that had been inspired by the daily-news programming of the sixties. Action-adventure hours were dominated by violent cops-and-robbers stories of the inner city (e.g. Aaron Spelling's *The Rookies,* Cy Chermak's *Ironside*), while sitcoms were wandering away from traditional suburban nuclear-family pastoralism to postsixties irony (e.g. *The Mary Tyler Moore Show, M*A*S*H*). In *The Waltons,* Rich saw a chance to rehabilitate family sentimentalism for prime time by synthesizing a new genre. *The Waltons* resurrected good old-fashioned family warmth by repackaging it for the post–*Leave It to Beaver* generation.

Plagued by the economic catastrophes of the Great Depression, the multigenerational inhabitants of Walton's Mountain cling together and transcend their material poverty with the riches of mutual love and respect. More insistently realistic than *The Beverly Hillbillies* or *The Andy Griffith Show,* but less socially conscious than an episode of *S.W.A.T.* featuring international terrorism, *The Waltons* satisfied a yearning for a vision of family that fans of Archie Bunker or Hawkeye Pierce had perhaps already given up on. Can the family afford a fine turkey this Christmas? Can John-Boy be spared from family chores to go off to college to take up the writing trade? "Didn't need no welfare state / Everybody pulled his weight . . ." *The Waltons* was truly America's "all in the family" legend, even if Norman Lear (see Chapter 4) had sarcastically purloined the title.

Perhaps because it stood alone in prime time for its lack of neurotic shrieking or gratuitous killing, *The Waltons* won the Emmy as outstanding continuing drama of 1973. In terms of popularity, it beat the popular *Flip Wilson Show* in its time period during the premiere season and finished nineteenth overall in the prime-time ratings. In 1973–74 it rose to Number Two — right behind *All in the Family*. While Lear's boisterous, outspoken sitcom sparked a national debate, no one dared raise a critical voice against John-Boy and company. Rich had struck an American gusher in *The Waltons* that was more valuable than oil: an unimpeachable slice of apple pie.

Understandably, *The Waltons* begat many offspring at Lorimar. The saga of the large, extended family, featuring an assortment of ongoing multi-episode substories, became a trademark of shows listing Lee Rich as executive producer. At the height of *The Waltons'* success in 1974, Rich and Hamner teamed again for *Apple's Way*. Once again the result was a serious-minded reexamination of what had been a topic of sitcom burlesque in the sixties. George Apple (Ronny Cox) is a Los Angeles architect who gives up life in the big city to return to his ancestral home in Appleton, Iowa: *Green Acres* without the Paul Henning (see Chapter 2) grain of salt. As in *The Waltons*, the patriarch is surrounded by his large, multigenerational family. The focus is on the kind of community that can only emerge from the love of the land growing in harmony with the love of each other. George Apple spends an episode sitting in the branches of a tree, protesting against its being chopped down.

Lacking the righteousness of *Apple's Way*, *Eight Is Enough* (ABC, 1977–81) was more successful commercially. Like *The Waltons*, this show was an adaptation of the autobiographical memoir of one of its members, in this case Washington newspaper columnist Tom Braden, the guy who in so-called real life used to play The Liberal on *Crossfire* (CNN, 1985–present). The family name was changed to Bradford; the setting was moved to Sacramento to tone down the political stuff from federal to state government; and when the actress who played Mrs. Bradford, Diana Hyland, died with only five episodes in the can, Tom (Dick Van Patten) became a single-parent widower.

In a sense in *Eight Is Enough* we find *The Waltons* some forty years after the Great Depression: a happy, well-adjusted suburban California family whose teenage children have the luxury of being more worried about finding dates than finding dinner. Tragedy, of course, can still strike, and often does. Mom dies. Eldest son David (Grant Goodeve) legally separates from his wife. Tommy (Willie Aames) gets a pimple. But Dad enters the Sacramento singles scene and finds Abby (Betty Buckley), whom he eventually marries. Daughter Susan (Susan Richardson) marries a baseball player and has a baby. Tommy discovers a good dermatologist. *Eight Is Enough*, with its contemporary setting and its muted but audible laughtrack, is a leap in the direction of situation comedy from the docudramatic pathos of *The Waltons*. The hour-long program did quite well in the ratings, spending four seasons among the top twenty-five programs.

The next major step for Lee Rich, for Lorimar, and, as it turned out, for American television was *Dallas* (CBS, 1978–91). While *Dallas* may appear to be a radical departure from Rich's three previous programs, the theme of strength through family emerges more powerfully stated than ever. Set midway between the Appalachian schmaltz of *The Waltons* and the West Coast station-wagonism of *Eight Is Enough*, *Dallas* brought the TV family into the age of arbitrage, leveraged buyouts, and ruthless multinational economics. The Ewings, like the Waltons and the Bradfords, have their disagreements, but all live together under the same roof and stand together in times of crisis.

Dallas established the continuing drama or "soap opera" (which had since the radio era been considered a daytime programming format) as a viable genre for prime-time television. While *The Waltons* and *Eight Is Enough* presented evolving families experiencing major transformations over the seasons, each of the episodes of these shows was essentially a self-contained unit insofar as the major crisis introduced at the top of the hour was brought to narrative climax by the end of the hour. The storylines of *Dallas*, however, extended across the traditional lines of the weekly episode. Multiple storylines branched out in every direction, with little regard for the episodic climax that had been a basic orthodoxy of American prime-time broadcasting. The season's end cliff-hanger became a prominent feature of the show. When J. R. Ewing (Larry Hagman) was shot at the end of the 1979–80 season, buttons, bumper stickers, and bookies all over the country that summer were suddenly asking, "Who shot J.R.?" The episode that revealed the identity of the would-be assassin that autumn was the most anticipated single episode of a TV series since Lucy gave birth to Little Ricky in 1953, earning an 80 percent share of the viewing audience during its Friday-night time period. It would be the most watched TV series episode in history until the final installment of *M*A*S*H* in 1983.

Dallas changed the warp and woof of prime-time drama. Similarly formatted shows ranging from Steven Bochco's *Hill Street Blues* (NBC, 1980–88) to Aaron Spelling's *Dynasty* (ABC, 1981–90) appeared on the other networks and constituted a new staple of prime-time programming. *Knots Landing* (CBS, 1979–present) was a direct spin-off of *Dallas*. It meant another big hit for Lee Rich and Lorimar. This series transplanted Gary Ewing, the youngest brother of J.R. and Bobby, from Southfork to a housing tract cul-de-sac in a Southern California suburb. The only one of Jock Ewing's sons to eschew the life of a wheeling, dealing tycoon, Gary (Ted Shackleford) chooses to leave East Texas along with his wife Val (Joan Van Ark) to escape the rat-race pressures of the Ewing Oil empire. Less mythic than the tale that spawned it, *Knots Landing* found the mellowest of the Ewing brothers selling cars at a local dealership. The show was slow to catch on, but it finally cracked the Top Twenty in its fourth season. It also began to receive a critical respect that had eluded most other nighttime soaps, as it developed a focus on human relationships rather than on the fantastic economic and political intrigues that set the narrative contexts for such shows as *Dallas* and *Dynasty*.

Falcon Crest (CBS, 1981–90) made for a third Lorimar soap opera mega-hit. The show was specifically designed by Lee Rich for the *Dallas* audience. Rich demanded that CBS place the show in the time slot immediately following *Dallas*. The network agreed to this, and the two shows dominated the Friday evening nine-to-eleven-o'clock hours for most of the eighties. Earl Hamner, Jr., who had done *The Waltons* for Rich, coproduced *Falcon Crest*, proving that the creator of John-Boy and Grandpa was ready to bring the American family saga to the down-and-dirty, greed-ridden, amoral eighties. Oil turned to wine in *Falcon Crest* as the locale shifted from the East Texas oilfields to the fictional Tuscany Valley (i.e. Napa Valley) grape country of Northern California. The Channing family was under the iron rule of its matriarch Angela (Jane Wyman), whose ruthlessness arguably surpassed that of J. R. Ewing himself.

Rich also tried several nighttime soap projects that weren't quite so successful as these. *The Secrets of Midland Heights* (CBS, 1980–81) took place in a Midwestern college town. When the show failed after only several months, its star Lorenzo Lamas was shipped over to *Falcon Crest*, where he achieved major success as a TV heartthrob in the role of Angela's son Lance. Three other *Midland Heights* players were moved to yet another new Lorimar soap, *King's Crossing* (ABC, 1982). This series, aimed at younger viewers, focused on two teenage girls whose parents move them back to the small California town of their birth after ten years in Chicago. *Flamingo Road* (NBC, 1981–82) was only slightly more successful. Based on the 1949 film starring Joan Crawford and Sydney Greenstreet, which in turn was adapted from a novel by Robert Wilder, *Flamingo Road* took place amid the political, economic, and moral corruptions of a small town in South Florida.

Rich did not restrict his prime-time work to soap operas. He also introduced more than his share of traditionally formatted series. In *Doc Elliot* (ABC, 1974), yet another urban professional forsakes the city for the country. James Franciscus plays a New York doctor who sets up practice in rural Colorado as a kind of four-wheel-drive Marcus Welby. *The Blue Knight* (CBS, 1975–76), based on a character created by Joseph Wambaugh, starred George Kennedy as an aging inner-city beat cop. (Rich was already at this time working on an adaptation of Wambaugh's novel *The Choir Boys*, which would be released to theaters a year later.) *Hunter* (CBS, 1977; not to be confused with the later series starring Fred Dryer) was a spy thriller starring Franciscus and pre-*Dynasty* Linda Evans as secret agents. *The Waverly Wonders* (NBC, 1978), one of Lorimar's only sitcoms, featured Joe Namath incompetently playing an incompetent high school history teacher who incompetently coaches the incompetent school basketball team in a small Wisconsin town. *The Young Pioneers* (ABC, 1978) was not about members of a Communist youth organization but was, rather, a Western, an Earl Hamner story of two just-married teenagers who settle in the Dakota Territory after the Civil War.

The list of unremembered Lee Rich series throughout the 1970s is actually quite long: *Kaz*, starring Ron Leibman as an ex-cop and ex-con turned lawyer; *Big Shamus, Little Shamus*, starring Brian Dennehy as a house detective at an Atlantic City casino trying to bring up a teenaged son; *Studs Lonigan*, a series based on James T. Farrell's novel about an Irish-American family in Chicago during the Roaring Twenties. In sharp contrast to the decade-long runs of the soap operatic family sagas — *The Waltons, Dallas*, and *Knots Landing* — none of these non–soap operas managed to last longer than a single season on network TV.

Rich did somewhat better as the executive producer of a formidable body of made-for-TV movies and miniseries. He employed several of his favorite writers on these projects, including Earl Hamner, and it is again difficult to isolate Rich's creative input from that of his collaborators. Quick on the heels of *The Waltons'* success, an urban/ black version of the rural/white tale was coproduced by Rich and Hamner as a two-hour pilot for a possible series. *A Dream for Christmas* (ABC, 1973) featured an all-black cast in a story about a preacher in a poor neighborhood of Los Angeles whose church is about to meet the wrecking ball. It was not, however, as successful as the *Waltons* Christmas movie pilot, and Rich never got the go-ahead for series production.

In the midseventies Rich turned his attentions to the horror story, which was experiencing a box-office revival on theater screens following the successes of such films as *Rosemary's Baby* and *The Exorcist*. *Don't Be Afraid of the Dark* (ABC, 1973) is the story of a demonic creature inhabiting an old mansion. In *Bad Ronald* (ABC, 1974) the demon inhabiting the house takes the more recognizable form of a teenaged murderer. *The Stranger Within* (ABC, 1974) is a kind of *Rosemary's Baby* knockoff, with the unholy, unborn fetus controlling the activities of the host/mother. By the time we get to *Conspiracy of Terror* (NBC, 1975), satanism has infiltrated an entire middle-class suburb, à la *The Stepford Wives*.

Of course any producer of soap operas is no stranger to characters struggling with medical (including mental) problems, and this type of generic pathos was understandably a favorite source of grist for Lorimar's telefilm mill. *Eric* (NBC, 1975) docudramatizes the story of a boy with cancer. *A Matter of Life and Death* (CBS, 1981) follows a nurse dealing with terminally ill patients; it also has the distinction of being perhaps the only movie adaptation ever made of a *60 Minutes* segment. *Long Journey Back* (ABC, 1978) concerns the recuperation of a young girl who has suffered multiple handicaps in a bus accident. *Some Kind of Miracle* (CBS, 1979) features a newspaper reporter who is paralyzed for life in a surfing mishap. *A Perfect Match* (CBS, 1980) synthesizes a pair of misery-of-the-week genres: a woman who gave up her child for adoption learns that the child is the only one who can supply her with a lifesaving bone-marrow transplant. Probably the best remembered of Rich's disease opuses was the award-winning *Sybil* (NBC, 1976), a docudrama starring Sally Field as a woman with sixteen personalities; Joanne Woodward costarred as the shrink.

Spouse death was another favorite Lorimar theme. While most TV widows had been wacky sitcom moms who went out on dates and spent little time mourning their dear departeds, Lorimar focused on the more tragic angles of the situation in *Do Not Fold, Spindle, or Mutilate* (ABC, 1971); *The Crooked Hearts* (ABC, 1972); and *Widow* (NBC, 1976). Abandoned unwed mothers, practically a subgenre unto themselves, were the subject of *The Girls of Huntington House* (ABC, 1973). Most of these sudsy tearjerkers were generally more in the realm of tabloid exploitations than muckraking exposés. But Rich did manage to stir up his share of controversy with *Helter Skelter* (CBS, 1976), a five-part miniseries on the rise and fall of the Manson family, with specific and graphic attention paid to the sensational Tate-LaBianca murders.

Lee Rich served as president of Lorimar Productions from 1969 through 1986. Having built a portfolio rife with disease, family strife, and personal tragedy, Rich may be a symbol to some of what went wrong with television drama after the disappearance of the live golden-age anthology dramas of the fifties. The viewer of the Lorimar program is, generally speaking, seduced into strong personal identification by a sequence of quick and slick emotional manipulations, only to be dragged through the muck of pathos and, once exhausted, left with little or nothing in the way of spiritual catharsis or even satisfying insight.

Others may see in Rich's work a focusing of the public spotlight on the troubling issues that affect most people sometime during the course of their lives. From that angle Rich may have offered millions of atomized viewers some sense of belonging or of a sharing of burden in his yarns. In any case, while winning the disdain of soap-bashers, the man behind *Dallas* and *Falcon Crest* also won an assortment of prestigious honors, including an Emmy, a Peabody, two Christopher medals and four Humanitas awards.

In most arts, breakthroughs in form are valued over breakthroughs in content. This is usually not the case, however, in commercial TV, and Lee Rich's reputation is a case in point. In terms of the historical development of television narrative, the ratings successes of Rich's prime-time "continuing drama" soap operas were absolutely essential in paving the way for others to get the chance to work in that form. Some of television's most critically acclaimed dramas, including Steven Bochco's *L.A. Law* (see Chapter 20) and Bruce Paltrow's *St. Elsewhere,* were built on the narrative model created, developed, and proved by Lee Rich at Lorimar. While Bochco and Paltrow were the recipients of much-deserved critical praise for the intelligence and grace they brought to the form, Lee Rich, the form giver, is likely to remain a name associated with the easy buck.

In 1986 Rich left Lorimar, which was later sold to Warner Communications, to become chair and CEO of MGM/United Artists.

LEE RICH: SELECTED VIDEOGRAPHY

Series (Executive Producer)

Rat Patrol (ABC, 1966–68)
Hey Landlord (NBC, 1966–67)
Super Six (NBC, 1966–69)
Super President and Spy Shadow (NBC, 1967–69)
The Good Life (NBC, 1971–72)
The Waltons (CBS, 1972–81; movie specials through 1982)
Doc Elliot (ABC, 1974)
Apple's Way (CBS, 1974–75)
The Blue Knight (CBS, 1975–76)
Hunter (CBS, 1977)
Eight Is Enough (ABC, 1977–81)
The Waverly Wonders (NBC, 1978)
The Young Pioneers (ABC, 1978)
Kaz (CBS, 1978–79)
Dallas (CBS, 1978–91)
Knots Landing (CBS, 1979–present)
Studs Lonigan (NBC, 1979)
Big Shamus, Little Shamus (CBS, 1979)
The Secrets of Midland Heights (CBS, 1980–81)
Skag (NBC, 1980)
Flamingo Road (NBC, 1981–82)
Falcon Crest (CBS, 1981–90)
King's Crossing (ABC, 1982)

Movies Made for Television and Miniseries (Executive Producer)

Do Not Fold, Spindle, or Mutilate (ABC, 1971)
Pursuit (ABC, 1972)
The Crooked Hearts (ABC, 1972)
Don't Be Afraid of the Dark (ABC, 1973)
A Dream for Christmas (ABC, 1973)
Dying Room Only (ABC, 1973)
The Girls of Huntington House (ABC, 1973)
The Stranger Within (ABC, 1974)
Bad Ronald (ABC, 1974)
Returning Home (ABC, 1975)
The Runaway Barge (NBC, 1975)
The Runaways (CBS, 1975)

Conspiracy of Terror (NBC, 1975)
Eric (NBC, 1975)
Helter Skelter (CBS, 1976)
Sybil (NBC, 1976)
Widow (NBC, 1976)
Killer on Board (NBC, 1977)
Green Eyes (ABC, 1977)
Desperate Women (ABC, 1978)
A Question of Guilt (CBS, 1978)
Long Journey Back (ABC, 1978)
A Man Called Intrepid (NBC, 1979)
Young Love, First Love (CBS, 1979)
Some Kind of Miracle (CBS, 1979)
Mr. Horn (CBS, 1979)
Mary and Joseph: A Story of Faith (NBC, 1979)
Reward (ABC, 1980)
A Perfect Match (CBS, 1980)
Marriage Is Alive and Well (NBC, 1980)
Killjoy (CBS, 1981)
A Matter of Life and Death (CBS, 1981)
Our Family Business (ABC, 1981)
This Is Kate Bennett . . . (ABC, 1982)
Two of a Kind (CBS, 1982)
One Cooks, the Other Doesn't (CBS, 1983)

19. STEPHEN J. CANNELL

_____ _____ _____ _____ _____ _____ _____ _____

Action/Adventure Mogul

In the 1980s Stephen J. Cannell defined the state of the art of the prime-time action/adventure hour. No one was more prolific as a series creator (both individually and collaboratively), or as a writer, producer, executive producer, or even as a studio head. As if all these roles in the production process were not enough, he has publicly stated that he would one day like to own a string of television stations. It is conceivable that before the end of the century Cannell may be able to singlehandedly shepherd a program concept from the whimsy of his own imagination all the way to the living room of the viewer — without having to suffer anyone's editing but his own. Should he accomplish such a masterpiece of the art of the deal, he will have brought about an unprecedented opportunity to demonstrate the possibilities of commercial television as a means of personal expression.

Whatever additional accomplishments the future may bring, it is safe to say that Cannell has already secured his place in American broadcasting history as a maestro of the TV crime series. Jack Webb had set the tone and style of such programming during the fifties with his white, middle-aged, no-nonsense crimestoppers. In the late sixties and early seventies, Aaron Spelling refined the genre by integrating the video police force racially, sexually, and generationally. By the late seventies there could be no doubt that the torch had been passed to Cannell. From *The Rockford Files* (NBC, 1974–80) to *The A-Team* (NBC, 1983–87) to *Wiseguy* (CBS, 1987–90), Cannell's extensive work came to thoroughly dominate the aesthetics of action/adventure television.

Stephen J. Cannell is a member of a rare Hollywood breed known as Southern California natives. Born in Pasadena in 1941 to a well-to-do family prominent in the furniture business, he struggled through his schooling with a severe case of dyslexia: reading words backward, writing words backward, unable to spell with anything approaching normal aptitude. There was little to suggest that he would one day become a competent, much less a wildly successful, professional writer. It was only with great difficulty and with the support of an affluent and understanding family that he managed to complete a bachelor's degree at the University of Oregon in Eugene.

Out of college, he spent the next four years working in the family's furniture business. Uninspired by the day-to-day administration of his father's ottoman empire, however, Cannell gave his nights to working on television scripts. In 1968 he managed to peddle one of them to *It Takes a Thief*. Still in his twenties, he was hired as a writer and story editor by Universal Television.

Throughout the sixties and seventies Universal was the quintessential video assemblyline factory, grinding out a staggering quantity of critically undistinguished — and sometimes indistinguishable — programming. Formed in 1964 from the old Revue studio, which had been MCA's production arm during the early years of television, Universal quickly became a leading supplier of programs to all three networks. In fairness, the company should be credited with several formal innovations during the late sixties; it pioneered such packaging devices as the made-for-TV movie, the rotating "umbrella" series (see Chapter 17, on Levinson and Link), and the miniseries. But on the whole, Universal earned a reputation for epitomizing everything that critics tend to assail the medium for: quantity over quality, speed of execution over attention to detail and, of course, bottom-line profits *über alles*.

For Cannell, as for so many televisionmakers of his generation, the frantic Universal assemblyline proved to be an invaluable site for on-the-job training. The studio held orders for so much material that young, inexperienced rookies were frequently given chances to direct or produce episodes or entire series years before they might have earned such chances elsewhere. Cannell quickly graduated from apprentice to journeyman, traversing the Universal lot, pen in hand, writing episodes during the late sixties and early seventies for such series as *Adam 12, Ironside, Columbo, The D.A., Madigan, Jigsaw,* and *Escape.*

His steady productivity on the lot was soon recognized by management, and Cannell won the chance to produce his own program concepts at Universal before reaching the age of forty. He created (or cocreated) no less than eight series for the studio: *Chase; The Rockford Files; Baretta; City of Angels; Baa Baa Black Sheep; Richie Brockelman, Private Eye; The Duke;* and *Stone.* In these Universal action shows, Cannell established the insistences of a signature style that he would continue to develop throughout his career: macho male camaraderie among rightminded heroes too profoundly individualistic to be establishment figures, high-speed chases (by land, air, or sea), mountains of twisted metal, and the triumph of Good (though not necessarily the Establishment) over Evil.

Cannell's many collaborations during this period brought him into contact with the acknowledged masters of the TV crimeshow. *Chase* (NBC, 1973–74), for example, was coproduced by Universal and by Jack Webb's Mark VII Productions. Cannell wrote the pilot and Webb (see Chapter 12) directed. The series starred Mitchell Ryan as Chase Reddick, a police captain who presided over four young undercover cops who comprised a special unit that took cases nobody else wanted or could handle. The series, though unsuccessful, provides a missing link between Aaron Spelling's *Mod Squad* (ABC, 1968–73), the first prime-time series based on the co-option of youthful nonconformists into the struggle against crime, and Cannell's own future hit, *21 Jump Street* (Fox/syndication, 1988–present). Prototypical elements of *The A-Team* can also be found in *Chase.* The members of Reddick's group were all macho action specialists: a Vietnam helicopter pilot, a race-car driver, a motorcycle champion, and an attack-dog trainer.

After the quick demise of *Chase,* Cannell left the shop of one TV action/adventure pioneer to work at the bench of another, Roy Huggins (see Chapter 13). Huggins became Cannell's mentor during the early seventies. Their first project together was *Toma.* Loosely based on the real-life experiences of Newark undercover detective David Toma, the series starred Tony Musante as a Serpico-like master of disguises whose unorthodox but effective police methods tend to upset the bureaucratic brass. By no means a spectacular hit, *Toma* performed well enough for ABC against such tough competition as *The Waltons* and *The Flip Wilson Show* so that the network chose to renew. Musante, however, unhappy with the hamster wheel of weekly TV production, simply upped and quit. At first the plan was to recast the part and call the program *Toma Starring Robert Blake*. But Blake was uncomfortable with the idea of stepping in to fill a role that had been cast off by another actor. So Cannell was given the job of creating a new character and series out of the ashes of the old; the result was *Baretta*.

Tony Baretta, like David Toma, was an urban detective of Italian descent, unorthodox in approach, wary of authority, a master of disguises and dialects, and decidedly more at ease and more effective when working alone. Unlike Toma, however, Baretta had neither wife nor children nor white-picket-fence home in New Jersey but, instead, lived alone in a seedy downtown Los Angeles boarding house. The switch in locales was particularly significant for Cannell. The Southern California boy delighted in animating his story-telling with regional detail: place-names, dialect, and all kinds of local color. This would become an even more salient feature of Cannell's next project with Huggins: *The Rockford Files*. Huggins, collaborating with Cannell and Meta Rosenberg, had based the *Rockford* concept on a previous hit, the Western series *Maverick* (ABC, 1957–62), hoping for a contemporary urban variation on the old Western.

In production, *Rockford* became Cannell's show. Its success afforded him the chance to fully develop his personal, idiosyncratic style. Cruising around Los Angeles in an energy-crisis-unrepentant, fading gold Pontiac Firebird, Jim Rockford is a modern-day Sam Spade, a reluctant mercenary in the war against crime who practices the grim trade of fighting evil because it just happens to be the only thing he's any good at. Armed with a portable printing press and a set of blank business cards in his glovebox, Jim knows that in a hypocritical society obsessed wtih image — and oblivious to substance — he can create whatever instant credentials are necessary to go walking through otherwise closed doors. When that doesn't work, he's ready to pick the lock. Neither a right-wing ideologue (à la Webb's Joe Friday) nor a bleeding-heart do-gooder (à la Spelling's rookie Patrolman Willie Gillis), Rockford is arguably the first detective to arrive in prime time schlepping something resembling existentialist baggage. The show was a bona fide success both critically and commercially. It won Cannell his first Emmy, and by the time the series left the air, he found himself running on the inside track.

In 1976 Cannell and Huggins launched their final collaborative effort, *City of Angels*. Loosely adapted from Roman Polanski's film *Chinatown* (1974), the program starred Wayne Rogers as a 1930s L.A. private investigator. Of all Cannell's detective shows, none was a more direct homage to his idol, Raymond Chandler. With its hardboiled dialogue and art deco L.A. settings, *City of Angels* was arguably Cannell's most aesthetically ambitious effort. The audience, however, failed to respond, and the series only lasted half a season. Cannell learned a bitter lesson about art and mass culture.

His next series, *Baa Baa Black Sheep* (NBC, 1976–78) was a World War II adventure concerning Gregg "Pappy" Boyington, the Marine flying ace who had written an autobiography of the same title. For the first time, Cannell found himself the undisputed boss of a project, serving as executive producer and chief writer. A mischievous carouser who was almost as effective at upsetting the Marine Corps brass with his off-duty antics as he was at shooting down Japanese Zeros, Pappy (Robert Conrad) was very much an archetypal Cannell hero. In fact Pappy's entire squadron (the "Black Sheep") was a collection of rowdy misfits whose only virtue was the wallop they packed in defeating the Japanese in spectacular dogfights over the Pacific.

Prefiguring *The A-Team*, *Baa Baa Black Sheep* was held together by the glue of macho male bonding. The show featured a dozen male regulars, all pilots and mechanics, one more raucous and uncontrollable than the next — and not a single woman could be found in the cast. Though ratings were poor, the show managed to be renewed largely owing to NBC's disastrous last-place finish that season. Returning for 1977–78 under the title *Black Sheep Squadron*, the revamped show featured a bevy of nurses listed in the credits as "Pappy's Lambs." It was scheduled, however, against Aaron Spelling's "T&A" classic *Charlie's Angels* and disappeared post haste.

Richie Brockelman, Private Eye (NBC, 1978) was a collaboration with Steven Bochco that was done two years before Bochco achieved fame as the creator and producer of *Hill Street Blues* at MTM. It starred Dennis Dugan as a novice L.A. private eye. At age twenty-three, the baby-faced Richie could pass for a high school student and often did so to work on youth-oriented cases. The show was first presented to the public on a special two-hour *Rockford Files* episode, but it never caught on. Cannell, however, would one day reprise the "baby-face detective" as the central premise of the *21 Jump Street* series.

Tenspeed and Brownshoe (ABC, 1980) was the first program to bear the independent studio imprimatur of Stephen J. Cannell Productions. Borrowing from the *Richie Brockelman* concept, the series concerned the mild-mannered, quixotic Lionel Whitney, nicknamed Brownshoe (Jeff Goldblum), whose love of hardboiled detective fiction leads him, against the wishes of his family, to become a private eye rather than a stockbroker. As if this self-reflexive autobiographical flourish by the producer/writer were not enough, the scripts contain generous references to Brownshoe's favorite novelist, none other than one Stephen J. Cannell. Brownshoe would even go so far as to offer "direct quotations" from "Cannell." His partner Tenspeed (Ben Vereen) is a Rockford figure, a streetwise ex-con who takes the job mainly to fulfill a parole agreement. Cannell had another ratings dud on his hands, however, and now found himself deeply in debt. The 1980–81 television season was the first in six years to open without a Cannell show in prime time, and the producer seemed to be reaching the end of his tether.

Letting go of his obsession with Los Angeles private eyes, Cannell's next venture was a radical departure from crimeshow verisimilitude. *The Greatest American Hero* (ABC, 1981–83) was another Stephen J. Cannell production and the first to bear the now familiar company logo that features Cannell pecking away at a typewriter that launches the written page out onto the video screen at the end of every episode. Borrowing an idea from the old *Green Lantern* comic-book series, Cannell created Ralph Hinkley (William Katt), a mild-mannered all-American boy who is visited by aliens one night and given a costume that endows its wearer with superhuman powers. Ralph's troubles begin when he misplaces the suit's instructions, forcing him to learn how to use it by trial and error. As if flying into brick walls and landing in swimming pools were not bad enough for the would-be superhero, he must contend with Bill Maxwell (Robert Culp), an uptight Watergate-era federal agent who becomes his sidekick.

Both *Tenspeed and Brownshoe* and *The Greatest American Hero* received industry accolades and varying degrees of critical acclaim, but neither was a hit — and a hit was what Cannell desperately needed. As the 1982–83 season opened, Stephen J. Cannell Productions, with a payroll of 450 employees, was flirting with financial disaster. The failure of its newest series, *The Quest* (ABC, 1982), put the operation even further in the hole. This international intrigue fantasy concerned four young Americans who must compete to take over a tiny principality somewhere in Europe when its hereditary ruler, their distant relative, dies. It came and went in less than a month. Cannell and his studio were teetering at the brink. The normal disparities between art and life would soon, however, vanish, as one and all were miraculously saved by none other than *The A-Team* (NBC, 1983–87).

The *A-Team* project began inauspiciously enough. In the midst of all his financial problems, Cannell found himself forced to fulfill an obligation that lingered on the books from his old Universal contract.

To that end he signed an agreement with MCA, Universal's distribution arm, to supply an action/adventure hour. The program that resulted was *The A-Team;* it went on to become one of the top-rated shows in television, finishing as high as Number Four in the national Nielsens. It was the loftiest commercial height that Cannell had hit thus far.

The genesis of the *A-Team* concept has become part of the lore of TV programming history. Brandon Tartikoff, the head of NBC Entertainment, had supposedly been impressed by the 1981 Australian film *The Road Warrior* and was said to be trolling for a series that would put its vigilante themes into play in a contemporary American setting. Cannell, who had previously mentioned the as yet unrealized *A-Team* idea to Tartikoff, received the following Zen memorandum from the NBC programming chief: *"The A-Team: Mission: Impossible, The Dirty Dozen* and *The Magnificent Seven,* all rolled into one and Mr. T drives the car."*

If *The Greatest American Hero* was an attempt to give Jimmy Carter's "malaise-ridden" post-Vietnam America a schleppy but well-meaning hero it could relate to, *The A-Team* was much more a bold Reagan-era plunge into historical fantasy. The premise of the series is succinctly stated by an unseen narrator at the opening of each episode: "Ten years ago a crack commando unit was sent to prison by a military court for a crime they didn't commit. These men promptly escaped from a maximum security military stockade to the Los Angeles underground. Today, still wanted by the government, they survive as soldiers of fortune. If you have a problem, if no one else can help, maybe you can hire . . . the A-Team."

Contemporaneously with Sylvester Stallone, Cannell helped initiate a historical revision of the Vietnam era that would become a central theme of American popular culture during the 1980s. The question of whether the waging of the war in the first place was right or wrong was dismissed as a moot point beneath the dignity of further discussion. Instead, exclusive focus was aimed at two tragic aspects of the war: 1) the corruption of the desk-jockey administrators who had handcuffed America's fighting men, and 2) the resulting wounds — both psychological and physical — that those men were subsequently forced to endure for the rest of their lives.

In the case of the A-Team, guilt for some shadowy, unexplained crime had been foisted on an innocent bunch of crack GI's whose only purpose had been to do the right thing. The government (or, as Reagan campaign rhetoric had termed it, "Big Government") had framed "our boys" for an atrocity, when it was the government itself that had committed the crime. After breaking out of the stockade, the Team members reveal themselves as the moral equivalent of post-Watergate Robin Hoods. Free from the constrictions of the "Establishment" Army, they establish themselves as a kind of private-enterprise free-lance army, available to save anyone who just might need their services in the free market of salvation.

Like Jim Rockford, the members of the A-Team were considered rascals by a rascal society. The bureaucrats who play by the book are exposed as spineless jellyfish, while the wild, unfettered nonconformists emerge as the dynamic force that gets things done and thus advances the cause of humanity. The symbolic appeal of this neo-cowboyism would soon become apparent enough in the news from Wall Street, from Main Street, and from executive suites around the world. As in Ayn Rand's *Atlas Shrugged* (1959) and Ivan Reitman's *Ghostbusters* (1984), we learn that it is only when talented people eschew hypocritical bleeding-heart institutions — and go into business for themselves — that their personal potentials, as well as the potential of society itself, can be realized.

Leading the team is Hannibal Smith (George Peppard), a master of disguises à la Toma or Baretta. Driving the customized van that serves as the Team's headquarters is B. A. Baracus (Mr. T). B. A., which officially stands for "Bad Attitude," is on the surface the biggest, meanest, most intimidating member of the group. But underneath all that gold jewelry we find an oh-so-human soul sensitive enough to share Erica Jong's fear of flying. Face Peck (Dirk Benedict) is the Rockford-like "good conman," the archetypal character who seems to dominate Cannell's imagination. Like The Professor in *Gilligan's Island,* he displays a genius for procuring trash that can be refashioned into high-tech appliances, in this case usually tactical or frontal-assault weapons. The team originally had a female member, but as in *Black Sheep Squadron,* this was only a kind of afterthought in the mythic locus of a Cannell male-bonding fantasy. Eventually the character was dropped without even so much as a plot explanation.

The success of *The A-Team* changed the way that Cannell made television. Abandoning the craftsmanlike personal approach that had characterized each project from *Rockford* to *The Greatest American Hero,* he sent his studio into assemblyline production. Cannell himself began to refer to the company's work as the "manufacturing" of television programs. By the mideighties he would be supplying the networks with as many as six prime-time series in a single season.

Hardcastle and McCormick (ABC, 1983–86) was of a political piece with *The A-Team.* Hardcastle (Brian Keith) is a judge who, throughout his career, has been forced to let criminal after criminal go free because of the corruption of a justice system that honors human rights "technicalities" over human horse sense. Now that he has retired, however, he is unshackled from those constraints and sets out, in free-lance Robin Hood style, to nail the perverse criminals that the "system" had forced him to let go. Along with his protégé McCormick (Daniel Hugh-Kelly), an ex-convict, he goes about the business of dispensing justice via the private sector — justice that he could not grant while hog-tied to the public bench.

These themes grew in intensity throughout the eighties: the three *Rambo* films (1982, 1985, 1988) and *The Equalizer* on TV, the Bernhard Goetz affair and the invasions of Grenada and Panama in the news. In fact, Stephen J. Cannell Productions linked itself directly to the Rambo phenomenon by securing the licensing rights to the merchandising operations inspired by the films, including action toys, chewing gum, lunch boxes, and so on. The financial rewards of the jingoist vigilante revival provided the capital for a string of new projects.

Riptide (1984–86) was added to NBC's Tuesday-night lineup in the slot directly following *The A-Team*. It cracked the Top Fifteen in its first season. The series featured three Vietnam veterans (Perry King, Joe Penny, and Thom Bray) living in and operating a detective agency out of a cabin cruiser moored in a Southern California harbor. If Rockford had lived in a beaten-up beachside mobile home, these eighties private detectives were managing to show a bit more yuppie class. Once again a group of capable American fighters — this time two romantic leading men and a computer nerd — must wait until they are free of government service to become noble entrepreneurs in the fight against evil.

Hunter (NBC, 1984–91) proved to be one of Cannell's longest-lasting if least-celebrated hits. Here Cannell deviates a bit from his new formula. Rick Hunter (Fred Dryer) is a cop, not a private eye. Perhaps more remarkable for a Cannell show, his partner is of all things a woman, Dee Dee McCall (Stephanie Kramer). In the style of Clint Eastwood's Dirty Harry (whom he resembles in both body and soul), Hunter is more than willing to break the rules to nab a perpetrator. One of his characteristic acts (introduced in a first-season episode written personally by Cannell) is to knock a suspect unconscious and then to suggest to his partner that the scum be read his rights before he wakes up. With more "free" cops like Rick Hunter, we might not need the A-Team. Or Judge Hardcastle could retire in peace.

In 1987 Cannell scored a coup by supplying the new Fox television network with its first genuine hit series: *21 Jump Street*. A kind of *Mod Squad* for the "just say no" generation, the show follows the exploits of a group of teen-idol cops who do their undercover work posing as high school students. Elevating the once stigmatized profession of "narc" to the status of the friend and protector of American youth, the *Jump Street* cops are both within and without the official police department. They constitute a kind of junior A-Team with badges who have dedicated themselves to keeping kids safe from parental abuse, drugs (not only crack and heroin, but steroids and marijuana as well), unsafe sexual practices, and the other threats that have made being an American teenager in the waning years of the twentieth century such a thoroughly dangerous and enervating experience. Fox was so pleased with *21 Jump Street* that the network bought a spin-off from Cannell, sight unseen. *Booker* (Fox, 1989–90) is an unambiguous Cannellian tale. The show's focus is a young cop who has left the police force and become an investigator for the Teshima Corporation.

In the midst of these successes, Cannell continued to crank out his share of failures as well: *Stingray* (NBC, 1986–87), *J. J. Starbuck* (NBC, 1987–88), and *Sonny Spoon* (NBC, 1988–89) were but three of a spate of private-eye losers in the late eighties. But in 1987 he introduced his most critically acclaimed series since *The Rockford Files: Wiseguy* (CBS, 1987–90). The obvious innovation of *Wiseguy* was Cannell's introduction of the "arc" structure to prime-time series television. This is a formatting hybrid that introduces elements of nighttime soap opera (e.g. *Dallas, Hill Street Blues*) into the content of the traditional action/adventure series. A *Wiseguy* story might extend for eight or ten weeks by making use of direct, episode-to-episode narrative continuity. This "arc" would then come to narrative climax. It would be followed by one or two self-contained episodes, usually concerning the hero's personal life, which in turn would be followed by another extended story, or arc. In a sense, Cannell had created a generic formula for presenting fresh miniseries concepts within secure continuing series structures.

For all its formal innovation, *Wiseguy* was very much "high Cannell" in its content. Vinnie Terranova (Ken Wahl), an Italian-American from the streets of Brooklyn, is an undercover agent for the federal Organized Crime Bureau, or OCB. He is sent to jail at the federal penitentiary in Newark, New Jersey, for a crime never committed (a variation on the Rockford etiology) in order to establish a credible identity in the criminal world to serve as his cover for the infiltration of underworld organizations. Though his immediate boss (Jonathan Banks) and his contact man, a wheelchair-bound Vietnam vet code named Uncle Mike (Jim Byrnes), are emphatically good guys, the brass at the OCB is, predictably, filled with corrupt bureaucrats who care little about the fates of the brave agents who put their lives on the line every day.

With its intelligent dialogue, its attempts at thick characterization, and its socially critical swipes at current events, *Wiseguy* is perhaps best understood as a high-IQ adaptation of *The A-Team* aimed at an upmarket audience. Given the shift in television's commercial emphasis from gross numbers to target demographics, *Wiseguy* might very well have been an augur of the future of TV crime. Like Steven Bochco's *Hill Street Blues* and Donald Bellisario's *Magnum, P.I.*, *Wiseguy* was a network television series capable of offering dramatic moments that were competitive with the theatrical releases offered as counterprogramming by HBO and Showtime.

Cannell has long passed mere auteur status in American television. He is a bona fide impresario well on his way to becoming a mogul. As the chair and CEO of the Cannell Studios, he sits atop Stephen J. Cannell Productions (program development, production, merchandising), North Shores Studios (a huge studio and office facility in nonunion Vancouver, British Columbia, where he does much of his shooting), Cannell Films of Canada (a Canadian TV production company), Image Point Productions (a studio that produces nationally aired television commercials), and Cinecal (a television production equipment rental outfit). In addition, he controls a television syndication company, Televentures, in partnership with Tri-Star Pictures. Cannell Communication, the newest arm of his video empire, is a company that has been formed to buy, own, and operate television stations. By cutting out one middleman after the next in an industry riddled with middlemen, he is, indeed, in a position to redefine the very concept of personal expression in the commercial television medium.

Though Cannell's career has been, by any standard, phenomenal, it also illustrates many of the ironies inherent in American TV production. He originally left the corporate behemoth of Universal to become an independent producer in order to gain artistic control over his own work. But television is expensive to produce, and to support the luxury of his independence he has had to take on more projects than he might have cared to. The more series that he placed on the air, the less attention — and therefore less control — he could assert. His escape from Universal ultimately resulted in his fashioning a corporate entity not unlike the one from which he had fled. While his name may now sit atop the company's letterhead — as well as atop its flashy office building on Hollywood Boulevard — Cannell is paradoxically no longer able to claim full artistic control over the production-line output of Stephen J. Cannell Productions.

STEPHEN J. CANNELL: SELECTED VIDEOGRAPHY

Itinerant Writing

Mission: Impossible (CBS, 1966–73)
Ironside (NBC, 1967–75)
It Takes a Thief (ABC, 1968–70)
Adam 12 (NBC, 1968–75)
Columbo (NBC, 1971–77)
The D.A. (NBC, 1971–72)
Madigan (NBC, 1972–73)
Jigsaw (ABC, 1972–73)
Escape (NBC, 1973)
Chase (NBC, 1973–74)

Staff Assignments at Universal (Creating/Writing/Producing)

Toma (ABC, 1973–74)
The Rockford Files (NBC, 1974–80)
Baretta (ABC, 1975–78)
City of Angels (NBC, 1976)
Baa Baa Black Sheep/Black Sheep Squadron (NBC, 1976–78)
Richie Brockelman, Private Eye (NBC, 1978)
The Duke (NBC, 1979)
Stone (ABC, 1980)

Series by Stephen J. Cannell Productions

Tenspeed and Brownshoe (ABC, 1980)
The Greatest American Hero (ABC, 1981–83)
The A-Team (NBC, 1983–87)
Hardcastle and McCormick (ABC, 1983–86)
The Rousters (NBC, 1983–84)
Riptide (NBC, 1984–86)
Hunter (NBC, 1984–91)
The Last Precinct (NBC, 1986)
Stingray (NBC, 1986–87)

J. J. Starbuck (NBC, 1987–88)
21 Jump Street (Fox/syndicated, 1987–present)
Werewolf (Fox, 1987–89)
Wiseguy (CBS, 1987–90)
Sonny Spoon (NBC, 1988–89)
UNSUB (NBC, 1989)
Booker (Fox, 1989–90)
Top of the Hill (CBS, 1989)
The Commish (ABC, 1991–present)
Palace Guard (CBS, 1991)
Scene of the Crime (CBS, 1991–present)
Silk Stalkings (CBS, 1991–present)

Movies Made for Television

Scott Free (NBC, 1976)
Dr. Scorpion (ABC, 1978)
The Jordan Chance (CBS, 1978)
The Night Rider (ABC, 1979)
Nightside (ABC, 1980)
Midnight Offerings (ABC, 1981)
Brothers in Law (ABC, 1985)

20. STEVEN BOCHCO

Yuppie Catharsis

For many well-educated, well-heeled Americans, Steven Bochco is the producer who made watching prime-time television a respectable activity during the 1980s. More a radical rehabilitator than a revolutionary, Bochco seized upon two of TV's most familiar bargain-basement dramatic formats — the cop show and the lawyer show — and refashioned them into a pair of designer originals: *Hill Street Blues* and *L.A. Law*. Bochco's success served as both artistic inspiration and commercial prototype for the exceptional leap forward in prime-time serial drama during the eighties that would include such programs as *St. Elsewhere, Moonlighting, thirtysomething,* and *The Wonder Years*.

It is perhaps apropos that a man credited with raising the standards of despised genres in a despised medium was himself raised on the spoils of the fine arts. The son of a concert violinist, Bochco took a degree in theater arts at Carnegie-Mellon University (then still known as Carnegie Tech) and quickly headed for Hollywood, where he found contract work at Universal in the mid-1960s. "Universal in those days . . . was sort of like a sausage factory," Bochco recalls. "They used every single part of the pig to make a product. Nothing got thrown out."

Indeed, the novice writer's first assignment was to add forty-five minutes of "filler" to a fifty-two-minute episode of *Bob Hope's Chrysler Theatre* to prepare the property for rerelease in Europe as a theatrical film. Thus Bochco's first screen credit came as cowriter to Rod Serling, the original author of the teleplay, though he had never so much as met his famous collaborator. Bochco went on to build a yeoman's résumé as a writer and producer at Universal during the course of the next decade. In 1968 he joined the writing staff of *The Name of the Game*. Set in the offices of "Crime Magazine," this umbrella vehicle featured alternating episodes about the publisher (Gene Barry), a crack investigative reporter (Tony Franciosa), and an editor (Robert Stack). Bochco wrote for the Robert Stack cycle.

Producers Richard Levinson and William Link (see Chapter 17) gave Bochco a significant break when they hired him as story editor and chief writer for *Columbo*, an alternating feature of another umbrella series, the *NBC Mystery Movie*. *Columbo*, as noted earlier, differed from most crimeshows on television in that it contained virtually no action sequences beyond the murder scene, which ritually occurred in the opening moments of the show. This lack of crashing cars and gunfire placed extraordinary responsibilities on the writer. Bochco honed his skill at sustaining dramatic interest with little more than verbal repartee, a talent that would come to full flower years later in *L.A. Law*. Humor, which had rarely if ever been an intentional feature of "classic" hardboiled TV copshows such as *Dragnet* or *Hawaii Five-O*, would emerge as a salient virtue of the Bochco style.

Though virtually unknown by the public, Bochco was all over prime time during the 1970s. He wrote multiple episodes for *McMillan and Wife*, which starred Rock Hudson as the millionaire police commissioner of San Francisco. Moving from Nob Hill to Beacon Hill, he continued to specialize in crimestyles of the rich and rational as associate producer of *Banacek*, which featured George Peppard as a chauffeur-driven Polish-American private eye who investigates phony annuity claims for Boston insurance companies.

Bochco's 1973 graduation from writer to producer was inauspicious. In *Griff* he caught Lorne Greene between *Bonanza* and the Alpo dogfood campaign as a retired LAPD cop who opens up shop as a private detective in Westwood. It was a ratings dud for ABC. Likewise, his next venture, *Delvecchio*, died on the vine at CBS. Despite *Delvecchio*'s failure, however, Bochco did manage to secure several important connections that would help point the way toward his later successes. Several members of the *Delvecchio* cast, including Charles Haid and Michael Conrad, impressed Bochco and would be called upon again to populate the ranks of *Hill Street Blues*. Perhaps most significant, he came into contact with Michael Kozoll, a Universal contract writer who had been assigned to the series. Kozoll would become his chief collaborator in the creation of *Hill Street Blues*.

Bochco's next — and last — project at Universal also had some bearing on his preparation for his coming breakthroughs. The studio teamed him with Stephen J. Cannell, then another of its rising stars, to do *Richie Brockelman, Private Eye*, a *Rockford Files* spin-off. Richie was young, gifted, and fresh out of college, an appropriate hero for the upscale demographic group that would become Bochco's most appreciative audience in the 1980s. The show won critical acclaim but not ratings. Though he had come up with his third flop in a row at the Universal "sausage factory," Bochco was moving toward his personal revision of prime-time formula drama: up-to-date sociopolitical remark set in a comedy of middle-class manners.

Having spent a dozen years with Universal, Bochco left the company in 1978 to go to work for MTM Enterprises. Though MTM was a new kid on the block of television production — the studio had only been formed in 1970 to produce *The Mary Tyler Moore Show* — it had gained a remarkable reputation for flexibility and quality under the leadership of Grant Tinker. For the first time in his career, Bochco was given the opportunity to work outside the formulaic confines of the Universal crimeshow. He wrote for *The White Shadow*, a socially conscious drama set at an inner-city high school. He cowrote *Vampire*, a movie-of-the-week adaptation of Bram Stoker's *Dracula* that aired on ABC. He collaborated with Bruce Paltrow and Mark Tinker on a pilot for a new medical series to be known as *Operating Room*. Though *Operating Room* never went into regular production, Paltrow and Tinker stuck with docshow work and eventually came up with *St. Elsewhere*.

Meanwhile, returning to his life of crime, Bochco gained full authorship status at MTM in 1979 as executive producer of *Paris*. This prestigious but ill-fated project starred James Earl Jones as an intellectual Los Angeles police captain who moonlights as a professor of criminology. There were elements of a dress rehearsal for *Hill Street Blues*: "*Paris* fed into what *Hill Street* finally became," Bochco points out, "because what I began to do on *Paris*, to an even greater degree than on *Delvecchio*, was to try to frame the thing in the context of a man's personal life." Comparing the James Earl Jones character to *Hill Street*'s Captain Frank Furillo, he added, "Woody Paris was a man with an enormous amount of responsibility and very little authority. He was a true kind of middle-management guy."

The story of the genesis of *Hill Street Blues* has been much written about in both the popular and academic presses. Fred Silverman, then president of NBC Entertainment, had seen the rushes to portions of *Fort Apache, The Bronx,* director Daniel Petrie's raw look at the lives of cops in a South Bronx police precinct. In January 1980 Silverman approached MTM and specifically asked if Bochco could deliver a cop series in the style of the Petrie film. Bochco, now bearing the onus of a spate of failures in the genre, had actually been working with Michael Kozoll on a series concept about the lives of the guests at a ritzy hotel (an idea that Aaron Spelling would realize several years later as *Hotel*).

Determined not to fail with another cops-and-robbers knockoff, Bochco made a set of celebrated demands concerning production autonomy and freedom from network censorship before agreeing to take on the assignment. Winning these assurances from a desperate NBC, which was languishing in last place in the ratings for the first time in the company's history, he came up with a show that broke the mold of the time-honored TV cop formula: multiple centers of audience identification; complicated personal lives; overlapping dialogue; hand-held camera shots; busy, crowded mise-en-scènes. Though some scholars have attributed certain of these innovations to the work of Robert Butler, who directed the *Hill Street Blues* pilot and several of its early episodes, Bochco takes personal credit for them, claiming that all these features were called for directly in the script that he and Michael Kozoll had written. According to Bochco, the two of them had been greatly influenced in creating the style for *Hill Street* not by the Hollywood feature film *Fort Apache,* which had so impressed Fred Silverman, but by a little-known, independently made documentary, *The Police Tapes,* directed by Alan and Susan Raymond, which presented candid scenes from the daily lives of South Bronx cops and was originally shown on public television.

Hill Street's ensemble cast was personally recruited by Bochco. Charles Haid (Officer Andy Renko) and Bruce Weitz (Detective Mick Belker) had both been among his college classmates. James B. Sikking (Lt. Howard Hunter) was an old friend of the family. Faye Furillo, the captain's ex-wife, was played by Bochco's wife, Barbara Bosson. Actors Kiel Martin, Michael Warren, Joe Spano, and Michael Conrad had all appeared in Bochco vehicles. Of the major roles, only the actors of the show's two biggest, Daniel J. Travanti and Veronica Hamel, had never worked with him previously.

In January 1981 *Hill Street Blues* premiered on NBC as a "second season" replacement. From the critics' point of view, it was the hottest thing to hit prime time since Norman Lear's Archie Bunker had first started hurling racial epithets around a sitcom living room a decade ago. Like *All in the Family* (also an "experimental" midseason replacement), *Hill Street* won immediate critical acclaim and a shelf full of Emmys. As was also the case with the Lear sitcom, *Hill Street* would need more time than was usually accorded a network series to build an acceptable Nielsen score.

The radically decentralized narrative structure that Bochco created for *Hill Street Blues*, while not nearly as tangled as a Robert Bresson film or an episode of *General Hospital*, confused some viewers and, in so doing, delighted others. The squadroom scene that opened each episode was shot with a bumpy, nervous, hand-held camera. It just didn't look like network TV. Nor did it preach like network TV. Criminals walked on technicalities; the battered innocent often remained unavenged. After thirty-five years of cops-and-robbers and more cops-and-robbers, here was a copshow that didn't seem to be in pursuit of commercial television's traditional aesthetic enemy number one: the lowest common denominator.

The show embodied, but transcended, its generic setting, emerging as more of a high-IQ *Dallas* than an upscale *Dragnet*. If the cold, calculating J. R. Ewing had made the dispossessed working classes of service-industry America swoon with admiration, the cool/calm/collected white-collar Frank Furillo could elicit a similar response from software technocrats, Wall Street whiz kids, and the other disposable-income types that flourished during the Reagan era. A reformed alcoholic, Catholic and divorced, Captain Furillo was celebrated as the first American popular culture hero of Italian descent who was neither a prizefighter nor a gangster. Though he has chosen the low-yield profession of law enforcement, Frank is a precinct boss from middle-manager heaven. More stable and resourceful than the blue-collar men and women under his charge, more ethical and decent than his arrogant autocratic boss, Chief Fletcher Daniels (Jon Cypher), Frank displays decisiveness and personal sensitivity in equal measures.

Joyce Davenport (Veronica Hamel), whose love for Furillo is matched only by her passion for Miranda, is an idealistic lawyer, the public defender. Her support for the Bill of Rights, eccentric in the Reagan era, is only slightly more steadfast than her capacity to understand, give succor, and heal her "Pizza Man" in a world full of hate and corruption. Together, the two became the Couple of the Decade for the computer-crunching, mineral-water swigging, earth-toned bourgeoisie.

Hill Street thrived on the mythic socio-economic baggage of a stationhouse full of off-center, stereotype-subversive characters. Officer Andy Renko was a rare character on network television: a feisty C&W man, neither mesomorphic nor racist, but a decent, humane redneck plucked from the depths of America's Scots-Irish soul. His sincere friendship with his suave, black, big-city partner, Bobby Hill (Michael Warren), was neither patronizing nor contrived. Joe Coffey (Ed Marinaro) and Lucy Bates (Betty Thomas) were similarly paired. Coffey, a familiarly macho working-class neighborhood ladies' man, learns the art of platonic intersexual friendship from his partner Lucy, a strong, competent, caring woman who will give her all for a comrade but who refuses to be manipulated into bed. Mick Belker was another character not seen too often in American popular culture: a tough Jewish undercover cop who seemed to relish a gritty physical battle with evil. Belker, a virtual wild man on the job, was alternately pictured biting criminals and being *hokked* to death by his mother on the telephone.

For all its formal and technical innovations, the series' greatest strength was its unprecedented ability to present the police as harried Everypersons driven to (and sometimes over) the brink of personal neurosis by the pressures of modern inner-city life. In this way the characters were infinitely more complex — and therefore, in the context of television drama, more realistic — than Joe Friday, Eliot Ness, Charlie's Angels, or any of the one-dimensional gangbusters who had dominated the genre. Since the earliest days of the medium, TV crimefighters had been the object of ridicule; takeoffs on *Dragnet* or *Highway Patrol* had been de rigueur for stand-up comedians in the fifties. Bochco had elevated a television copshow into the realm of seriously regarded drama.

In some ways the commercial triumph of *Hill Street Blues* was even more remarkable than its artistic achievement. Having finished eighty-ninth in the Nielsen ratings during its first half season, the series seemed a sure candidate for the network dumpster. But a combination of several extraordinary factors saved it. Despite its low initial ratings — only about nine million homes were tuning in each week for the original episodes — network market research revealed that *Hill Street*'s audience, though tiny by the yardstick of prime-time tradition, was composed of a striking percentage of "POMs" (an industry acronym for "professionals, operatives, and managers"). With cable beginning to make significant inroads into network audience share, the old industry rule of seeking the largest possible audience without regard to particulars was becoming archaic. Demographics would be the key to profitability in the cable era. While the old "mass audience" standards would have disqualified a show like *Hill Street* as being of "limited appeal" in a three-way market, in TV's new thirty-way market the networks were freed to seek "class audiences" that lent themselves to target advertising. *Hill Street Blues,* in both form and content, was a "high end" or "upscale" product, a copshow with an options package, just the kind of thing that was favored by that group of high spending baby-boomers who had recently been tagged with the name "yuppies." Indeed, Bochco's cop opera became a magnet for advertising dollars from purveyors of luxury items such as expensive cars and jewelry.

Perhaps no better case can be made for the power of producer authorship in American television than a consideration of the consequences suffered by *Hill Street Blues* after Steven Bochco departed from the show following differences with the MTM brass in 1985. The Dickensian quality of the series — a wide variety of colorful characters in perpetually evolving narrative intercourse — was lost overnight. In the final two seasons, under the joint regime of Jeffrey Milch and David Lewis, the series became listless. Andy Renko was reduced to a pathetic overweight nebbish who was most often pictured fretting over when he might get his next donut. Lieutenant Hunter, the head of the S.W.A.T. team, became enmeshed in a multiepisode affair with an anthropologist who leaves him for a Papua New Guinea tribal chief. Lucy Bates spends half a dozen episodes filing papers to become foster parent to a young black neighborhood kid whose junkie mother cannot care for him; but then, once in place for a new plotline, the child mysteriously disappears from the show. Without Bochco at the helm, the show seemed like a sloppy imitation of itself.

Back in 1983, while *Hill Street Blues* was riding the crest of its popular and critical wave, Bochco attempted to parlay his ascending prestige into a new series for MTM and NBC. In *Bay City Blues,* he borrowed the narrative form of *Hill Street* to follow the fortunes of a minor-league baseball team in a mythical working-class city. NBC was wary of the concept from the outset. Sports dramas had no track record to speak of on prime-time TV. A few seasons earlier, CBS had attempted *The Bad News Bears,* a baseball-oriented comedy adapted from a blockbuster film, but it had failed dismally. Perhaps more ominous, working-class images were in decline as the worship of Wall Street seized the American imagination during the mideighties. Bochco, while still active on the *Hill Street* set, persevered with the project and produced eight episodes of *Bay City Blues.* They were dense, allusion-laden, and meticulously written in the MTM style of *Hill Street* and *St. Elsewhere*. But only four ever aired.

In an unusual move, NBC attempted to find an audience for *Bay City Blues* by promoting Bochco as the program's auteur. Network promos touted the new show as "from the creator of *Hill Street Blues*." Bochco himself even pitched the show in a promotional advertisement. At the same time, fearing a lack of interest from female viewers, NBC downplayed the bats and the balls, stressing instead *Bay City*'s obsessions with sex and human foibles. Nothing worked. With its eighteen regular cast members, its extraordinarily high outdoor production costs, and its overweening insistence on baseball as the great American metaphor for life itself, *Bay City Blues* never recovered from its opening day slump.

Many viewers were shocked when Steven Bochco was fired by MTM in 1985. But insiders knew that studio president Arthur Price had been feuding with Bochco over high production budgets for quite some time. Episodes of *Hill Street Blues* were costing more to produce than the studio was receiving in payment from NBC. This in itself was not unusual. Deficits are typically financed by studios on the premise that the sale of syndication rights to reruns of those series will ultimately bring profits. But some episodes of *Hill Street* were costing as much as two hundred thousand dollars more than MTM was getting from the network, putting an uncommon debt burden on the studio. Furthermore, because of the experimental form of *Hill Street*'s unsymmetrical narrative, it was not completely clear how the show might do in the world of perpetual reruns. Would it work on a Monday-through-Friday basis? Would it have to be recut into half-hour units, such as is often the preference of local stations shopping for syndication properties? By 1985 there were enough completed hours of *Hill Street* on the shelf to put together a reasonable syndication package. Why continue to be buried deeper in the hole by Bochco's overruns? The studio owned the series and felt it could continue to produce less expensive new episodes without him for as long as the ratings justified. Bochco was asked to leave.

From Delvecchio to Paris to Frank Furillo, Bochco's characters had been acquiring increasing amounts of responsibility and savvy but not very much power. They were decent, resourceful, and courageous but always somewhat marginal to the movers and shakers. Perhaps in the wake of his forced departure from *Hill Street*, Bochco felt the pain of that same lack of authority in his own career. He responded, in both art and life, by forming a new company to produce *L.A. Law*.

"*Hill Street* was for me always fundamentally a series about despair,"
Bochco told an interviewer. "*L.A. Law* is not about despair. This is
an upscale show about by-and-large successful people who truly impact on the environment. . . ." As an independent producer, Bochco
signed a deal with Twentieth Century–Fox. Terms were favor-
able. Fox got exclusive distribution rights to Bochco's work; Bochco
got the use of Fox's facilities, full artistic control, and a deal worth
millions.

The "make it look messy" production philosophy that had characterized *Hill Street* was altered to a "make it look trendy" style for
this shiny new courtroom drama. Cellular phones took the place of
handguns as the weapons of choice. If expensive location shots had
given *Hill Street* a penumbra of gritty realism, they had also been
the source of untenable production costs. With the producer now
responsible for his own bottom line, cheaper soundstage shooting
schedules prevailed. Tenements, police cruisers, and greasy-spoon
diners gave way to more cheaply assembled semitropical condos, air-
conditioned board rooms, and restaurants with wine stewards. Bochco
had returned from the naked city to the bourgeois crimebeat of Lieutenant Columbo.

Despite the shifting mise en scène and the change of genre, *L.A.
Law* owed its structural soul to *Hill Street* rather than to *Perry Mason,
Owen Marshall,* or *Mr. District Attorney.* The partners' meeting that
opens each episode serves precisely the same purpose as the *Hill
Street* roll call scene: the principals are assembled; their narrative
assignments are handed out; all depart in diverse directions, criss-
crossing socially and professionally for the balance of the hour. The
variation on a theme that epitomizes the relationship of the two series
is a function of Bochco's angle of vision. *Hill Street* had developed a
vantage point from which a middle-class audience might peer down-
ward at the underside of American inner-city life; *L.A. Law* would
maintain that same vantage point but pivot the viewing neck upward
for a glimpse at life in yuppie heaven. The series was previewed at
the Museum of Broadcasting in New York, as if it were a gallery
opening or a poetry reading rather than a lawyer show destined for
prime-time television.

L.A. Law, programmed in *Hill Street*'s (Bochco's?) old Thursday-
night time slot, became a hit almost immediately in the fall of 1986.
The cool, efficient hum of the McKenzie, Brackman corporate suite
was both counterpart and complement to the funky chaos of the Hill
Street stationhouse. Here was a show set on the extraordinary Amer-

ican Olympus that had materialized during the Reagan presidency. Gods and goddesses of capitalism — beautiful, rich, smart, sensitive, well-bred, tasteful, passionate, aloof, idealistic, pragmatic, creative, conventional — wheeling and dealing, defending and exploiting, committing and cocooning, making love and making money.

The grand old man of the company, Leland McKenzie (Richard Dysart) demonstrates familiar Bochcovian management skills: fair-minded but tough, a walking, talking synthesis of practical wisdom and serious beliefs. Unlike Furillo, however, McKenzie is armed for the eighties with a devastating pedigree and clout to match. In a curious way his untarnished image owes much to Douglas Brackman, Jr. (Alan Rachins), who does most of the managerial dirty work, counting the paper clips and scolding the unthrifty in the name of the bottom line.

Michael Kuzak (Harry Hamlin) is the nominal center of narrative focus. A darkly handsome Yalie with a pouting lower lip, Michael accepts his class privilege with a serene, almost casual sense of noblesse oblige that leads him to accept the most exciting of the *pro bono* cases. His continuing love affair during the early seasons with Assistant District Attorney Grace Van Owen (Susan Dey) provided a key dramatic link to the other side of the adversarial legal system, much as the Furillo-Davenport romance did for *Hill Street*. The trials and tribulations of the couple gave human dimensions to their functions in the massive tangle of the legal system. Later on, when Grace joins the firm, she takes up with Victor Sifuentes (Jimmy Smits), Michael's close friend and associate.

Ann Kelsey (Jill Eikenberry) and Stuart Markowitz (Michael Tucker), both full partners in the firm, are the bearers of the series' other important romantic torch. The unlikeliness of the union of the short, graying male tax expert and the glamorous, idealistic female litigator is played for all its worth against the fact of Eikenberry and Tucker's real-life marriage. Bochco has used the couple to explore issues ranging from genteel anti-Semitism (Ann's mother is dismayed by her daughter's marriage to a Jew) to the trials and tribulations of a low sperm count (after considering several options, the couple adopts a baby).

Arnie Becker (Corbin Bernsen), as the firm's divorce specialist, is a study in AIDS-era promiscuity, a sex addict whose protestations of loneliness do not make him any less an object of envy. Victor Sifuentes is a born-in-East-L.A. Chicano who leaves the public defender's office to join the firm and live life in the corporate fast lane, hoping not to forget his roots. Jonathan Rollins (Brian Underwood) is an arrogant black attorney fresh out of Harvard Law School whose penchant for courtroom pyrotechnics, while sometimes less than effective for his clients, makes for extremely good TV. In addition to the attorneys, other office personnel, such as office secretary Roxanne (Susan Ruttan) and Benny (Larry Drake), the firm's mentally retarded office boy, provide a variety of storylines.

Terry Louise Fisher, who cocreated *L.A. Law* and collaborated with Bochco during the first several seasons, is herself a former deputy district attorney, and there can be no doubt that her insider's experience of the legal system was one of the show's great resources in revitalizing television courtroom drama. But Fisher's departure from the series in 1987 left none of the noticeable effects on *L.A. Law* that Bochco's departure had caused *Hill Street Blues* in 1985. In 1989 Bochco himself left direct involvement with the series and changed his credit to "Executive Consultant," leaving direct management of the show to David Kelley. Kelley has done a strong job, adding several new characters and taking the show in creative directions, without destroying Bochco's basic concept.

The success of *L.A. Law* opened up even greater opportunity for Bochco. In 1988 he signed a contract with ABC to create no less than ten new series for the network, with seven to be delivered over a span of six years. The first fruit of this arrangement was *Hooperman*, a whimsical half-hour dramedy starring John Ritter and set in San Francisco, a locale Bochco had not visited in his television fiction since *McMillan and Wife*. Though differing from the soap-operatic format of his previous two hits, the Bochco imprimatur is unmistakable. A female officer is paired with a gay male partner. The precinct captain (played by Barbara Bosson) frets over her failed marriage. Hooperman is having a baby with his live-in girlfriend. Just a month after *Hooperman*'s debut, Bud Grant was fired as president of CBS Entertainment and Steven Bochco was offered the job. He refused the position — and the considerable power that went with it — preferring instead to continue working as an artist.

Steven Bochco Productions, now sporting an end-of-episode logo of Bochco's father performing on his fiddle, delivered a hit to ABC on the second try. *Doogie Howser, M.D.* (ABC, 1989–present) was filled with some things old and some things new. Douglas "Doogie" Howser (Neil Patrick Harris) learns calculus while he still has his baby teeth, blows away the SATs at twelve, and breezes through medical school before he can shave. As the pilot episode begins, another half-hour dramedy without a laughtrack, sixteen-year-old Doogie is a resident physician at the Eastman Medical Center. Cocreated by Bochco and David Kelley, the show has many elements, including the professional setting (a hospital), the raucous plotlines (Doogie is the only one available to perform emergency surgery on his own girlfriend), and even some of the faces (*Hill Street*'s James B. Sikking plays Doogie's doctor dad), that are by now familiar to the oeuvre. But *Doogie Howser* is also a departure, laced with moralizing (albeit post–Dr. Spock) atypical of Bochco's previous works. Just as Mork explicated what we were supposed to have learned at the end of every episode of Garry Marshall's *Mork and Mindy,* Doogie keys the evening's moral into his PC diary just before the final credits roll. The series also has more kid appeal than Bochco's previous works, many stories centering around Doogie, his teenage best friend, and their steadies. In an era of entrance exams to exclusive preschools, Bochco has adapted the style of *L.A. Law* to the fast-track adolescent.

In 1990 Bochco premiered *Cop Rock,* an audaciously innovative — and expensive — project that ended up laying an egg on the order of *Bay City Blues.* The concept for *Cop Rock* originated in a proposal from a team of theatrical producers who wanted to mount a production of *Hill Street Blues* as a Broadway musical during the late eighties. Although the adaptation scheme died on the drawing board, Bochco remained fascinated with the idea of creating a weekly prime-time police drama laced with production numbers in the style of the Broadway musical theater. "Why can't you do a musical drama on television?" he mused. "They do it in the theater all the time."

Bochco found out the answer to his question sooner than he had expected. Making the equivalent of an hour-long Broadway musical on an eight-day production schedule turned out to be a nightmare; many three-minute MTV videos take over a month to produce. Moreover, the added costs of the musical production numbers raised average episode costs to $1.3 million, approximately one-third more than the average copshow. ABC might have stuck with the project to see if, like *Hill Street Blues,* it might eventually catch on, but ratings were so poor that the network felt it could not chance it. Though some critics loved it, *Cop Rock* died by midseason. If nothing else, the project gained Bochco an accolade that is usually reserved for great novelists and European film directors but almost never for TV producers: his failures are as interesting as his successes.

STEVEN BOCHCO: SELECTED VIDEOGRAPHY

Itinerant Writing

The Name of the Game (NBC, 1968–71)
Columbo (NBC, 1971–77)
McMillan and Wife (NBC, 1971–77)
Banacek (NBC, 1972–74)
The White Shadow (CBS, 1978–81)

Series

Griff (ABC, 1973–74)
Delvecchio (CBS, 1976–77)
Richie Brockelman, Private Eye (NBC, 1978)
Paris (CBS, 1979–80)
Hill Street Blues (NBC, 1981–87)
Bay City Blues (NBC, 1983)
L.A. Law (NBC, 1986–present)
Hooperman (ABC, 1987–89)
Doogie Howser, M.D. (ABC, 1989–present)
Cop Rock (ABC, 1990)
Civil Wars (ABC, 1991–present)

Movies Made for Television

Lieutenant Shuster's Wife (ABC, 1972)
Double Indemnity (ABC, 1973)
The Invisible Man (NBC, 1975)
Vampire (ABC, 1979)

21. MICHAEL MANN

———————————

Knowing the Score

The evolution of the cops-and-robbers show followed a slow and steady trajectory from the black-and-white staccato of Jack Webb (*Dragnet*) to the multicolored glitz of Aaron Spelling (*Charlie's Angels*). But the rise of cable television in the eighties caused the genre to adapt in new directions that speeded up its evolution, or perhaps caused it to mutate radically. If Steven Bochco (*Hill Street Blues*) can be credited as the progressive rehabilitator of copshow substance, then Michael Mann (*Miami Vice*) must be recognized as the creator of a new style for the genre during a decade when style quite frankly seemed to count for more than anything else.

As the expansion of cable began to take its toll on network ratings during the Reagan years in the White House, broadcast executives tried various strategies to stem the erosion of their previously impenetrable domain. For an audience suddenly free to flip through the dozens of channels of a remote-controlled cable box, the movies on HBO and other new outlets were unquestionably more visually arresting and compelling than the familiar, flatly lit, simply blocked scenes of weekly TV series. One solution to this problem might be to air TV series that looked more like contemporary films. Hollywood directors, including Steven Spielberg, Tony Richards, Robert Altman,

Wes Craven, John Sayles, and, of course, David Lynch, were lured to (or in some cases back to) television with this purpose in mind. But none of these directors was as personally successful in transforming the look and feel of network TV as a one-time would-be English professor named Michael Mann.

Miami Vice (NBC, 1984–89) was arguably the first weekly television program in decades to actively seek a completely new video aesthetic for that old network standby, the copshow. Mann gave a level of attention to visual detail that had previously been reserved for the screens behind the popcorn stands. Complex camera angles, state-of-the-art editing, synaesthetic use of music with image, and elaborate color design all demonstrated Mann's willingness to ignore the limitations that had somehow remained the burden of the ugly little TV set, even in the age of the Trinitron and the Mitsubishi giant screen.

Miami Vice was among the first series to be produced and broadcast in stereo, thus helping to smash the forty-year hegemony of the tiny little monaural TV audiospeaker in the age of Dolby, Sensurround, and sixteen-speaker theater systems. Its success almost singlehandedly created the consumer market for stereo television. As is so often the case with technological innovation in the mass media, what begins as an imitation of an older medium emerges as a new artform. Indeed, Mann, as *Miami Vice*'s executive producer and occasional director, had at first defined his work as not so much making TV as making "minimovies." In the final analysis, however, he would change the way weekly action/adventure television was made.

Born in Chicago during the Second World War, Mann attended the University of Wisconsin at Madison, where he majored in English literature. Having planned a career for himself as an academic, he shifted his vocational attentions away from the English department after taking an undergraduate film class at Wisconsin during the sixties. In a 1987 interview, he told *Rolling Stone:* "I realized there was something passive about being a professor of English literature. It was about studying and analyzing and digesting what had already been written. And you know, what's the function of analysis? To design a tool to make the creation or production better? It is in other disciplines. It is not in English literature."

After graduating from Wisconsin, instead of seeking an advanced degree in literary studies, Mann crossed the Atlantic to enroll in the London Film School. While in Britain he worked on documentaries, short films, and commercials, directing the short subject *Jaunpuri*, which won the Juris Prize at the Cannes Film Festival in 1971. From there, it was off to Hollywood.

Mann arrived in Los Angeles in the early seventies with hopes of directing feature films. But after three years of knocking on studio doors, he had gotten nowhere. It was at about this time that his friend, Bob Lewin, a story editor for Aaron Spelling's *Starsky and Hutch*, taught him TV scripting structure and got him a job writing multiple episodes for the hit copshow. Though TV work had not originally figured in his plans, Mann suddenly found himself making a living in the industry.

Several of the roots of *Miami Vice* developed out of this experience at the Spelling studio. Starsky (Paul Michael Glaser) and Hutch (David Soul) were undercover partners, just as Sonny Crockett and Rico Tubbs would be. Visually, one was light, the other dark, and they dressed, drove, and at times even talked like pimps, dealers, and the other street scum they chased through the streets of their Sunbelt beat. They were often more at home with their underworld informants than they were with the solid citizens. The difference between the two undercover teams would be largely a matter of style — a matter that was, one might say, the salient difference between the seventies and the eighties: Starsky and Hutch wore jeans and drove a red '74 Dodge Charger with a white racing stripe; Crockett and Tubbs wore pastel designer fashions and drove a Ferrari Spider (upgraded mid-series to a Testarossa).

Mann followed his script work on *Starsky and Hutch* with several years of itinerant writing for copshows, including *Police Story* and *Bronk*. In 1976 he made a detour from his otherwise solid devotion to cops-and-robbers when he tried his hand at writing an ambitious *Waltons* knockoff called *Gibbsville*, which was based on John O'Hara's short stories about a reporter living in a small Pennsylvania mining town during the 1940s. But the show was canceled after less than two months. In 1978 Mann went back to work for Aaron Spelling, creating and producing his first weekly series, *Vega$*, starring Robert Urich.

Stylistically, *Vega$* is very much a midway milestone between *Starsky and Hutch* and *Miami Vice*. Somewhere between a gaudy muscle-car racing the back alleys of Los Angeles and an imported Italian sports car cruising the causeways of Biscayne Bay, we find Dan Tanna (Urich) at the wheel of his classic 1957 two-seat Thunderbird, tooling down the neon boulevards of Las Vegas. Tanna is a private eye on retainer to Philip Roth (Tony Curtis), the multimillionaire owner of a string of Nevada casinos (and a character who could have been named only by a former English major). In this ultraseventies concept, Tanna did not have a partner, as such, but rather a kind of support group: a schlmielish reformed criminal named Binzer (Bart

Braverman); an obligatory jiggle-era receptionist named Angie (Judy Landers); and Beatrice (Phyllis Davis), an older and wiser Gal Friday who supplemented her office income by teaching dancing courses to Las Vegas show girls.

"When I wrote Vega$, I had Kerouac in mind," recalled Mann, "and the drawings from (Hunter S. Thompson's) Fear and Loathing in Las Vegas." Despite these ambitions, however, the show's Las Vegas looked more like Roy Huggins's 77 Sunset Strip (see Chapter 13) than Jack Kerouac's On the Road. Though Mann had written the pilot film and had taken creator's credits for the series, the stamp of the Spelling studio was dominant and indelible. The mise-en-scène was bursting with busty chorus girls and television's version of exotic street characters. Even the episode titles — the first two were "Centerfold" and "The Games Girls Play" — epitomized the midseventies cosmology that Spelling (see Chapter 15) had created for ABC during the halcyon days of his partnership with the network.

Mann was frankly unhappy with all of this. He claimed that Vega$ had become too "sanitized" and left the show midseries. He had hoped to explore dramatic and visual territories that were beyond the limits of what the Spelling studio, at the peak of its dominance, was willing to tolerate. Ironically, only a decade earlier, Spelling himself had been an innovative force in the genre, adding black and female cops to previously all-white police forces.

Mann held fast to his desire of becoming a film director, and he moved back toward that pursuit after his disappointment with Vega$. Still not able to get a theatrical assignment, he directed several made-for-television movies. His notable achievement was The Jericho Mile (ABC, 1979), a telefilm that he directed and cowrote about a convict doing life at Folsom Prison who is training for a chance to compete as a runner on the U.S. Olympic track team. The film was shot on location at the penitentiary, and Mann uses actual inmates as extras to give it a realistic look — as well as to insure a peaceful set. The Jericho Mile was a critical success, nominated for an Emmy as the year's best drama. Mann and his script collaborator, Patrick J. Nolan, shared an Emmy for best writing in a limited series or special, and the film's star, Peter Strauss, won for best actor. Mann also received the Directors Guild of America's Best Director award for 1979. The following season, another Mann telefilm premiered on ABC. Swan Song, coproduced with former Starsky and Hutch star David Soul, was in some ways a knockoff of The Jericho Mile. The story concerned a downhill skier attempting to make a comeback after a personal disaster that has left his career in ruins. Mann had paid his dues and established his credentials. He now felt ready to fulfill his longtime career goal of becoming a bona fide movie director.

His first theatrical release was *Thief*, a visually and musically stylized story about the life of a professional burglar (James Caan). Mann wrote, directed, and produced the film, which costarred Tuesday Weld and Robert Prosky and included a cameo appearance by Willie Nelson. Dennis Farina, who would later become Mann's star in *Crime Story*, had a minor role as well. The film was something less than a hit, but elements of the musical scoring technique and the cinematography foreshadow the coming of *Miami Vice*. Mann's next movie, a World War II film titled *The Keep*, also made the bad guys its focus. It concerns a group of German soldiers who base themselves in a haunted ancient fortress to defend a mountain pass in the Transylvanian Alps of Romania.

Both films were commercially negligible, and this brought Mann to a crossroads in his career. Finally functioning as a director of theatrically released films, he might perhaps advance to more solid success in the medium through repeated effort. But television somehow remained the land of opportunity, and he would soon receive an offer he couldn't refuse. Industry legend has it that NBC programming chief Brandon Tartikoff, in his typically Zen style, had come up with a two-word story concept — "MTV Cops" — and had put out a contract on the idea for anyone who could execute it. At least one important producer, Stephen J. Cannell, seriously toyed with the idea but decided to pass.

The concept then landed on the desk of writer-producer Anthony Yerkovich, a member of the creative inner sanctum at MTM Enterprises, which was riding high on the success of *Hill Street Blues*. Michael Mann was starting up on yet another Hollywood movie when his agent sent over a pilot script by Yerkovich for a series then titled *Gold Coast*. Mann reportedly loved the script and saw its commercial possibilities, though at first he argued to do it as a theatrical release rather than as a made-for-TV movie functioning as a pilot for a series. But preparations were already abroad for a weekly series, and under some duress Mann agreed to sign on as executive producer of what would eventually be titled *Miami Vice*.

Brandon Tartikoff's call for "MTV Cops" was a tall order to fill. In the early eighties the establishment of MTV as a twenty-four-hour-a-day nationally subscribed cable phenomenon had sent shock waves through the mass-culture industry. Originally conceived of as merely a promotional tool for the selling of records and audiotapes, music videos had taken on a life of their own. Not only were they becoming a new form of salable software, but they were also proving the commercial viability of a kind of quick nonnaturalistic cutting style that had previously been anything but popular in American mass entertainment. Borrowing heavily from experimental film techniques and from television commercials, music videos somehow managed to avoid both the profound obscurities of the former and the even more profound banalities of the latter. Was there actually a way that the relentless hipness of this technique could be assimilated into an otherwise familiar prime-time narrative genre?

In *Miami Vice*, Mann indeed gave Tartikoff his "MTV Cops." The show became instantly notorious as a vehicle for "style" rather than content. Like Mann's feature films, many of the storylines were confusing in terms of traditional continuity. But that simply didn't seem to matter; the real point of the show was its sound and its look. Avant-garde filmmakers, especially the movement that had briefly flourished in the sixties around the likes of Stan Brakhage and Ken Jacobs, had dreamed of a nonnarrative art cinema, where the properties of human vision itself might become the subject of the camera. During this same period, the advertising agencies had promoted a visual tradition of cinema as psychology experiment, in which styles of dress, cuisine, transportation, and finally life itself would become subconsciously associated with the pleasures of the audiovisual text. Mann had somehow retrieved elements of both these extremes to the dead center of popular story-telling.

Using a pastel palette dominated by the pink and turquoise motif of a Miami Dolphins football uniform, Mann announced *Miami Vice* each week in an opening montage of flamingos, surf, and sky. In the episodes of the first several seasons, many sequences — be they romantic encounters or car chase shootouts — were visually choreographed with popular songs culled directly from the Billboard charts. *Time* critic Richard Zoglin noted that "unlike other TV shows that have utilized rock music, *Miami Vice* can spend more than $10,000 per episode in buying the rights to original recordings, rather than using made-for-TV imitations." Sixties rock star Al Kooper even took a credit on the crawl as "Guy Who Picks Music for the Show." In 1985 *USA Today* began listing the *songs* that would appear on *Miami Vice* that evening in its Friday morning edition.

Some of the musicians whose work was used regularly (Phil Collins, for example) appeared in guest-starring roles or in cameos. Borrowing a technique from *Rowan and Martin's Laugh-In,* Mann offered viewers unexpected personality tidbits from the great smorgasbord of mass culture. Lee Iacocca, having only recently saved Chrysler Corporation by the good graces of *Miami Vice*'s tax-paying audience, even appeared on an episode.

Scratch the pastel surface of *Miami Vice* and beneath it a viewer might find a premise that owed a lot to *Starsky and Hutch* and an assortment of other conventional precursors. White Miami undercover cop Sonny Crockett (Don Johnson) teams up with transplanted black New Yorker Rico Tubbs (Philip Michael Thomas), and together they act out the fantasies for which they are dressed: drug dealers, pimps, con artists, you name it. In public, style is all; in private, sensitivity and values rule. They live the ultimate fantasy of the Sunbelt Stud.

In typical copshow style, the unorthodox officers must answer for some of their more outrageous stunts to a boss who simultaneously admires their bravado but in his dedication to procedural decorum must chastise them and rein them in from their excesses. In this case the father figure is the serene, self-possessed Lieutenant Castillo (Edward J. Olmos). Shadowing Crockett and Tubbs, macho stars, are their female counterparts, Detectives Gina Calabrese (Saundra Santiago) and Trudy Joplin (Olivia Brown), and their comical "character" doubles Detectives Stan Switek (Michael Talbot) and Larry Zito (John Diehl).

If *Miami Vice* did contain any radical substance, it was the sense of hopelessness that hung like a cloud over the otherwise sunny South Florida locations. In Mann's world of conspicuous lifestyle, the bad guys often dress, drive, eat, and copulate in higher style than the good guys. Actors in a state-supported charade to infiltrate the world of the criminals, Crockett and Tubbs play out a devilish fantasy that is utterly incompatible with human decency. Which one for you, hypocrite voyeur? This question, asked by Mann of his audience, is not the kind of question that either a Joe Friday or a Hutch took home with him from the office. The level of anxiety could at times become too much for Sonny; one season he flipped out, no longer able to distinguish between his undercover persona and his "real" identity. Some viewers, much like Sonny, couldn't figure out what the hell was going on; others just dug the music and the visuals.

After faltering a bit during its premiere season opposite *Falcon Crest* on CBS, *Miami Vice* took off on the wings of its own inventiveness and cracked the Nielsen Top Ten during its second season. But the gods of marketing are fickle. As *Miami Vice*–inspired fashions started turning up at discount stores and Crockett and Tubbs wannabes started showing up at singles bars and high school proms, the series managed to quickly become a parody of itself. Watching a rerun of *Miami Vice* today may not be much different from looking at a videotape of *Saturday Night Fever*. NBC didn't help matters when, after the strong second season, the network thought the show powerful enough to take on CBS's perennial Friday-night ratings champ, *Dallas*, a program obviously targeted at more conservative dressers and consciousnesses. J. R. Ewing and company had little trouble in preventing a hostile takeover of their time slot in this battle of the Sunbelt lifestyles.

Mann continued to keep a hand in feature films during the *Miami Vice* production run, directing *Manhunter* (1986) and serving as executive producer for *Band of the Hand* (1986), which took place in Miami and was directed by *Starsky and Hutch*'s Paul Michael Glaser. But based on what he was accomplishing with *Miami Vice*, his attitude toward the relative possibilities of the boob tube and *le cinema* seemed to be changing. With *Vice* still in production, he made a commitment to become executive producer of a second TV series, which had been created by Chuck Adamson and Gustave Reininger: *Crime Story* (NBC, 1986–88). Though commercially marginal, this show would be his greatest artistic achievement.

Set in the early sixties in Chicago and Las Vegas, *Crime Story* exhibited remarkably fresh location shooting, editing, and narrative techniques. As in *Miami Vice,* music played an important role in the program, but this time instead of high-tech contempo, Mann cranked up the rhythm with a gush of doo-wap and girl-group oldies from the late fifties–early sixties. Strict attention to color, costume, automobile choices, and set design gave the series a robust period flavor that had been rare in weekly television.

Quinn Martin's *The Untouchables* (ABC, 1959–63) might be seen as an early model for *Crime Story*. The first thirteen episodes were in fact set in Eliot Ness's old stomping grounds of Chicago. Lt. Mike Torello (Dennis Farina), an "untouchable" cop, was locked in mortal cops-and-robbers combat with sleazy Ray Luca (Anthony Denison), a postwar Frank Nitti trying to consolidate his power in the Chicago underworld. Like Ness, Torello was in charge of a special unit of crack gangbusters, in this case known as the "Major Crimes Unit."

In the second season, Ray Luca, an all-American gangster if there ever was one, follows the advice of Horace Greeley, and the examples of Bugsy Siegel and Vito Corleone, moving his operation to the opportunity-laden American West. In Las Vegas, the stark film noir–ishness of Ness versus Nitti collides emphatically with the Sunbelt tones of *Miami Vice* to become the televisually gorgeous struggle of

Torello and Luca amid the neon blues and flaming pinks of the famed desert oasis.

The passion with which Mann told *Crime Story* is perhaps attributable to the fact that he was examining autobiographical roots. Chicago had been Mann's hometown in so-called real life; Las Vegas had been the fictional locale of his first TV creation. Dennis Farina, whom Mann had cast in the lead, was a fellow Chicago native who had grown up in the city during the same period. Farina brought other credentials to the role of Torello as well. He had spent eighteen years as an officer of the Chicago Police Department, beginning his acting career in the early eighties while still carrying a badge. Having also appeared in both *Thief* and *Manhunter*, he became in effect Michael Mann's on-camera persona.

Crime Story never achieved the ratings success of *Miami Vice*, at least partially due to its misfortune in being put up against ABC's *Moonlighting*, which was reaching the peak of its mass-cult phenomenology during the 1986–87 season. As the final episode of the first season of *Crime Story* was being shot, cancellation seemed imminent to Mann, and in one of the most hyperbolic self-reflexive storylines ever broadcast, he had Ray Luca nuked by an atomic bomb. After a spectacular shootout with Torello on the Vegas Strip, Luca escapes with the help of his flunky Paulie, a Clemenza-like gangster/clown brilliantly overplayed by John Santucci. Ever the schlmiel, Paulie leads Ray to a suitably out-of-the-way shack in order to lay low. Unfortunately, the desolation of the hideout can be explained by the fact that it sits on a piece of Nevada desert maintained by the Atomic Energy Commission for above-ground nuclear testing.

To everyone's surprise, not least of all Mann's, NBC reversed itself and renewed *Crime Story*, despite its low ratings. In a trope of post-Einstein deus ex machina, Ray and Paulie reappear the following fall, having miraculously survived the blast. Though able to make the Atomic Energy Commission's Geiger counters sing, they return to plague Torello once again after several wacky episodes of detoxification, rest, and relaxation in a government facility. By the end of the second season, Luca has moved his base of operations yet again, this time to a mythical Latin American country where he plans to develop a narcotics operation under the protection of a corrupt dictator. *Crime Story* ends just as it is approaching the historical beginnings of the cocaine problem that would be the informing spirit of *Miami Vice*. Torello, Luca, and Paulie go down together in a plane crash; this time there is no reprieve from the network programmer.

In Mann's next major television project, he stuck with his favorite theme of cops, robbers, and drugs but moved from fiction toward docudrama. *Drug Wars: The Camarena Story* (NBC, 1990) was an ambitious six-hour, three-part miniseries concerning the career of Enrique "Kiki" Camarena, an undercover agent for the United States Drug Enforcement Administration who had been brutally executed in Mexico by dealers. Based on the nonfiction bestseller by Elaine Shannon, the show followed Camarena through vast fields of marijuana, poppies, and government corruption in Mexico.

Mann will perhaps always be associated in the public mind with the stylistic innovations of *Miami Vice*. But his willingness to experiment with the video synthesis of music and image should not overshadow the richness of his description and the depth of his critique of post–World War II American culture that is always part and parcel of his work. Mann effectively uses prime-time television as a form of personal expression. "It's as if he views his role on *Miami Vice* and *Crime Story* as executive producer *slash* auteur," wrote critic Elvis Mitchell in 1986. "He provides the shows with an overwhelming vision — a point of view."

MICHAEL MANN: SELECTED VIDEOGRAPHY

Itinerant Writing

Police Story (NBC, 1973–77)
Starsky and Hutch (ABC, 1975–79)
Bronk (CBS, 1975–76)
Gibbsville (NBC, 1976)

Series

Vega$ (ABC, 1978–81)
Miami Vice (NBC, 1984–89)
Crime Story (NBC, 1986–88)

Movies Made for Television and Miniseries

The Jericho Mile (ABC, 1979)
Swan Song (ABC, 1980)
Drug Wars: The Camarena Story (NBC, 1990)

22. DRAMA

Honorable Mention

Donald Bellisario

A native of western Pennsylvania, Donald Bellisario took his college degree from Penn State University before moving on to a career in advertising. He spent fourteen years in the industry as an account executive for the Bloom Agency, and then as a director of television commercials. In the early seventies he left Madison Avenue for Hollywood, taking a job at Universal Studios, where he got the chance to work alongside other budding TV producers. His first jobs were scriptwriting assignments for action/adventure series such as Glen Larson's *Switch*, Steve Bochco's *Delvecchio*, and Abby Mann's *Kojak*. He soon graduated to the position of line producer, turning out weekly episodes for Stephen J. Cannell's *Baa Baa Black Sheep* and *The Rockford Files*, and for Glen Larson's *Battlestar Gallactica*. In 1980 Bellisario cocreated *Magnum, P.I.* (CBS, 1980–88) with Larson. He then took on full authorial responsibility as the series' executive producer. *Magnum* was not only a tremendous hit but also a critical success that inspired accolades from professors as well as reviewers across the country. The show was a post-Vietnam reexamination of the "trouble in Paradise" myth that had been the focus of several earlier TV crimeshows set in Hawaii, such as Roy Huggins's *Hawaiian Eye* and Jack Lord's *Hawaii Five-O*. It starred Tom Selleck as an introspective private detective given to a kind of macho existential musing that was expressed in frequent diarylike voiceover monologues. *Airwolf* (various, 1984–87), which followed, was a more conventional action series by Bellisario, starring Ernest Borgnine and Jan-Michael Vincent as the copilots of a super high-tech attack helicopter. In 1989, however, Bellisario introduced his most innovative series to date, *Quantum Leap*, a sci-fi adventure about a scientist who travels through time by inhabiting the bodies of other people. Despite the cartoonish-sounding concept, the show plays against type by seriously addressing such issues as racism, sexism, and the plight of the physically handicapped in its storylines.

Glenn Gordon Caron

Caron began his TV career writing episode scripts for such crime series as *Murder, She Wrote* and *Remington Steele*, both of which concerned female detectives. In 1985 Caron created and produced the first series of his own, *Moonlighting* (ABC, 1985–89), which also concerns a female private eye. Maddie Hayes (Cybil Shepherd) is a top fashion model who is cheated out of her personal fortune by a scoundrel manager. When the dust clears, the only holding left in her portfolio is an unprofitable detective agency. David Addison (Bruce Willis), the Blue Moon Detective Agency's chief employee, convinces her to keep the place and to try to make a go of it. As the show evolved, the scripts became increasingly ironic and self-reflexive. Dialogue often seemed more concerned with analyzing the nature of the TV crimeshow genre than with solving the crime at hand. David and Maddie's relationship became a model for contemporary video romance, echoed, for example, by the Ted Danson–Kirstie Alley relationship on *Cheers*. Caron swore off television work amid the tumultuous personality battles that characterized the production run of the series — battles that ultimately led to its demise despite its high ratings. His departure from the TV industry was, however, only brief. In 1991 he made a deal with ABC; the network agreed to buy three new series from Caron's Picturemaker Productions company by 1995.

Michael Landon

Born Eugene Orowitz in 1937 in the Forest Hills section of New York City, Landon was raised in Collingwood, New Jersey. Critic Tim Brooks describes the environment of Landon's youth as "a tension-filled home in a white Protestant neighborhood" that, according to Landon, "wasn't very friendly to a skinny little Jewish kid." His ability to throw the javelin won him a track-and-field scholarship to the University of Southern California. But after an injury ended his sports career, he turned to acting. One of his first roles was as the title player in the camp classic film *I Was a Teenage Werewolf* (1957). But he found more regular work in TV Westerns during the heyday of that genre, playing guest parts on such series as *Jim Bowie, Wanted: Dead or Alive*, and *Tales of Wells Fargo*. His major break came in 1959 when he was cast in the role of Little Joe in *Bonanza*. Landon made good use of his time during *Bonanza's* fourteen-year production run, not only by developing his craft as an actor but by taking the opportunity to write and direct episodes as well. He also learned the whys and wherefores of producing a popular, family-oriented, prime-time television series for commercial TV. He put all this experience together to become the coproducer, director, writer, and star of his own show, *Little House on the Prairie* (NBC, 1974–83), an adaptation of the Laura Ingalls Wilder books about small-town family life on the Western frontier. Landon followed *Little House* with *Father Murphy*, which starred Merlin Olsen posing as a Roman Catholic priest while running an orphanage in the Dakota Territory just after the Civil War. With *Highway to Heaven* (NBC, 1984–89), Landon scored his first hit set in contemporary times. At this point he had established a reputation as a master of "family television" as well as something of a tyrant on the set, the latter perhaps an inevitable result of his holding half a dozen positions of responsibility — from executive producer to star. In *Highway to Heaven* he plays a probationary angel on a weekly mission from God to help the poor, the abused, and/or the otherwise troubled. Landon also did a handful of TV movies over the years, one of them based on his autobiographical experiences as a teenage athlete. He was the recipient of numerous honors, including a prestigious Founder's Award Emmy. In 1991, while working on a new series titled *Us*, he was diagnosed with inoperable cancer of the pancreas and liver and died a few months later.

Bruce Paltrow

A product of the Long Island suburbs of New York City, Paltrow left home to study theater at Tulane University in New Orleans, where he took a bachelor of fine arts degree in 1965. Returning to the New York area after college, he began a career as a free-lance writer, and eventually he produced several off-Broadway plays. His first television work was a made-for-TV movie titled *Shirts/Skins* (1973), which concerned inner-city basketball players. In 1977 he joined the production staff of MTM Enterprises on the West Coast. Working in collaboration with Mark Tinker, John Masius, John Falsey, and Joshua Brand, Paltrow created, occasionally directed, and took executive producer credits for *The White Shadow* (CBS, 1978–81), a series about a white, former NBA player who is coaching a basketball team at a predominantly black high school in Los Angeles. Continuing to work with the same collaborative team at MTM, Paltrow went on to produce *St. Elsewhere* (NBC, 1982–88), a series that redefined the possibilities of that old generic standby, the doctor show. Set in a ghetto neighborhood of Boston, *St. Elsewhere*'s frank examinations of social issues as well as medical problems, along with its complex, multidimensional characters and plotlines, combined to make it one of the most satisfying dramas ever presented in the weekly series format. Picking up on the innovations in dramatic structure introduced several seasons before at MTM by Steven Bochco, *St. Elsewhere* is perhaps the missing link between *Hill Street Blues* and Zwick and Herskovitz's *thirtysomething*. In 1988 Paltrow set up a production facility in New York for a new series, *Tattinger's*, which focused on the life of an upper-crust restaurateur; it was, however, a disappointing wipeout.

Gene Roddenberry

Born in 1921 in El Paso, Texas, Gene Roddenberry was an airline pilot for Pan American before ever getting involved in the TV industry. In fact, his first writing credits came in articles he wrote for Pan Am's in-flight magazine. In 1949 he gave up professional flying, moving to Los Angeles to try his hand at TV. To support himself while writing scripts, he worked as an LAPD cop for five years. While still on the force, he sold a science-fiction script, "The Secret Defense of 117," to *Chevrolet Tele-Theatre*. By 1954 he resigned his position as an LAPD sergeant and began writing full time as a television writer. He sold over eighty scripts to such series as *Mr. District Attorney*, *Highway Patrol*, *Dr. Kildare*, and *Naked City*, winning a Writers Guild Award for his work as head writer on *Have Gun, Will Travel*, a popular Western starring Richard Boone. Roddenberry, of course, is best known as the creator and producer of *Star Trek* (NBC, 1966–69), which he once described as "just another horse opera, except they ride in a spaceship instead of on a nag. . . . *Wagon Train* to the stars." Though *Star Trek* just barely managed to hang on for three seasons in prime time, it achieved cult status in syndicated reruns, and eventually the old TV show gave life to a series of enormously popular theatrically released movies. The *Star Trek* phenomenon can be seen as the model for the many film adaptations of TV shows that followed, including *The Twilight Zone* and *The Jetsons*. In the seventies Roddenberry attempted various new sci-fi series for the networks, but none of them succeeded. In 1989, however, he returned as executive producer of *Star Trek: The Next Generation*, which has been a hit in first-run syndication. Roddenberry died in 1991.

Frederick W. Ziv

After completing his studies at the College of St. Joseph (Missouri) and taking a law degree at the University of Michigan, Ziv started his own radio production company, which packaged programs for such personalities as Red Skelton, Guy Lombardo, and Goodman Ace in the thirties and forties. Forming Ziv Television in 1947, he became known in the pioneer days as the leading independent supplier of thirty-minute, filmed-action "chase" series, such as *The Cisco Kid* (Western), *Highway Patrol* (copshow), *Sea Hunt* (underwater adventure), *Whirlybirds* (helicopter rescues), and *I Led Three Lives* (spy). All of these weekly programs were presented nationally in first-run syndication. Ziv's ability to successfully bypass the networks during the period of their greatest stranglehold over the medium was extraordinary. His unequaled accomplishments in this regard served as an example to other independents, including David Wolper (see Chapter 28), while also helping to nudge the networks toward greater investment in action telefilm series. In 1959 Ziv sold off the company; eventually it became a faceless division of United Artists. Ziv returned to the Midwest to pursue academic interests as Distinguished Professor of Radio, Television, and Theater Crafts at the University of Cincinnati. He has written two books about the entertainment industry: *The Business of Writing* and *The Valiant Muse*.

PART THREE

Other Genres

23. THE EDGES
OF PRIME TIME

_____ _____ _____ _____ _____ _____ _____ _____

Gamesters,
Soapsters,
Documentarians

Our focus thus far has been on prime-time television (i.e. the most-watched hours). According to the A. C. Nielsen Company, during the period from eight to eleven o'clock each evening (seven to ten o'clock central and mountain times), more Americans are watching television sets than are engaging in any other known human activity. On the positive side, we can perhaps speak of the programs broadcast during these hours as constituting a truly national drama, the likes of which have never been achieved before in the history of civilizations. On the down side, we may have revealed ourselves as a nation of semifunctional zombies, sitting there slack-jawed and wide-eyed, staring at the flicker of a stream of weightless transmissions, rendered incapable of the interactive communication with our fellow beings that once distinguished us as a species. One suspects that the truth lies somewhere along a vast spectrum of less spectacular choices that divide these messianic polarities.

Perhaps it is more useful to think of prime-time TV in terms of the traditions of show business rather than of laboratory psychology. Prime time is to television what "the big time" or "playing the Palace" was to vaudeville. It is where the big bucks and the colossal fame lie;

it is at the top of a profession that measures success almost exclusively by these yardsticks.

Each of the chapters that follow is dedicated to a producer who has worked in a genre that is marginal to the "big time" of prime-time television: gameshows, daily soap operas, and documentaries. In going outside of prime time, we are not attempting to cover authorship in all genres of television. To do that, we would certainly need a chapter on Lorne Michaels who, as producer of *Saturday Night Live*, almost singlehandedly redefined late-night American television, and another one on Joan Ganz Cooney, the moving force behind *Sesame Street*, who did the same for children's programming.

Instead, we specifically chose those producers working in marginal genres who had managed to influence the character of prime-time television. Mark Goodson's gameshows survived the quiz scandals of the late fifties to become a prime-time genre unto themselves. Irna Phillips's lifelong work in developing the daytime soap opera for radio and television made her an important source for the narrative techniques of such prime-time hits as *Dallas, L.A. Law,* and *thirtysomething*. David Wolper, alarmed that his beloved documentary form was being nudged out of prime time in favor of fictional genres, was forced to reconsider how history might be portrayed on television; one of the results was a docudramatic miniseries called *Roots*.

Did we leave anybody out? Certainly.

24. MARK GOODSON

_____ __ __ ___ ___ __ _____

The Gameshow King

In 1949 CBS was still signing off the air on Sunday nights at 10:15 P.M. When the network decided to fill out its prime-time lineup to 11:00 P.M. the following season, it bought an inexpensive gameshow that had been created by a radio announcer named Mark Goodson. The series, titled *What's My Line?* premiered in February 1950. It would be telecast live, fifty-two weeks a year, in that same time slot for the next seventeen seasons. By the late 1950s, Goodson's studio had grown to the point where it was churning out as many as fifty half hours of nationally aired game programming per week. Some four decades later not a single television season has gone by without at least one gameshow created and produced by Mark Goodson on the air.

Unlike the competition during the 1950s, including such quiz vehicles as Louis G. Cowan's *The $64,000 Question* and Jack Barry and Dan Enright's *Twenty-One*, Goodson avoided big money prizes and instead based his concepts on deductive parlor-room guessing games played by celebrity panelists. Rather than the high-anxiety drama of watching contestants in isolation booths risking tens of thousands of dollars in their quest for the ultimate jackpot, Goodson's viewers were offered a brand of playful verbal badinage that ranged in substance from diverting chitchat to occasional tests of erudition. As a result of this less sensational approach, Mark Goodson emerged from the quiz show scandals of the late 1950s unscathed — and thus became the undisputed king of the gameshow genre.

Born in Sacramento to Russian immigrant parents on January 24, 1915, Goodson grew up on a chicken farm near Hayward, California. When he was seventeen his father moved the family to Berkeley, where he opened up a health-food emporium, the first such store in a town that would later become famous for whole-grain retailing. Goodson stayed in town to attend college at the University of California, graduating Phi Beta Kappa in 1937. After leaving school, he pursued his childhood dream of a career in radio. Like Paul Henning (see Chapter 2) and so many other pioneer TV producers, Goodson got an on-the-job broadcasting education as a jack-of-all-trades at a local radio station. His duties at KFRC in San Francisco included announcing, newscasting, directing, and spinning platters.

Locally made radio programming was not unusual during this period, and while at KFRC he created and produced two gameshows for the station, *Pop the Question* (local, 1939) and *The Quiz of Two Cities* (local, 1941–44). The latter was particularly innovative and it helped make Goodson's name. Broadcast simultaneously on KFRC and on KHJ–Los Angeles, the quiz pitted contestants from the rival California cities in competition with each other. It won Goodson some recognition — and eventually a job in New York, the center of network radio production.

Goodson began his big-time radio career as a writer for Kate Smith's popular NBC variety show in 1941. But he already had designs upon becoming a program auteur. In 1943 he made a deal to obtain the files of a well-known professional marriage counselor, and from them he created, produced, and directed the soap opera *Appointment with Life* for the ABC radio network. Though the show didn't make it through the season, Goodson's experience helped him up the ladder, especially in a situation where many established radio professionals were going off to war. In 1944 he became the line producer of a running radio soap opera titled *Portia Faces Life*.

But Goodson's passion remained the gameshow, and after this brief detour into the soap-opera world, he returned to it to stay. It was during this period, the midforties, that he met Bill Todman, who was to become his longtime business partner. Though Todman's background was principally as a radio writer, he became, in effect, Goodson's business agent, making the deals with the ad agencies, the networks, and the stars, freeing Goodson to concentrate on the creative side. In 1946 Todman sold Goodson's first network game, *Winner Take All* (1946–49), to CBS radio, and the partnership was formalized into Mark Goodson–Bill Todman Productions.

Some other Goodson-Todman radio shows included *Hit the Jackpot* (CBS, 1948–52), hosted by Bill Cullen, a game in which viewers mailed in cards for the chance to be called by phone and asked to repeat a "mystery phrase" to win prizes that included trips, furniture, DeSoto cars (the show's sponsor), and even a gold-plated lawnmower valued at three thousand dollars. *Beat the Clock* (CBS, 1950–54), hosted by Bud Collyer, awarded prizes to contestants who could perform unusual feats within a specified number of seconds. Relying heavily on the use of visual stunts, this radio show was a natural for television. It premiered on CBS Television in 1950 and remained a daytime television fixture until the 1970s.

Goodson-Todman's first prime-time series was *What's My Line?* The concept was an elegantly simple one. A contestant would come out on stage and "sign in" on a blackboard. The profession of the contestant would then be revealed to the home audience by superimposition: "Plumber," "Nuclear Physicist," "Prison Guard," or whatever. (In 1972 Jimmy Carter appeared on the show, listing his job as "Governor of the state of Georgia.") Each of the four panelists would then be given the opportunity to ask the contestant "yes or no" questions until receiving a "no" answer. Parlor wit was emphasized over cash excitement: the most a contestant could win was fifty dollars!

Almost as much a talkshow as a gameshow, *What's My Line?* featured on its panel such raconteurs as Random House chief Bennett Cerf, a publisher who had overseen the publication of works by such authors as William Faulkner, Sinclair Lewis, and Eugene O'Neill; Dorothy Kilgallen, the syndicated columnist of the *New York Daily Mirror*; and poet Louis Untermeyer. An extraordinary range of personalities made guest appearances on the panel as well: radio satirist Fred Allen; Governor Harold Hoffman of New Jersey; Kitty Carlisle, the former diva who would go on to become the head of the New York State Council on the Arts. The show's host, John Charles Daly, was himself a nationally known newsman; his was the voice that had interrupted programming over the CBS Radio Network on the morning of December 7, 1941, to announce that the Japanese had attacked Pearl Harbor. Even while acting as host of *What's My Line?* for CBS-TV on Sunday nights, he was the anchor of ABC-TV's daily fifteen-minute national newscast as well as the network's vice president in charge of news, special events, and public affairs.

The most popular feature of *What's My Line?* was the "mystery guest" segment, which came at the conclusion of each thirty-minute episode. The panelists, dressed as ever in high-society evening clothes, put on their masked-ball blindfolds. A famous celebrity then came onstage and signed in, leaving the blindfolded panel to guess who it was. The mystery guests typically attempted to disguise their voices while answering questions. More than two thousand such guests appeared on the series over the years. They included such personalities as Phil Rizzuto, Ronald Reagan, Bette Davis, Walt Disney, Carl Sandburg, and Elizabeth Taylor.

Also in 1950, Goodson-Todman introduced the TV version of *Beat the Clock* as a CBS daytime program. Bud Collyer was host of both the television and radio versions of the show. Contestants competed for the usual array of washer-dryers, patio furniture, and other glamorous prizes by performing stunts: "You've got forty-five seconds to beat the clock!" Water balloons, cream pies, and massive quantities of Jell-O figured heavily in the mise-en-scène. It can be argued that *Beat the Clock* remains the model for a genre of children's gameshows that rely extensively on the technique of making a mess (e.g. *Wonderama* and *Teenage Double Dare*). The stunts used on *Beat the Clock* were all pretested by the show's staff, which included a would-be actor named James Dean in his first steady show-business job. A decade before Vanna White was even born, Bud Collyer's attractive blond assistant Roxanne (Dolores Rosedale) became a celebrity and media darling.

Beat the Clock notwithstanding, the structural foundation of most of the Mark Goodson gameshows of the 1950s was typically the guessing of a secret — a name, an occupation, a word, etc. In this regard, *I've Got a Secret* (CBS, 1952–67) epitomized the Goodson formula. A prime-time discursive gameshow, much like *What's My Line?*, *I've Got a Secret* consisted of a host (Garry Moore) and a four-member celebrity panel who tried to divine each contestant's "secret." At various points during the show's long history, regular panelists included Steve Allen, Henry Morgan, Bess Myerson, Bill Cullen, and Betsy Palmer. The "secrets," which were whispered into the host's ear (and simultaneously revealed to the home audience by superimposition), might consist of anything: three contestants, named William William, Herbert Herbert, and George George, were all from Walla Walla, Washington; a woman had been Greta Garbo's maid; a man could play the William Tell Overture by slapping his own cheeks. Again the money was small; a winning contestant took home eighty dollars and a carton of Winstons.

As the Goodson-Todman empire grew, the studio took on the efficiencies of a factory. Gil Fates acted as line producer for both *What's My Line?* and *I've Got a Secret,* the company's two major money-making hits. John Daly was employed as host of a second prime-time program, *It's News to Me* (CBS, 1951–54). In this game a clue, such as a photograph, was provided by the host. Four celebrity panelists would then describe a recent news event that was suggested by the clue. Three of them were lying; the other was describing a real event. The contestant had to guess who was telling the truth. It is perhaps worth noting that in 1954, during the final months of the show, none other than Walter Cronkite replaced Daly as the host of *It's News to Me.*

Mark Goodson's salad days on network television coincided directly with the McCarthy era, and even a gameshow producer could not fully escape the consequences of this. In a 1991 article for the *New York Times Sunday Magazine,* Goodson finally came forward to discuss his own involvement in the blacklists. For example, *What's My Line?* panelist Louis Untermeyer was sacked by Goodson when CBS began to get mail regarding his work for the Joint Anti-Fascist Refugee Committee during the thirties and his participation in the 1948 May Day parade in New York. Abe Burrows, the Broadway and Hollywood writer who was a panelist on Goodson's *The Name's the Same,* had at one time participated in programs sponsored by a California Communist "front" group; he, too, was fired. But it gradually became apparent to Goodson that if a stand were taken, the witch-hunters might back down. Henry Morgan, a panelist on *I've Got a Secret,* was named as a Communist sympathizer in *Red Channels* magazine, the blacklister's bible. However, Garry Moore, the show's host, threatened to quit if Morgan were let go. The network relented in that case, and Morgan remained an *I've Got a Secret* regular for the show's entire fifteen-season production run.

Meanwhile, the hits just kept on coming in the midfifties. *The Price Is Right* (NBC, 1956–63; ABC, 1963–65), was an epic test of consumer knowledge that originally aired in both daytime and prime-time editions. It was hosted by Bill Cullen, a familiar Goodson-Todman interlocutor. Four contestants, seated at a panel, were shown fur coats, cars, silver services, jewelry, and other prizes described in exorbitant detail by announcer Don Pardo (these descriptions were often written by the manufacturer's public-relations staff). The contestant who bid "closest to the suggested retail price without going over" it got to take the object of consumer envy home.

In *To Tell the Truth* (CBS, 1956–67), three contestants claimed to be a certain person who had accomplished some remarkable feat:

climbed Mt. Everest, swum the English Channel, gotten a taxicab during a rush-hour rainstorm at Manhattan's Grand Central Station. Celebrities questioned the trio and attempted to ferret out the truth-teller from the pretenders. The panel was composed of a typical Goodson pool of Broadway personalities: Kitty Carlisle, Orson Bean, Polly Bergen, Hy Gardner, Peggy Cass, Tom Poston, and Hildy Parks.

Both of these shows eventually became part of the woodwork of American culture. *The Price Is Right,* after a hiatus of several years, was altered and revived. The "panel" set was gone, and in its place contestants were chosen from the studio audience and exhorted by announcer Johnny Olsen to "come on down!" to the stage, making the show look a bit more like Monty Hall's *Let's Make a Deal.* The revival has been more successful than the original. The newer hour-long *Price Is Right,* hosted by Bob Barker, has aired on CBS daytime for over twenty years. *To Tell the Truth* has been resurrected several times, including a 1991 NBC morning revival hosted by Alex Trebek. In this case, almost nothing has been changed from the original. Phrases such as, "What is your name, please?" and, "Will the real [So-and-So] please stand up?" have become part of the American language.

Though Goodson was in no way implicated in the quiz-show scandals of the late 1950s, it became increasingly difficult for him (or anyone) to place any kind of gameshow on prime-time television in the aftermath of the revelations that contestants had been coached on some of TV's most popular contest shows. But Goodson-Todman continued to have success with daytime programs during the sixties. *Password,* hosted by Allen Ludden, was another decades-long hit. In yet another variation of the Goodson formula, two teams, each composed of a celebrity and a normal human being, competed against each other, attempting to guess a secret word from single-word clues provided by their partners. *The Match Game,* hosted by Gene Rayburn during its original 1962–69 run on NBC, challenged contestants to guess the responses of a celebrity panel. The program was revived during the seventies, a period that saw the rise of increasingly lewd and vulgar television programming, including the extremely popular toxic gameshows of Chuck Barris (see next chapter), such as *The Gong Show* and *The Newlywed Game.* Goodson went with the Barris flow in *The Match Game* revival. Whereas a typical round of the original *Match Game* might be something like, "What is your favorite color?" a typical seventies *Match Game* clue might be, "The lady at the grocery store told Mr. Smith to stop squeezing her *blank*." This kind of "question" would be greeted with giddy shrieks of shock from the audience — every single time. The answer given by the celebrities might typically be "boobs," and, in fact, that same answer might come up in response to any number of clues during any given episode. Whereas once the likes of Bennett Cerf and Kitty Carlisle graced the Goodson panel, *The Match Game* featured professional gameshow personalities such as Charles Nelson Reilly and Brett Sommers.

Goodson was doing so well coasting along on his "classics" that a string of failures hardly seemed to matter. But, in fact, the maestro seemed to be losing his magic touch by the midsixties. A succession of Goodson-Todman shows, including *Snap Judgment, Call My Bluff,* and *He Said, She Said* all came and went with uncharacteristic speed. Goodson rebounded from these failures in the midseventies with *Tattletales,* a show hosted by Bert Convy. Here again, he borrowed from rival Chuck Barris. *Tattletales* was a thinly masked copy imitation of *The Newlywed Game.* Instead of using downscale couples as contestants, Goodson relied on his trademark technique of using celebrities. The game, however, was the same: the players attempted to guess the responses of their spouses to questions that ranged from indelicate to obnoxious.

Goodson-Todman's next truly smash hit did not occur until the debut of *Family Feud* on ABC daytime in 1976. In this show, two families compete against each other by guessing the results of a public-opinion survey taken among the members of a TV studio audience. In some ways *Family Feud* is more a test of personal mediocrity than of knowledge. The question might be, say, "What is your favorite vegetable?" A contestant might answer "tomato." Scientifically speaking, a tomato, of course, is a fruit and not a vegetable. But if enough respondents in the survey answered "tomato," the answer would be "correct." Thus "normalness" is rewarded at the expense of excellence. In this regard *Family Feud* is a potent self-reflexive metaphor for the age of television, lending perhaps a new spin to the old adage "A little knowledge is a dangerous thing."

Richard Dawson, *Family Feud*'s original host, projected a smarmy show-biz personality that fell somewhere between the brainless sincerity of Wink Martindale and the raunchy cynicism of Chuck Barris. A good portion of *Family Feud* was devoted to small talk between Dawson and the contestants. Viewers were treated to whole minutes of Dawson's insistent practice of kissing each of the mothers, sisters, grandmas, and aunts who competed on the show. Mark

Goodson — as well as the TV gameshow and perhaps American culture — had come a long way from the Algonquin-like banter of the
black-tie panelists of *What's My Line?*

Goodson and Todman dabbled in other genres over the years —
but strictly as "hands off" investors. As far back as 1949 they produced
The Front Page for CBS, an hour-long dramatic series about newspaper reporters, which was based on the Ben Hecht Broadway play.
The show starred John Daly. Had *The Front Page* not been canceled
so quickly, Daly might never have hosted *What's My Line?* Goodson-
Todman also produced *The Web*, a New York–based golden-age anthology drama. This series was composed exclusively of adaptations
of short stories written by members of the Mystery Writers of America. Other non-gameshows under the company's banner included *The
Rebel*, a Western starring Nick Adams; *Philip Marlowe*, a series based
on the Raymond Chandler private eye; and *The Don Rickles Show*,
a comedy-variety show during the late sixties. None of these efforts
was particularly successful.

Bill Todman died in 1979, and since then Goodson has continued
to run the company, which is now called Mark Goodson Productions.
During the eighties, Goodson brought several new gameshows to the
air, including *Mindreaders*, *Blockbusters*, *Child's Play*, and *Trivia
Trap*. None of these was a hit — and Mark Goodson can no longer
be said to dominate the television gameshow. (During the eighties,
it can be argued, that distinction passed into the hands of Merv Griffin,
the creator of *Wheel of Fortune* and *Jeopardy*.) But a look at daytime
television in the 1990s reveals that Goodson's original concepts —
some of them almost a half century old now — are still there, at the
center of the genre, endlessly revived, altered, updated, and recycled
by Goodson (and copied by his competitors). No longer the king, he
remains the indisputable father of the television gameshow.

MARK GOODSON: SELECTED VIDEOGRAPHY

Gameshows

Winner Take All (CBS, 1948–52)
What's My Line? (CBS, 1950–67; syndicated, 1968–75)
Beat the Clock (CBS, 1950–58; ABC, 1958–61; syndicated, 1961–
    74; CBS, 1979–80)
By Popular Demand (CBS, 1950)
It's News to Me (CBS, 1951–54)
Two for the Money (NBC, 1952–53; CBS, 1953–57)

I've Got a Secret (CBS, 1952–67; syndicated, 1972; syndicated, 1976)

The Fred Allen Show/Judge for Yourself (NBC, 1953–54)

What's Going On? (ABC, 1954)

Make the Connection (NBC, 1955)

Choose Up Sides (NBC, 1956)

The Price Is Right (NBC, 1956–63; ABC, 1963–65; revived as *The New Price Is Right*, syndicated, 1972–74; CBS, 1972–present)

To Tell the Truth (CBS, 1956–67; syndicated, 1969–77; NBC, 1990–present)

Play Your Hunch (CBS, 1958–59; ABC, 1959; NBC, 1959–63)

Split Personality (NBC, 1958–59)

One Happy Family (NBC, 1961)

Number Please (ABC, 1961)

Say When! (NBC, 1961–65)

Password (CBS, 1961–67; syndicated, 1967–69; ABC, 1971–75; revived as *Password Plus*, NBC, 1979–82; revived as *Super Password*, NBC, 1984–87)

The Match Game (NBC, 1962–69; CBS, 1973–79; syndicated, 1975–81)

Missing Links (NBC, 1963–64; ABC, 1964)

Get the Message (ABC, 1964)

Call My Bluff (NBC, 1965)

Snap Judgment (NBC, 1967–69)

He Said, She Said (syndicated, 1968)

Tattletales (CBS, 1974–78; syndicated, 1977; CBS, 1982–83; syndicated, 1983–present)

Now You See It (CBS, 1974–75)

Showoffs (ABC, 1975)

Family Feud (ABC, 1976)

Double Dare (CBS, 1976–77)

The Better Sex (ABC, 1977–78)

Card Sharks (NBC, 1978–81; syndicated, 1982–present)

Mindreaders (NBC, 1979–80)

That's My Line (CBS, 1980–81)

Blockbusters (NBC, 1980–82)

Child's Play (CBS, 1982–83)

Body Language (syndicated, 1984)

Classic Concentration (NBC, 1987–present)

Non-Gameshows from Goodson-Todman Productions

The Front Page (CBS, 1949–50) — drama series
The Web (CBS, 1950–54; NBC, 1954–57) — anthology series
Jefferson Drum (NBC, 1958–59) — Western
The Rebel (ABC, 1959–61) — Western
The Richard Boone Show (NBC, 1963–64) — anthology series
Branded (NBC, 1965–66) — Western
The Don Rickles Show (ABC, 1968–69) — variety series
Philip Marlowe (ABC, 1969–70) — detective series

25. CHUCK BARRIS

Life's a Dirty Game

The successes of Mark Goodson's lighthearted, talkshow-like gameshows aside, the gameshow has had an extremely difficult history. The America that was waking up to TV after World War II had already substantially changed from a rural to a metropolitan society. But the ethos of a previous era continued to dominate public mores and to find expression in local blue laws. Las Vegas was still, for the most part, a radical theory of desert industrialization; Atlantic City, a place to go to the beach. There was not a single legal public lottery in the United States during the 1950s, and fewer than a dozen states even allowed pari-mutuel horse racing; Miami, with its jai alai frontons and dogtracks, raised the eyebrows of Northern visitors as America's version of a Caribbean sin city.

By the late fifties, however, the emerging suburban bourgeoisie had loosened up considerably amid the comforts of split-level utopia. *Playboy* magazine stood tall on the racks, while *Look* and *Colliers* decomposed into collective memory. Traditionally dry counties in the South and the Midwest went wet. Italian movies began to appear in Main Street theaters. The accumulation of postwar wealth seemed to make imperial Romans of the once pious Jeffersonian yeomanry. With bread plentiful, circuses seemed in order. It was in this context that television spat forth the big-money, prime-time quiz program.

The strike-it-rich excitement of shows such as *The $64,000 Question* and *Twenty-One* became a docudramatic metaphor for a society that found itself abruptly emerging from the deprivations of economic depression and total war into the gaudiest consumer bonanza the world had ever seen. While it was clear that Ralph Kramden would never achieve financial security driving a bus, Charles Van Doren was carting home tens of thousands of dollars each week just for being so goddamned smart.

At the height of its vogue, however, the quiz show self-destructed in a disgraceful scandal that would rival the Black Sox World Series of 1919 in the mythopoetics of American dreaming. The contestants, it was revealed, had been coached. What had seemed like a demonstration of meritocracy at work in the clean, new, high-tech America of IBM and Xerox was revealed as just another rigged game. As so often happens in a nation founded by theological radicals, the fist of a resurgent superego took the opportunity to pummel the frenzied id back into the underground.

The tragic prime-time quiz show was survived, however, by its poor relation, the daytime gameshow. With downscaled prizes (washers and dryers and weekends in Mexico rather than wads of cash) and a tendency to emphasize luck as well as brains, gameshows — from *Beat the Clock* to *Wheel of Fortune* — managed to survive the scandal. Companies that made gameshows, such as Goodson-Todman Productions and Merv Griffin Enterprises, were careful to cultivate Disney-like images of family wholesomeness. Perhaps this antiseptic aesthetic would have remained the fate of all TV gameshows if Chuck Barris had not come along to prove that the humiliation of contestants could be as sleazy — and as popular — a public spectacle as panting for cash.

Born in Philadelphia during the fateful year of 1929, Chuck Barris was educated at the University of Miami and the Drexel Institute of Technology. By the midfifties he was toiling far and wide in the vineyards of mass culture: he joined an NBC management trainee program; he worked on promotion of the Floyd Patterson–Ingemar Johansson heavyweight championship fight; he wrote the hit tune "Palisades Park" for Freddy Cannon and the Dreamers. By the end of the decade he was swiveling in a Hollywood office chair as ABC's West Coast director of daytime programming.

Bored with balancing the marketing demands of the national grocery conglomerates against the supply of gameshows and soap operas offered by the production companies, Barris began to develop his own programming ideas. In 1965 he left ABC to form Chuck Barris Productions. The company's first show, *The Dating Game* (ABC, 1965–73), was an unqualified hit. The concept was elegantly simple. An eligible bachelor (or, occasionally, a "bachelorette") questioned three candidates for a "dream date," all of whom were concealed from view. From the lilting refrains of Herb Alpert and the Tijuana Brass on the soundtrack to the orange bathtub flowers that dominated the set to the prom tuxedoes sported by host Jim Lange, the show was a polyester daydream of adolescent sexual double entendre and giddy ca-ca talk that cannot be wholly discounted as an element of the "sexual revolution" of the sixties.

The Newlywed Game (ABC, 1966–74; syndicated, 1977–80) picked up where *The Dating Game* left off, extending Barris's exploration of American mating rituals beyond the threshold of legal union. Once again, the smirking, sneering infantile sexual double entendre figured largely in the show's appeal. Four couples, each married less than a year, were assembled to compete for recreational vehicles, major appliances, matched pit-group furniture, and other prizes of a lifetime. The neophyte husbands and wives were isolated from each other while host Bob Eubanks posed questions such as, "What will your husband say is his favorite thing to dip his cruller in each morning?" or "Fill in the following: I wish my wife knew how to take better care of my *blank*." The audiences roared. The husbands and wives would then be reunited, and the couple whose answers matched most often "won."

Both *The Dating Game* and *The Newlywed Game* enjoyed long runs on daytime TV and in syndication. Moreover, they also managed the considerable trick of making the transition to prime time and becoming successful there as well. Barris claimed that the reason for the success of the two shows was that "the television audience could identify with the contestants. Almost everybody had, at one time or another, dated, and many were married. And if they weren't married, they had parents who were, and who knew what marriage was all about. Everyone could relate to what the contestants on *The Dating Game* and *The Newlywed Game* were going through: the discomfort, the embarrassment, the relief, the anger, the humor, and, sometimes, the thrilling conclusions that dating and young married couples both suffer and enjoy."

The Newlywed Game thrived on the sophomoric themes of American show business. Mother-in-law questions, for example, were a staple (e.g., "What kind of horse would your wife say your mother most resembles?"). Barris, never blind to an opportunity, spun off yet another show, based on this subgenre of *Newlywed Game* questions: *How's Your Mother-in-Law?* (ABC, 1967–68). Hosted by game-show myth Wink Martindale, the show featured three celebrities who attempted to "rate" the mothers-in-law of three noncelebrity couples, all of whom supplied the panelists with the most personal and shocking details about their mothers that they could come up with. Barris, with his usual clinical precision, described the concept as an opportunity to put "the legendarily frightening and meddlesome battle-ax on the hot seat."

The Family Game (ABC, 1967) was the fourth and final variation on the theme that had started with *The Dating Game*. This time children were asked embarrassing questions — by Bob Barker — about their parents. Like *How's Your Mother-in-Law?* the show was a failure in the ratings and Barris began to turn his attention toward comedy-variety.

Operation Entertainment (ABC, 1968–69) was Barris's first hour-long variety series. It was also his first show designed specifically for prime-time as opposed to daytime television. During the dog days of the Vietnam War, Barris announced that he wanted "to produce a 'Bob Hope Christmas Show' for our troops every week on ABC-TV." He claims to have told ABC's vice president for nighttime programming, "I want to do a one-hour weekly variety show from army and navy bases. I want lots of stars, and sexy models, a big Les Brown–type band. I want to have thousands of servicemen sitting in front of the stage, whistling and hooting and hollering. . . . I know there's no way I can get Hope. But I don't need him. . . . Each week, instead of Bob Hope, I'll have a big star hosting the show. Flip Wilson, James Garner, Don Rickles, those kinds of stars. Not only will the program be a gigantic hit for the network . . . but it's a hell of a patriotic gesture."

Debuting in time for the Tet Offensive, *Operation Entertainment* brought such stars as Rich Little, Tim Conway, Jimmy Dean, Ray Charles, Ed Ames, the Operation Entertainment Girls, and the Terry Gibbs Band to the military bases of the world and the living rooms of North America. The show was over, however, a lot sooner than the war.

Barris continued to dream of reviving comedy-variety in prime time. He produced several specials for CBS, including one for Mamas and Papas star Cass Elliot in 1973. His most ambitious effort during the period was *Your Hit Parade* (CBS, 1974). Based on the old hit series of the same name that had begun on radio in the thirties and continued on to TV in the fifties, the Barris version mixed nostalgic presentations of standards with the contemporary music of the seventies. The combination proved deadly, alienating rather than satisfying fans of both types of music.

The most long lived comedy-variety series that Barris was able to put together was *The Bobby Vinton Show* (syndicated, 1975–78). Made in Canada, the series had all the trappings of a classical fifties variety package: its own backup singers, collectively called The Peaches; its own band, the Jimmy Dale Orchestra; a group of nondescript sidekicks to play in sketches; and a stable of stand-up comics, including Foster Brooks, John Byner, and Henny Youngman. Featuring Bobby "Mr. Lonely" Vinton cavorting through the studio audience with microphone in hand, singing a mixture of Tin Pan Alley, fifties pop ballads, and polka classics to a studio audience obviously thrilled to be this close to a show-business legend, the show achieved a viewership whose demographic profile would have turned the publicity department of the Social Security Administration green with envy.

Barris continued churning out gameshows even as he was making his foray into comedy-variety. *The Game Game* (syndicated, 1969) picked up on a growing national interest in pop psychology. Here three celebrities and one contestant attempted to match answers to highly subjective (and of course sexually suggestive) questions with "normative" answers supplied by a rather mysterious source referred to on the show as the "Southern Institute of Psychology." *The Parent Game* (syndicated, 1972) was a variation on the theme of the failed *Family Game* concept, mixed with a bit of the failed *Game Game* concept. This time parents would try to match their answers about child rearing with the "correct" answers supplied by a child psychiatrist. As late as 1979 Barris was still plugging away with this stuff when he introduced *Three's a Crowd,* in which both wives and secretaries were asked to predict how their husbands/bosses would answer (often sexually suggestive) questions.

Barris hadn't come up with a breakaway hit in any format since his early successes with *The Dating Game* and *The Newlywed Game.* With *The New Treasure Hunt* (syndicated, 1974–77), he began to move in a different direction. Like *Your Hit Parade, The New Treasure Hunt* was a revival of a long-canceled old show, in this case a fifties gameshow starring Jan Murray. In the original, Murray would ask contestants questions, and the winners would be sent on a "treasure hunt," which allowed them to choose to open one of thirty treasure chests. Barris revised the show with his personal touch by eliminating the quiz entirely and just sending the contestants scampering around trying to imagine in which of the treasure chests lay twenty-five grand. The prize they found was usually something more like a headless doll or fifty pounds of chili beans and a can of Glade. At the end of the half hour a stone-faced uniformed security guard would reveal the location of the loot.

The New Treasure Hunt was as much a self-reflexive parody of gameshows as it was a gameshow. Requiring no mental or physical skills at all, it established the marketability of what amounted to a gameless gameshow. In his next project, Barris took that principle a step further. *The Gong Show* (NBC, 1976–78; syndicated, 1976–80) self-consciously tested the intelligence and sensibility of the viewer. With its emcee, its celebrity panel, and its contestants, it looked like a typical afternoon gameshow. It might even be mistaken for a talent-scout revival, on the order of the old Ted Mack or Arthur Godfrey programs. But on closer inspection many of the acts turned out to be pros imitating amateurs, and others turned out not to be acts at all. Caught at the right moment, it even looked like an old-time 1950s comedy-variety series. Confusion? Deception? Contestant self-degradation? It proved to be the triumph of Chuck Barris's career.

To understand the popularity of *The Gong Show*, it is necessary to consider the historical context of the show's appearance on television during the late seventies. This was a particularly boring period in prime time. The burst of "relevance" energy that had awoken television from its decades of McCarthy-induced sleep during the early part of the decade was petering out, as shows such as *All in the Family*, *M*A*S*H*, and *Mod Squad* were losing ratings points to the likes of *Happy Days*, *Three's Company*, and *Charlie's Angels*. The sophisticated yuppie operas of the eighties, series such as *Hill Street Blues*, *St. Elsewhere*, and *thirtysomething*, had yet to make their target demographic influences felt.

While prime time was struggling through this period of retrenchment, the creative action shifted to the "marginal" hours. NBC, floundering in last place for the first time in its history, had the least to lose in experimenting with new forms of programming during non–prime-time slots. The network led the way in this regard, with late-night satires such as *Saturday Night Live* and *SCTV Comedy Network*. *The Gong Show*, aired daily at noon, must be seen as part of this strategy of attempting to break loose from the wooden programming pieties that had dominated American commercial television since its inception.

In terms of traditional values and decorum, *The Gong Show* went out of its way to be vulgar, cheap, and irreverent. Over the course of each episode's half hour, seven or eight acts would perform on stage to be judged by a panel of three celebrities, which included at various times such talent as Jaye P. Morgan, Jamie Farr, Arte Johnson, Rex Reed, Phyllis Diller, Rip Taylor, Steve Garvey, and *$64,000 Question* alumna Dr. Joyce Brothers. At any time during a performance, a judge could get up and strike the gong, which symbolically served the function of the old "hook" that was used in vaudeville to pull a bad act off the stage. If the act could survive its performance without being gonged, the judges then rated it on a scale of one to ten. The performer with the most points received the grand prize: a check for $516.32 (this skyrocketed to $712.05 in the nighttime version that was added in 1978).

Upon occasion, the lineup would include a legitimate act or two. Luanne, for example, was a bona fide amateur singer whose appearance on *The Gong Show* led to a role in the Broadway production of *Annie*. Pee-Wee Herman made his first national television appearance on the show. But usually the acts were more like purposeful displays of silliness, tastelessness, and/or exhibitional stupidity than demonstrations of talent. One contestant whistled "Swanee River" through her nose; another played the trumpet through his navel. The Popsicle Twins were two scantily clad teenage girls who did nothing but lick orange popsicles in a suggestive manner. Physical abnormality was a popular theme, and heavy women, especially, were paraded across the screen singing and dancing. Such performances only served to stimulate the screaming, jeering studio audience to further abuse ("Gong 'em!"). The snickering double entendres of *The Dating Game* and *The Newlywed Game* seemed like primitive attempts at contestant humiliation by comparison. Barris, who hosted the show himself, described the sadistic pleasures of *The Gong Show* this way: "The Christians (the act and the host) versus the lions (everybody else), right there on the boob tube for everyone to watch. *The Gong Show* gave the little person his or her moment in the spotlight — and the consequences thereof. The rest of the world was given the opportunity to be jealous and to kick the shit in the little person's face."

The auteur is being somewhat generous in this description by including himself among the Christians. It was not unusual for him as emcee, dressed in gaudy tux and face adorned with brainless smile, to kick an act off the stage with the toe of his boot before the gong had even sounded.

The Gong Show made Chuck Barris, for the first time in his career, a star. John Barbour, later one of the hosts of *Real People* (NBC, 1979–84), had originally been scheduled to be the host. But Barbour was unable to understand the campy gestalt that was essential to the program, leading Barris, the worried producer, to step in and personally take over. Barris became so thoroughly identified with *The Gong Show* that an attempt to use an alternate host, Gary Owens, on the evening version had to be abandoned, leaving Barris with more work than he cared to do.

If the viewing public associated *The Gong Show* with Barris, so did critics, academics, and other guardians of Kultur, scores of whom jumped on the program and its popularity as more evidence of the death of Western civilization and the primary role that TV was playing in the unfortunate murder. But "the gong" had indeed found its way into American idiom, and the format was borrowed by high schools and social organizations all over the country as the exciting new form of what had so recently been the tired old amateur show. Barris even directed a film, generically titled *The Gong Show Movie*, in an attempt to enshrine his creation into an epic tale of American show business. The resurgence of "amateur" shows on national TV — from "Stupid Pet Tricks" on *Late Night with David Letterman* to *Ed McMahon's Star Search* to *America's Funniest Home Videos* — can be traced directly to Barris's sarcastic resuscitation of the genre.

Barris had always grounded his work on deriving aesthetic pleasure from the embarrassment or humiliation of "regular" people who are set free to make fools of themselves by means of the technological monolith of the national television system. If most television producers seemed obsessed with consumerist glamor, sexual voyeurism, and the slick representation of sensationalistic violence, Barris exploited the cavalier boredom that an overdose of such product can inspire. Teenagers, especially, enjoyed the funky aroma of Barris's revolt against the antiseptic atmosphere that was so thoroughly dominating mass-culture production values in the late seventies.

In *The $1.98 Beauty Contest* (syndicated, 1978), Barris discovered the lower limits of the descendantal aesthetic he had created. Each week six female contestants would compete for a title and prizes. As in *The Gong Show*, contestants ranged from familiar contenders to those whose qualifications placed them outside the mainstream of the genre's traditions. Once again, obese women were singled out for particular ridicule, especially during the swimsuit competition. The talent competition was a kind of micro–*Gong Show* embedded in each episode's center.

The $1.98 Beauty Contest made no secret of its connections to *The Gong Show*; it was clearly a Chuck Barris production. The host, Rip Taylor, was a frequent *Gong* panelist, and the judges included Jaye

P. Morgan, Jamie Farr, The Unknown Comic, and many other Barris repertory players. At the end of each episode Taylor, as the anti–Bert Parks, would bellow out the *$1.98* themesong ("You can win the prize, you take the cake . . .") as the winner took her victory walk down the runway. Interestingly, this was not Barris's first exploration of the beauty-contest genre. Earlier in his career, he had created *Dream Girl* (ABC, 1966–67), which was an attempt at a "legit" weekly prime-time pageant. Of course, that was before Barris had proved the commercial viability of self-degradation.

By the end of the seventies, Barris's talent and/or luck had burned out. *The Chuck Barris Rah-Rah Show* (NBC, 1978) was an hour-long variety package, hosted by Barris, that included big-name acts such as Cab Calloway, Chuck Berry, Jose Feliciano, Henny Youngman, and The Coasters, along with an interspersing of *Gong Show* freaks and losers. It didn't last two months. Like Sherwood Schwartz (see Chapter 3) and several other TV producers who have found themselves out of creative capital, Barris went into a baroque period of remaking and repackaging his early hits. During the mideighties, new versions of *The Dating Game* and *The Newlywed Game* appeared in national syndication, but little else. Also like Sherwood Schwartz, Barris was moved to write his autobiography as he was running out of TV concepts. As ready to scramble traditional literary genres as he had been to mix video formats, Barris wrote *Confessions of a Dangerous Mind,* which he characterized as "an unauthorized autobiography." A bizarre synthesis of fact and fiction, the book included detailed information on how Barris had worked as an assassin for the CIA while producing *The Gong Show.*

In 1985 ABC allowed him his own self-congratulatory retrospective special, *Anything for a Laugh: Twenty Years of the Best of the Chuck Barris Shows.* Barris hosted the show with full *Gong Show* accoutrements, but he seemed to be growing a little tired of the whole thing. *The Love Connection* was by now asking frank sexual questions of its dating couples that would have made Jim Lange blush. *Star Search,* with its TV spokesperson competition, made the objectification of women on *The $1.98 Beauty Contest* seem halfhearted. Irony and hipness, the qualities that Barris had tried to mine from the depths of slapstick lasciviousness, were everywhere on television by now, and the "greatest hits" of TV's original schlockmeister had come to seem primitive by comparison.

CHUCK BARRIS: SELECTED VIDEOGRAPHY

Series

The Dating Game (ABC, 1965–73; syndicated, 1973; 1977–80)
The New Dating Game (syndicated, 1986)
The All New Dating Game (syndicated, 1987)
The Newlywed Game (ABC, 1966–74; syndicated, 1977–80)
The New Newlywed Game (ABC, 1984)
How's Your Mother-in-Law? (ABC, 1967–68)
The Family Game (ABC, 1967)
Operation Entertainment (ABC, 1968–69)
The Game Game (syndicated, 1969)
The Parent Game (syndicated, 1972)
Your Hit Parade (CBS, 1974)
The New Treasure Hunt (syndicated, 1974–77)
The Bobby Vinton Show (syndicated, 1975–78)
The Gong Show (NBC, 1976–78 daytime; syndicated, 1976–80
   nighttime)
Three's a Crowd (syndicated, 1977)
The $1.98 Beauty Contest (syndicated, 1978)
The Chuck Barris Rah-Rah Show (NBC, 1978)
Leave It to the Women (syndicated, 1981)

Specials

The Cass Elliot Special (CBS, 1973)
The Chuck Barris Special (NBC, 1977)

26. IRNA PHILLIPS

_____

Queen of the Soaps

The "soap opera," so named for the household cleansers that have been among its chief sponsors for most of this century on radio and TV, can be seen as a by-product of the general spread of literate culture to a widening circle of social classes over the last three hundred years. With roots traceable to Restoration theater (see, for example, William Congreve's *The Way of the World*) via English "penny dreadful" novels and American daytime radio serials, the television soap opera flourished during the 1980s to an unprecedented degree. Transcending its ghettoization in the commercially marginal hours of afternoon broadcast, the soap opera exhibited a profound effect on the formal character of many of the most ambitious and prestigious prime-time series, including shows such as *Dallas, Hill Street Blues, Dynasty*, and *St. Elsewhere.*

Even since the earliest days of the broadcast media, there has been a special kind of disrespect reserved for the soap opera by most critics and many nonfans. The hyperbolic use of music as a mood punctuator has helped make the genre the definitive televisual incarnation of melodrama (which literally means, from a Greek root, "a drama performed with the accompaniment of music"). But this scorn may have less to do with content analysis than with audience analysis.

Considered a "woman's" or, even worse, a "housewife's" entertainment, the modern soap has drawn more than its share of derision from the men who have written the history and criticism of Western drama and literature. If Charles Dickens's plots are complex and comprehensive, soap operas are convoluted and distended; if Congreve and Moliére are the immortal satiric masters of social manners and class detail, soap operas are sophomorically obsessed with the banalities of everyday bourgeois life. And yet, at the same time, this very perception of the TV soap opera as "female" has also made it possible for women to dominate its production to a greater degree than any other video (or, for that matter, cinematic) genre.

Credit for the adaptations and inventions that brought about the broadcast soap opera must go in great part to one producer, Irna Phillips. Having begun her career as a radio pioneer in the thirties, she was responsible, along with a handful of colleagues and collaborators, for churning out millions of lines of dialogue and thousands of hours of programming. Phillips was so successful, with so many programs running on the networks at once, that she was known to hang giant storyline charts on the walls of her office to keep her plotting responsibilities clear for a half dozen or more soap operas that she might be working on at any given time. As the Zen mistress of suds, she eventually came to the point at which she could plot her stories conceptually and farm out the actual scriptwriting to "dialoguers," who would deliver shooting scripts for her approval. She became known in the industry as "The Queen of the Soaps."

Born just after the turn of the century, Irna Phillips was one of ten children in a Jewish family growing up in the Midwest. She received a master of arts degree in drama from the University of Illinois and went on to postgraduate studies at the University of Wisconsin. From 1925 to 1930 she worked as a teacher in the Dayton, Ohio, public school system, telling stories and teaching drama and theater history to children. There is, perhaps, a fine line between teaching in a classroom and acting on a stage, and Phillips continued to hold out hopes for a career in the theater while teaching in the late twenties. In 1930, having won several acting roles for radio productions at WGN in Chicago, she was finally able to leave the classroom to pursue a full-time career in show business.

After spending some time as a staff writer for a daytime talkshow titled *Thought for the Day*, she created what is generally regarded as the first daytime serial specifically targeted for women, *Painted Dreams*. Phillips not only wrote all the episodes but starred in the show as well. Home and family were the principal themes, and both bore autobiographical echoes from the writer's life. The large immigrant Jewish family of Phillips's youth became an Irish immigrant family, with Phillips playing the role of Mother Moynihan. In 1933 she urged WGN, a local Chicago station owned by the *Chicago Tribune* ("World's Greatest Newspaper"), to sell the program to a national network. WGN's management refused, and Phillips took the company to court, claiming *Painted Dreams* as her own property. While the case lingered in court, she went on to sell a new show to NBC radio's Red Network, titled *Today's Children*. In this thinly disguised knockoff of *Painted Dreams*, Mother Moynihan became Mother Moran, and much of the story remained the same. To the degree that *Today's Children* can be considered the first incarnation of the broadcast network soap opera, Irna Phillips must be considered the inventor of the genre.

While Phillips never married, her shows were emphatic in their defense of marriage, home, and the nuclear family. For example, in an episode of *Today's Children*, one of the daughters is reluctant to get married, to which Mother Moran replies in her thick brogue, "When you're paintin' your dreams, be careful of the colors you're goin' to be usin', 'cause sometimes you make a mistake and the colors that you think are goin' to look good don't look so good in the finished picture. . . . There are three colors that have stood the test of time. They are the colors that are the foundations of all the dreams of all men and women in the world: the colors of love — family — home."

Phillips adhered to this philosophy throughout her career as a dramatist. As late as 1972, some forty years after the premiere of *Today's Children*, she told *Broadcasting* magazine that "relationships don't have to be sordid to be interesting. I'm [always] trying to get back to the fundamentals: for example, the way in which a death in the family, or serious illness, brings members of the family closer together, gives them a real sense of how much they're dependent on each other."

Phillips found her commitment to the family *über alles* in no way incompatible with commercialism. Even her first local Chicago effort, *Painted Dreams*, was specifically structured to fit the needs of its sponsor, Montgomery Ward and Company. Robert C. Allen, in *Speaking of Soap Operas*, offers the following quotation from Phillips's original proposal for the program: "Any radio presentation which is sponsored, must actually sell merchandise. . . . It is my plan [for *Painted Dreams*] to have an engagement, the wedding in June, the trousseau, the furnishing of a home, actually occur via the air. This is the first step in developing the feature as a merchandising vehicle, and this plan opens an avenue to merchandising any article which may be sold by mail order or through the other retail outlets of Montgomery Ward and Company."

This willingness and savvy in pleasing both audience and sponsor went a long way in helping to establish the soap opera as a viable genre of commercial mass culture. *Today's Children* became a hit for NBC radio; by 1938 it was the highest-rated daytime program on the air. That same year *Painted Dreams* emerged from its legal entanglements and was bought by CBS radio. However, the court settlements prohibited Phillips from further involvement with the property. Much to Phillips's pleasure, *Painted Dreams* would never approach the popularity of its stepchild, *Today's Children*.

The importance of Phillips's personal relationship to her work was further demonstrated that same year. Following the death of her real-life mother, who had served as the inspiration for Mother Moran, Phillips insisted on canceling *Today's Children*, despite the fact that it had hit the top of the ratings. Her sponsor, Pillsbury, was understandably upset about losing the hit, but rather than fight her in court the company promptly bought her next radio creation, *Woman in White*, whose main character was a nurse. Phillips had done it again; the new series would remain in production for a decade. (Interestingly, in 1943, some five years later, after perhaps absorbing the sting of the loss of her mother, Phillips would bring *Today's Children* back into production.)

Along with other soap producers working in Chicago, especially the husband-and-wife team of Frank and Anne Hummert, Irna Phillips helped to establish the city as a major national production center for American radio in the thirties and forties. As her career began to blossom, she continued to create new series at a prodigious rate. The consistency of the conceptual framework she maintained in these programs became synonymous with the structural traits that came to be associated with the entire genre.

Phillips's *The Guiding Light*, which premiered on NBC radio in 1937, is still on the air, a regular feature of the daily CBS afternoon television schedule in the 1990s. Interestingly, the series began as the story of a small-town minister and his flock. The minister, Reverend Ruthledge, became Phillips's on-air persona. Through him she preached her gospel of devotion to traditional family values and the righteousness of a Victorian code of conduct. In *Tune In Yesterday*, John Dunning recalls that "running through the fabric of the early *Guiding Light* was the philosophy of Reverend Ruthledge and his church — the goodness of life, the inspiration of the American way.

Sometimes Miss Phillips even devoted the entire 15 minutes to the Ruthledge sermon."

While the idea of an unmarried Jewish woman speaking through the masque of a married male Protestant minister may seem bizarre, media historian J. Fred MacDonald suggests that much of Phillips's success can be traced to "her careful understanding of the women who comprised her audience." She was a careful reader of fan mail, and she actively solicited the opinions and views of female listeners, which she would then integrate into her stories. MacDonald quotes Phillips from an interview she gave to *Variety* in 1940, in which she states that the average American woman seeks "to build securely for herself a haven, which means a husband, a family, friends, and a mode of living — all wrapped up neatly and compactly into a tight little ball with the woman as the busy center of the complete, secure little world." The basis of dramatic tension in her stories, suggests MacDonald, is the introduction of threat after threat to this fragile ideal. The constant defeat of these threats becomes the wellspring of listener satisfaction.

The Guiding Light and its spin-off, *The Right to Happiness* (which itself ran on radio for over twenty years), firmly established Phillips's reputation. Two other Phillips radio hits, *The Road of Life* and *Woman in White,* were among the first soap operas to focus on doctors and nurses. Several critics have noted that the insistent focus of soap operas on the medical profession may be at least partly attributable to Irna Phillips's own hypochondriac tendencies. The popularity of these medi-soaps was also instrumental in shifting the broader focus of the entire genre away from poor, often immigrant, families (such as the Morans in *Today's Children*) to upscale, educated, professional people. This remains the major class setting of soap-operatic narrative some fifty years later.

During the 1940s Phillips dominated the afternoon airwaves. Most soap operas were still fifteen minutes in length during this period, and in 1946 four popular Irna Phillips series were presented consecutively each day over NBC under the umbrella title of *The General Mills Hour.* General Mills, the giant food and household-wares corporation, also sponsored a fifth Phillips show, not part of the package, titled *Lonely Women.* The program, set in real time during the Second World War, addressed itself to the plight of women separated from their men; it had an almost exclusively female cast. But this avant-garde experiment failed, barely lasting a season. Phillips's last great radio hit was *The Brighter Day.* Like *The Guiding Light, Brighter Day* concerned a small-town clergyman and his congregation. This time the preacher of Phillips's gospel was Reverend Richard Dennis, a widower bringing up four daughters.

But even as *The Brighter Day* was rising to the top of ratings, radio was passing the mantle of mass-culture story-telling on to television, and Phillips, though at first skeptical about TV, proved equal to the task of the transition to the new medium. She began her television career in 1949 by adapting her old radio hit, *Today's Children*, into *These Are My Children* for NBC. By 1954 three Phillips series, *The Guiding Light*, *The Brighter Day*, and *The Road of Life* were all being broadcast daily over the NBC television network. Direct sponsorship had always been an important feature of soap-opera production, and Phillips ended her longtime radio association with General Mills as she moved over to television production. She entered the TV era by making a deal with another giant domestic products marketer, Procter and Gamble.

Phillips introduced her first two thirty-minute programs, *As the World Turns* and *The Edge of Night*, in the fall of 1956. They were her most popular efforts to date. Throughout much of its first fifteen years on CBS, *As the World Turns* was the highest-rated program on daytime TV. In 1965, taking note of ABC's success with *Peyton Place* (a nighttime twice-a-week soap for which Phillips served as consultant), CBS attempted a short-lived, prime-time spin-off of *As the World Turns* titled *Our Private World*. *As the World Turns* epitomized the work of Irna Phillips. It focused on doctors and lawyers in a small Midwestern town ("near Chicago") called Oakdale. It was built on the structuring principle of following the lives of two WASPish families, one solidly upper-middle-class (the Lowells) and one just slightly less well-to-do (the Hugheses). No matter what happened, the emphasis of plot resolution always valorized the primacy of the family in American life.

Phillips added another hit to her collection with *Another World* (NBC, 1964–present). The title of this program refers to what Phillips characterized as the "other world" of dreams, feelings, and aspirations that each of us — and each of the program's characters — carries within us parallel to the material world in which we are forced to live. Though Phillips left active involvement with *Another World* during the late sixties, she achieved yet another milestone when her creation became the first daily sixty-minute soap opera in the history of American broadcasting. NBC even experimentally expanded the format to ninety minutes during 1979–80 but decided to return to hour-long episodes the following season. *Another World* would eventually spawn two spin-offs: *Somerset* (NBC, 1970–76) and *Texas* (NBC,

1980–82), which was an afternoon attempt to cash in on the *Dallas* craze.

Right on the heels of *Another World* came *Days of Our Lives*, which premiered on NBC in 1965. The series, which was cocreated by Phillips, Ted Corday, and Allan Chase, distinguished itself with its famous hourglass-in-the-sky symbol and the dulcet tones of Macdonald Carey announcing, "As sands through the hourglass, so are the days of our lives." It was another Irna Phillips mega-hit, and it remains in production some three decades later.

By the late sixties, the cultural rumblings of the civil rights movement were beginning to be felt in network TV programming, and Phillips, despite her reputation as a principal engineer of what at the time seemed to be the soap opera's structural conservatism, attempted to bring her work into appropriate new territory. Her last project, *Love Is a Many Splendored Thing* (CBS, 1967–73), was conceived by Phillips as an extension of a 1955 Oscar-winning film of the same title, which had been directed by Henry King. A modern retelling of the Madame Butterfly tale, the movie was the story of a Eurasian doctor (Jennifer Jones) and a white American war correspondent (William Holden) who fall in love in Hong Kong during the Korean War period. CBS, however, insisted that the key theme of interracial romance be dropped. After some forty years of creating commercially successful soap operas for the networks on both radio and TV, Phillips quit the project in anger over an artistic-control issue. *Love Is a Many Splendored Thing* finally reached the air in 1967 as a tepid imitation of her original concept. Its six-year run was not very successful by the standards that Irna Phillips had set for the genre.

The "Queen of the Soaps" would continue to actively write episodes for her array of running hits until her death in 1974. But she was not able to update soap narrative to reflect the changes in race relations and sex relations that were overtaking American culture. That job would fall to Irna Phillips's protégé and heir, Agnes Nixon (see next chapter).

IRNA PHILLIPS: SELECTED SOAPOGRAPHY

Radio

Painted Dreams (WGN-Chicago, 1930–33)
Judy and Jane (NBC, 1932–43) — writer only
Today's Children (NBC, 1933–38; 1943–50)
The Road of Life (NBC, 1937–59)

The Guiding Light (various, 1937–56)
Woman in White (various, 1938–42)
The Right to Happiness (various, 1939–60)
Lonely Women (NBC, 1942–43)
Masquerade (NBC, 1946–57)
The Brighter Day (NBC, 1948–52)

Television

These Are My Children (NBC, 1949)
The Guiding Light (CBS, 1952–present)
The Road of Life (CBS, 1954–55)
The Brighter Day (CBS, 1954–62)
The Edge of Night (CBS/ABC, 1956–84)
As the World Turns (CBS, 1956–present)
Another World (NBC, 1964–present)
Days of Our Lives (NBC, 1965–present)
Love Is a Many Splendored Thing (CBS, 1967–73)

27. AGNES NIXON

─ ─ ─ ─ ─ ─ ─ ─ ─

Soap Opera Goes Post-Victorian

Agnes Eckhardt was born in Nashville, Tennessee, on December 10, 1927, to a father who made his living in "burial garments." Raised a Roman Catholic, she attended St. Mary's College in South Bend, Indiana, but transferred to Northwestern University midway through her studies. While still at Northwestern, she sold her first radio play and was soon hired by Irna Phillips (see previous chapter) as a dialogue writer for the Chicago-based soap opera *Woman in White*. In a short time, however, she left Chicago for New York, where she began a career in prime-time television, writing additional dialogue lines throughout the fifties for a wide range of golden-age anthology dramas, including *Studio One, Robert Montgomery Presents, The Armstrong Circle Theatre, The Hallmark Hall of Fame, Cameo Theatre, Somerset Maugham Theatre,* and *Philco Television Playhouse.*

As the golden age of live, prime-time anthology drama disintegrated in the rush toward weekly filmed series, the center of TV production was moving from New York theaters to Hollywood soundstages. Agnes Eckhardt, however, had married Robert Nixon, who was happily employed in Philadelphia, and she was not willing to make a move to the West Coast at the risk of her personal life. Her opportunities as a prime-time drama script doctor continued to dry up in the early sixties.

It was at about this time that Irna Phillips, Nixon's old boss from Chicago radio, called her and asked her to start writing for *The Guiding Light*, a New York–based daytime soap opera. With New York just a ninety-minute train ride away, Nixon accepted the offer, and she eventually became the program's head writer. This would be the start of a long career in TV soap operas in association with Irna Phillips. Her involvement in the Phillips soap empire grew as she took on writing assignments for *As the World Turns* and *Another World*.

Juggling her responsibilities as a dramatist and a mother, Nixon found herself in the peculiar position of a housewife writing programs designed for housewives. In a nonfictional account of the behind-the-scenes production of *All My Children*, novelist Dan Wakefield quoted Nixon's recollection of this period in her life: "When the children were small . . . I was writing and changing diapers too — I had to give up the bridge clubs and ladies' luncheons, the civic work — the only thing I . . . [did was] . . . go to PTA or go see my son and daughters in school sports."

By the late sixties, Nixon's reputation as a soap-opera scriptwriter was second only to that of Irna Phillips herself. There is evidence to make the case that Agnes Nixon was actually eclipsing her old mentor. In 1968, for example, Procter and Gamble asked her to come in and take over *Another World*, an Irna Phillips soap opera that had abruptly fallen down in the afternoon Nielsens. Nixon did what Phillips had been unable to do. Her introduction of several new characters and a whole set of new storylines propelled *Another World* from a precarious position at the edge of cancellation to Number Two in the daytime ratings. Nixon now found herself in a position to create and produce her own daytime serials.

Agnes Nixon is usually given credit for bringing "relevance" to what had been for decades the insufferably stodgy "Ken and Barbie" world of the soap opera. While the earliest of radio soaps had included immigrant characters, especially large immigrant families whose mothers had thick accents suitable for the aural medium, television soap opera had developed as a virtually all-WASP domain. Even the sitcom, which was dominated by shows such as *Father Knows Best* and *Donna Reed* during the fifties, had produced some sampling of ethnic variety. But there had never been a Ricky Ricardo, much less a Kingfish Stevens or a Molly Goldberg, in the prim and proper middle-class settings of the afternoon soaps.

One Life to Live, the first show created, produced, and written by

Agnes Nixon, debuted on ABC in 1968. The 1968–69 season was a significant one in that it saw the success of several topically oriented programs that had broken longtime TV taboos. Examples include *Rowan and Martin's Laugh-In*, which contained within its electronic slapstick bits and bites of political and social humor; *Julia*, the first sitcom starring a black performer in a title role since the cancellations of *Amos 'n' Andy* and *Beulah* in 1953; and *60 Minutes*, the CBS News documentary series that occasionally featured controversial exposés and muckraking pieces among its segments.

"When I created *One Life to Live*," Nixon disclosed to Dan Wakefield, "I achieved one of my personal ambitions, which was to take soap operas out of WASP Valley." Hoping to "force people to examine their own prejudices," Nixon even developed a story on *One Life to Live* about a light-skinned black woman who passed for white during the first months of the program. Viewers were as shocked as the fictional characters when the revelation of her race was made public. Blacks, Jews, ethnic Poles — groups virtually absent from twenty years of daytime TV soap opera — were all written into prominent storylines of the show.

Another innovation implemented by Nixon during this period was on-location shooting. Ever since coming to television, soap operas had been claustrophobically shot on one or two sets, usually rooms of a family home or wards of a hospital. In *One Life to Live*, Nixon took the soap opera's cameras to an actual New York City drug rehabilitation center, where one of the program's principal characters worked as a doctor. Actual residents of the center were used as extras, and in some cases they were invited to discuss their lives in "vérité" sequences that were used as part of the show.

Nixon followed up the success of *One Life to Live* with another hit, *All My Children*, which also served her as a vehicle for airing topics that were new to daytime television. Between the two series, such issues as abortion, infertility, the efficacy of getting a pap smear (a plotline that is credited with moving thousands of viewers to do just that), clinical depression, child abuse, and the problems of returning Vietnam War veterans all made their way into daily storylines. Sensitive social issues, once thoroughly absent from the romantic entanglements and betrayals that dominated soap opera narrative, became a familiar convention of TV soap operas. Nixon had done for the soap opera what Aaron Spelling (see Chapter 15) was doing for the copshow during the late sixties and what Norman Lear (see Chapter 4) would do for the sitcom during the early seventies.

It is interesting to note that despite all the "socially conscious" content innovations that Nixon had crammed into *All My Children,* the narrative framework of the series did not deviate notably from the "classic" soap-opera structure that Irna Phillips had developed back during the radio era. *All My Children,* like *Today's Children,* focused on two suburban families, the Tylers and the Martins, who lived in Pine Valley, about an hour's drive from New York City (Phillips, of course, preferred the Chicago suburbs). The maintaining of these familiar conventions was probably a factor in making *All My Children*'s inventive content more easily palatable for traditional soap audiences. By the late seventies, *One Life to Live* had become the highest-rated serial on daytime television. It continued to command a large audience even after it relinquished the Number One position to Gloria Monty's rejuvenation of *General Hospital* at the end of the decade, when that show's "Luke and Laura" storyline provoked unprecedented popularity and media attention.

Nixon continued to introduce successful innovations to the soap-opera craft in *All My Children,* some of which probably helped increase the general audience for this type of programming. Glitzy production stunts, including on-location trips to the Caribbean island of St. Croix, were written into storylines. Soap opera was no longer treated as the stepchild of television drama. Famous guest stars, including Elizabeth Taylor, Joan Crawford, and Carol Burnett, began popping up in cameo roles on regular weekday episodes. Conversely, the soap opera began to produce its own crop of recognized stars, including David Hasselhoff of *The Young and the Restless,* who broke away from daytime drama to become the star of Glen Larson's prime-time action-adventure series *Knight Rider.*

In the seventies, as more and more women left the home to join the wage-earning work force, the demographic spectrum of the soap-opera audience began to expand and feature other groups, especially college students, an audience that contained the genre's first significant male component. Agnes Nixon was particularly successful in welcoming these new viewers. Not surprisingly, Nixon's next series, *Loving* (ABC, 1983–present), was set on the campus of the mythical Alden University. She cocreated the show with Douglas Marland, whom she had worked with writing episodes for *The Guiding Light* and *Another World.* Marland would become her principal collaborator for the rest of her career.

As a programming format that is utterly dependent for success on audience intimacy with character and plot, a soap opera is an extremely difficult type of program to introduce. Nixon and ABC emphatically addressed this problem by launching an aggressive promotional campaign for *Loving* months before its premiere. Steamy, sexually provocative promos were presented during all parts of the daily broadcast schedule. The night before the daytime debut, a special two-hour movie version of *Loving*, starring Geraldine Page and Lloyd Bridges (neither of whom was a player in the series), was aired to generate interest.

Just as Irna Phillips had spent much of her time in Chicago, even after her creations had moved off to the production centers on both coasts, Agnes Nixon chose to remain based in the Philadelphia area. Seldom visiting the sets of her shows, she would draw out her plotlines and give them to dialoguers for execution, making final checks on shooting scripts. Having spent an early portion of her career working in anthology drama, Agnes Nixon was only once tempted to return to prime time in a major project. The British program *Upstairs, Downstairs* had been presented in the United States on PBS's *Masterpiece Theater* during the early seventies. It had been one of the most critically acclaimed shows ever to air on American television and, relative to public television's normal audience share, one of the most popular as well. The similarities between *Upstairs, Downstairs* and the American soap form were obvious, and high hopes were expressed by some industry executives that some kind of synthesis could be achieved between the finely wrought, literate dialogue of the British production and the popularity of the masscult soap format. In 1975 CBS had tried *Beacon Hill*, a thinly disguised American knockoff of *Upstairs, Downstairs*, which essentially moved the World War I London story of *Upstairs, Downstairs* to a 1920s Boston row house. That show was a quick failure in the ratings. But in the same spirit, Agnes Nixon made her return to prime time with *The Manions of America* (ABC, 1980), which she cowrote with *Upstairs, Downstairs* creator Rosemary Anne Sisson. Built upon typical soap-operatic structure, the six-hour series followed the lives of two families. Set in the nineteenth century, the program contained two clans of American immigrants — one Irish, the other German — who establish family financial dynasties in Nixon's home turf, Philadelphia. Nielsen numbers were only lukewarm, however, and Nixon returned to daytime duties.

AGNES NIXON: SELECTED SOAPOGRAPHY

Radio

Woman in White (NBC/CBS, 1938–42, 1944–48)

Television

WRITER FOR PRIME-TIME ANTHOLOGY DRAMAS
Studio One (CBS, 1948–58)
Robert Montgomery Presents (NBC, 1950–57)
Armstrong Circle Theater (NBC/CBS, 1950–63)
Cameo Theatre (NBC, 1950–52, 1955)

SOAP OPERAS
Search for Tomorrow (CBS/NBC, 1951–86)
As the World Turns (CBS, 1956–present)
Another World (NBC, 1964–present)
One Life to Live (ABC, 1968–present)
All My Children (ABC, 1970–present)
Loving (ABC, 1983–present)

PRIME-TIME MINISERIES
The Manions of America (ABC, 1980)

28. DAVID WOLPER

_____

From Documentary to Docudrama

When viewers think of documentary television today, they tend to think of grant-funded PBS series such as *Frontline* and *Nova*. But this was not always the case. During the first decades of American television, there was no Public Broadcasting System, and yet the documentary was a familiar prime-time programming genre to the TV audience. During this period (from the late forties to about 1970) the responsibility for making documentary television was taken quite seriously by the three commercial networks. Still piling up the cash that was accruing from their precable oligopoly, the majors dutifully fulfilled their broadcast license obligations with critically acclaimed — though often low-rated — series such as *CBS Reports*, *NBC White Paper*, and *ABC Close-up*.

By the 1970s, however, the networks were backing away from this type of programming. In addition to having poor ratings, advocacy-oriented documentaries were proving to be more trouble than they were worth. Fred Friendly's *CBS Reports*, for example, produced a trio of muckraking programs that were particularly embarrassing to the American agricultural and food-retailing industries: "Harvest of Shame," an exposé of the shocking conditions under which migrant farm-worker families were forced to live; "The Silent Spring," an indictment of the use of agricultural pesticides, which was based on the book by Rachel Carson; and "Hunger in America," a program that dared insinuate that such a thing existed amid the official plenty of the period. Buzz words such as "liberal media" and "left-wing propaganda" were directed at the network. The specter of FCC censorship was raised under the banner of calls for "fair journalism." Sponsor boycotts and law suits were threatened.

The rise of PBS gave the networks an easy out from this increasingly unwanted responsibility. CBS, NBC, and ABC gradually cut back their production of hour-long documentary programs and instead went over to "magazine" formats. *Sixty Minutes* (CBS, 1968–present) was the prototype. Stories were typically limited to about fifteen minutes in length. The sting of controversial muckraking pieces was ameliorated by the mixing in of upbeat "lite" fare: interviews with celebrities, the showing off of a child prodigy, the heartwarming success story of a backyard inventor. The network news departments in effect gave up making advocacy-oriented documentaries. That function now fell to the Corporation for Public Broadcasting, whose grant decisions could make or break a PBS project.

One consequence of this extremely limited, bureaucratically controlled market for documentary television has been a scarcity of independent commercial producers working in the genre. The one glaring exception to that rule in the history of American TV has been producer David Wolper. With nearly six hundred hours of television to his credit, including historically based fictional programs as well as documentaries, Wolper must be counted among the most prolific television producers of all time.

David L. Wolper was born in New York City on January 11, 1928. His father was an immigrant Russian Jew who supported the family as a bill collector for a jewelry company and as a real estate agent. Growing up on East Fifty-second Street in midtown Manhattan, Wolper was attracted to show business early in life, spending his boyhood watching nightclub comedians, playing in a band, and working in the Catskills during summer vacations. He attended New York University for less than a year before dropping out to seek his fortune in the film business.

While still in his teens, Wolper and a friend, Jim Harris, came up with a scheme to invest their life savings in buying the American distribution rights to an Italian "art film" titled *The Miracle of Monte Casino*. The film bombed, Wolper lost his shirt, and the family shipped him off to Drake University in Des Moines, Iowa, for another shot at college. At the age of twenty, he transferred from Drake to the University of Southern California, with the intention of becoming a film major. But Wolper was never to receive his college diploma. Once again, he dropped out to chase a film-distribution scheme. In partnership with Harris (who would later go on to become Stanley Kubrick's producer for *Paths of Glory* and *Lolita*), Wolper formed Flamingo Films in 1949. It was one of the first companies ever to attempt to distribute motion pictures to local television stations.

For two years Wolper and Harris crisscrossed the country, visiting most of the nation's hundred-plus operating television stations, attempting to peddle the broadcast rights to their small portfolio of films. The partners were so successful that while still in their early twenties they were able to sell their tiny operation to a larger company and gain management positions in the merged corporation, which was called Motion Pictures for Television. This was the beginning of a successful business career that took Wolper to positions as an officer at the Continental Bank and Trust Company of Los Angeles before the age of thirty.

The story of how David Wolper started to produce his own documentary films is the stuff of which American show-business legends are made. While in New York on bank business in 1958, Wolper ran into a Russian film distributor from whom he had bought some East Bloc cartoons back in the early fifties. He showed Wolper footage of Russian space rockets blasting off — footage that had never been seen outside the Soviet Union. Wolper bought the films, formed his own production company, left the bank, and began a new career.

With the Russian films in hand, Wolper had already accomplished the hard part of the project he had in mind. He contacted the Department of Defense and NASA for the rights to use footage of American missile launches, which these agencies were only too happy to grant gratis in return for the publicity. He then obtained footage from the archives of Robert Goddard, the rocket pioneer. The main job was to write a script that would verbally string the film clips together with a voiceover monologue. Mike Wallace was hired as the narrator. The Shulton Company, makers of Old Spice after-shave, came on board as sponsors.

Thus Wolper was able to offer his program, *The Race for Space*, to the networks as a fully sponsored, completed project. He assumed that they would jump at the chance to air this kind of wholesome, noncontroversial, "educational" documentary. But he was wrong. All three networks held fast to their unofficial rule of airing only "in-house" documentaries that were produced by their own news departments.

Wolper, however, refused to be thwarted. He used his many contacts around the country to put together an ad hoc network of dozens of stations, including independents in the large markets as well as network affiliates in smaller cities that were willing to preempt network programming in favor of *The Race for Space*. It was the first time that the syndication method had been used for the debut of a documentary special. Wolper won several awards and, in a bit of period-media confusion, *The Race for Space* was the first TV program ever to be nominated for an Oscar (best documentary).

Wolper capitalized on this success by immediately going into full-scale studio production. In 1961 he completed a pair of films on black athletes: *The Rafer Johnson Story*, concerning the Olympic gold medalist track star, and *Biography of a Rookie*, which spotlighted the career of rising Dodger baseball star Willie Davis. His ability to circumvent network control by going into direct first-run syndication forced the networks to reconsider their "in-house" policy, and soon the corporate giants who had scorned him were among Wolper's best customers. *Hollywood: The Golden Years* was bought by NBC. ABC then outbid NBC for two more Wolper studies of American film history: *Hollywood: The Great Stars* and *Hollywood: The Fabulous Era*. Following this trio of popular specials that made economical (and emphatically noncontroversial) use of Hollywood's bottomless pit of film footage, NBC commissioned Wolper to do a weekly documentary series for the 1962–63 season, *Hollywood and the Stars*. American film history would continue to be a favorite subject for Wolper throughout his career, from his *Legend of Marilyn Monroe* (1964) to his *Moviola* series for NBC (1980).

Wolper's newly won acceptance at the networks did not prevent him from continuing to use independent syndication to his advantage. *Biography* (1961–64) was a weekly half-hour syndicated series focusing on twentieth-century celebrities from Winston Churchill and Adolf Hitler to Babe Ruth and Knute Rockne. The series won four Peabody Awards. Mike Wallace once again served as Wolper's on-air voice and, in this case, as a script consultant as well. *Biography* exemplified what was now emerging as the Wolper documentary technique. Compiled historical footage of the major political and cultural events and personalities of the twentieth century was cheap and abundant — and mostly there for the taking. Wolper mined this resource in ways that the network news departments had never imagined, often developing program ideas out of the available footage rather than the other way around. Moreover, Wolper had a talent for slipping past controversy. He avoided outright advocacy positions, such as had been the trademark of Edward R. Murrow on *See It Now*. The Wolper documentary was presented to its audience as an objective (or, better yet, "educational") lesson in history.

The Making of the President, 1960 (ABC, 1963) was Wolper's most celebrated work to date. Based on Theodore H. White's Pulitzer Prize–winning book, this film followed the presidential race between John F. Kennedy and Richard Nixon. As with *The Race for Space*, Wolper went to the networks with a completed program and a full sponsorship commitment, in this case from Xerox Corporation. But despite their newfound willingness to buy other Wolper products, the networks were reluctant to buy this program. It was one thing to air Wolper's documentaries about Clark Gable and Judy Garland; it was quite another for them to go outside the in-house news department for material on the president of the United States. The news directors of all three networks turned down the program. But Leonard Goldenson, then head of ABC, stepped in to overrule his news department, buying the program for prime-time broadcast. It won Emmy Awards for music, editing, and writing, and was the first ABC show ever to win in the "Super Emmy" category of "Program of the Year." It was also the beginning of a strong unofficial relationship between Wolper and ABC that would endure to mutual advantage for many years to come.

The Making of the President, 1960 made David Wolper into a celebrity. Major articles on the producer appeared in *Time* and *Newsweek* as well as in broadcasting industry journals and magazines. Combining elements of his earlier career as a film distributor and his more recent vocation, he maintained a growing collection of stock news footage around which he could construct future documentaries. *Four Days in November* (1964) covered the assassination of John Kennedy. President Lyndon Johnson personally commissioned Wolper to produce *A Thousand Days*, a celebratory survey of the Kennedy Administration that was aired for the party faithful at the 1964 Democratic Convention and simulcast to the nation (as convention coverage) by all three major networks. When Theodore White wrote *The Making of the President, 1964*, Wolper was right there with the TV adaptation for ABC.

In 1965 the first of Wolper's *National Geographic* programs was aired. Produced in direct collaboration with the National Geographic Society, the series opened the Society's huge film archives to Wolper's cut-and-paste technique. One of the episodes featured ocean explorer Jacques Cousteau, which in turn led to the first-ever documentary spin-off: *The Undersea World of Jacques Cousteau*. Wolper reminisced on the origins of the Cousteau series in Leonard Gold-enson's autobiography, *Beating the Odds:* "One day I was looking at some underwater footage on television, and I said, 'A TV screen looks like a fish tank. The fish look like they're alive, swimming around in my tank. It would make a great series, an underwater thing. I'm going to make a deal with Jacques Cousteau.' "

Though a personal friend of the Kennedy family, Wolper was approached by both Democrats and Republicans to make campaign films. Among his credits in this area were propaganda pieces for New York City mayor John V. Lindsay and California governor Edmund G. Brown. In 1970 Wolper released *The Unfinished Journey of Robert Kennedy* from a script written by Kennedy confidant Arthur Schlesinger, Jr.

In a short period of time, less than ten years, Wolper had virtually invented the role of the independent, commercial TV documentary producer. But Wolper also showed himself to have an astute understanding of the changing nature of the TV business. As documentaries became an increasingly endangered species, a phenomenon caused at least in part by the increasingly polarized atmosphere in the America of the late sixties, Wolper began evolving toward a different aesthetic synthesis for the presentation of historical events on the medium: the docudrama. Wolper described the philosophy behind this shift in his work in a book he later wrote about the making of *Roots:* "I'm out there selling information, but as everyone knows, I've always tried to place entertainment into my films. I don't agree with many highbrow intellectuals who feel that by putting entertainment into educational films it somehow corrupts them. I believe very strongly that the way to educate the American people is put entertainment into informational films. I know that the American public wants to be educated, but they want to be educated their way. They want to be educated in an entertaining manner, so I give it to them their way."

One of his first steps in this direction occurred in a 1971 special for NBC, *Say Goodbye.* Ostensibly a documentary about the preservation of endangered animal species, the film included a graphic and moving scene of a polar bear being illegally hunted and killed. But it turned out that Wolper had "re-created" the event by staging it for the camera with an actor. Hunting and firearms organizations claimed that this re-creation discredited the entire film. But in terms of public perception, the point was essentially academic. Re-creations of reality would quickly become a feature of Wolper's work. Today they are a common technique in commercial documentaries and even on weekly "news" broadcasts.

That same year, Wolper launched *Appointment with Destiny*, a series dealing mostly with events that occurred before the advent of film technology. If Wolper had begun his production career by mining the archives for stock footage of historical events, he now had the resources — and some would say the nerve — to create his own archival material. The show presented "newsreel" re-creations of such historical events as the assassination of Lincoln, the crucifixion of Jesus, and Lee's surrender to Grant at Appomattox. This concept is traceable to the series *You Are There* (CBS, 1953–57), hosted by Walter Cronkite, in which a CBS newsman would appear as an "on-the-scene" reporter at such events as the Wright brothers' launching of the first airplane, Lincoln's delivery of the Gettysburg address, and the fall of Troy.

Though this kind of programming was denounced by some academics as a burlesque of serious historiography, others saw it as a way to bring historical information to a public that was becoming increasingly dependent upon television for its knowledge of all subjects. In any case, Wolper's fame and prestige continued to spread. In 1973 he was commissioned by the American Heritage Publishing Company to make a series of specials on American history. In 1974 President Gerald R. Ford named Wolper to his advisory council on the American Revolution bicentennial.

In the midseventies, Wolper became as deeply involved in fictional drama as he was in documentary work. While producing *Visions of Eight*, a series of eight films about the 1972 Olympics by eight distinguished directors, he came up with the idea of using extra footage from the project to make a fiction film set in Munich during the 1972 Games. *The 500-Pound Jerk* (CBS, 1973) followed the story of a hillbilly weightlifter, a Russian female gymnast, and a greedy advertising man who is trying to exploit their newly won Olympic fame. Sportscaster Howard Cosell appeared in the role of himself, helping to further promote the emphatically documentary feel created by the use of filmed footage of actual events.

In 1974 Wolper collaborated with film director Stanley Kubrick to create *Dramatic Nonfiction TV*, a syndicated series that consisted mainly of re-creations for television of famous trials. Episodes included *The Trial of Julius and Ethel Rosenberg* and *The Court-martial of Lieutenant William Calley*. Though the events covered in these programs were themselves extremely controversial, Wolper was able to avoid the problems usually associated with commercial broadcast of such material by using actual court transcripts for the basis of his scripts; the "record" was merely "read," the embellishments of writers and film editors notwithstanding.

Perhaps it was inevitable that Wolper would at some point try his hand in the area of the weekly prime-time fiction series. In 1974 he premiered his first such program, *Get Christie Love!* for ABC. It was the first copshow ever to cast a black woman in the leading role. Teresa Graves starred as a no-nonsense detective in LAPD's Special Investigations Division. In familiar TV copshow style she worked undercover and stretched the rules in the name of justice. Because she was a beautiful woman, her undercover assignments often took her into prostitution and other forms of street crime that allowed the camera to capture her in provocative dress. While *Get Christie Love!* failed to make it back for a second season, a related premise involving three white women, Aaron Spelling's *Charlie's Angels* (ABC, 1976–81), would do better in the ratings.

Also in 1974, Wolper made a move into situation comedy, collaborating with James Komack on *Chico and the Man* (NBC, 1974–78). Taking its cues from the "relevance" sitcoms of Norman Lear (see Chapter 4), the series concerned the relationship between crotchety old Anglo widower Ed Brown (Jack Albertson) and ambitious young Chicano entrepreneur Chico Rodriguez (Freddie Prinze). Imitating the look and feel of Lear's *Sanford and Son*, which took place in a Watts junkyard, *Chico and the Man* was set in an East Los Angeles car repair garage. The show was a quick hit, placing third in the ratings. In the middle of production for the third season, however, Prinze, the show's star, committed suicide. A new actor was tried in the role, but the show didn't make it through a fourth year. Another Wolper-Komack sitcom was *Welcome Back, Kotter* (ABC, 1975–79). Based loosely on the experiences of its star, Gabriel Kaplan, who had himself been a remedial student at a Brooklyn high school, the series launched the career of John Travolta. *Welcome Back, Kotter* spent its first two seasons in the Top Twenty but, in a sense, became a victim of its own successes as its stars either left the show to make movies or aged beyond credibility.

Wolper achieved only limited success with these and several other weekly dramatic series. His big breakthrough in prime-time fiction would occur in a genre of fictional programming more closely related to his area of expertise: the historically based miniseries. His first such project was *Sandburg's Lincoln* (NBC, 1974–75), an Emmy

Award–winning adaptation of the poet's biography of the tragic life of the sixteenth U.S. president. The miniseries as such did not yet exist on American television. The six hour-long episodes of *Sandburg's Lincoln* were spread out over an entire season by NBC, making the program more like a collection of specials than a series. Given the famous attention-span problems of the American television audience, this structure tended to work against the success of the project.

This scheduling obstacle would be overcome in the presentation of Wolper's most famous work, *Roots* (ABC, 1977). Based on the novel by Alex Haley, which was still being written when the scripting for the TV adaptation began, *Roots* follows the life of Kunta Kinte (LeVar Burton) and his descendants. Kunta Kinte is a West African, a Gambian born in 1750 and captured by slave traders at the age of seventeen. Surviving his deportation in chains to America, he is auctioned off into slavery. The twelve-hour narrative follows him through his attempts to escape and through the growth of his family across a hundred years of history to the end of the Civil War and the freeing of his descendants from slavery.

Mixing fact and fiction in a crucible of historical myth, *Roots* was a perfect property for Wolper. ABC programming chief Fred Silverman, however, was not so sure about how a series featuring graphic depictions of the brutal treatment of blacks by whites would play in Peoria — or at least in all parts of town. Silverman slotted the show for telecast in late January, before the start of the crucial February "sweeps" period, when ratings are used to set ad prices. His decision to air the twelve-hour program in two-hour and one-hour segments over the course of eight consecutive days was seen by some as a scheduling strategy designed to help the network have done with this potential ratings disaster as quickly as possible and to thereby cut its losses. Could the network really have expected a large audience using a programming technique that had never been tried before?

Roots, of course, confounded all negative commercial predictions. The first installment of the program turned out to be the lowest rated of the eight parts. The show, with its intimate portrayals of the evils of slavery, including whippings and the forced separations of children from mothers, caused a national sensation. Viewership did not fade away as some network executives had feared, but instead grew geometrically. It is estimated that over a hundred million Americans, nearly half the population of the country, watched the final installment one week after the premiere. And critical notices were as good as the box office. The series, its production staff, and its actors all won

Emmys, Humanitas citations, and other awards. The miniseries was suddenly established as a viable genre that would become a staple of network programming for most of the next decade.

On the personal level, Wolper felt that his docudramatic technique of mixing history with fiction was redeemed. "ABC News took a poll immediately after *Roots*," he proudly told television historian Michael Winship, "and it showed that people were more sympathetic to the plight of blacks because they had seen the roots of where all the problems came from."

Others disagreed. The presentation of the historical atrocities of the eighteenth and early nineteenth centuries, they argued, did little to raise the consciousness of white viewers concerning the evils of racism in the twentieth century. In fact, by showing the shocking excesses of the past, *Roots* may have had the effect of "congratulating" contemporary white America for having done away with these inhuman excesses. In his book *Blacks and White TV*, historian J. Fred MacDonald points out that while the show was based on the novel of an African-American writer, its executive producer (Wolper), as well as most of its scriptwriters and production personnel, were all white. The story of black America, in effect, remains to be told by black Americans on TV. "The *Roots* phenomenon failed to catalyze a new Golden Age for blacks in American television," wrote Mac-Donald. "When the applause ended, black actors returned to the familiar roles."

In 1979 ABC aired *Roots: The Next Generations*. Based on the success of the original, Wolper's sequel had a much larger budget. Fourteen hours long, it featured such Hollywood stars as James Earl Jones in the role of Alex Haley and Marlon Brando, who won an Emmy for his portrayal of American Nazi Party leader George Lincoln Rockwell, whom Haley had once interviewed for *Playboy* magazine. With the commercial track record of *Roots* behind him, Wolper had no trouble with network censors in depicting such subjects as lynchings, the harassment of interracial married couples, and black separatism, including a screen portrayal of Malcolm X, whose autobiography Haley had coauthored.

While the sequel didn't break the ratings records set by the first *Roots*, it was a blockbuster hit by any normal standard, with all seven of its two-hour episodes scoring among the Top Eleven prime-time programs for the week. In 1988, in one more attempt to cash in on the *Roots* mythology, Wolper reunited two of the original actors, LeVar Burton and Louis Gossett, Jr., in their roles as Kunta Kinte and Fiddler, in a Christmas movie set on a slave plantation in 1775 Virginia.

Roots and its sequel proved to be a difficult act to follow for Wolper. In the 1980s he tried to make a similar miniseries project out of Ruth Beebe Hill's best-selling novel, *Hanta Yo,* an eight-hundred-page opus concerning three generations of an American Indian family. Whatever Wolper's intentions, the project caused a storm of controversy before ever getting to the air. Native American activists accused the book, written by a white woman, of being full of errors regarding Indian history and culture. Groups including the Black Hills Treaty Council, the Pine Ridge Sioux Tribal Council, the National Advisory Council on Indian Education, and the American Indian Historical Society all made public protests. An organization specifically designed to challenge the project, the Ad Hoc Committee to Stop "Hanta Yo," was formed. Far from becoming a Native American version of *Roots,* this miniseries became a political quagmire for Wolper. It was shortened from nine hours to five. Wolper disassociated himself from the Hill book on which it was originally supposed to be based; the title was changed to *The Mystic Warrior.* Five years in the making, the beleaguered show finally aired over two nights to ratings far below what had been hoped for.

The Civil War, from D. W. Griffith's *The Birth of a Nation* to Wolper's *Roots* to Ken Burns's *The Civil War* (see next chapter), has always been a box-office draw in American popular culture. Wolper hoped to rebound from the "Hanta Yo" disaster with his own Civil War epic, *North and South.* The miniseries was aired on ABC in November 1985, and its preplanned sequel, *North and South Book II,* was presented by the network the following May. Taken as a whole, the project was Wolper's most ambitious to date, some twenty-four hours in length. The show's putative stars were Patrick Swayze and Kirstie Alley, but neither of them had yet achieved superstar fame. *North and South*'s biggest draw consisted of its bevy of big-time stars who appeared in cameo roles. They included Elizabeth Taylor, Robert Mitchum, Gene Kelly, Jean Simmons, and Jimmy Stewart, to name only a few.

Wolper had gone to great lengths to make *North and South* a ratings winner, and he had indeed succeeded in coming back from the "Hanta Yo" fiasco. But nevertheless the miniseries, as a genre, was going into decline in the mideighties. In an article that he wrote for *TV Guide,* Wolper in effect wrote an epitaph for the genre that he had helped to invent. He stated that miniseries tended to fall into at least one of three categories. The first of these was the adaptation of a best-selling novel, which by its very nature has wide-reaching preproduction public recognition. Several of Wolper's own works fell into this category, including (Alex Haley's) *Roots*, (Colleen McCullough's) *The Thorn Birds*, and (John Jakes's) *North and South*. The second category he characterized was "sociological significance," citing the fact that monumental historical issues such as the enslavement of African-Americans and the Nazi Holocaust of the Jews always tend to stir great public interest. The third category was the family saga that reached across generations. No matter how epic or distant the historical event, it could always be brought home to the individual viewer on the level of its significance to an individual family. To be truly successful, Wolper concluded, a miniseries ought to fit into at least two of these categories, if not all three. Again, *Roots* was the exemplar. Though dormant in the late eighties, the miniseries did show some signs of life with the ratings and critical successes of the five-part Western *Lonesome Dove* in 1988.

With so much work carrying the imprimatur of his production supervision, Wolper has obviously had different degrees of direct involvement with specific projects. As early as the midsixties, his company had grown to the point where it maintained offices in three cities and employed over two hundred staff workers. Wolper, like Lee Rich (see Chapter 18), is a prime example of the impresario as auteur. Quincy Troupe, who wrote a book about the production of *Roots*, reported that Wolper selects and determines the general approach to all his projects and puts together the staffs for each production. Wolper also keeps a close eye on editing, which is, after all, where he started in the first place.

DAVID WOLPER: SELECTED VIDEOGRAPHY

Dates with designated networks refer to original air dates. Other works were released in syndication, which means that air dates varied from city to city and so date of release is given.

Documentary Specials

The Race for Space (1958)
Project: Man in Space (1959)
Hollywood: The Golden Years (NBC, 1961)
Biography of a Rookie (1961)
The Rafer Johnson Story (1961)

D-Day (NBC, 1962)
Hollywood: The Great Stars (ABC, 1963)
Hollywood: The Fabulous Era (ABC, 1963)
Escape to Freedom (1963)
Krebiozen and Cancer: Thirteen Years of Bitter Conflict (1963)
The Passing Years (1963)
The Making of the President, 1960 (ABC, 1963)
December 7: The Day of Infamy (1963)
Ten Seconds That Shook the World (1963)
The American Woman in the Twentieth Century (1963)
The Battle of Britain (1964)
The Yanks Are Coming (1964)
Berlin: Kaiser to Khrushchev (1964)
The Trial at Nuremberg (1964)
The Legend of Marilyn Monroe (1964)
And Away We Go (1964)
France: Conquest to Liberation (1965)
Korea: The 38th Parallel (1965)
Prelude to War (1965)
Japan: A New Dawn Over Asia (1965)
007: The Incredible World of James Bond (NBC, 1965)
Let My People Go (1965)
October Madness: The World Series (1965)
Race for the Moon (1965)
The Really Big Family (1965)
Revolution in Our Time (1965)
The Bold Men (ABC, 1965)
The General (ABC, 1965)
Teenage Revolution (ABC, 1965)
The Way Out Men (ABC, 1965)
In Search of Man (ABC, 1965)
The Thin Blue Line (ABC, 1965)
Revolution in the Three R's (ABC, 1965)
Pro Football: Mayhem on a Sunday Afternoon (ABC, 1965)
The Making of the President, 1964 (CBS, 1966)
Wall Street: Where the Money Is (CBS, 1966)
Destination Safety (1966)
China: Roots of Madness (1966)
A Nation of Immigrants (1966)
Men from Boys (1966)
Do Blondes Have More Fun? (ABC, 1967)
Untamed World (1967)

The Dangerous Years (1967)
California (1967)
Sophia (1967)
On the Trail of Stanley and Livingstone (ABC, 1968)
The Secret Musical Life of George Plimpton (1968)
Los Angeles: Where the Action Is (1968)
The Making of the President, 1968 (CBS, 1969)
The Unfinished Journey of Robert F. Kennedy (ABC, 1970)
Say Amen (NBC, 1971)
They've Killed President Lincoln (1971)
Here Comes Tomorrow: The Fear Fighters (1972)
The Trial of Julius and Ethel Rosenberg (1974)
The Court-martial of the Tiger of Malaya: General Yamashita (1974)
The Court-martial of Lieutenant William Calley (1974)
The Unexplained: The UFO Connection (1976)
Mystery of the Great Pyramids (1977)
Roots: One Year Later (1978)
Opening and Closing Ceremonies of the 1984 Olympic Games (ABC, 1984)
Statue of Liberty "Liberty Weekend" Centennial Celebration (1986)

Documentary Series

Biography (1961–64; revived in production 1979–80)
The Story of . . . (1962–63)
Hollywood and the Stars (NBC, 1963–64)
National Geographic (various, 1964–75)
Men in Crisis (1965)
The March of Time (1965–66)
The World of Animals (1966–68)
The Rise and Fall of the Third Reich (ABC, 1968)
The Undersea World of Jacques Cousteau (ABC, 1968)
Men of the Sea (1971)
Plimpton! (ABC, 1971–73)
Appointment with Destiny (1971–73)
Competitors (1972)
Explorers (1972–73)
American Wilderness (1973)
American Heritage (1973–75)
Primal Man (1973–75)
Smithsonian (1974–75)

This Week in the NBA (1974)
Moviola (NBC, 1980)
David L. Wolper Presents (A&E, 1990–present)

Fictional (Historically Based) Miniseries

Sandburg's Lincoln (NBC, 1974–75)
Roots (ABC, 1977)
Roots: The Next Generations (ABC, 1979)
The Thorn Birds (ABC, 1983)
The Mystic Warrior (ABC, 1984)
North and South (ABC, 1985)
North and South Book II (ABC, 1986)
Napoleon and Josephine: A Love Story (ABC, 1987)

Fictional Prime-Time Series

Chico and the Man (NBC, 1974–78)
Get Christie Love! (ABC, 1974–75)
Welcome Back, Kotter (ABC, 1975–79)
Casablanca (NBC, 1983)

Movies Made for Television

The 500-Pound Jerk (CBS, 1973)
The Morning After (ABC, 1974)
Unwed Father (ABC, 1974)
Death Stalk (NBC, 1975)
I Will Fight No More Forever (ABC, 1975)
Brenda Starr (ABC, 1976)
Collision Course (1976)
Victory at Entebbe (ABC, 1976)
Agatha Christie's "Murder Is Easy" (CBS, 1982)
His Mistress (NBC, 1984)
The Betty Ford Story (1987)
Roots: The Gift (1988)

Entertainment Specials

A Funny Thing Happened on the Way to the White House (ABC, 1966)
A Funny Thing Happened on the Way to Hollywood (1967)
Movin' with Nancy (1967)
Monte Carlo, C'est La Rose (1967)
With Love, Sophia (1968)

The Ice Capades (1968)
Make Mine Red, White, and Blue (NBC, 1972)
Of Thee I Sing (1972)
Love from A to Z (1974)
Yes, Virginia, There Is a Santa Claus (1974)
American Spirit (1975)
Small World (NBC, 1982)

29. KEN BURNS

The Art of the Artifact

In the fall of 1990, the Public Broadcasting System achieved its highest ratings ever as an estimated thirty-nine million Americans tuned in to the telecast of Ken Burns's *The Civil War*. The eleven-hour documentary series was telecast in one- and two-hour segments across nine consecutive prime-time evenings. If David Wolper's *Roots* and *North and South* miniseries had proven that America's fascination with slavery and the Civil War had survived into the television era, Ken Burns had accomplished a more remarkable feat. He had captured the imagination of a nationwide audience without the benefit of a romantic love story, a filmed action sequence, or even the profile of a Hollywood heartthrob. Burns had somehow convinced millions of viewers — their remote-control units always at the ready — to sit still for eleven hours of careful examination of still photographs and other artifacts, complemented by a soundtrack dominated by nineteenth-century music and unseen actors reading quotations from the diaries of long-dead soldiers, poets, and politicians. PBS vice president Barry Chase put it this way in an interview with the *Los Angeles Times:* "Burns has the ability to make inanimate objects and pictures move without doing so literally. If you're talking about history and historical events prior to the time there were moving pictures, there is no one who is his peer." The few "moving pictures" that did appear in the mammoth program were mostly talking heads — and most of those were the heads of college professors. Large numbers of Americans watched anyway; rumors of resurgent attention span were briefly rampant.

Celebrity came quickly to Ken Burns on the heels of the broadcast. Within weeks, reporters from all over the world were visiting his Walpole, New Hampshire, home/studio, making him the subject of dozens of newspaper and magazine features. Hollywood, usually aloof to grant-funded producers, showed interest, beckoning him onto the talk circuit, including an appearance on *The Tonight Show*. But contrary to the general perception that the baby-faced documentarian had suddenly "come out of nowhere," Burns had been at work long and hard at his craft when the media blitz came knocking at his door in the fall of 1990.

Born in Brooklyn, New York, in 1955, Burns grew up in Ann Arbor, the son of a University of Michigan anthropology professor. He left the Midwest to attend Hampshire College in the Connecticut River Valley region of western Massachusetts. New England would become his lifelong home and a subject for much of his work. Completing a B.A. in film studies and design at the age of twenty, his senior thesis film at Hampshire, *Working in Rural New England* (1975), won an award from the National Trust for Historic Preservation. His acute interest in the region also led him to make *The Quabbin,* a documentary concerning political infighting over the establishment of water rights in the area by the Metropolitan District Commission of Boston, some ninety miles away.

In 1975 Burns formed a collective with a group of his Hampshire College classmates with the stated purpose of making films of their own choosing, independently of both the New York foundation bureaucracies and the Hollywood corporate bureaucracies. They named themselves Florentine Films in honor of their mentor at Hampshire College, Professor Elaine Mayes, who resided in the tiny hamlet of Florentine, Massachusetts. Amy Stechler, who joined Florentine soon after, became one of Burns's chief collaborators, and eventually the two were married.

Florentine projects in the late seventies were eclectic, including a portrait of Herman Melville and an exploration into the mysteries of ancient Irish art. Burns was well on his way to developing a documentary style capable of penetrating topics of the precinema era in ways that were not only of interest to the academic cognoscenti but were equally appealing to the curious and thoughtful from all walks of life. Moreover, he was able to reach a general audience without resorting to the clumsy — often embarrassing — technique of "historical reenactments." The potential of documentary television to bring history into the lives of millions of citizens had always been a promising feature of the medium. But the increasing tendency of producers to hire actors from central casting and dress them up in historical drag to act out "the great scenes" was proving of limited value in realizing this noble dream. Ken Burns was, in effect, helping to rescue TV documentary from these doldrums.

Burns's first major breakthrough to a national television audience came in 1982 with *The Brooklyn Bridge,* which was made to commemorate the centennial of John Roebling's monumental attempt to span the East River with a suspension bridge connecting the then independent cities of New York and Brooklyn. It was in this project that Burns's style came to first full flower. David McCullough, a Yale professor who had written a book on the bridge, served as a consultant, an on-screen informant, and the narrator. Amy Stechler Burns wrote the narration. Photographs, paintings, daguerreotypes, and other artifacts of the event were scrutinized by Burns's camera. Readings from the personal papers, diaries, and letters of John Roebling, and of his son Washington Roebling (who took over the project in mid-construction after his father's death), constituted a key component of the soundtrack. The building of the bridge was examined not only in terms of its significance as an engineering feat but also as an occasion in the spiritual life of the American nation. In terms of subject matter, *The Brooklyn Bridge* was an ideal project for Burns, allowing him to bring his keen personal obsession with the American nineteenth century to a topic of public interest.

Stylistically, *The Brooklyn Bridge* was a milestone in the evolution of Burns's "rephotographing" technique: the close examination of still photographs, drawings, and other artifacts with a moving-picture camera. Burns demonstrated an extraordinary talent for cinematically fingering, even caressing, century-old black-and-white stills with his camera. Critic Judith Michaelson has described the effect of Burns's work in this regard as his ability to "make [the picture] come alive, to coax out its life."

The Brooklyn Bridge was an unqualified success in terms of both critical reaction and viewer popularity (albeit skewed to the expectations of a PBS broadcast). Its historical accuracy; its presentation of diverse, sometimes opposing, viewpoints on issues; and the consistency of the aesthetic vision of its auteur all challenged the traditional hostility of academic historians to television as a medium for documentation and learning. In a rare gesture toward a person not holding a university position, the Society of American Historians bestowed membership on the filmmaker. As had been the case with David Wolper's *The Race for Space* a quarter of a century earlier, *The Brooklyn Bridge* was nominated for an Oscar, despite the fact that it had been made specifically for the homescreen.

Three projects, all presented on PBS, followed in quick succession. *The Shakers: Hands to Work, Hearts to God* (1985) examined the history of this uniquely American religious and social community. Pledged to lifelong celibacy, the Shakers could only survive as a community through the recruitment of new members. Having flourished briefly in the late nineteenth century in communal settlements in the Berkshire Mountains of Massachusetts and the Upper Hudson River Valley of New York, the Shakers became known and respected for the magnificent quality of their industry, especially their furniture. Several elderly survivors of the community gave fascinating on-camera interviews. A book adaptation, coauthored by Ken and Amy Stechler Burns, followed.

Huey Long (1986) found Burns wandering a bit afield from his demonstrated historical and geographical interests. Leaving behind, for the moment, his genius loci of nineteenth-century New England and New York for the twentieth-century Deep South, Burns explored the career of Louisiana politician Huey Long. The controversial Long, a populist whose motto was "Every Man a King!" at one point simultaneously held both a U.S. Senate seat and the governor's chair in Louisiana. Seen by some as a crypto-fascist demagogue and by others as a friend to "the little guy" during the devastating years of the Great Depression, Long was eventually assassinated on the steps of the state capitol in Baton Rouge. In statements to the press, Burns compared Long to Shakespeare's Macbeth, as a "tragic character" whose ambitions had conjured evil from his soul.

This project provided Burns with ample opportunity to add historical motion-picture footage to his repertoire of documentary sources. In addition to newsreel footage of the bombastic "Kingfish" on the speaker's podium, Burns made use of docudramatic reenactments, editing clips from Robert Rossen's *All the King's Men*, a Hollywood adaptation of Robert Penn Warren's novel on Huey Long, which had won the Best Picture Oscar for 1950. Dramatic readings by Robert Penn Warren from his novel were a highlight of the film, of historical significance in and of themselves. Perhaps most important for Burns, it was his first foray into the myths and symbols of the

American South, an experience that would prove invaluable to the making of *The Civil War.*

The Statue of Liberty (1985) was a more familiar Burns subject. Like *The Brooklyn Bridge,* the film was made in conjunction with the centennial of a nineteenth-century symbol of American self-image, and it included both the story of the construction of the symbol and interviews with various informants on the significance of the finished product. New York governor Mario Cuomo finds the gift from France a "symbol of the intention toward equality," while novelist James Baldwin replies that "to black Americans, the Statue of Liberty is a bitter joke." The documentary was nominated for both an Oscar and an Emmy. Interestingly, David Wolper (see previous chapter), the other great independent American TV documentarian, had produced *Liberty Weekend* for commercial television, a glitzy — and superficial — tribute by comparison.

Burns premiered two new works on PBS during 1989. *Thomas Hart Benton* was a ninety-minute portrait made on the occasion of the centennial of the painter's birth. Benton, we learn, was an American artist who wanted his paintings of American landscapes hung in saloons, "where the ordinary man could appreciate them." The subject matter gave Burns the chance to use his signature camera technique on dozens of paintings by Benton and other "Hudson River School" artists. He also edited in footage from a 1953 episode of *Person to Person,* which found Edward R. Murrow interviewing Benton at his home.

The Congress was yet another project in conjunction with an historical anniversary: the bicentennial of the United States Congress. Burns used the occasion not only to describe the history and workings of the institution, but also to highlight the construction of the capitol building, especially the dome and the interior. Since much of the work took place during the Lincoln Administration, research on *The Congress* contributed ultimately to the making of *The Civil War.* Such notables as Derek Jacobi, Alistair Cooke, Garrison Keillor, Arthur Miller, Julie Harris, and Kurt Vonnegut performed off-camera voiceover roles. The film was premiered before the full complement of members of the U.S. Senate and House of Representatives at a special screening at the National Theater in March of 1989.

Work on *The Civil War* had actually begun in bits and pieces as far back as 1984. Burns later revealed to interviewers that he had been warned away from the project by several filmmakers and historians who had attempted similarly epic documentaries but had been stymied by the magnitude of the subject. In the book adaptation of *The Civil War,* Burns cites this caveat from no less a chronicler of the period than Walt Whitman: "Future years will never know the seething hell and the black infernal background, the countless minor scenes and the interiors of the secession war; and it is best they should not. The real war will never get in books." But, of course, television did not exist as an option for telling that story during Whitman's lifetime, nor had a documentarian ever developed a camera style so suited to the subject matter as had Ken Burns. The project "just called me," Burns told Judith Michaelson.

With his reputation for producing high-quality television documentaries capable of winning wide public interest and acceptance, Burns was able to secure adequate funding for *The Civil War* from various private-sector sources as well as public sources. Key to the project was a million-dollar grant from the General Motors Corporation. Other major contributors included the National Endowment for the Humanities, the Corporation for Public Broadcasting, the Arthur Vining Davis Foundation, the John B. and Catherine T. MacArthur Foundation, and Dr. Max King Morris.

David McCullough, who had worked with Burns on so many of his projects, was senior creative consultant and series narrator, and several big-name actors agreed to play off-screen voiceover roles for a fraction of their normal fees: Jason Robards, who had narrated *The Statue of Liberty,* as General Ulysses S. Grant; Julie Harris as a Richmond society lady whose wartime diary served as a revelatory window into Southern homefront life; Morgan Freeman as the philosopher and freed slave Frederick Douglass; and Sam Waterston as President Abraham Lincoln. Geoffrey C. Ward collaborated with Burns on the script for the series as well as on a book of the same title that was released in connection with it. WETA-TV of Washington, D.C., served as the administering PBS station.

The soundtrack of *The Civil War* was a remarkable piece of work in its own right. New recordings of period compositions constituted the first exposure for many viewers to nineteenth-century popular music. A dirgelike violin piece emerged as Burns's aural signature. Simple sound effects, such as creaking wagon wheels and the patter of rain, were used to aesthetically animate the movement of large armies across the landscape. The on-camera appearances of Civil War historian and novelist Shelby Foote were particularly effective. Foote, who has made the subject his life's work, emerged as a passionate storyteller whose vast knowledge of the period and its personalities literally gushed forth across the screen. He was "the presiding spirit of our project," Burns told the press. Foote, too, became an overnight media celebrity.

Not all historians, including several who were involved with the project, were happy with the outcome. Barbara J. Fields and Eric Foner, both professors of American history at Columbia University, disavowed their involvement in the production. Dr. Fields complained to the *New York Times* that Burns had given too much credence to the mythic military prowess of the Southern generals (especially Robert E. Lee and Stonewall Jackson) at the expense of telling the full story of the horrors of slavery. The further implication of the charge was that Burns had flattered Southern whites at the expense of portraying the war as a struggle against the barbaric oppression perpetrated (in large part by the ancestors of white middle-class Southern PBS subscribers) against the enslaved ancestors of millions of African-Americans. Burns denied these charges, claiming that he had set out to tell a many-sided story, "a Homeric epic," and that he had accomplished that goal to his satisfaction. In an interview with the *New York Times*, Burns remarked, "If I told you that I had been working on a film that was about the Imperial Presidency, a developing women's movement, an ever-present civil rights question, incompetent generals, military contractors who sold shoddy goods to the government at inflated prices, about Wall Street speculators who traded on inside information and made millions, about flag desecration, you would say, 'You are making a piece about contemporary America.' But I am making a piece about the Civil War, and every one of these issues reverberates today."

Ken Burns's mantel is filled with accolades. In addition to the PGA's Producer of the Year award for *The Civil War*, Burns has collected a Peabody, a Golden Globe, a D. W. Griffith Award, and first-place honors from various film festivals around the country. Perhaps the most remarkable of these is the People's Choice Award for best miniseries, which he won for *The Civil War*. This award is voted for by viewers — not critics or industry people — and it marked the first time a "straight" documentary, as opposed to a docudrama, had ever won in that category.

Burns has not sat still since his *Civil War* triumph. *Empire of the Air*, a ninety-minute history of American radio, a collaboration with Morgan Wesson and Tom Lewis, is scheduled for a 1992 PBS debut. He has also made a commitment to a PBS documentary series titled *American Lives*. Burns will make some of the episodes himself

(Thomas Jefferson, Mark Twain, and Abraham Lincoln are all in the works) and act as executive producer for others, including the premiere episode, *Lindbergh*, a film by Stephen Ives.

Burns has also announced his next major miniseries project: a history of baseball. Calling the sport "the Rosetta stone of America" and claiming that "if you understand it, you can understand our country," he has defined the task in his usual epic terms. As the singular national star of serious American TV documentary production, Burns has had no trouble getting more than adequate funding for what could be his most popular subject matter yet. His reputation is also winning him the cooperation of the living makers of baseball history — the players, sportswriters, fans, umpires, and team owners — as well as access to the important institutions holding artifacts awaiting the perusal of his camera. Ironically, Ken Burns has expressed some interest in turning his attention one day to docudramatic feature films, much as David Wolper did in the middle of his career. Not yet forty years old, Burns has several times mentioned a desire to do an historically accurate bio-pic feature film on the life of Sam Houston.

KEN BURNS: SELECTED VIDEOGRAPHY

Dates given on these programs indicate television premiere dates. Several were released as theatrical films prior to telecast.

Documentary Specials

The Brooklyn Bridge (PBS, 1982)
The Shakers: Hands to Work, Hearts to God (PBS, 1985)
The Statue of Liberty (PBS, 1985)
Huey Long (PBS, 1986)
The Congress (PBS, 1989)
Thomas Hart Benton (PBS, 1989)
The Civil War (PBS, 1990)
Empire of the Air (PBS, 1992)

Afterword

Television credits were once merely indecipherable; they are now occasionally practically invisible. In an effort to stem the rampant channel surfing that has become standard operating procedure for so many viewers, three of the four major broadcast networks adopted retrenchment policies with regards to screen credits in 1994. ABC called for procedures to eliminate opening theme songs; NBC squeezed the end credits of their series onto the right half of the screen while promotional or even program codas play on the left; and CBS has in some cases dispensed with the closing credit crawl entirely. As a result, it is more difficult than ever for viewers to find out who is responsible for the television program they have just watched.

At the same time, perhaps by design, some of the biggest movers and shakers in television production have become household names since the first edition of this book appeared in 1992. When Vice President Dan Quayle took on single mother Murphy Brown during that year's election campaign, it was Diane English, the show's creator-producer, who responded rather than star Candice Bergen. English was suddenly thrust into the position of a Hollywood soldier in the American culture wars, and, given the circumstances, rightfully so. When Linda Bloodworth-Thomason and her husband Harry took time off from making *Evening Shade* and their other sitcoms to produce their friend Bill Clinton's bio-film for the Democratic National Convention, yet another prime-time producer had burst out of the TV section and into the front-page news.

While the political visibility of the television producer was on the rise during the early 1990s, so apparently was the status of working in this once bottom-end medium. The work of big name Hollywood directors popped up all over prime time as never before. The *artistes du cinema*, however, were not exactly embraced by the home-screen faithful. David Lynch's *Twin Peaks* (ABC, 1990) made a spectacular nova, but had burned out and disappeared before the end of its second season. Lynch's other two TV projects, the documentary series *American Chronicles* (Fox, 1990) and the surrealistic sitcom *On the Air* (Fox, 1992) were cancelled so quickly that they are not likely to ever become *Jeopardy* clues, not even in the "Very Hard TV Trivia" category.

Other cinema *auteurs* fared no better on the video waves. Oliver Stone's heavily promoted mini-series *Wild Palms* was unable to win its time period. Tim Burton's *Family Dog*, Robert Townsend's *Townsend TV*, Penny Marshall's *A League of Their Own*, and Robert DeNiro's *Tribeca* all bombed, none lasting an entire season. Barry Levinson's *Homicide: Life on the Streets* made it back for a second try, but it has had more trouble earning rating points than critical acclaim. Even Steven Spielberg's *Seaquest DSV* is struggling for air at the bottom of the Nielsen deep-blue sea.

While feature film directors were finding that slumming in the vast wasteland wasn't as easy as it looked, some of the old TV hands covered in the first edition of this book were adding to their resumés. With *L.A. Law* finishing an eight-year run on NBC, Steven Bochco revisited the territory of his watershed hit, *Hill Street Blues,* and came up with a new top ten, critically acclaimed series, *NYPD Blue*. In the eighties, Bochco had almost singlehandedly delivered the hourlong continuing drama from the gossipy sensationalism of Lee Rich's *Dallas* and Aaron Spelling's *Dynasty,* and he came to the rescue of the genre once again with his new ABC hit. Recognizing the new economic realities of the cable environment, he built *NYPD Blue* around two star characters rather than a dozen. Citing the fact that he must compete for viewers with cable movies that are free of the traditional network content restrictions, Bochco gave double meaning to "Blue," showing naked derrieres, both male and female, and using language that might once have gotten a station license revoked.

Aaron Spelling, by far TV's most versatile and prolific producer, took prime time by storm yet again by inventing a new subgenre and populating it with a trilogy of hits for Fox in the early 1990s. In *Beverly Hills 90210, Melrose Place,* and *Models, Inc.* Spelling had overhauled the "jiggle TV" of the 1970s for Generation X. The objectification of men as sex objects had achieved equal status with the objectification of women over the last two decades, and the male stars of Spelling's teen soaps were sold with the same successful technique that the producer had pioneered for the female stars of his T & A classic, *Charlie's Angels* (ABC, 1976–81).

After a slow start, *Beverly Hills 90210* became one of the cornerstones of Fox's schedule. The earnest "relevance" of the contemporary dialogue and issue-oriented plots recalls the early Spelling who gave TV *The Mod Squad* in the late 1960s. Spelling's new shows, however, are very much designed for the 1990s. The offcamera antics of star Shannen Doherty have given the show more promotion in the tabloids (both print and video) than money could have bought. The up-to-the-minute hairstyles and attitudes have already presaged the show's future as a camp classic in twenty-first century syndication. In these turgid hourlong soaps, Spelling is creating a kind of Prozac-era *Brady Bunch* that is likely to keep future historians, anthropologists and TV knock-off artists glued to their sets.

In situation comedy, Diane English added another series, *Love and War,* to her impressive portfolio. In it, she continues to explore familiar, insistent themes. Once again we have a single female professional, with a sexually ambiguous name, living in a go-go cosmopolis, fighting to make it in a man's world; this time it is Dana (Annie Potts), a New York restaurateur, (It was Wally at the debut, but a miscast Susan Dey left the show in its first season). But unlike such previous English efforts as *Murphy Brown* and *My Sister Sam,* the focus of this will they?/won't they? sitcom is Relationship rather than Career.

Norman Lear, who reinvented situation comedy with *All in the Family* during the 1970s, has not been nearly as successful as Spelling or English in keeping up with the fickle whims of network audience share. Essentially sticking with the didactic, issue-oriented living room badinage that made him famous, he has struck out no less than three times in the 1990s: *The Powers that Be,* a parlor-room political comedy starring John Forsythe as a smile-button U.S. Senator from the Midwest; *Sunday Dinner,* in which a family of grown children come to Dad's house each week to wage demographic dialogue war on each other; and *704 Hauser Street,* which revisits Archie Bunker's old house, now occupied by an African-American family with, of all things, a liberal father and an outspoken conservative son who dates a white girlfriend.

The most interesting new TV auteur to arrive in the last several years is, without doubt, David Kelley. A protégé of Steven Bochco, he worked with the maestro on both *L.A. Law* and *Doogie Howser, M.D.*, striking off on his own for the first time with *Picket Fences*, a serious, high-tone hourlong drama whose occasional flights of whimsy conjure such unlikely extremes as *The Andy Griffith Show* and *Twin Peaks*. Kelley has staked out ethical and religious concerns as the show's major dramatic themes and *Picket Fences* won two consecutive "Best Drama" Emmies. As we go to press during the 1994–95 season Kelley enters the hospital field with *Chicago Hope*. He has demonstrated the potential to bring that genre back to the heights of *St. Elsewhere* if the audience will let him.

Selected Bibliography

Books

Adler, Richard. *All in the Family: A Critical Appraisal.* New York: Praeger, 1979.

Allen, Robert C. *Speaking of Soap Operas.* Chapel Hill: University of North Carolina Press, 1985.

Alley, Robert S., and Irby B. Brown. *Love Is All Around: The Making of the Mary Tyler Moore Show.* New York: Delta, 1989.

————. *Murphy Brown: The Anatomy of a Sitcom.* New York: Delta, 1990.

Alvarado, Manuel, and Edward Buscombe. *Hazel: The Making of a Television Series.* London: British Film Institute, 1978.

Barnouw, Erik. *Tube of Plenty: The Evolution of American Television.* 2nd edition. New York: Oxford, 1990.

Barris, Chuck. *Confessions of a Dangerous Mind.* New York: St. Martin's, 1984.

Becker, Howard. *Art Worlds.* Berkeley: University of California Press, 1982.

Bedell, Sally. *Up the Tube: Prime-Time TV in the Silverman Years.* New York: Viking, 1981.

Berle, Milton, with Haskell Frankel. *Milton Berle: An Autobiography.* New York: Delacorte, 1974.

Bishop, Jim. *The Golden Ham: A Candid Biography of Jackie Gleason.* New York: Simon and Schuster, 1956.

Brooks, Tim, and Earle Marsh. *The Complete Directory to Prime-Time Network TV Shows, 1946–Present.* 4th edition. New York: Ballantine, 1988.

Broughton, Irv. *Producers on Producing.* Jefferson, N.C.: McFarland, 1986.

Brown, Les. *Les Brown's Encyclopedia of Television.* New York: New York Zoetrope, 1982.

Burnett, Carol. *One More Time: A Memoir*. New York: Random House, 1986.

Buxton, Frank, and Bill Owen. *The Big Broadcast — 1929–1950*. New York: Avon, 1972.

Cantor, Muriel. *The Hollywood TV Producer: His Work and His Audience*. New York: Basic Books, 1971.

Cantor, Muriel, and Suzanne Pingree. *The Soap Opera*. Beverly Hills: Sage, 1983.

Castleman, Harry, and Walter J. Podrazik. *Harry and Wally's Favorite TV Shows*. New York: Prentice-Hall, 1989.

Caughie, John, ed. *Theories of Authorship: A Reader*. London: Routledge and Kegan Paul, 1981.

Chayefsky, Paddy. *Television Plays*. New York: Simon and Schuster, 1955.

Christensen, Mark, and Cameron Stauth. *The Sweeps*. New York: William Morrow, 1984.

Clum, John M. *Paddy Chayefsky*. Boston: Twayne, 1976.

Daly, Marsha. *Michael Landon: A Biography*. New York: St. Martin's, 1987.

Dunning, John. *Tune In Yesterday*. Englewood Cliffs, N.J.: Prentice-Hall, 1976.

Einstein, Dan. *Special Edition: A Guide to Network Television Documentaries and Special News Reports, 1955–79*. Metuchen, N.J.: Scarecrow Press, 1987.

Eisner, Joel, and David Krinsky. *Television Comedy Series*. Jefferson, N.C.: McFarland, 1984.

Elliott, Philip. *The Making of a Television Series*. London: Constable, 1972.

Ellis, John. *Visible Fictions — Cinema: Television: Video*. London: Routledge and Kegan Paul, 1981.

Engel, Joel. *Rod Serling: The Dreams and Nightmares of Life in the Twilight Zone*. Chicago: Contemporary Books, 1989.

Esslin, Martin. *The Age of Television*. San Francisco: Freeman, 1982.

Feuer, Jane, Paul Kerr, and Tise Vahimagi, eds. *MTM "Quality Television."* London: British Film Institute, 1984.

Gianakos, Larry James. *Television Drama Series Programming: A Comprehensive Chronicle*. Vols. 1–5. Metuchen, N.J.: Scarecrow Press, 1978, 1980, 1981, 1983, 1987.

Gitlin, Todd. *Inside Prime Time*. New York: Pantheon, 1983.

Goldenson, Leonard H., with Marvin J. Wolf. *Beating the Odds: The Untold Story Behind the Rise of ABC*. New York: Scribner's, 1991.

Green, Joey. *The Unofficial Gilligan's Island Handbook*. New York: Warner Books, 1988.

Gregg, Rodman, ed. *Who's Who in Television*. Beverly Hills: Packard House, 1987.

Hill, Doug, and Jeff Weingard. *Saturday Night: A Backstage History of Saturday Night Live*. New York: William Morrow, 1986.

Intintoli, Michael. *Taking Soaps Seriously*. New York: Praeger, 1984.

Kaminsky, Stuart M., with Jeffrey H. Mahan. *American Television Genres*. Chicago: Nelson-Hall, 1985.

Levinson, Richard, and William Link. *Off Camera*. New York: New American Library, 1986.

————. *Stay Tuned: An Inside Look at the Making of Prime-Time Television*. New York: St. Martin's, 1981.

McCarty, John, and Brian Kelleher. *Alfred Hitchcock Presents: An Illustrated Guide to the Ten-Year Television Career of the Master of Suspense*. New York: St. Martin's, 1985.

MacDonald, J. Fred. *Blacks and White TV: Afro-Americans in Television Since 1948*. Chicago: Nelson-Hall, 1983.

————. *Don't Touch That Dial! Radio Programming in American Life from 1920 to 1960*. Chicago: Nelson-Hall, 1979.

McNeil, Alex. *Total Television*. Revised ed. New York: Viking Penguin, 1984.

Marc, David. *Comic Visions: Television Comedy and American Culture*. Boston: Unwin Hyman, 1989.

————. *Demographic Vistas*. Philadelphia: University of Pennsylvania Press, 1984.

Marill, Alvin H. *Movies Made for Television: The Telefeature and the Mini-Series, 1964–1986*. New York: New York Zoetrope, 1987.

Marx, Arthur. *Red Skelton: An Unauthorized Biography*. New York: Dutton, 1979.

Museum of Broadcasting. *Richard Levinson–William Link: Seminars at the Museum of Broadcasting, October 1983*. New York: Museum of Broadcasting, 1983.

Navasky, Victor S. *Naming Names*. New York: Viking Penguin, 1980.

Newcomb, Horace, ed. *Television: The Critical View*. 3rd ed. New York: Oxford, 1987.

Newcomb, Horace. *TV: The Most Popular Art*. Garden City, N.Y.: Anchor/Doubleday, 1974.

Newcomb, Horace, and Robert S. Alley. *The Producer's Medium*. New York: Oxford, 1983.

O'Connor, John E., ed. *American History/American Television*. New York: Ungar, 1983.

Perry, Jeb. *Universal Television: The Studio and Its Programs, 1950–80*. Metuchen, N.J.: Scarecrow Press, 1983.

Ravage, John. *Television: The Director's Viewpoint*. Boulder, Colo.: Westview Press, 1978.

Rose, Reginald. *Six Television Plays*. New York: Simon and Schuster, 1956.

Sarris, Andrew. *The American Cinema: Directors and Directions, 1929–1968*. New York: Dutton, 1968.

Schatz, Thomas. *Hollywood Genres*. New York: Random House, 1981.

Scheuer, Steven H. *Who's Who in Television and Cable*. New York: Facts on File, 1983.

Schwartz, David, Steve Ryan, and Fred Wostbrock. *The Encyclopedia of TV Game Shows*. New York: New York Zoetrope, 1987.

Schwartz, Sherwood. *Inside Gilligan's Island: From Creation to Syndication*. Jefferson, N.C.: McFarland, 1988.

Seldes, Gilbert. *The Public Arts*. New York: Simon and Schuster, 1956.

Serling, Rod. *Patterns: Four Television Plays with the Author's Personal Commentary*. New York: Simon and Schuster, 1957.

Sklar, Robert. *Movie-Made America*. New York: Vintage, 1975.

Sorensen, Jeff. *The Taxi Book*. New York: St. Martin's, 1987.

Stedman, Raymond W. *The Serials: Suspense and Drama by Installment*. Norman: University of Oklahoma Press, 1971.

Stock, Rip. *Odd Couple Mania*. New York: Ballantine, 1981.

Strait, Raymond. *James Garner*. New York: St. Martin's, 1985.

Terrace, Vincent. *Encyclopedia of Television Series, Pilots, and Specials, 1937–1973*. New York: New York Zoetrope, 1986.

Thompson, Robert. *Adventures on Prime Time: The Television Programs of Stephen J. Cannell*. New York: Praeger, 1990.

Thompson, Robert, and Gary Burns, eds. *Making Television: Authorship and the Production Process*. New York: Praeger, 1990.

Toll, Robert C. *The Entertainment Machine*. New York: Oxford, 1982.

Wakefield, Dan. *All Her Children: The Real Life Story of America's Favorite Soap Opera*. Garden City, N.Y.: Doubleday, 1976.

Ward, Geoffrey C., with Ric Burns and Ken Burns. *The Civil War: An Illustrated History*. New York: Alfred A. Knopf, 1990.

Watson, Mary Ann. *The Expanding Vista: American Television in the Kennedy Years*. New York: Oxford, 1990.

Whitfield, Stephen E., and Gene Roddenberry. *The Making of Star Trek*. New York: Ballantine, 1968.

Wicking, Christopher, and Tise Vahimagi. *The American Vein: Directors and Directions in Television*. New York: Dutton, 1979.

Winship, Michael. *Television*. New York: Random House, 1988.

Wolper, David, with Quincy Troupe. *The Inside Story of TV's "Roots."* New York: Warner Books, 1978.

Wooley, Lynn, Robert Malsbary, and Robert G. Strange, Jr. *Warner Brothers Television*. Jefferson, N.C.: McFarland, 1985.

Articles

Arden, Darlen. "Celebrity of the Month: Stephen J. Cannell." *Entrepreneur*, October 1982.

Ashley, Franklin. "On Location with *North and South*." *TV Guide*, November 2, 1985.

Attanasio, Paul. "Fit for a Kingfish: *Huey Long* a Superb Documentary." *Washington Post*, February 12, 1986.

CBS Television Network Press Information (on Paul Henning and *The Beverly Hillbillies*), September 13–19, 1962.

Christensen, Mark. "Bochco's Law." *Rolling Stone*, April 21, 1988.

Clark, Kenneth, "Cannell: Why *A Team* and *Riptide* Are Hot." *Chicago Tribune TV Week*, July 29, 1984.

Davis, Donald M. "Auteur Film Criticism as a Vehicle for Television Criticism." *Feedback* 26:1 (summer 1984).

Duncan, Dayton. "A Cinematic Storyteller." *Boston Globe Magazine*, March 19, 1989.

Fanning, Deidre. "What Stuff Are Dreams Made Of?" *Forbes*, August 22, 1988.

Frost, David. "Q & A: Garry Marshall Interviewed by David Frost." *Panorama*, October 1980.

Gerard, Jeremy. "Producers Carsey and Werner: What Have They Done for Us Lately?" *New York Times Magazine*, November 23, 1990.

Goodson, Mark. "If I'd Stood Up Earlier . . . ." *New York Times Magazine*, January 13, 1991.

Klemesrud, Judy. "From Rah-Rah Cheerleader to *Soap*'s Creator." *New York Times*, June 17, 1978.

Koch, Neal. "Steve Bochco: Prime-Time Renegade." *Channels*, November 1989.

Lichter, S. R., and L. S. Rothman. "From Lucy to Lacey: TV's Dream Girls." *Public Opinion*, September–October 1986.

McMurran, Kristin. "Mark Goodson: Wizard of Games." *People*, May 14, 1984.

Marc, David. "TV Auteurism." *American Film*, November 1981.

Margulies, Lee. "On the Job with . . . Stephen J. Cannell." *Continental*, September 1980.

"Michael Mann Interview." *Rolling Stone*, May 14, 1981.

Michaelson, Judith. "A *Civil War* for the Masses." *Los Angeles Times Calendar*, July 22, 1990.

Mitchell, Elvis. "*Miami Vice* Losing Its Virtue." *Rolling Stone*, March 27, 1986.

Nixon, Agnes. "Coming of Age in Sudsville." *Television Quarterly* 9 (1970).

Phillips, Irna. "Writing On: Irna Phillips Mends with Tradition." *Broadcasting*, November 6, 1972.

Pollan, Michael. "The *Vice* Look." *Channels*, July–August 1985.

Powers, Ron. "Glory, Glory." *Gentleman's Quarterly*, September 1990.

Rober, Paul Coyle. "The Fugitive." *Emmy Magazine*, November–December 1982.

"Roundtable: Stephen J. Cannell." *View*, March 1985.

Self, Robert. "Robert Altman and the Theory of Authorship." *Cinema Journal* 25:1 (1986).

Shindler, Merrill. "Okay, Cannell, Come Clean!!" *Los Angeles Magazine*, October 1983.

Shruers, Fred. "Can 80 Million Chinese Be Wrong?" *Rolling Stone*, March 24, 1988.

Silverman, Jeff. "Mr. Write." *US*, February 24, 1986.

"Steven Bochco Interview." *Rolling Stone*, March 13, 1986.

Turran, Kenneth. "How to Tell TV's Good Videos from the Bad Ones." *TV Guide*, August 10, 1985.

Waters, Harry F. "Family Feuds." *Newsweek*, April 23, 1990.

Waters, Harry F., with Jane Huck. "The Merchant of Mayhem." *Newsweek*, March 12, 1981.

Whitney, Dwight. "*Hanta Yo* Controversy: The Warpath Runneth Over." *TV Guide*, May 19, 1984.

Wolper, David. "Yes, *A.D.* and *Space* Died — But Don't Bury the Mini-Series Form Yet." *TV Guide*, October 5, 1985.

Zoglin, Richard. "The Civil War Comes Home." *Time*, October 8, 1990.

———. "Cool Cops, Hot Show." *Time*, September 16, 1985.

Index